The Courts, the Church and the Constitution

THE COURTS, THE CHURCH AND THE CONSTITUTION

Aspects of the Disruption of 1843

LORD RODGER OF EARLSFERRY
A Lord of Appeal in Ordinary

The Jean Clark Memorial Lectures

EDINBURGH UNIVERSITY PRESS

Edinburgh University Press Ltd
22 George Square, Edinburgh

Typeset in Goudy by
Norman Tilley Graphics Ltd, Northampton
and printed and bound in Great Britain by
CPI Antony Rowe, Chippenham, Wilts

A CIP record for this book is available from the British Library

ISBN 978 0 7486 3754 6 (paperback)

Contents

The Clark Foundation for Legal Education, 5 February 1992.
Jean Clark (Chairman), front row, centre.

Foreword

Jean Clark was born in 1918. A native of Troon, she was educated at St George's School, Edinburgh. She went on to Edinburgh University and graduated MA, LLB in 1943. Soon after, she was admitted as a solicitor and then worked in private practice for many years.

In 1967 a far-sighted President of the Law Society of Scotland appointed Jean to be the Deputy Secretary in charge of the then fledging Public Relations Department and of what was to become the enormously successful Postgraduate Education Department. Jean's care and attention to detail were important elements in the success of both. On a more personal level, behind a quiet and efficient manner, she hid a delightfully mischievous sense of humour, particularly about the pretensions of the great ones of the earth, most of whom, as it turned out, she could have bought out three times over. It was a great loss to the Law Society when she retired in 1980.

Few had suspected that, through her father, one of the founders of Saxone Shoes, Jean was a woman of considerable wealth. But, in fact, during her lifetime she used her wealth to support many good causes and charities – for which she was awarded the MBE. In 1991 she established the Clark Foundation to promote the Law of Scotland and support 'lawyers' who wished to further their studies. The Foundation has been pursuing that aim now for seventeen years.

When Jean died in 2001, she left additional funds to the Foundation. The Trustees decided that the Jean Clark Lectures should be established in her memory. She would have been delighted that, in 2007, the three lectures in the inaugural series were delivered by Lord Rodger of Earlsferry.

Through the Lectures and its other work, the Clark Foundation strives to support the development of Scots Law in ways which are a fitting memorial to a modest but remarkable woman.

Kenneth Pritchard
Chairman of the Clark Foundation
April 2008

Preface

In one sense, the origin of these lectures goes back to the day, about thirty years ago, when, in the (then) dusty back room of Wildy's shop in Lincoln's Inn Archway, I picked up a copy of Robertson's two-volume report of the Court of Session proceedings in the first *Auchterarder* case. Some years later, I bought a copy of Orr's report of the *Free Church* case in the House of Lords. But I would never have got round to writing anything based on these finds without the invitation of the Trustees of the Jean Clark Foundation to deliver the inaugural series of lectures in memory of the late Jean Clark in May 2007. In retrospect at least, I am grateful to them for that stimulus.

The text of the lectures has been substantially revised for publication. In particular, I have added footnotes and expanded the first lecture to cover the *Stewarton* case, which I had to omit from the oral version for reasons of time. Nevertheless, the lectures remain simply lectures: they do not pretend to be the much-needed modern authoritative account of the crisis.

The theme is a constitutional crisis, not only for the Church of Scotland, but also for the courts, and indeed for the country as a whole. What makes the cases which I discuss unusual, if not unique, is the vast amount of available material about them in special law reports, newspapers, pamphlets, books and memoirs. Read in moderation and duly sifted, this material allows us to see how the highly intelligent judges, lawyers and ministers of the day devoted their very best efforts to a subject which was of vital importance to the life of Scotland and of the United Kingdom. Whether they would have admitted it or not, they were all having the time of their lives. Although I have tried to be objective, as a judge, I am instinctively more sensitive to the plight of the judges than their colleague, the non-intrusionist sympathiser, Lord Cockburn, or the authors of the many other, often entertainingly partisan, accounts.

I am grateful to the Trustees for agreeing to the topic, even though – as I realised – they would probably have preferred something rather different. I also appreciate their financial and other assistance in arranging for the lectures to be published by Edinburgh University Press. My main point of contact was with the Chairman of the Trustees, Kenneth Pritchard. Along with Professor Paul Beaumont, he took immense pains with the practical arrangements for the delivery of the lectures in Aberdeen University on 1–3 May 2007, starting on the three-hundredth anniversary of the United Kingdom. Lord Mackay of Clashfern kindly agreed to preside at the lectures, on a subject about which he knows far more than the lecturer. Behind the scenes, the Pritchards and the Mackays provided me with every kind of assistance and encouragement over the three days in Aberdeen. Sir David and Lady Edward were equally supportive, David having, months before, lent me various books on the Disruption and ecclesiastical history. He and James Mackay also agreed to read a revised version of the lectures, as did Lord Bingham of Cornhill, the Senior Lord of Appeal in Ordinary, Colin Mackay, of BBC Radio Scotland, Sheriff Andrew Bell and Philip Barton, of the Victorian Bar. I have tried to take account of the resulting suggestions, but I alone am responsible for the views expressed.

Among others who have helped in different ways I should mention Lord Hope of Craighead, who has a family connection with two of the main characters in the story and who showed me various items relating to them. John Summers, my judicial assistant at the time of the lectures, verified a number of points for me. Victoria Ailes, my judicial assistant when the text was being prepared for the press, cheerfully and expertly checked the legal citations and helped with the Table of Cases. My thanks also go to my sister, Dr Christine Rodger, two former Procurators of the Church of Scotland, Lord Davidson and Lord Hodge, and to the present Procurator, Laura Dunlop QC. The Depute Clerk of the General Assembly of the Church of Scotland, the Rev. Dr Marjory MacLean, kindly lent me a copy of her unpublished thesis on 'The Crown Rights of the Redeemer'. Lady Davidson provided a number of texts and Frank Cranmer a copy of his unpublished article on the *Percy* case. My former Oxford colleague, Peter Skegg, now Professor of Law in the University of Otago, helped with the Free Church settlement in Dunedin. Members of staff of the British Library, the London Library, the House of Lords Library (especially Andy Zelinger), the National Library of Scotland, the Advocates Library, the Edinburgh Central Library and Glasgow University Library all smoothed my path. So, too, did Esmé Watson, the commissioning editor, and Eddie Clark at Edinburgh University Press, my copy-editor, Helen Johnston, and Moyra Forrest, who prepared the index.

Finally, I am grateful to the Keeper of the Advocates Library for permission to refer to, and quote from, a number of letters in the Advocates' Manuscripts Collection in the National Library of Scotland.

Alan Rodger
27 February 2008

Note on the Terminology

At the time of the Disruption in 1843, as today, the Church of Scotland was organised in a hierarchy of **courts**, with the higher courts having power to review the decisions of lower courts.

At the lowest level was the **kirk session**, comprising the parish minister and his elders. They had jurisdiction over the members of the congregation in matters of discipline.

Above the kirk session was the **presbytery**, made up of the ministers of the parishes within the area covered by the presbytery, for example Glasgow or Edinburgh. The eighty-two presbyteries exercised discipline over the ministers in their area and also ordained and admitted presentees to office as parish ministers. Part of the procedure for the appointment of a minister involved a **call** from the congregation, inviting the person concerned to become their minister. (The status of such calls was disputed.) One of the purposes of the **Chapels Act**, passed by the General Assembly in 1834, but held to be invalid by the Court of Session in 1843, was to include ministers of churches, other than parish churches, as members of the presbytery and higher courts.

Above the presbyteries were the seventeen **provincial synods**, made up of the ministers who were members of the presbyteries within the area covered by the particular synod, for example Glasgow and Ayr or Lothian and Tweeddale. Synods, which usually met twice a year, were abolished in 1992.

Above the synods, and forming the highest court in the Church, was the **General Assembly**, which met in Edinburgh for about ten days each May. It was made up of **Commissioners**, the majority being ministers, and the rest **elders**, appointed annually by the presbyteries. The composition of the General Assembly therefore changed from year to year. The General Assembly was not only the highest court, but was also a forum for debate and a legislature, having the power to pass Acts of Assembly. The presbyteries could send **overtures** (proposals) for discussion by the General Assembly. By virtue of the **Barrier Act** (1697), Acts of the General Assembly were binding on the Church only if they had first been agreed to by a majority of the presbyteries.

Each General Assembly appointed a **Commission of Assembly**, made up of a number of its Commissioners who were given authority to conduct any business (especially legal business) which the General Assembly did not have time to complete, or which arose during the year before the next General Assembly met.

The Church of Scotland was the **Established Church** in Scotland, organised into parishes covering the whole of the country. As the Established Church, the Church of Scotland was officially recognised and protected by the State. The fundamental dispute between the civil courts and the Church came to be over the claim of the Evangelical majority in the Church that, despite its peculiar legal position as the Established Church under the Constitution, it should enjoy independence from any interference by the State and, in particular, by the State courts in any spiritual matters (**spiritual independence**). Proponents of that claim often accused their opponents of **Erastianism**. Using the term rather loosely, they meant that their opponents were in favour of undue subservience of the Church to the State.

For the sake of brevity, I have used the term '**the Disruption cases**' to refer to the various court cases, between 1835 and 1843, which eventually led to the Disruption. In quoting from them and other contemporary materials, I have occasionally modernised the punctuation and capitalisation.

Abbreviated References

Auchterarder Report   Robertson, Charles, *Report of the Auchterarder case: the Earl of Kinnoull and the Rev. R. Young, against the Presbytery of Auchterarder*, two volumes (Adam & Charles Black, Edinburgh, 1838).

Bayne   Bayne, Peter, *The Free Church of Scotland: Her Origin, Founders and Testimony* (2nd edition, T. & T. Clark, Edinburgh, 1894).

Bryce   Bryce, Alexander, *Ten years of the Church of Scotland: from 1833 to 1843: with historical retrospect from 1560*, two volumes (William Blackwood & Sons, Edinburgh and London, 1850). The historical retrospect is separately paginated. The references to volume 1 in the footnotes are to the account which begins after that retrospect.

Buchanan   Buchanan, Robert, *The Ten Years' Conflict*, two volumes (Blackie, Glasgow, 1849).

Cairns   Cairns, David Smith, *Life and Times of Alexander Robertson MacEwen D.D.* (Hodder & Stoughton, London, 1925).

Cameron   Cameron, John Kennedy, *Scottish Church Union of 1900: Reminiscences and Reflections* (The Northern Counties Newspaper and Printing and Publishing Company Limited, Inverness, 1923).

Candlish Memorials   Wilson, William, and Rainy, Robert, *Memorials of Robert Smith Candlish* (A. & C. Black, Edinburgh, 1880).

Chalmers, *What ought*   Chalmers, Thomas, *What ought the Church and the People of Scotland to do now?* (William Collins, Glasgow, 1840).

Cockburn Journal   *Journal of Henry Cockburn, being a continuation of the memorials of his time 1831–1854*, two volumes (Edmonston & Douglas, Edinburgh, 1874).

Cunningham	Cunningham, John, *The Church History of Scotland, from the commencement of the Christian era to the present century*, two volumes (A. & C. Black, Edinburgh, 1859).
Disruption Worthies	Wylie, James Aitken (ed.), *Disruption Worthies: A Memorial of 1843*, two volumes (new edition, Thomas C. Jack, Edinburgh and London, 1881).
Free Church Appeals	Orr, Robert Low (ed.), *The Free Church of Scotland Appeals 1903–4* (Macniven & Wallace, Edinburgh; Hodder & Stoughton, London, 1904).
Guthrie	Guthrie, David Kelly, and Guthrie, Charles John, *Autobiography of Thomas Guthrie, D.D.*, two volumes (Daldy Isbister & Co., London, 1874).
Hanna	Hanna, William, *Memoirs of the life and writings of Thomas Chalmers*, four volumes (Sutherland & Knox, Edinburgh, 1849–52).
Henderson	Henderson, George David, *Heritage: a Study of the Disruption* (2nd edition, revised, Oliver & Boyd, Edinburgh and London, 1943).
Hetherington	Hetherington, William Maxwell, *History of the Church of Scotland from the introduction of Christianity to the period of the Disruption in 1843*, two volumes (7th edition, Johnston & Hunter, Edinburgh, 1852).
Inglis	Anonymous [Inglis, John], 'The Present Position of the Church of Scotland' (1840), *Blackwood's Magazine*, 46, pp. 573–91 (Part I) and pp. 799–812 (Part II).
Lethendy Report	Robertson, Charles Gordon (ed.), *Report of the Proceedings of the Court of Session in the Lethendy Case, the Rev. Thomas Clark … against the Presbytery of Dunkeld and the Rev. Andrew Kessen* (Blackwood & Sons, Edinburgh, 1839).
Life of Rainy	Simpson, Patrick Carnegie, *The Life of Principal Rainy*, two volumes (Hodder & Stoughton, London, 1909).
Macfarlane	Macfarlane, James, *The Late Secession from the Church of Scotland* (William Blackwood & Sons, Edinburgh and London, 1846).
Moncreiff	Moncreiff, Sir Henry Wellwood, *The Free Church Principle: its Character and History* (Edinburgh, 1883).

Omond	Omond, George William Thomson, *The Lord Advocates of Scotland: Second Series 1834–1880* (Andrew Melrose Ltd, London, 1914).
Robertson	Robertson, James, *Observations on the Veto Act* (W. Blackwood & Sons, W. Whyte and Co., A. Brown & Co., Edinburgh; L. Smith, Aberdeen; Smith, Elder & Co., London, 1840).
Ross	Ross, Kenneth Rankin, *Church and Creed in Scotland* (Rutherford Studies, Series One, Rutherford House, Edinburgh, 1988).
Stewart and Cameron	Stewart, Alexander and Cameron, John Kennedy, *The Free Church of Scotland: A Vindication* (William Hodge & Co., Edinburgh and Glasgow, n.d. [1910]), reprinted as *The Free Church of Scotland: The Crisis of 1900* (Knox Press, Edinburgh, 1989).
Stewarton Report	Bell, John Montgomery et al. (eds), *Report of the Stewarton Case, William Cuninghame and others ... against the Presbytery of Irvine* (Thomas Clark, Edinburgh, Saunders & Benning, London, 1843).
Taylor Innes	Innes, Alexander Taylor, *Chapters of Reminiscence* (Hodder & Stoughton, London, New York, Toronto, 1913).
Turner	Turner, Alexander, *The Scottish Secession of 1843: being an examination of the principles and narrative of the contest which led to that remarkable event* (Paton & Ritchie, Edinburgh; Thomas Murray & Sons, Glasgow, 1859).
Watt	Watt, Hugh, *Thomas Chalmers and the Disruption* (Thomas Nelson & Sons Ltd, Edinburgh, London etc., 1943).
Wilson	Wilson, John, *An Examination of the claims of the Free Church as advanced by the Rev. R. Buchanan, D.D. in his 'Ten Years' Conflict'* (Paton & Ritchie, Edinburgh, 1850).

When citing law reports I have used the standard abbreviations. They are explained in the annual volumes of the *Current Law Case Citator* (Sweet & Maxwell, London and W. Green, Edinburgh), as well as in the *Cardiff Index to Legal Abbreviations*, which is available on the internet.

Table of Cases

References are to pages in the main text where the footnote occurs.
References to the main discussion of a case appear in bold type.

LECTURE I

The Road to the Disruption

Shortly after half-past two in the afternoon of Thursday, 18 May 1843, in St Andrew's Church in Edinburgh, the Marquis of Bute took his place as Lord High Commissioner to the General Assembly of the Church of Scotland.[1] The retiring Moderator, Dr Welsh, led the assembled ministers and elders in prayer. Then – according to a carefully prepared plan[2] – he begged permission to read out a long protest. He began by declaring that, in consequence of certain proceedings affecting their rights and privileges, which had been sanctioned by the government and legislature, 'there has been an infringement on the liberties of our constitution, so that we could not now constitute this court without a violation of the terms of the union between Church and State in this land, as now authoritatively declared.'[3] When he had finished reading, about three-quarters of an hour later,[4] Dr Welsh bowed to the Lord High Commissioner, took his hat and walked out of the church. He was followed by some 200 ministers.[5] Along George Street they went, down Hanover Street and on to the Tanfield Hall in Canonmills,[6] through crowds mostly waving and cheering but just occasionally hissing.[7] When they arrived at the hall at about a quarter to four, many more ministers and elders were waiting to join them. There they set themselves up as the General Assembly of what soon came to be known as the Free Church of Scotland. The famous Dr Thomas Chalmers, economist, social philosopher and reformer, and a mighty preacher, was elected as the first Moderator.

Given the popular excitement, for some ministers at least, 'if it was hard to go out, it was harder to stay in.'[8] Back in St Andrew's Church, though considerably shaken by the size of the exodus, the remaining ministers and elders tried to set about the business of the General Assembly of the Established Church of Scotland as if not too much had happened. They elected Principal M'Farlan as their Moderator and he took the chair 'amid the mingled applause and disapprobation of the audience.'[9] To one observer looking down on the proceedings from the gallery, however, it was like looking into a grave.[10] The Disruption had finally come to pass.

After the Disruption – 'the most important event in the whole of Scotland's nineteenth-century history'[11] – the new Free Church quickly proved to be a vigorous and hostile rival to the Established Church. With 474 out of 1,195 ministers, including most of the leading figures, eventually signing the Deed of Demission,[12] the Church of Scotland was split in two. So was much of Scottish society.[13] The consequences can still be detected today – if only in the Free Church, United Free Church and Free Presbyterian Church buildings which are dotted over the landscape of Scotland.

The story of that day, of the events leading up to it and of the sufferings endured after it, was one on which Free Church writers loved to dwell. The bookcase of many a Scottish household used to contain a copy of Brown's *Annals of the Disruption*[14] – 'that most sentimental of books'[15] – or of a similar work written in what some might regard as a quietly triumphalist tone.[16] The tale is less familiar today but, even though we have to go back to the time of *Pickwick Papers* and *Oliver Twist*, it is one that should still be told not only to Scots lawyers, but to anyone with an interest in the British constitution. For at the very heart of those events was a series of decisions of the Court of Session and House of Lords in what would nowadays be described as judicial review proceedings. Indeed, the Disruption occurred because of those decisions.

Outwardly, most of the decisions concerned an unpopular system by which patrons – the Crown or local landowners – presented men to become parish ministers without necessarily consulting the wishes of the parishioners. Of course, that specific problem was finally solved long ago by the abolition of patronage.[17] But, as the cases went on, year after year, another general issue, of perennial interest far beyond the confines of the Church, came to dominate them.

When the Church defended the cases, it argued that, under the con-stitution of the Church of Scotland as enshrined in the Treaty of Union of 1707 and the implementing legislation, in all spiritual matters the Church of Scotland and her courts were not subject to the jurisdiction of the Court of Session or House of Lords. The Church courts were sovereign in their own ecclesiastical sphere and could ignore any decisions of the secular, that is, civil, courts which intruded into that sphere. So, where a statute applied within that ecclesiastical sphere, the civil courts could do nothing to make the Church courts comply with it. The majority of the Court of Session and then the House of Lords rejected that claim. The Government and Parliament backed them. The result was the Disruption, when those ministers and members who felt unable to accept what they saw as a loss of their 'spiritual independence' from the State courts left the Established Church, while proclaiming that the Free Church was now the true historic Church of Scotland.

It is appropriate to mark the three-hundredth anniversary of the Act(s) of Union by concentrating in this lecture on some of the constitutional aspects of the dispute – in particular, on how the Church reacted to the judgments of the courts and on how those who eventually left the Established Church saw the constitutional position.[18] Nowadays, we tend to think of constitutional disputes as involving some issue as to the powers of the executive or of the legislature. Even today, however, the Church of Scotland has its place in the constitution of the United Kingdom. Make no mistake: the battle which developed all those years ago between the courts and the majority party in the Church was in every sense a constitutional struggle and was regarded as such at the time, even if the two sides saw the issue differently.

For the majority party in the Church, the Court of Session and House of Lords were defying the constitution as laid down in the Act of Union. Lord Moncreiff encapsulated that position when he asked whether the church:

is not an essential and component part of the constitution of the realm, whose independent powers, judicial and legislative, are even more sacred and inviolable than the powers and jurisdiction of the highest civil and criminal courts of the country. These may be changed or taken away, as they have often been. The others cannot be invaded in any vital point, without a direct breach of what is fundamental and essential in the political state of the United Kingdom.[19]

By contrast, the majority judges and the House of Lords thought that the Church was defying the authority of the law of the land. When the presbytery of Auchterarder complained of the hardship of being held liable in damages for acting according to their consciences, Lord Campbell declared:

I do not think, my Lords, that where the law is clear, the hardship of being obliged to obey it is a topic that can be listened to in a Court of Justice. There can be nothing more dangerous than to allow the obligation to obey a law to depend upon the opinion entertained by individuals of its propriety, that opinion being so liable to be influenced by interest, prejudice, and passion; the love of power, still more deceitful than the love of profit; and that most seductive of all delusions, that a man may recommend himself to the Almighty by exercising a stern control over the religious opinions of his fellow men.[20]

The resulting clash could be presented to the public in stark terms. For, instance, at one point in 1839, Hugh Miller, the main public apologist for the dominant party in the Church, seemed to warn, or threaten, the judges that they should consider their fate in a revolution that they risked provoking:

> But the aged judges, the wealthy patrons, the delicately nurtured aristocracy of Scotland, the men who have so much to lose, which in a popular con-vulsion could not fail to be lost, nay, even the more eloquent orators, and more vigorous thinkers of the age, who have yet to give their first proof of military talent – what fate do they augur to themselves![21]

Three years later Dr Chalmers warned the judges that, in trampling on the liberties of the Church courts, they were engaged in 'a sort of genteel chartism' which the multitude below might follow and so embark on a course of anarchy.[22] Addressing a meeting of tradesmen in January 1843, the Rev. Dr James Begg earned loud cheers when he worked himself up to a ringing declaration that 'The foundation principles of the Constitution have been subverted, and, no matter whether that is done by mobs or patrons, by judges or senators, in that consists not only the beginning, but the very essence of Revolutions.'[23] On the other side, a week later, Dean of Faculty Robertson declaimed to the judges of the Court of Session:

> But, my Lords, if there is to be a secession – if they will separate from the State – do not let those parties imagine they can shake the fabric of our glorious constitution. … If they will not read your Lordships' judgments in calm deliberation, let them read them in the imploring looks and the tearful eyes of their wives and children. If, however, it must be otherwise – while I cannot look upon the alternative without distress – I can look upon it without dismay; for I know that not only will the constitution stand unshaken, and that the majesty of the law will not be dethroned, but that there are numbers, equal in learning, in zeal, and in piety, to those who may secede, ready and sufficient to supply the wants of the Established Church of Scotland.[24]

Rather more sedately, John Inglis, the future Lord President of the Court of Session, protested against fallacies couched in loose and popular language being addressed to a portion of the community that 'neither their education nor their mental habits have fitted … to sit in judgment on a question of constitutional law.'[25]

Though largely forgotten by law students and practising lawyers today,[26] this, then, is easily the most important constitutional dispute to have confronted the Scottish courts since the Union.

In order to understand how the constitutional crisis developed, we have to pay some attention to the actual dispute on patronage which came before the courts. Its origins are to be found in the time when the idea of a Union between England and Scotland was under discussion in Scotland.[27] The Church of Scotland was initially suspicious. It feared that, if Scotland and England were united, this would threaten the recently attained position of the presbyterian church as the Established Church in Scotland. To avoid that danger, the Scottish commissioners were forbidden to discuss the position of the Church when negotiating the terms of Union. In addition, the Scottish parliament passed the Protestant Religion and Presbyterian Church Act 1707[28] ('the Act of Security'), under which 'Presbyterian Church Government and Discipline' was to 'Remain and Continue unalterable.' The terms of that Act and the Establishment which it embodied were to be observed 'as a fundamentall and essentiall Condition' of the Treaty of Union as ratified, confirmed and approved by the Scottish[29] and English[30] parliaments.

Less than five years after the Union, however, the United Kingdom Parliament passed the Church Patronage (Scotland) Act 1711[31] which made a significant change in the government of the Church of Scotland by reintroducing a system of patronage. That is to say, the Crown or a local landowner could nominate a man, who had been licensed by the Church as a preacher, to fill a vacancy for a minister in a parish. In terms of section 1 of the Act, the presbytery was obliged to receive and admit those who were presented in the same way 'as the persons or ministers presented before the making of this act ought to have been admitted.' Although the point was disputed, this was interpreted as being a reference back to a provision in an Act of the Parliament of Scotland, 1592 c. 116, under which presbyteries 'be bound and astricted, to receive and admit quhatsumever qualified Minister, presented be his Majestie, or laick patrones.' In other words, the presbytery could check to see that the person presented was 'qualified' – the term was not defined. But, if he was indeed 'qualified', the presbytery was bound to receive and admit him. No mention was made in the Act 1592 c. 116 of what was to happen if the presbytery failed to carry out this duty. A widely held view, however, was that the only sanction was to be found in the next Act of the same year, c. 117, under which the patron was entitled to retain the fruits of the benefice if the presbytery failed to perform its duty.[32] In 1814 this provision had been amended to give the right to the fruits to the Church Widows' Fund.[33]

The Patronage Act was bitterly resented by the Church and was denounced as being incompatible with the guarantees in the Act of Union. Indeed, each year until 1784, the General Assembly would formally protest about the passing of the 1711 Act. To no avail: the Act remained on the statute book and, for many years in the later eighteenth century, little attention was paid to the views of the congregations.

One feature of this controversy about the Patronage Act is particularly worth noticing. During the first hundred years after it was passed, the Court of Session dealt with many disputes under the Act. But no one, whether counsel or judge, suggested that the court could solve the problem by simply holding that, since the Treaty of Union had made the government of the Church of Scotland unalterable, Parliament had had no power to pass the Patronage Act and so it was not to be regarded as law. This is a factor to be taken into account when considering the well-known remarks of Lord President Cooper in *MacCormick* v *Lord Advocate*[34] about a possible power in the Court of Session to hold an Act of Parliament invalid because of its inconsistency with a guarantee in the Act of Union.

Lord Cooper famously declared that 'The principle of the unlimited sovereignty of Parliament is a distinctively English principle which has no counterpart in Scottish constitutional law.'[35] He did not deign, however, to explain what the Scottish position was. Despite this, especially in the debates before 1998, supporters of devolution tended to rely on the same idea.[36] It always seemed likely, however, that, on investigation, the actual position regarding sovereignty in pre-Union Scotland would turn out to be quite complex. Thanks to more recent research,[37] we now have a clearer picture and it does indeed appear that the position was by no means straightforward. While Stair considered that the Court of Session had a power not only of interpretation but of derogation of Acts of Parliament,[38] the seventeenth-century judges themselves acknowledged that they 'could not be Judges to annul an Act of Parliament, which was clearly conceived and had no difficulty in the interpretation' because 'it was not within their Judgment to decide, whether it was justly or unjustly Statute.'[39]

But could the judges have annulled an Act of Parliament on the ground that it was inconsistent with some previous statutory provision which was said to be 'fundamentall' or 'unalterable'? In England, the doctrine of the sovereignty of Parliament would have suggested that they could not. When the terms of the proposed Union were under consideration, there was indeed considerable discussion in Scotland as to whether, by declaring a provision to be 'fundamentall', a legislature could prevent its subsequent repeal or alteration.[40] There appears to have been a range of views, among politicians and theorists at least. By its very nature, the issue is not one that practitioners or judges would have had much, if any, occasion to consider in court. But the failure to challenge the Patronage Act suggests that in those days there must have been a settled view among Scottish practitioners and judges that an Act of Parliament could not be challenged on the ground that, by reason of the Act of Union, it was beyond the powers of Parliament. With the exception of the *Factortame*[41] line of decisions relating to European Community law, the courts have adhered to that position on the sovereignty of Parliament ever since.[42] Of course, in a spirit of 'never say never', some of the speeches in the House of Lords in the first foxhunting case, *R (Jackson) v Attorney General*,[43] contain characteristically bold, or cautious, speculations about the possible fate of a provision passed by the House of Commons alone and purporting to extend the life of Parliament, contrary to the Parliament Acts 1911 and 1949. Having easily resisted the temptation to join in those speculations in my speech, I shall equally easily continue to resist it on this occasion.[44]

Back in the eighteenth century, the Church of Scotland was dominated by ministers appointed under the system of patronage who were well educated, rather effective in debate with the rationalist critics of the day, good at composing elegant sermons, and of some social standing – but rather lacking in enthusiasm. They came to be known as 'Moderates'.[45] By the beginning of the nineteenth century a spirit of change was abroad in the Church.[46] The 'Evangelicals', as they were called, thought that a more vigorous, and indeed more popular, approach was needed if the Church was not to haemorrhage members to more dynamic churches outside the Establishment.[47] Until his sudden death in 1831, the Evangelicals were ably led by the Rev. Andrew Thomson, who was a renowned preacher and the first minister of St George's, the great new church standing in Charlotte Square, at one end of Edinburgh's fashionable New Town.[48] After 1831 the leadership of the Evanglicals passed to Dr Chalmers. Year by year, the Moderates and Evangelicals eyed one another warily across the floor of the General Assembly, as the strength of the Evangelical party increased. In 1834 the Evangelicals took control of the General Assembly.

By that time, in the heady atmosphere after the passing of the Reform Act of 1832, opponents of patronage[49] were flooding the new Parliament with petitions demanding its abolition. Taylor Innes captures the mood:

> It was now the third[50] decade of the nineteenth century. All around there was a warm wave of revolution or reform. The Catholics had been emancipated. Parliament had been reformed. The new electorate seemed to have made up its mind that in Scotland, too, there should be no exclusive Church privileges and no Church penalties. In 1833, in Edinburgh alone, 846 persons were prosecuted for a Church tax; and those imprisoned and liberated were carried in triumph to their homes.[51]

Inside the Church the Evangelicals, too, felt that that it was wrong for lacklustre Moderate ministers to be 'intruded' on congregations without their consent. Those who took this view were known as 'non-intrusionists'.

What was to be done? Some favoured the total abolition of patronage as wrong in principle. Others – conscious, perhaps, that they themselves were the products of patronage[52] – argued that the system was not fundamentally unsound: all that was needed was to find a way for the congregation to express its views about the suitability of the man presented by the patron.

Although for many years the General Assembly had taken a lax view of the relevance of any dissent of the congregation to the induction of a particular presentee, Dr Chalmers and others thought that any problems with the operation of patronage could be solved by the Assembly changing tack and giving weight to parishioners' objections. The perceived difficulty with this proposed remedy was that, with the composition of the Assembly fluctuating from year to year, different Assemblies might take different views and the position might well not settle down for some time. A more decisive solution was needed.[53]

The General Assembly of the Church had power to pass legislation, somewhat in the same way as other corporations,[54] such as local authorities, have powers to pass by-laws. So the Evangelical party finally decided to propose such an Act which would give increased power to congregations to reject presentees. The Act would then be ratified by the Church as a whole and enacted by the General Assembly under the Barrier Act. This course was advocated by Lord Moncreiff, who was not only a Court of Session judge but a prominent Whig, an elder of St George's, and one of the lay leaders of the Evangelical party in the General Assembly. He was, in fact, opposed to the abolition of patronage and saw this kind of legislation as a way to head off demands for the popular election of ministers.[55] By contrast, radical opponents of patronage criticised the idea of such an Act, on the ground that it would be the first measure to have been adopted by the Church which acknowledged the lawfulness of patronage.[56] Subsequently, one strand of criticism was indeed that, by abandoning the Church's traditional opposition to patronage as being fundamentally inconsistent with the parishioners' right of election and by trying, instead, to regulate it, Lord Moncreiff and the other authors of the Veto Act had brought patronage into the realm of ecclesiastical law. They should therefore bear the blame for creating the conflict with the civil law which engulfed the Church.[57]

When Lord Moncreiff and his allies decided to proceed by passing an Act, they were well aware that Moderate opponents would challenge it on the basis that an Act of the General Assembly could not interfere with the rights of patrons and presentees under the ordinary civil law of the land.

The Evangelicals were confident of seeing off the challenge. In part, their confidence was based on the stance of Lord Moncreiff, with his store of learning on ecclesiastical law.[58] His friend, the Lord Advocate, Francis Jeffrey, had also made reassuring noises about the kind of Act they had in mind.[59] So had another of his friends, the Solicitor General for Scotland, Henry Cockburn, who had voted for an earlier version of the Act put forward by Dr Chalmers in 1833.[60] At their instigation, Lord Moncreiff was summoned to London to give evidence to a House of Commons committee on patronage in March 1834. While in London, he stayed with yet another old friend, the Lord Chancellor, Lord Brougham.[61] Jeffrey and Brougham took the opportunity to discuss with Lord Moncreiff what evidence he should give.[62] According to Jeffrey, Lord Moncreiff's evidence, in which he referred to the possibility of the General Assembly legislating on the point, was 'most impressive and apostolic' and had a decisive effect on the Committee.[63]

A couple of months later, meeting in the Tron Church[64] in Edinburgh on 27 May 1834, on the motion of Lord Moncreiff, the General Assembly passed an 'Act on the Calling of Ministers' and, with it, 'terminated the reign of Moderatism in the Church of Scotland.'[65] The Act was given interim effect and, the following year, became a fully fledged Act of the Church by the operation of the Barrier Act. In effect, the Act and the accompanying Regulations meant that, if a majority of male[66] communicant heads of families in a parish objected to the presentee, even without giving reasons, the presbytery was bound to reject him. In this way the male heads of families had a veto on any appointment.[67] Hence the nickname, 'the Veto Act', which stuck, despite the repeated protests of its supporters. Shades of Mrs Thatcher's Poll Tax. Reassuringly for the Evangelicals, both the Attorney General, Sir John Campbell,[68] and Lord Chancellor Brougham[69] went out of their way to express their support for the Act. More ominously, both Lord President Hope and Lord Justice Clerk Boyle voted against it in the General Assembly.[70] Still more ominously, the Lord President's son, John Hope, the Dean of the Faculty of Advocates, had his dissent specially recorded.[71]

Two days after passing the Veto Act, the Assembly went on to deal with another matter that was destined to cause trouble.[72] Scotland was divided up, for both ecclesiastical and civil purposes, into parishes. The ministry of the Church was organised on the basis of these parishes, each parish having a church, a minister of that church, a manse and, in landward parishes, some land, known as the 'glebe', which the minister could cultivate. It was settled that the church, the churchyard, the manse and the glebe were subject to civil, as opposed to ecclesiastical, law. The heritors (landowners) of the parish paid a duty, known as a 'teind', and the minister was entitled to be paid his stipend out of the teinds of the parish. But, with the growth in population and its movement into the towns and cities, by the beginning of the nineteenth century this traditional parish structure was proving unsuitable. In many areas it would have been simply impossible for the minister to look after all the people in his parish. In theory, the difficulties could have been overcome by asking the Court of Session to reorganise the existing parishes and to create new parishes under the Act anent Plantation of Kirks etc. 1707.[73] But the procedure under the Act required the consent of landowners possessing at least three-quarters of the valued rent of the parish and, in practice, that consent was hard to obtain.

Therefore, when faced with the need for additional church accommodation, some local communities simply raised funds, built a new church and secured the services of a minister whose stipend they also had to pay. Many of these ministers were young and enthusiastic Evangelicals, eager to spread the gospel to people who had previously been beyond the reach of the Church. The Church would recognise these churches as 'Chapels of Ease'. The ministers of Chapels of Ease saw themselves as being at a disadvantage by comparison with parish ministers, however: they had no definite sphere in which to work, had no kirk session and could not sit as members of the presbytery. 'In other words, they were permitted to teach but not to rule.'[74] In an age of Church Extension,[75] these complaints could not be ignored indefinitely. Into this matter, too, party rivalries obtruded. The Evangelicals tended to favour, and the Moderates to oppose, giving full rights to the ministers of the Chapels of Ease because so many of them were Evangelicals who would reinforce the strength of that party in the church courts, especially in the General Assembly. In the 1833 General Assembly the Moderates narrowly defeated a proposal to deal with the problem. It was to be their last great victory.

The following year, the General Assembly, with its new Evangelical majority, passed the so-called Chapels Act,[76] which in effect put the ministers of Chapels of Ease on an equal footing with ordinary parish ministers. They were to be enrolled in the presbytery and to be eligible to sit in all the courts of the Church. Kirk sessions were to be formed and each church was to have a district assigned to it as a parish *quoad sacra* – for ecclesiastical purposes only. For all civil purposes, the old parishes would remain the same. Since it had become clear that the Government was not going to provide the Church with funds to endow new churches, this was the best that could be done.

With the Veto Act and the Chapels Act in place, the stage was set for the constitutional battles that were to be played out in a society where public interest in Church questions was already intense.[77] The occasion for the first battle, in what was to prove a long war, soon presented itself in a dispute over patronage.[78]

The patron's right of presentation under the Patronage Act was part of the civil law of the land and could be bought and sold with the land to which it was attached. The Veto Act was liable to reduce the value of that right by making the outcome of any presentation less certain. Even after the Act, however, in practice most of the patrons' nominees were inducted. But not all. In September 1834, little more than three months into the new regime, the Earl of Kinnoull presented 'Mr Robert Young, preacher of the Gospel, residing at Seafield Cottage, Dundee' to be the parish minister at Auchterarder.[79] Unfortunately, after Mr Young had preached on two Sundays, only two people signed his call and, when an opportunity was given to the male heads of families to express their view under the Veto Act, 287 out of a possible 330 recorded their dissent from Mr Young's call. After an adjournment for two weeks for reflection, all but one of the opponents adhered to his dissent. In terms of the Veto Act, the presbytery then held that the call was not a good one. Mr Young appealed on certain procedural points to the synod and from there to the General Assembly of 1835. On the motion of Lord Moncreiff,[80] his appeal to the Assembly was, in substance, dismissed. The case was remitted to the presbytery, which proceeded to reject Mr Young. This time, though an appeal to the synod was marked, he did not proceed with it.[81] Before we lose sight of Mr Young as an individual, it is right to mention that, when he was eventually appointed after the Disruption, he proved a successful and respected parish minister of Auchterarder until his death in 1865.[82]

In his appeal to the synod, Mr Young had been represented by George Patton, the future Lord Justice Clerk. Before the General Assembly, Mr Patton remained one of his counsel, but he was led by Thomas Maitland, who later became Lord Dundrennan. At some stage Mr Young's case came to the attention of the Dean of the Faculty of Advocates, John Hope, the ultra-fervent supporter of the Moderates who had spoken and voted against the veto in the General Assembly. Robert Whigham, another advocate and long-time Moderate member of the Assembly, also became involved. Between them, in October 1835, Hope and Whigham raised an action in the Court of Session on behalf of Lord Kinnoull and Mr Young, challenging the decision of the presbytery of Auchterarder to reject Mr Young.[83] The General Assembly backed the presbytery.

In their summons the pursuers sought declarators (that is: declarations) that Mr Young had been validly presented to the parish and that the presbytery were 'bound and astricted to make trial of the qualification of the pursuer, and are still bound so to do.'[84] The pursuers also included a conclusion (that is, a claim) that, since the presbytery had unlawfully rejected Mr Young, the heritors of the parish should be ordained to pay him the minister's stipend 'in time coming, during the life of the pursuer.'[85] In its defences the presbytery pointed out that no such conclusion could properly be directed against it since the presbytery had nothing to do with the payment of stipend.[86]

Faced with that objection, counsel for the pursuers confined themselves to asking the court to grant a declarator that the presbytery was bound to make trial of Mr Young's qualifications. The presbytery responded by contending that, when not accompanied by the pecuniary conclusion relating to the stipend, this conclusion raised no issue of civil law, but only one of ecclesiastical law.[87] The majority of the court rejected that submission.[88]

Another rather technical point attracted Lord Fullerton and Lord Moncreiff. In their summons the pursuers simply relied on the presbytery's statutory duty under the Act 1592 c. 116 to make trial of Mr Young's qualifications. They did not mention the Veto Act or have a conclusion asking the court to pronounce on its validity.[89] By contrast, the presbytery had, of course, to refer to the regulations made in relation to the Veto Act in order to explain why it had rejected Mr Young and why, in its view, the rejection had been lawful.[90] The pursuers simply argued that this defence was bad since the Veto Act had been *ultra vires* the General Assembly and so could not provide any legal justification for what the presbytery had done. Nevertheless, because the pursuers had not framed their pleadings so as to raise the issue of the validity of the Veto Act, and the General Assembly was not a party to the proceedings, Lord Fullerton and Lord Moncreiff considered that the court should not rule on the validity of the Act.[91] This somewhat over-refined argument, which really ignored the realities of the situation, did not find favour with the majority judges, or indeed with Lord Jeffrey.[92] The House of Lords also rejected it.[93] So the issue of the validity of the Veto Act was in fact determined in the proceedings, even though there was no conclusion in the summons relating to the point and, therefore, no mention of the Act in the court's formal order.[94]

Counsel's arguments before all the judges of the Court of Session took ten days in November and December 1837. The hearing does not appear to have attracted much attention at the time. To those familiar with the ways of modern courts the proceedings are notable for the very few interruptions from the judges. Since Lord Cockburn comments on Lord Jeffrey's usual tendency to intervene during hearings,[95] it may be that, because all the judges were sitting, they felt the need to exercise restraint if the hearing was not to be interminable.[96]

The argument for the pursuers was essentially simple. Taken in conjunction with the Act 1592 c. 116, the Church Patronage (Scotland) Act 1711 provided that, if, after taking him on his trials, the presbytery found that a presentee was indeed qualified to serve as a minister, then the presbytery was bound to induct him into the charge. It was therefore its statutory duty to take him on trial.[97] In so far as the Veto Act cut across that statutory duty, it should simply be ignored. The Court of Session should accordingly declare that, by refusing to take trial of Mr Young's qualifications, the presbytery had acted illegally and in violation of its statutory duty.

It is important to remember that the pursuers had not proceeded with an appeal against the presbytery's final decision to reject Mr Young as parish minister of Auchterarder. So the case raised a question about the power of the Court of Session in these circumstances to review a decision of the presbytery, as a court. But, strictly speaking, it raised no issue about the power of the Court of Session to review a judgment of the General Assembly, as a court deciding an appeal relating to the induction of a presentee. That question was to come before the Court of Session in later proceedings.[98] On the other hand, the case was treated as raising an issue about the power of the General Assembly, as a legislature, to legislate in relation to the induction of a presentee. In that connection counsel for the Church argued that the Veto Act could not be *ultra vires*, since it had actually done nothing more than the Assembly could have done in a series of decisions in its judicial capacity.[99] To deal with that argument, the judges sometimes strayed into the issue of the Court of Session's power to control the General Assembly in its judicial capacity.[100]

The presbytery's principal defence was radical. While making various points about the proper interpretation of the Patronage Act, the presbytery's main thrust was to challenge the jurisdiction of the Court of Session to deal with the matter. The argument started from the fact that the case concerned the procedure leading to the possible ordination of Mr Young as a minister. Ordination was a spiritual matter and so, the argument ran, everything relating to it lay within the exclusive (spiritual) jurisdiction of the Church courts which, as courts of the Established Church, were an important, distinct and indeed unalterable element in the constitution of Scotland as found in the Act of Union. The General Assembly, at the top of that separate court structure, was just as much a national supreme court in ecclesiastical matters as the Court of Session or House of Lords was in civil matters or the Court of Justiciary in criminal matters. So, even if the presbytery was bound by the Act 1592 c. 116 'to receive and admit' Mr Young, that statutory obligation related to a spiritual matter within the exclusive jurisdiction of the Church courts. If the pursuers were unhappy with the presbytery's decision to reject Mr Young, their only remedy was to appeal to the synod and then to the General Assembly, whose decision would be final. Even if the Court of Session considered that the decision of any of the Church courts was wrong, it could not interfere to put it right or even to declare that it was unlawful – just as the (civil) Court of Session could not interfere to correct a decision of the (criminal) Court of Justiciary that it thought was wrong. Quite simply, it was no business of the Court of Session.

Andrew Rutherfurd, the talented but haughty Solicitor General for Scotland in Lord Melbourne's ministry,[101] put the point for the presbytery in this way:

> There is no question, my Lords, that in this country the majesty of the law is all in all: the majesty of the monarch is but a reflex of the majesty of the law. But the majesty of the law shall then be best consulted when the different courts of this country keep themselves in the exercise of their powers, within their proper jurisdiction; and do not commit encroachments on the peculiar provinces of each other. ... It would be 'confusion worse confounded,' and not only would the majesty of the law be insulted and degraded in such a contest, but law itself would be lost or destroyed, were those courts, which are her authoritative organs, to come to a conflict, which the constitution, not deeming possible, has provided no means of determining, but which could only be settled apparently by the weight of the mace, and the physical force of the officers and apparitors of the court.[102]

So stated, this was a formidable argument and one which the minority judges in the Court of Session accepted and applied, time and again, as the same point came up in case after case.[103] But it was bedevilled by a qualification which greatly complicated matters. As the General Assembly and presbyteries must have known very well when they passed the Veto Act, it did inevitably affect 'in some degree' the civil interests of individuals.[104] In so far as it did so, the Church admitted that the Court of Session had jurisdiction. In effect, therefore, you could have two courts dealing with the same issue, one with its civil and one with its ecclesiastical effects. For the Moderates, John Inglis dismissed the idea that there could be ever be room for a collision of this kind between the Court of Session and the Church courts: 'Collision! This is the collision between a sovereign and his subject, between the law and the lieges, between the judge and the litigant.'[105]

On the Church's approach, however, interpreting and applying a statute in one way, the General Assembly might authorise someone's induction as the minister of a parish, while, interpreting and applying the same statute differently, the Court of Session might simultaneously hold that he was not entitled to occupy the manse or to cultivate the glebe. The General Assembly would be deciding on 'the spiritualities', the Court of Session on 'the temporalities'. Both decisions would be 'correct' and the Court of Session had no jurisdiction to force the Church courts to apply its interpretation. In theory, therefore, a time could come when, all over Scotland, Established Church manses lay empty and the glebes untended, when presentees idled away their time without a charge, and when the ministers admitted to the charges by the presbyteries could not claim the stipend for carrying out their duties in the parish and would have to be supported from funds raised by their parishioners.[106] It would amount to creeping disestablishment.[107]

There was, of course, a further complication which even the most determined apologists for the doctrine admitted was difficult to resolve: who had the final say on whether some particular matter fell to be regarded as civil or ecclesiastical – the Court of Session or the Church courts?[108]

When the judges came to announce their decision in February and March 1838, the court room was unusually crowded and a number of Edinburgh ministers were there to see the outcome.[109] They had a long wait ahead of them since the judges took six days to deliver their judgments, which ran to about a quarter of a million words.[110] By a majority of eight to five, they found in favour of the pursuers and against the presbytery.[111] By the time the old and frail Lord Glenlee made a special trip to court to give his opinion on 6 March, the Church was plainly in difficulties. The courtroom and its gallery were filled with spectators, including leading clerical figures, eagerly watching the drama unfold. Something of the tension within the court emerges from the different reactions when it turned out that Lord Glenlee was supporting the presbytery. The majority judges suddenly stopped being studiously courteous to him, while Andrew Rutherfurd, the Solicitor General, turned to the bench and looked to Lord Moncreiff, 'with the smallest possible wink – small, yet marked enough to say, "Is that not capital?"'[112]

The majority of the judges rejected the Church's argument on jurisdiction. They held that, since the Veto Act had led to Mr Young's rejection as the parish minister, it had interfered with both pursuers' patrimonial interests – a very elastic concept[113] – and so with their civil rights. This was enough to bring the matter into the jurisdiction of the Court of Session. But, critically, they also held that, where the statute said that the presbytery was bound to take a presentee on trials, the Court of

Session had jurisdiction to decide whether the presbytery had performed that duty and the Church courts had no power to contradict that determination.

The opinion of Lord President Hope may be taken as embodying the majority view. He had to remark, he said,

> that in every civilized country, there *must* be some court or other judicature, by which every other court of judicature may be either compelled to do their duty, or kept within the bounds of their own duty. Without this the greatest public confusion must follow, and often great injustice to individuals.[114]

By passing the Veto Act the Church had purported to give

> supreme and omnipotent control of heads of families over the *civil and patrimonial and parliamentary* rights of the patron and his presentee. It is sometimes said that Parliament is omnipotent; but our Church goes a step farther, and plays viceroy over Parliament itself.[115]

In short, the Lord President is saying that the Court of Session must be able to step in, not only to stop such interference with the civil rights of patrons and their presentees, but also to maintain the authority of Parliament. Already, right at the very outset, he is emphasising the wider, constitutional, significance of the issue which all these Disruption cases raise. That same constitutional dimension is seen in the references that he and other judges make to major English constitutional cases, such as *Burdett* v *Abbott*,[116] *Stockdale* v *Hansard*[117] and *Ashby* v *White*.[118]

In his judgment, Lord Gillies commented:

> If the Church can pass resolutions like that against intrusion, the effect of which, as the defenders say, is to render a political matter an ecclesiastical matter, and to convert the one into the other; and if, in virtue of such resolutions, the Church is entitled to pass laws like the *veto* act, regulating such matters; and if finally these matters are to *take end* in the church courts, their powers are indeed transcendant.[119]

The view of the minority judges on the crucial question of the jurisdiction to control the presbytery can be seen from Lord Jeffrey's declaration that:

> though a court should act *ultra vires*, still if it were acting within its own proper province, or in relation to that class of cases or interests to which it alone was competent, no other court can encroach upon that province, or go beyond its own, either to correct or to declare that excess or illegality – the remedy in such an extremity being in parliament alone.[120]

One legal critic spoke of Lord Jeffrey

> displaying the same ingenuity and brilliancy as a judge, which he has so

often displayed as a reviewer, in bolstering up an infirm cause. But even his as well as the others' arguments on this head are very similar to those by which the House of Commons and its advocates lately sought, though happily without success, to establish the total exemption of *their* functionaries from the jurisdiction of courts of justice, about as candid, about as rational, and about as constitutional.[121]

The majority judges also resolved the question of *Kompetenz-Kompetenz*, as it is called today in European law circles, against the Church. They held that the Church courts could not determine the extent of their own ecclesiastical jurisdiction. It was for the Court of Session to fix the appropriate dividing line between civil and ecclesiastical matters. Perhaps the point of view of the majority was put most succinctly by Lord Wood in the later *Stewarton* case. He said that the question whether anything ecclesiastical does or does not fall within the independent and exclusive jurisdiction of the Church is itself 'a civil, not an ecclesiastical question – and it is one which the Supreme Court has jurisdiction to entertain and decide.'[122] Just because the Court of Session had no ecclesiastical jurisdiction, it did not follow that it had no jurisdiction to determine whether

> in any matter ecclesiastical in which the Church asserts its power to act and judge, the Church really possesses such power or not. I think that that is a question which legitimately falls within the jurisdiction of the Court.[123]

The opposing view of the Church, that it could determine the scope of its own exclusive ecclesiastical jurisdiction, left it open to the criticism that it was claiming a sacred and unique right:

> that authority, when exercised within the ecclesiastical department as defined by ecclesiastics, is superior to the civil power, even should the exercise of their authority be followed with secular effects of great temporal concern. In regard to the secular evil, they tell their opponents that they must rest without redress, if it arises from an ecclesiastical concern that can be settled only under the jurisdiction of the Church. When contrasted with spiritual interests, which are of importance in the eye of the Church, patrimonial interests are to be set aside and forgotten, as things that were, but now are lost and for ever, at the bidding of churchmen.[124]

When the decision of the Court of Session was finally announced, the leaders of the Evangelical party in the Church professed themselves horrified by the majority judgments. They had assumed that the Established Church of Scotland and her courts were a separate and independent element in the British constitution of 1707. It now turned out that the Acts which she passed and the decisions which her courts reached were subject to review by the Court of Session if, in its view, they interfered with a civil right. The cry went up: the Court of Session is encroaching on the territory of the Church and her courts and threatening her very spiritual independence. In the General Assembly debate on 23 May 1838, a few months after the decision, Dr Robert Buchanan[125] rallied his troops in colourful language. He referred to the spiritual independence of the Church as being

> inscribed, and that not unfrequently, in characters of blood, on many of the brightest and most memorable pages of our ecclesiastical history. Like some ancient banner which has been borne in triumph through many a hard fought field, it hangs honoured and venerated within our church's armoury. ....[126]

A clear warning of troubles ahead was to be found at the end of the resolution which the Assembly passed at Dr Buchanan's instigation: the Assembly would 'firmly enforce obedience upon all office-bearers and members of this church, by the execution of her laws, in the exercise of the ecclesiastical authority wherewith they are invested.'[127] To judge by the language of both sides,[128] the Court of Session and the Church seemed ready for war. As happens in many conflicts, the generals on both sides were soon to become household names in Scotland.

Even this particular battle might not yet be lost for the Evangelicals. The day after the debate on the *Auchterarder* decision, on the recommendation of the Procurator of the Church, Robert Bell, the General Assembly authorised him to appeal to the House of Lords as soon as it appeared expedient to do so.[129] At the same time, Mr Bell reminded the Assembly that 'the funds of the Church were in a very low state, and that it would be necessary to devise some means for raising subscriptions for that purpose.' As their opponents did not fail to point out,[130] despite the outcome of the previous day's debate, by the act of appealing, the Evangelical party might appear to be impliedly recognising the very jurisdiction of the civil courts that they were simultaneously denying. But, for the Evangelicals, the appeal was to be seen as relating only to the temporalities, such as the stipend, which would be divorced from the ministerial office and so 'bereave' the parish of Auchterarder 'of the inestimable benefits of the National Establishment' if the decision of the Court of Session stood.[131]

In marking the appeal, the Church's advisers may have hoped for a favourable reception from Lord Brougham who, when Lord Chancellor, had gone on record as approving the Veto Act.[132] But he was now in the political wilderness and sniping at his former friends. He was scarcely to be relied on for consistency. In the event, Lord Brougham ditched the Whig companions of his Edinburgh youth, Lord Moncreiff, Lord Jeffrey and Lord Cockburn. Along with Lord Chancellor Cottenham, he resoundingly upheld the majority of the Court of Session. In the course of an extempore speech lasting over three hours,[133] Lord Brougham rejected the presbytery's argument on jurisdiction in summary fashion: '... I have no doubt whatever upon that.'[134] He continued:

> Then it is said, you have no means of carrying into effect the decree of the Court of Session, albeit supported by the authority of the House of Lords, which is a decision of Parliament in its judicial character upon the subject. In other words, although you say the presbytery have acted wrong – although you say that their reason for rejecting is of no avail whatever – although you say the law is contrary to what they have supposed it to be – and although you say ... let the presbytery induct immediately, for it has no grounds for refusing – still it is affirmed that the presbytery may persist in refusing, and must prevail. My Lords, it is indecent to suppose any such case.[135]

Lord Chancellor Cottenham was equally clear on the point. If the General Assembly had legislative power to make any regulations it pleased on the admission of ministers and if any appeal from the decisions of presbyteries lay only to the self-same General Assembly, no means would exist of questioning the legality of its enactments. 'This is but a mode of describing pure despotism.'[136] The Church had tried to meet this objection by arguing that under the constitution any remedy lay not with the civil courts but with Parliament. Lord Cottenham demolished that argument:

> Those who contend that there is no remedy for the wrong which has been committed in any existing law, suggest that redress can be obtained only by application to Parliament. But if the right be already established by statute, and if the wrong consist in a violation of the right so resting upon the authority of Parliament, it is not easy to conceive in what manner Parliament may be able hereafter, with more success, to secure the objects of its enactments: certainly not without a more direct and important interference with the powers, legislative and judicial, claimed by the Assembly, than the judgement of the Court of Session can be supposed to effect.[137]

Worse still from the point of view of the Evangelical party in the Church – in a move that seems to have taken even the Moderates by surprise – their Lordships indicated that the only 'qualifications' which the presbytery could take into account when deciding whether to receive and admit a presentee were his 'literature, life and manners'.[138] So it could not apparently consider any other objections to the presentee's suitability for a particular parish – such as an inability to speak Gaelic in a Gaelic-speaking area. Leading Moderates soon argued that these observations were *obiter dicta* and therefore not binding.[139]

The speeches in the House of Lords ran over from 2 to 3 May 1839. With the General Assembly due to start later in the month, the decision was the main topic of conversation.[140] How was the Assembly to react to this complete rejection of the presbytery's case by 'the supreme court'?[141] 'Coteries of lawyers and divines debated in libraries and drawing-rooms what was to be done.'[142] Back in 1833–4, Dr Chalmers had been doubtful about the wisdom of adopting the Veto Law and had only been persuaded to support the 'blunder', as he later called it, by the advice of Lord Moncreiff and Henry Cockburn.[143] After the decision of the Court of Session in 1838, Dr Chalmers had favoured the Evangelicals defusing the situation by repealing the Veto Act.[144] In the immediate aftermath of the decision of the House of Lords, Dr Chalmers was inclined to maintain that position. But eventually he came to the view that the *obiter* remarks of the Lord Chancellor and Lord Brougham, about the narrow range of qualifications which a presbytery could consider, meant that simply repealing the Veto Act and relying on the presbytery's power to reject unqualified presentees would not solve the problem. His critics claimed that Dr Chalmers' will had been overborne by one of the younger, forceful, Evangelical leaders as late as the Monday before the Assembly began.[145]

At all events, Dr Chalmers submitted to the Assembly a series of resolutions which he protested – perhaps too much – were his own work.[146] The debate on his resolutions and two others took place on 16 May in an atmosphere of great excitement. The Tron Church was crowded, ladies having taken their place in the galleries at five in the morning, even though the debate was not due to begin until noon.[147] It did not finish until two the following morning when Dr Chalmers' resolutions were adopted. His speech, which he read while leaning on a staff,[148] had lasted close on three hours and ended in his near collapse – a sign, perhaps, of the strain he was under.[149]

Dr Chalmers' new, unrelenting, attitude to the courts and the veto came through when he declared that the Church must organise its affairs according to its own statute book:

> Now, it was by the deliberate voice and judgment of the Church that this law [the Veto Law], so obnoxious in other quarters, found its way there; and though it never should be consented to by the State it must continue to be our regulator till rescinded by the same power to which it owes its enactment, and on no other considerations I trust than those of principle and of the public weal. Whether a law is to be established or repealed by us, let me never see the day when we shall be constrained to either the one or

the other by a force *ab extra*, or by any principle whatever distinct from our own spontaneous views of what is best for the interests of Christ's kingdom.[150]

In other words, the Church should not repeal the Veto Act just because of the judgments of the House of Lords or the Court of Session, but only if Parliament would not legislate to bring it into line with the civil law and the Church itself thought it right to repeal it.[151] When, the following year, it became clear, however, that Parliament was not going to legislate, Dr Chalmers reverted to his original position. He again favoured repealing the Veto Act and leaving it to the presbyteries and the General Assembly to consider the sufficiency of calls on a case-by-case basis.[152]

Though hailed as a 'magnificent oration'[153] and 'a masterpiece'[154] by two of his biographers, Dr Chalmers' marathon speech to the 1839 Assembly struck his opponents and some of his former supporters rather differently – in short, as involving a morally doubtful change of front. In the debate, one of those opponents, Dr Bryce, was brave enough to say that, when he saw how those who had advocated appealing to the House of Lords then hesitated to give effect to its decision dismissing their appeal, 'he felt inclined to doubt whether he was speaking to honest men and clergymen.'[155] For his pains, he was howled down.[156] Dr Cook, the leader of the Moderates, complained that the adoption of Dr Chalmers' motion would stamp the Church as rebels against the law of the land. That was not well received either.[157] One observer acknowledged the great impact of Dr Chalmers' speech on the Assembly, but noted that it had 'little logical texture, and no legal grasp.'[158] Another critic subsequently accused him of 'almost supercilious' neglect of statutes and of treating them as 'the playthings of imagination',[159] while the young Earl of Dalhousie left the Assembly, declaring that Dr Chalmers had gained a victory which, 'though brilliant, has not been, morally, a bloodless one.'[160] In the *Presbytery of Strathbogie* case, the following February, Lord President Hope was able to make the obvious, but still telling, point that, if the judgment of the House of Lords had gone the other way, the judges in the House of Lords 'would then have been Solomon and Daniel in the eyes of the Church courts.' As it was, the Church courts absolutely refused to obey the judgment. In point of 'candour and fairness', the Lord President considered it 'no better than the old shuffle, "Odds, I win – evens, you lose."'[161]

Although one of Dr Chalmers' resolutions instructed the presbytery of Auchterarder to offer no further resistance to the claims of Mr Young or his patron to the emoluments of the benefice, this was really a meaningless concession since 'it [was] in law impossible for any man to possess himself of the emoluments of a benefice without induction by the presbytery'[162] –

and the General Assembly was resisting any idea that Mr Young should be inducted.

With Dr Chalmers signed up and with the Rev. Robert Candlish having stepped into the arena,[163] the dominant party in the Church was now set on a collision course with the civil courts over their respective roles in the constitution. Neither side would readily back down.

On the very day when the General Assembly was debating the resolutions on the *Auchterarder* case, a little further up the High Street the Court of Session was busy administering a new blow in the *Lethendy* case.[164] The atmosphere in which the majority judges felt themselves to be operating comes out when Lord Medwyn complains of how

> in consequence of protection having been afforded, as I humbly think, legally and constitutionally, in support of civil interests, a cry is raised in our land that the civil court is interfering with the independence of the Church; and presbyteries resolve, and prayer meetings are held to pray against such Erastian oppression and invasion of Church rights. Some attempt, I think, should be made to disabuse the public mind from the misconception with which it is poisoned, and the true state of the case should be broadly and plainly stated.[165]

Stripped of detail,[166] the case concerned a situation where there were two rivals for appointment as minister in the united parishes of Lethendy and Kinloch. Under the Veto Act the presbytery of Dunkeld had rejected the first choice, a Mr Clark, when a majority of the male heads of families opposed him. But he obtained an interdict from the Court of Session against anyone else being appointed to the vacancy. Despite this, a new presentation was issued by the Crown in favour of a Mr Kessen. The presbytery was about to induct Mr Kessen when Mr Clark obtained an interim interdict against it doing so. In June 1838 the matter came before the interim body, the Commission of the General Assembly, which ordered the presbytery to proceed with his ordination. Mr Clark obtained further interdicts against Mr Kessen and the presbytery. The matter was again taken to the Commission. It again ordered the presbytery to proceed to Mr Kessen's ordination – without delay. In the face of dire threats from Dean of Faculty Hope about the retribution that awaited them,[167] a majority of the presbytery decided to proceed and did indeed ordain Mr Kessen in defiance of the orders of the Court of Session.

In short, when faced with conflicting orders in the shape of interdicts of the Court of Session and a deliverance of the Commission of the General Assembly, the majority of the presbytery had decided to ignore the orders of the civil court and to obey the order of the Church body. With the concurrence of the Lord Advocate, Mr Clark raised proceedings (a petition and complaint) against the majority of the presbytery and Mr Kessen for their breach of the interdicts of the Court of Session.

A variety of preliminary arguments having been disposed of,[168] the defence became, classically, one of superior orders:[169] the ministers had disregarded the interdict of the Court of Session in obedience to the orders of their superior in the hierarchy of Church courts, the Commission of the General Assembly.[170] As with all such defences, it presupposed, of course, that there were indeed two separate and legitimate sources of authority – the State, represented by the Court of Session, and the Church, represented by the Commission. The supposed dilemma lay in having to choose between two conflicting orders, each of which they could regard as compelling. But no civil court, however sympathetic to the ministers' predicament,[171] could ever accept that there could be such a rival source of lawful competing orders within the one state. Certainly the Court of Session did not. For Lord Meadowbank, who chose to be as sententious as possible:

> It would be strange, indeed, if those whose pre-eminent duty it is to instruct the people in the duty of subjection to the law, should alone be left at liberty, not only to set its tenets and its courts at defiance, but themselves to proceed with impunity to give resistance of the legal and constitutional orders and appointments of the highest authority in the State.[172]

Even Lord Jeffrey, who was indeed sympathetic to the claims of the Church, accepted that, on the majority view, 'it is quite right that [the court's] authority should now be vindicated, by finding that its violation was unjustifiable, and without warrant of law.'[173] As often happens with the defence of superior orders, there was a suspicion that the ministers were really hiding behind the Commission: the logic of their position was that the Commission, which had ordered them to proceed with the ordination, was the real wrongdoer. Lord Justice Clerk Boyle was 'much afraid, however, that the desire of merely obeying the deliverance of the Commission had not much effect upon the minds of [the] majority.' He surmised that they had voluntarily chosen to act on their own opinion of the law.[174]

The offending ministers and Mr Kessen were ordered to appear before the Court of Session three weeks later. In one of the great set pieces in the Disruption drama – ministers of the Church standing resolutely before judges in their robes of office representing the State and worldly power[175] – they made two statements to the court,[176] the terms of which had already been published. They did not actually apologise. After some debate behind the scenes, the Court decided not to impose any punishment and just to warn the ministers. A significant factor may well have been that the judges were anxious to avoid raising the stakes by making martyrs out of the ministers.[177] Having warned them, Lord President Hope added a personal address.[178] 'Dreadful' was how Lord Cockburn described it later that day to his friend, Andrew Rutherfurd, by now the Lord Advocate.[179] The Lord President sought to persuade the ministers of their need to submit to civil authority. Warming to his theme, he referred to Christ's appearance before the Sanhedrin when He did not dispute that court's jurisdiction over Him.[180] 'N.B.,' Lord Cockburn said to the Lord Advocate in the same letter, 'He did not say what Christ would have done if interdicted from inducting an apostle.'

Faced with an essentially similar dilemma when a vacancy arose at Marnoch in Aberdeenshire, the presbytery of Strathbogie followed the opposite course. After much toing and froing,[181] at the beginning of December 1839 the majority, comprising seven ministers, decided to disobey the orders of the General Assembly and, instead, to obey the Court of Session and take the presentee, Mr Edwards, on trial.[182] If anything, this caused even greater havoc. Because they had decided to obey the civil courts rather than the General Assembly, a week later the seven ministers were suspended by the Commission of Assembly.[183] Two months after that, the Court of Session set aside their suspension and backed up its order with interdicts that were widely ignored.[184] Dr Chalmers thought that the insurrection of the seven ministers was being orchestrated (by the Dean of Faculty, John Hope) to produce anarchy in the Church. So Strathbogie was 'the arena on which the battle of the Church is to be fought.'[185] For the Moderates, the proceedings taken by the Evangelical majority against the Strathbogie ministers assumed 'a peculiarly serious and alarming aspect to all the clergy who coincided with them in their opinions and principles.'[186] In other words, who's going to be next for such treatment?

Matters dragged on,[187] but eventually in December 1840 the Court of Session ordered the presbytery actually to admit Mr Edwards to the charge.[188] On a snowy day in January 1841, even though they had been suspended by the Assembly, the seven ministers making up the majority of the presbytery proceeded with the induction in the parish church at Marnoch. The scene – humble but dignified country people watching the confrontation with 'the recusant presbyters' before withdrawing silently from the church, never to return – was to become another set piece in the saga of those times.[189] In May of the same year the General Assembly declared the admission of Mr Edwards to have been null and void and directed the presbytery to proceed with the induction of another presentee, the Rev. David Henry[190] – which a minority of the presbytery did. For the offence of seeking the protection of the Court of Session against the Commission of Assembly, the General Assembly went on to depose the seven ministers from their office as ministers and to declare their churches vacant.[191] At the urging of Dean of Faculty Hope, Moderate colleagues ignored the deposition and quickly joined the deposed ministers in dispensing communion[192] – for which offence they were suspended for nine months by the 1842 General Assembly.[193]

The Court of Session responded to the deposition of the Strathbogie Seven[194] by suspending the General Assembly's sentence and interdicting any steps to fill the purported vacancies in the parishes.[195] Subsequently, by a majority, the Court of Session affirmed its jurisdiction to reduce the decree of the General Assembly deposing the ministers.[196] They also found, unanimously, that, by admitting Mr Henry to the charge in Marnoch, the ministers making up the minority of the presbytery were in breach of interdict.[197] There matters stood when the Disruption brought hostilities to a close.[198]

Whatever the non-intrusionists might say in public, they were aware that their stance and the turmoil it was causing were not going down well with much of enlightened opinion in Scotland.[199] While Dr Chalmers and his colleagues might think that the Church had acted 'with caution and well-weighed consideration in the midst or her embarrassments', as he himself realised, many in society had the honest impression that their style of proceeding had been 'the most wayward and outrageous.'[200] There was a danger that, because of these events, the leaders of opinion in Scotland would become disillusioned with the Established Church and, deeming it valueless, leave for the waiting arms of the Episcopal Church.[201] The press was all but universally hostile – even the radical press, which wanted patronage abolished, denounced the Evangelicals for adopting their belligerent stance from the safety of the Establishment. For the Glasgow Herald 'The Church professes obedience to the law, and yet does not obey it.'[202]

On 2 June 1841, a week after the Strathbogie ministers were deposed, more than 700 people – a record number – attended a meeting in the Assembly Rooms in Edinburgh to support them.[203] The Tory Sheriff Anderson, a supporter of the Moderates and future Lord Advocate,[204] mocked the position of the majority in the General Assembly:

I have heard of opposition to the law, of rebellion against the law, being considered as punishable offences; but it lies with the Church of Scotland in the present day to introduce this new offence into the category of crimes – obedience in matters of civil right to the civil judicatories of the country.[205]

Two days later, a rival meeting in support of the non-intrusionists, chaired by the (seventh) Duke of Argyll and attended by the Lord Provost, attracted a smaller audience. Even at the end, *The Scotsman* noted, the room was not much more than one-third full, 'one half of those present being ladies!'[206] Nevertheless, strong words were spoken, not least by Sheriff Monteith[207] who drew cheers when he declared that, if the Church fell in her struggle with the civil courts of Scotland, she would not fall alone: 'it would only be the commencement' – he said it advisedly – 'of a struggle which would convulse the empire[208] to its upmost limits.'[209]

Really repeating a point made by Sheriff Monteith,[210] *The Witness* newspaper, the mouthpiece of the non-intrusionists, noted that the supporters of the Strathbogie ministers at the earlier public meeting had included known Episcopalians. It also calculated that over 400 of the 766 names in the published list of the ministers' supporters were members of the legal profession. The 'cuckoo cry' of 'the law of the land' would have most influence with them, it said. The fact that lawyers were so prominent in the list showed 'how little [the ministers were] sympathised with by other classes.'[211] But the author – presumably the editor, Hugh Miller – may well have missed the point. The very fact that Episcopalians were sufficiently alarmed to turn out suggests that many informed people with no direct interest in the dispute considered that the General Assembly had threatened the very fabric of the constitution by punishing the ministers for having recourse to the Court of Session and for then obeying the orders of the highest civil court in Scotland. Nor could a cheap jibe diminish the significance of the fact that so many lawyers thought so too.

In May 1842, amidst scenes of great excitement,[212] on the motion of Dr Chalmers, the General Assembly adopted a Claim of Right or, more precisely, a 'Claim, Declaration, and Protest'. It had been drafted by yet another advocate, Alexander Dunlop.[213] Only after many closely printed pages of recitals do we eventually reach a claim as of right, followed by a declaration and then a protest in these terms:

> And they PROTEST, that all and whatsoever acts of the Parliament of Great Britain, passed without the consent of this Church and nation, in alteration of, or derogation to the aforesaid government, discipline, right, and privileges of this Church (which were not allowed to be treated of by the commissioners for settling the terms of the union between the two kingdoms, but were secured by antecedent stipulation provided to be inserted, and inserted in the Treaty of Union, as an unalterable and fundamental condition thereof, and so reserved from the cognizance and power of the federal legislature created by the said Treaty), – as also, all and whatsoever sentences of courts in contravention of the same government,

discipline, right and privileges, are, and shall be, in themselves, void and null, and of no legal force or effect; and that, while they will accord full submission to all such acts and sentences, in so far – though in so far only – as these may regard civil rights and privileges, whatever may be their opinion of the justice or legality of the same, their said submission shall not be deemed an acquiescence therein, but that it shall be free to the members of this Church, or their successors, at any time hereafter, when there shall be a prospect of obtaining justice, to claim the restitution of all such civil rights and privileges, and temporal benefits and endowments, as for the present they may be compelled to yield up, in order to preserve to their office-bearers the free exercise of their spiritual government and discipline, and to the people the liberties, of which respectively it has been attempted, so contrary to law and justice, to deprive them.[214]

This represents the most extreme statement of the position of the Church. It actually declares that the Acts of Parliament dealing with the government, etc. of the Church which Parliament had passed after the Act of Union, without the consent of 'the Church and nation', are 'void and null, and of no legal force or effect.' The same applies to judgments in contravention of the same government, etc. In other words, the Patronage Act and all the judgments of the Court of Session and House of Lords on the Veto Act are void and have no legal effect. But, even though it makes that claim, the Church does not suggest that the Patronage Act could or would be declared null and void by the Court of Session. Moreover, the Church stops short of drawing the conclusion that it can simply ignore the offending legislation and judgments: it will submit to, but not acquiesce in, the judgments of the civil courts on civil rights and privileges. So, in this version of its stance, the Church does not even accept the decisions of the civil courts on civil matters touching the Church, but looks forward to a day when 'there shall be a prospect of obtaining justice' and the Church will be able to reclaim its civil rights.

Even though, one might think, its extreme language and claims were more likely to alarm than to persuade,[215] the declaration was very much for public consumption and directed, in particular, at the Government and Parliament. Privately, the Evangelical leaders, including the draftsman, did 'not entertain the most remote expectation of the State listening to any, even the most reasonable, demands they might make.'[216] Despite the confident tone of the declaration, the realities of the situation were indeed rather different. In the general election the previous year the Tories had swept to power and Peel was now Prime Minister.[217] The stream of litigations involving the Church continued. In August 1842 the House of Lords again confounded the professed expectations of the non-intrusionists[218] by holding that the Earl of Kinnoull and Mr Young were entitled to claim damages for the presbytery of Auchterarder's failure to carry out its duty to take Mr Young on trial.[219] The argument of the presbytery, that the only remedy was the withholding of the fruits of the benefice, was all but laughed out of court.[220]

The leaders of the Evangelical party realised that the situation could not continue. The court actions were draining their financial resources and exposing them to the risk of fines and to liability in damages. Enforcing their discipline against ministers who disagreed with them was presenting the Church – and the Evangelical party, in particular – in a very unattractive light. So the Evangelical leaders called a Convocation of sympathetic ministers to reinforce their commitment and to work out a plan of action.[221]

The trouble was that the Evangelicals were divided about how to proceed. Some thought that, if their approaches to the Government and Parliament did not succeed, they should dissolve their union with the State and leave the Established Church. Others, notably the Rev. James Begg, thought that their duty was to remain in the Established Church and – despite all the difficulties – to fight on, by purging the Church, mercilessly, of those who supported Erastian views about the right of the State to control it.[222] This second possible course of action opened up a long vista of tit-for-tat lawsuits between the warring factions. Precisely these two competing views were to surface in the Convocation, which then had to decide between them. It was by no means certain in advance that the bulk of the Evangelical ministers would follow if the leaders decided to leave the Established Church.[223]

The Convocation met in Edinburgh over a seven-day period in November 1842. Only ministers took part. The Convocation adopted two sets of resolutions which were published. But the actual proceedings were kept secret and observers could only guess at the train of the discussions leading to the resolutions.[224] It was not until 1880 that a minute prepared by one of the ministers who was present was published.[225] For a lawyer, at least, it gives an interesting insight into the way the constitution and the guarantees in the Act of Union were regarded. It is all the more interesting because, at the outset, the meeting decided not to admit John Hamilton and Alexander Dunlop, the two advocates who had been the non-intrusionists' most prominent legal advisers. It was felt that there was no want of information on the subject in the group.[226] That was no idle boast: the record of their debate suggests that the participants had a remarkable grasp of law and politics, which would not be easily matched in any legal or other assembly today.

The first task of the meeting was to decide what their real grievance was. Was it non-intrusion or their loss of spiritual independence? Predictably, the answer was: their loss of spiritual independence as a result of the decisions of the Court of Session and now of the Supreme Court (in other words, the House of Lords).[227] They focused on the recent decision of the House of Lords in the second *Auchterarder* case,[228] holding that the presbytery's failure to take Mr Young on trial gave rise to a liability in damages enforceable in the civil courts.[229]

What was their duty in these circumstances? That depended on the status of the decisions of the civil courts. This in turn depended on how you looked at the constitution. On the position adopted by the non-intrusionists, the decisions of the civil courts, interfering with the spiritual matter of ordination, were a violation of the constitutional guarantee in the Act of Union that the government of the Church of Scotland would remain and continue unalterable. Now that these decisions had been taken by the courts, where did that leave the constitutional guarantee?

Note the special nature of the constitutional problem, as the members of the Convocation perceived it. We are used to situations where a legislature or a member of the executive is said to have violated some guarantee in a constitution. As we have seen already,[230] the passing of the Church Patronage (Scotland) Act 1711 was regarded as an example of the use by Parliament of its legislative power in breach of one of the guarantees in the Act of Union. What makes the discussion among the ministers in their Convocation unusual is that they are confronting a very different problem. They are trying to work out what happens if – as they saw it – the judges, who should be the very people to uphold the constitution, themselves violate one of the guarantees which it embodies. Of course, you can say that, once the House of Lords had decided the point, its decision had to be treated as a proper application, rather than as a violation, of the constitution. The attempt of ministers of the Church to indoctrinate 'the rulers' on the interpretation of statutes might therefore appear rather quixotic.[231] But, especially when a distinguished minority of the Court of Session had taken a different view on closely argued grounds, it was understandable that people continued to believe that the victorious view was wrong and that the error should be corrected.

There is nothing inherently improper about such an attitude, which can be compared with the attitude of the government and parliament of Barbados to certain decisions of the Privy Council on the mandatory death penalty. Looking at the decisions on equivalent provisions in other Caribbean constitutions, they foresaw that the Board would rule that the mandatory death penalty was inconsistent with the constitution of

Barbados. They rejected that interpretation and passed an Act amending section 15 of the constitution to reinforce what they saw as the correct position and to try to head off any decision to the contrary.[232]

Some of those present at the Convocation did indeed simply argue that the constitution could not be altered – that, by its very nature, the Act of Security could not be violated – and so the decisions of the courts were not law.[233] They were really following the line so defiantly declared in the Claim of Right six months before. More pragmatic voices, however, replied: 'This is all very well in theory.[234] But, don't argue against the facts: the Act is broken, and we cannot force the State to keep it.'[235]

According to Dr Candlish, the theory that there were co-ordinate courts, civil and ecclesiastical, *was* the constitution. But the decisions of the civil courts had changed this aspect of the constitution. *Prima facie* the civil courts declared the mind of the State and this was, at last, known as a result of the decision of the House of Lords in the second *Auchterarder* case. Now they must go to the legislature and ask for the law, as so declared, to be changed. They should tell the legislators that, if Parliament did not say anything to the contrary, the State would be taken to have spoken through the decisions of the courts of law.[236] Dr Gordon, a former Moderator, took much the same view, arguing that silence on the part of the State, that is, the Government and Parliament, would make law, by carrying you back to the last recorded and unrepealed utterance of the courts.[237]

As anticipated, Dr Begg – who was something of a Scottish nationalist *avant la lettre*[238] – considered that the silence of the Government and Parliament should be seen rather differently.[239] For him the constitution was supreme – above law. The rights in the constitution were rights of subjects which rulers had no right to touch. Under the constitution, the Church was placed outside the power of the civil courts and their duty as ministers was therefore to stand out against the civil courts. As long as the Government and Parliament remained silent on the topic, even if the State threw the weight of the secular arm against the Church, their duty was not to abandon, but to stand by, the Church.[240]

Dr Chalmers also distinguished between current or ordinary law and constitutional law. If they conflicted, and an appeal was made to con-stitutional law and the State kept silent or, *a fortiori*, gave civil effect to the change made by the ordinary law, then he would defer to the change. But, while deferring, the Church should admonish the State as to her duty. If rules laid down by the courts violated the constitution of a State, there tended to be a strong feeling of sympathy with the resistance of the people to the aggression, and a lively joy if they triumphed. But Christianity would control these feelings. If the State looked on benignantly at the aggression of the civil courts against the Church courts, then persecution had begun and the rule of Scripture would apply: 'if they persecute you in one city, flee into another.'[241] In other words, if Parliament would not pass legislation to vindicate the ministers' view of the constitution, they should leave the Established Church and set up a new church.

The speakers appear to have proceeded on the basis that the courts were to be treated as the voice of the State for the purposes of interpreting the constitution.[242] But, if the interpretation adopted by the courts really amounted to a change in the constitution, then that change was always subject to the ratification of the other organs of the State – the Government and Parliament. It would only be if they, in effect, adopted the courts' interpretation that this interpretation would become definitive and, in this way, the constitution would actually be changed. But how was one to know if the Government and Parliament had actually approved the change? Did they have to do so positively? Was it enough if, when the matter was drawn to their attention, they did nothing? Or did it have to be drawn to their attention more than once?

The majority view was that once was enough. In other words, if the Church asked the Government and Parliament to legislate to reinstate the previous understanding of the constitutional position and they refused – or even if they simply ignored the request and did nothing – that would be a proper basis for concluding that the constitutional position was indeed as the courts had declared it. That position, with the Church at the mercy of the courts, would be intolerable. The ministers would therefore have to leave the Established Church.

Initially, Dr Begg remained unconvinced that, if there was no response from the Government or Parliament, his duty was to leave, rather than to stay at his post and fight from the inside for the spiritual independence of the Church. Admittedly, if the ministers stayed at their posts, they would have to enforce the discipline of the Church against those who disobeyed the orders of its superior courts on the point.[243] Plainly, even Begg, who spoke ingeniously,[244] recognised that this was a potentially unattractive aspect of his position. Dr Guthrie skilfully exposed the highly undesirable consequences of any attempt to follow that line.[245] Gradually Begg's supporters deserted him until, isolated, he too gave way and agreed that he would have to leave the Established Church if their demands were ignored.

With that, the Convocation had completed its work and, after a meeting in the Evangelical stronghold, Lady Glenorchy's Chapel (then situated near the North Bridge), to announce its resolutions to the public, the members set off back to their parishes to spread the news and to prepare for the Disruption. Soon some of them would be on the road once more, travelling across Scotland to stir up support[246] – while continuing to draw a stipend as ministers of the very Established Church that they were doing their best to undermine in the event of a parting of the ways.[247] For, as we have seen, they were realistic enough to appreciate that, so long as the Church was perceived to be defying the law of the land, the Government and Parliament were not going to help them. Indeed the whole drift of the proceedings in the Convocation had been to prepare men's minds for expulsion.[248]

January 1843 brought two significant developments. First, as anticipated, Peel's Government firmly rejected the Claim of Right and the other representations made on behalf of the Church.[249] Second, the Court of Session inflicted yet another blow. This time the court struck down the Chapels Act that had purported to put the ministers of Chapels of Ease on a footing of equality with ordinary parish ministers and to provide for *quoad sacra* parishes to be attached to their churches.[250]

The dispute centred on the small town of Stewarton in Ayrshire. So the litigation came to be known as the *Stewarton* case.[251] The problem had begun in August 1839, at a time when the powers of the General Assembly had already been put under scrutiny in the *Auchterarder* and *Lethendy* cases. In terms of an Act of the General Assembly passed earlier that year,[252] the minister, Mr Clelland, and the congregation of the United Synod church in Stewarton were accepted into the Church of Scotland. Mr Clelland was enrolled as a member of the presbytery of Irvine. Steps were also taken towards creating a kirk session and allocating a *quoad sacra* parish to the new church – all as envisaged by the Chapels Act. The patron and the heritors of the parish intimated their opposition and then raised proceedings in the Court of Session to stop these moves and to challenge Mr Clelland's right to sit in the presbytery. As usual, the proceedings were long and complicated. During them, a rival congregation succeeded in its claim to the church building and Mr Clelland demitted the charge and left for England. Another minister, Mr Latta, was chosen to succeed him, but in March 1841 the court granted an interim interdict against the presbytery admitting anyone to the new parish and against receiving him as a member of the presbytery. The General Assembly of that year appointed a special commission to which the presbytery was to apply for direction and advice. In the meantime, Mr Latta had died. On 29 June 1841, despite the interdict, the presbytery decided to go ahead with the procedure for admitting a new minister, if the special commission agreed.

Because of its importance, the Lord Ordinary reported the case to the Court, which ordered that a hearing should be held before all the judges.

That hearing did not begin until 21 June 1842,[253] a few weeks after the General Assembly which had adopted the defiant Claim of Right.

As usual, the first line of the presbytery's defence was a denial of the jurisdiction of the Court of Session. Its written case on the point was drafted by Alexander Dunlop, the author of the Claim of Right, in his capacity as junior counsel for the presbytery. Characteristically, he had put the point in strong terms – so strong indeed that, to some of the judges, part of what he said seemed disrespectful to the court.[254] The matter was raised by Lord President Boyle at the conclusion of Mr Rutherfurd's submissions for the presbytery on 28 June but, at the suggestion of Lord Justice Clerk Hope, consideration of the point was postponed.[255] At a special hearing convened later in the week, Rutherfurd appeared and, having assured the judges that no disrespect had been intended, read out a minute explaining the position of the presbytery. Dunlop then addressed the judges and confirmed that no disrespect had been intended: he had merely sought to ensure that nothing was said that would compromise the presbytery's position that only the Church courts had jurisdiction in the matter.[256] The terms of the minute did not completely satisfy the judges and Rutherfurd had to put in a further minute withdrawing the two offending paragraphs in the presbytery's case. With that, the judges were content.[257]

At the end of the hearing in presence on 28 June, the Lord President had indicated that, since the consulted judges could not, at that stage of the session, form their opinions on the merits of such an important case, 'the Court were under the painful necessity of delaying to give judgment till next session.'[258] When the court reassembled in November after its four-month vacation, however, there was still no sign of a judgment. With the Convocation imminent, there had already been mutterings about the court's delay in giving judgment.[259] More delay was to come. Lord Gillies had resigned during the vacation and his replacement, Lord Wood, was installed on the day the Convocation ended. The Lord President announced that arrangements would have to be made to secure his views on the case.[260] So it was only on Friday, 20 January 1843 that the court finally gave judgment.[261] Not unexpectedly,[262] by a majority of eight to five,[263] it came down against the Chapels Act.[264]

Predictably, the majority of the judges rejected the presbytery's argument on jurisdiction and, equally predictably, the minority accepted it. For most of the judges it meant going over much the same ground as in the previous cases.[265] The non-intrusionists' old foe, John Hope, now Lord Justice Clerk Hope, must have relished the opportunity, however, to expound his version of the pro-jurisdiction argument in typically vigorous terms.[266]

The presbytery could, and did, emphasise how the Chapels Act should be seen as dealing only with internal church affairs and as explicitly recognising that the new parishes were *quoad sacra tantum* – for ecclesiastical purposes only. The chink, or indeed hole, in the presbytery's armour was that the ministers became members of the presbytery and that body dealt with certain matters that were undoubtedly civil rather than ecclesiastical: church buildings, manses, glebes and schoolmasters.[267] So the Church was claiming the right to alter the constitution of a body which had this role in civil matters. That might well be thought to give an entrée to the Court of Session. The fact that the Church had deliberately ignored the mechanism provided by Parliament for establishing new churches and altering parishes, and had only recently come up with the idea of *quoad sacra* parishes, was another potentially tricky aspect of its position.[268]

There were difficulties on the other side too. In particular, even supposing the Chapels Act was, in principle, open to attack in the Court of Session, it was far from clear that the patron and heritors had any very real civil interest which would give them a title and interest to mount that attack. As Lord Cockburn put it, no party had shown how he could lose one sixpence by what had been done.[269] The patron's civil right was to appoint a minister for the whole parish and, at most, it could be argued that, if a new *quoad sacra* parish were created, that would affect his civil right by cutting down the area for which he was appointing. As for the heritors, the argument was that they had a civil interest in being under the discipline of the minister and kirk session of their parish church, rather than under a different minister in a different church. To be frank, that interest does not look very civil. In any event, it was far-fetched to suggest that anyone was going to be prevented from continuing to attend the parish church if they wanted to. Nevertheless, the majority accepted versions of these arguments.[270] The minority picked them apart.[271]

The decision constituted another severe setback for the Evangelical party. Indeed its potential effects ran wider and deeper than the *Auchterarder* cases. Within a few days Dr Candlish had denounced the decision as containing 'nothing but the naked assertion of jurisdiction by the civil courts in matters which are wholly ecclesiastical.'[272] At the heart of the decision lay a rejection of the Church's claim to spiritual independence from the civil courts and, by January 1843, that was all that really mattered. Those who were going to leave the Church were confirmed in their intention to do so. As, indeed, they were when, in March, both Houses of Parliament declined to intervene to help the Church, even though a majority of the Scottish MPs had voted in favour.[273] When the Evangelicals first appealed to the House of Lords in the

Stewarton case and then withdrew the appeal, their opponents thought that this might be a device to create more confusion over the status of ministers of Chapels of Ease as commissioners to the forthcoming General Assembly.[274]

At last, in May, that long-awaited General Assembly came round and most of the ministers who had attended the Convocation, and others too, left the Established Church. Although their departure was portrayed at the time, and subsequently, as a triumphant moment, the Rev. William Cunningham was certainly not wide of the mark when he said to a Glasgow audience a few weeks later, 'It is true that in a certain sense we have been beaten in this controversy' but added that 'neither have our opponents gained their leading object.'[275] Subsequently, that most cerebral of Free Church lawyers, Taylor Innes, even expressed the view that 'in not sitting still until they were driven out by the sword, the Disruption Fathers committed the same mistake as did James VII and II.'[276] At the time, however, it did not seem to those who went out that they had made a mistake. Rather, when, Sunday by Sunday, large open-air congregations gathered in glorious summer weather, they felt that God's grace was at work in the land.[277]

In rather a nice *Nachspiel*, during that same summer of 1843, Parliament passed the Benefices (Scotland) Act 1843. It regulated the exercise of patronage by giving presbyteries power to act on objections to the qualifications of the patron's presentee. In its terms the Act purported to be declaratory of the existing law.[278] The peers who had delivered judgment in the *Auchterarder* appeals protested that the law in the Bill was actually completely different from the law as established by the House of Lords in its judicial capacity.[279] They therefore moved, unsuccessfully, to have the declaratory words omitted.[280] In the end, Lord Cottenham and Lord Campbell entered a protest against the Third Reading.[281] But the Bill became law and ushered in an era of comparative peace in the Established Church.

In conclusion, I return briefly to the Convocation in November 1842. To judge by the way that the Act of Union has been approached since their day, it could be said that the ministers made a pretty good shot at assessing its significance. In particular, they rightly saw that, although, in their view, the Court of Session had actually stripped away the guarantees in the Treaty of Union, they could not say that the Treaty had been formally repealed. Nor could they ask Parliament to re-enact it. Most importantly, 'You cannot well ask Parliament to pass a law promising not to violate it in future.'[282] The ministers' conclusion was that, to regain their freedom, they had to set up a church that was not subject to the particular laws that the

Court of Session had enforced against the Established Church. That did not mean, of course, that the new church would be beyond the reach of the civil law. As the Free Church was to be reminded in the *Cardross* litigation,[283] that was very far from the case. Indeed, some sixty years later, the constitutionalist minority in the Free Church was to use the civil law of the land in a daring and successful strike against the new United Free Church.[284]

The members of the Convocation were right, however, to see the Act of Union as a statute apart, because of the guarantees for Scotland that it contains. These are certainly standards by which actions of the executive, the legislature and the courts can be judged. Parliament is therefore understandably reluctant to be seen to meddle with the Act.[285] As Dr Chalmers indicated, and others after him have also thought, an action which violated one of those guarantees might well be expected to meet with popular opposition. Of course, some of the provisions, such as those on the oaths to be taken by professors in the universities, came to seem outdated and their repeal was generally welcomed. But in other cases, even if – as the majority of the Convocation clearly thought – Parliament could alter the guarantees in favour of Scotland in the Act of Union, there would be a political price to pay for making an unwelcome alteration in them. It is significant that, since the Disruption, the Scottish courts have rarely been called upon to apply those guarantees and have, in fact, never done so.[286] Despite this, in practice, 300 years on, the guarantees still remain effective to prevent various constitutional changes which would not be supported by public opinion in Scotland.

NOTES

1. The minister of St Andrew's was not, however, present: Macfarlane, pp. 135–40.
2. For the preparations, see Watt, pp. 290–5; Hetherington vol. 2, pp. 521–2; Turner, pp. 349–52. The aim was to take action before disputes about the roll of commissioners – especially the inclusion of ministers of *quoad sacra* parishes – could arise. Turner was originally a supporter of the non-intrusionist cause, but abandoned it and became one of the 'Forty Thieves'. For the emergence of that party, see Henderson, pp. 89–90. Turner is duly recorded in the Second Class in J. McCosh, *The Wheat and the Chaff Gathered into Bundles* (James Dewar, Perth, 1843), p. 54. McCosh lists the way the ministers of the Church went at the Disruption and singles out for particular attention those, like Turner, in the Second Class, who deserted the non-intrusionist cause and remained in the Establishment. Hetherington was a stout ally of Dr Candlish.
3. *Proceedings of the General Assembly of the Free Church of Scotland at Edinburgh, May 1843* (John Grey & Son, Edinburgh, 1853), p. 12. The text of the Protest was largely the work of Alexander Dunlop: Hetherington vol. 2, p. 522.
4. *The Times*, 22 May 1843, p. 7.

5. *The Scotsman*, 20 May 1843, p. 2; Buchanan vol. 2, pp. 593–608; Bryce vol. 2, pp. 358–70; Turner, pp. 352–6; Hetherington vol. 2, pp. 522–6; T. Brown (ed.), *Annals of the Disruption* (McNiven & Wallace, Edinburgh, 1876–84), Chapter IX; J. Dodds, *Thomas Chalmers: A Biographical Study* (William Oliphant & Co., Edinburgh, 1870), pp. 267–75; D. Macleod, *Memoir of Norman Macleod D.D.* (Daldy, Isbister & Co., London, 1876), pp. 197–8, reproducing two letters of the Rev. Norman Macleod, to his sister, Jane, dated 18 May 1843; W. Arnot, *Life of James Hamilton D.D., F.L.S.* (James Nisbet & Co. London, 1870), pp. 219–27; A. Beith, *Memories of Disruption Times* (Blackie & Son, London, Glasgow and Edinburgh, 1877), Section V (containing some telling detail, such as Lord Advocate McNeill changing back into mufti and watching events from a window: see p. 179); Sir John H. A. Macdonald, *Life Jottings of an old Edinburgh Citizen* (T. N. Foulis, London, Edinburgh and Boston, 1915), pp. 63–7. According to the *Caledonian Mercury*, 20 May 1843, p. 2, there were cheers mingled with a few hisses when the ministers emerged, but 'along the line of procession, which was crowded by no means densely, there were no expressions of applause or the reverse.' See also p. 64 below.
6. An award-winning building, Tanfield House, at present owned by Standard Life, now stands on the site. A plaque records the events of 1843. The hall, which had been built as a gas works, was used for the annual General Assembly of the Free Church until 1856.
7. Hilton points out that the walk-out from St George's fits into a series of 'theatrical' events that were typical of the age: B. Hilton, *A Mad, Bad, and Dangerous People? England 1743–1846* (Clarendon Press, Oxford, 2006), p. 34.
8. Macleod, *Memoir of Norman Macleod D.D.*, p. 188. Macleod was another of the Forty Thieves.
9. The opposition was due to his support for the Strathbogie ministers: *The Scotsman*, 20 May 1843, p. 2; *Caledonian Mercury*, 20 May 1843, p. 4 ('amidst cheers and hisses on the part of the audience'). See also Beith, *Memories of Disruption Times*, pp. 188–9. The hitch is airbrushed out of the accounts in Bryce vol. 2, pp. 363 and 370, and Turner, p. 365, who refers to 'the venerable father whom the unanimous Assembly called to occupy their chair.' On the Strathbogie ministers, see pp. 24–5 and 77–9.
10. Referred to by C. N. Johnston (later Lord Sands), 'Doctrinal Subscription in the Church of Scotland' (1905) 17 Juridical Review 201, at p. 208. Something of the atmosphere of the 'residual' Assembly comes over in the letters of the Rev. Norman Macleod to his sister, dated 23, 25 and 27 May 1843, and in his Journal entry dated 2 June 1843: Macleod, *Memoir of Norman Macleod D.D.*, pp. 198–200 and 200–3, respectively.
11. M. Fry, *Patronage and Principle: A Political History of Modern Scotland* (Aberdeen University Press, Aberdeen, paperback edition, 1991), p. 52.
12. The signing ceremony took place on Tuesday, 23 May and is immortalised in the famous, if somewhat idealised, painting by David Octavius Hill, *The First General Assembly of the Free Church of Scotland; signing the Act of Separation and Deed of Demission – 23rd May 1843*. For the story of the picture, including an account of the Disruption, see J. Fowler, *Mr Hill's Big Picture: The Day that Changed Scotland Forever – Captured on Canvas* (Saint Andrew Press, Edinburgh, 2006). See also Arnot, *Life of James Hamilton D.D., F.L.S.*, pp. 225–7. Ministers and elders who were not present in Edinburgh at the time or who changed their minds and decided

to join the Free Church, after all, signed subsequently.

13. For the impact in the rest of Britain, see O. Chadwick, *The Victorian Church*, Part I (A. & C. Black, London, 3rd edition, 1971), pp. 224–6; S. J. Brown, *The National Churches of England, Ireland, and Scotland, 1801–1846* (Oxford University Press, Oxford, 2001), pp. 357–62.

14. Brown (ed.), *Annals of the Disruption* (n. 5).

15. Henderson, p. 114.

16. The self-congratulatory attitude of many Free Churchmen in the years after the Disruption infuriated their counterparts in the Established Church: see, for instance, Wilson, pp. 246–8.

17. Church Patronage (Scotland) Act 1874.

18. See, more generally, M. Fry, 'The Disruption and the Union', in S. J. Brown and M. Fry (eds), *Scotland in the Age of the Disruption* (Edinburgh University Press, Edinburgh, 1993), p. 31.

19. Auchterarder Report vol. 2, p. 329.

20. *Ferguson v Earl of Kinnoull* (1842) 1 Bell 662, at p. 733; 9 Cl. & F. 251, at pp. 324–5.

21. H. Miller, *The Whiggism of the Old School, as exemplified by the Past History and Present Position of the Church of Scotland* (Edinburgh, 1839), p. 29.

22. 24 May 1842, *Proceedings of the General Assembly of the Church of Scotland 1842*, pp. 120–1.

23. J. Begg, *Reply to Sir James Graham's Letter; being the Substance of an Address delivered in Roxburgh Church on Thursday Evening, 19th January 1843 at the Request of the Edinburgh Tradesmen's Association for Advancing the Interests of the Church of Scotland* (J. Johnstone, Edinburgh, 1843), p. 8. Watt, pp. 276–9, makes the point that the more flamboyant orations of this kind were not typical. The Court of Session delivered judgment in the *Stewarton* case the following day. See p. 33.

24. *Speech of the Dean of Faculty, in the Court of Session, on the hearing in presence of the whole court, in conjoined actions of reduction and suspension, of the sentence of deposition, The Presbytery of Strathbogie against the Rev. Dr Gordon and Others January 26, 1843* (W. Blackwood & Sons; Alex Macredie, Edinburgh, 1843), p. 13. *The Scotsman*, 28 January 1843, p. 4, gives a slightly different version of the passage, which the Dean may have revised for publication. One of the copies of the speech in the British Library has the manuscript comment on the title page: 'as wretched a harangue as was ever ventured on.'

25. Inglis, p. 573.

26. J. D. B. Mitchell, *Constitutional Law* (2nd edition, W. Green & Son, Edinburgh, 1968), p. 257, refers to the matter in a single sentence. See also the short accounts in *The Laws of Scotland: Stair Memorial Encyclopaedia* vol. 3 (1994), paras 1634 and 1636 (P. H. Brodie and Lord Mackay of Clashfern); vol. 5 (1987), para. 691 (Lord Murray). There is, of course, an authoritative account of the subject in F. Lyall, *Of Presbyters and Kings: Church and State in the Law of Scotland* (Aberdeen University Press, Aberdeen, 1980), Chapter III, and a shorter account in D. M. Walker, *A Legal History of Scotland Vol. VI: The Nineteenth Century* (Butterworths, Edinburgh, 2001), pp. 218–24.

27. For a recent account of the events leading to the Union, see M. Fry, *The Union: England, Scotland and the Treaty of 1707* (Birlinn, Edinburgh, 2006). The position of the Church is considered, in particular, at pp. 233–41.

28. c. 6.

29. Union with England Act 1707.
30. Union with Scotland Act 1706, section IV.
31. On the dating of this Act see Lyall, *Of Presbyters and Kings: Church and State in the Law of Scotland*, p. 199.
32. In particular, this was the view of Lord Kames, *Historical Law-Tracts* (Bell & Bradfute and John Fairbairn, Edinburgh, 4th edition, 1817), pp. 240–1, a passage which was much quoted.
33. Scottish Ministers' Widows' Fund Act 1814 (54 Geo. 3, c. clxix).
34. 1953 S.C. 396. Much of the opinion – in particular the idea that the court should regard a statute as impossible to construe, rather than look at the relevant White Paper – has a distinctly antique appearance.
35. 1953 S.C. 396, at p. 411.
36. See, e.g., S. Tierney, 'Scotland and the Union State', in A. McHarg and T. Mullen, *Public Law in Scotland* (Avizandum, Edinburgh, 2006), p. 25, at pp. 39–41.
37. J. D. Ford, 'The Legal Provisions in the Act of Union' (2007) 66 Cambridge Law Journal 106. See also J. Goldsworthy, *The Sovereignty of Parliament: History and Philosophy* (Clarendon Press, Oxford, 1999), pp. 165–73; C. Kidd, 'Sovereignty and the Scottish constitution before 1707' 2004 Juridical Review 225. For a full discussion of the background, see J. D. Ford, *Law and Opinion in Scotland during the Seventeenth Century* (Hart Publishing, Oxford and Portland, OR, 2007).
38. *Institutions of the Law of Scotland* 1.1.16; Ford, 66 Cambridge Law Journal 106, at p. 137.
39. *Earl of Rothes v Gordon of Hallhead and Cushny* (1622) Mor. 1 Brown's Supp. 4; *Town of Edinburgh v College of Justice* (1678) Mor. 3 Brown's Supp. 257, at p. 262; Ford, 66 Cambridge Law Journal 106, at pp. 136–7.
40. Ford, 66 Cambridge Law Journal 106, at pp. 128–39.
41. *R v Secretary of State for Transport ex pte Factortame Ltd (No 2)* [1991] 1 A.C. 603.
42. Indeed, in *Ferguson v Earl of Kinnoull* (1842) 1 Bell 662, at p. 721; 9 Cl. & F. 251, at p. 311, Lord Campbell explicitly held that 'we must consider [the 1711 Act] binding, although it has been said to be *ultra vires* of the British Parliament.' For the position adopted by the Church in the Claim of Right in May 1842, see pp. 26–7.
43. [2005] UKHL 56; [2006] 1 A.C. 262.
44. See J. Allan, 'The Paradox of Sovereignty: *Jackson* and the Hunt for a New Rule of Recognition?' (2007) 18 King's Law Journal 1.
45. For a fuller description of the Moderates, see Henderson, pp. 37–40; D. A. Mackinnon, *Some Chapters in Scottish History* (R. W. Hunter, Edinburgh, 1893), Chapter VII.
46. This period is beautifully described in Henderson, Chapter III. An interesting sketch of the period (albeit from a staunchly pro-Establishment standpoint) is to be found in Macfarlane, pp. 4–20. See also Brown, *The National Churches of England, Ireland, and Scotland 1801–1846*, pp. 59–61.
47. In these respects, the Evangelicals' criticisms of the Moderates were not dissimilar to the Tractarians' criticisms of the English High Church clergy: Hilton, *A Mad, Bad, and Dangerous People?*, pp. 472–3.
48. Thomson was the composer of, *inter alia*, the rousing and much-loved tune 'St George's Edinburgh', named after his church and used as a setting for 'Ye gates, lift up your heads on high', the version of Psalm 24 vv. 7–10 in the Scottish Metrical Psalter of 1650.

49. For the views of the Secretary of the Anti-Patronage Society, see J. Bridges, *Patronage in the Church of Scotland Considered* (John Johnstone, Edinburgh, Whittaker & Co., James Nisbet & Co., London, 1840).

50. Actually, the fourth decade.

51. A. Taylor Innes, *The Law of Creeds in Scotland* (2nd edition, William Blackwood & Sons, Edinburgh and London, 1902), p. 69. See also Cockburn Journal vol. 1, pp. 58–9, entry for 4 April 1834. For the wider picture, see Chadwick, *The Victorian Church* Part I, pp. 60–100 and 142–58; Hilton, *A Mad, Bad, and Dangerous People?*, pp. 524–32.

52. A vigorous and amusing attack based on this difficulty for non-intrusionist ministers was launched by Dr Lee in the Presbytery of Glasgow on 16 December 1840: R. H. Story, *Life and Remains of Robert Lee D.D.* (Hurst & Blackett, London, 1870) vol. 1, pp. 27–35.

53. Hanna vol. 3, pp. 350–2; Buchanan vol. 1, pp. 240–2.

54. *Cruickshank v Gordon* (1843) 5 D. 909, at p. 919 per the Lord Ordinary (Cuninghame). In *Percy v Board of National Mission of the Church of Scotland* [2005] UKHL 73; 2006 S.C. (H.L.) 1, at p. 29, para. 117; [2006] 2 A.C. 28, at p. 63, para. 117, Lord Hope of Craighead comments that the Church is not a body that has been incorporated by statute and goes on to say that 'its status in law is that of a voluntary association.' But the weight of authority is to the effect that the Established Church is, at the least, a common law corporation. In addition to the passage from Lord Cuninghame's opinion, see Bankton, *An Institute of the Laws of Scotland* 1.2.25: 'The established church is likewise a great corporation. ...' In *Earl of Kinnoull v Gordon* (1842) 5 D. 12, at pp. 62–3, Lord Fullerton repeatedly refers to the 'corporate character' of the Church and to the Church as 'an incorporated body'. See also *Cuninghame v Presbytery of Irvine* (1843) Stewarton Report, p. 70, per Lord Meadowbank and Lord Murray. Much of the argument of Inglis in his articles on the position of the Church is based on the proposition that the Church '*is in law an incorporation*' (emphasis as in the original) and that the Church is 'nothing but an incorporation, however harsh the phrase may sound': Inglis, p. 577. In Cockburn Journal vol. 2, p. 158, Lord Cockburn remarks that the Church has no 'corporate' property, but the fact that the Church did not hold property did not mean that it was not a corporation. In the first *Auchterarder* case, Lord Moncreiff asks rhetorically whether 'a church so formed and consolidated equally by statutes and by the usage of centuries ... is not something more than a mere corporation with power to make bye-laws ...': Auchterarder Report vol. 2, p. 329. In the same case Lord Cockburn also rejected the notion that the Court of Session could control the Church, as it could control a corporation in the admission of candidates, 'Because, in the *first* place, I really do not think that the Church of Scotland is a mere corporation ...': Auchterarder Report vol. 2, p. 410.

55. His attitude can be seen in his evidence to the House of Commons Committee in March 1834. See, for example, *Minutes of Evidence taken before the Select Committee on Church Patronage, Scotland*, 26 March 1834, pp. 189–90, Questions 1330, 1331 and 1332. In the first *Auchterarder* case he spoke of 'the deep conviction which I had formed, of the extreme inexpediency and danger of the measure of abolition demanded of Parliament': Auchterarder Report vol. 2, p. 276. His son, Sir Henry Wellwood Moncreiff, rather plays down this aspect in Moncreiff, pp. 314–25.

56. See, e.g., Turner, p. 169 n.

57. Wilson, *passim*.
58. Macfarlane, p. 59.
59. Letter to Dr Chalmers dated 13 May 1833: Hanna vol. 4, pp. 116–17. Jeffrey got into difficulties with other MPs of his own party who thought him obdurate and conservative in Church matters: I. G. C. Hutchison, A *Political History of Scotland 1832–1924* (John Donald, Edinburgh, 1986), p. 34. For his attitude, see also the letter of Lord Cockburn to Lord Murray, 22 April 1841: A. Bell (ed.), *Lord Cockburn: Selected Letters* (John Donald, Edinburgh, 2005), p. 167.
60. Moncreiff, pp. 233–4.
61. Moncreiff, p. 260.
62. Letter of Jeffrey to Cockburn, 22 March 1834: Adv. Ms. 9.1.10 f. 835 at f. 838r, National Library of Scotland.
63. Letter of Jeffrey to Cockburn, 27 March 1834: Adv. Ms. 9.1.10 f. 840r, National Library of Scotland.
64. The General Assembly met there from 1830 to 1840, to the growing displeasure of the Kirk Session: D. Butler, *The Tron Kirk of Edinburgh or Christ's Kirk at the Tron: A History* (Oliphant, Anderson & Ferrier, Edinburgh and London, 1906), pp. 288–91 and 333–8.
65. Hetherington vol. 2, p. 394
66. Lord Brougham drew attention to the sex discrimination: *Presbytery of Auchterarder* v *Earl of Kinnoull* (1839) Macl. & Rob. 220, at pp. 294–5; 6 Cl. & F. 646, at p. 701. See also Macfarlane, p. 54*, and A. Gordon, *The Life of Archibald Hamilton Charteris D.D., LL.D.* (Hodder & Stoughton, London, New York and Toronto, n.d. [1912]), p. 126 n. 1. There was also discrimination against single men: Cunningham vol. 2, p. 485 n. 1.
67. Especially in the North of Scotland, where comparatively few men were communicants, the measure could work capriciously. See Turner, pp. 182–4.
68. The Attorney General was speaking, the day after the vote in the General Assembly, at the hustings in the Edinburgh by-election prompted by Jeffrey's appointment to the bench following the death of Lord Craigie on 1 May 1834. See *The Scotsman*, 28 May 1834, p. 2. The fact that the Attorney General had expressed that view at the time did not prevent him subsequently accepting the brief for the pursuers in the first *Auchterarder* appeal to the House of Lords. As a judge, he upheld the decision of the First Division in the second *Auchterarder* appeal to the House of Lords in August 1842: *Ferguson* v *Earl of Kinnoull* (1842) 1 Bell 662, at pp 719–35; 9 Cl. & F. 251, at pp. 308–26.
69. House of Lords, 23 July 1834. See, e.g., Turner, pp. 170–1; Hanna vol. 3, pp. 361–2, noting that Dr Chalmers had been informed, and believed, that the Veto Law had been submitted to Lord Brougham and had received his imprimatur. It would not be surprising if Lord Moncreiff had sent a copy of his proposed law to his friend, the Lord Chancellor, or if he had told Dr Chalmers what had happened.
70. Cunningham vol. 2, pp. 458–60; J. Hope, A *Letter to the Lord Chancellor on the Claims of the Church of Scotland in regard to its Jurisdiction and on the Proposed Changes in its Polity* (William Whyte & Co., Edinburgh, John Murray, London, 1839), p. 55.
71. See, for instance, Bryce vol. 1, pp. 25–6
72. Buchanan vol. 1, pp. 268–77 and 316–48; Macfarlane, Chapter II; Wilson, Chapter V.
73. 1707 c. 10.
74. Buchanan vol. 1, p. 271.

75. On the significance of Church Extension for the whole matter, see D. Chambers, 'The Church of Scotland's Extension Scheme and the Scottish Disruption' (1974) 16 Journal of Church and State 263.

76. Its official title was 'Declaratory Enactment as to Chapels of Ease'. The text is reproduced in the Stewarton Report, Appendix, p. iii. The Act was opposed by, *inter alios*, Dr Chalmers and another leading Evangelical, Dr Gordon: Cunningham vol. 2, p. 464.

77. See Hutchison, *A Political History of Scotland 1832–1924*, pp. 15–25 and 37–48.

78. This, the first, *Auchterarder* case is treated in all the accounts of the Disruption crisis. See, for instance, Buchanan vol. 1, Chapter VIII and vol. 2, pp. 1–60; Bryce vol. 1, Chapter III and pp. 84–100; Macfarlane, Chapter IV; Bayne, Chapters XII–XV; Hetherington vol. 2, pp. 398–407.

79. Auchterarder Report vol. 1, Appendix, p. 35; Respondents' Case, Appendix, p. 15. For the suggestion that the Earl of Kinnoull actually had no right to make the presentation because he had never completed the necessary conveyancing procedures to give him a good title, see Gordon, *The Life of Archibald Hamilton Charteris*, pp. 128–9.

80. Hetherington vol. 2, p. 399.

81. One might have supposed that the failure to exhaust the mechanisms for appeal in the hierarchy of Church courts would have been an objection to the proceedings in the Court of Session, but that point does not seem to have been much pressed – perhaps because, as Lord Gillies noted, the presbytery had simply failed to perform a ministerial duty and so there was not really any exercise of judgment, against which to appeal: Auchterarder Report vol. 2, 43. The point was taken successfully by the defenders in *Lang v Presbytery of Irvine* (1864) 2 M. 823. The case is notable for Lord Deas ruffling Lord Ardmillan's Free Church feathers, at pp. 838–9.

82. He was ordained on 4 August 1843. For the outline of his career, see H. Scott, *Fasti Ecclesiae Scoticanae* (new edition) vol. 4 (Oliver & Boyd, Edinburgh, 1923), p. 260. According to A. G. Reid, *The Annals of Auchterarder* (D. Philips, Crieff, 1899), p. 290, 'He was an excellent scholar, an able and evangelical preacher, and a good and honourable man, the sole and only objection which could be brought forward against him was that his discourses were read.' The fact that he was slightly lame and had a slightly contorted hand may also have counted against him: Cunningham vol. 2, p. 467.

83. The summons was signeted on 5 October 1835: Auchterarder Report vol. 1, Appendix, p. 12.

84. Auchterarder Report vol. 1, Appendix, p. 10.

85. Ibid. vol. 1, Appendix, p. 11. To judge by the terms of his dissent to the Veto Act, the Dean seems, at that stage, to have harboured a belief that, though rejected under the Act, a presentee would be effectively presented to the benefice and would have 'a clear right to the stipend and all other rights appertaining thereto': Buchanan vol. 1, p. 316. It soon became clear, however, that the presentee had no right to the stipend unless he was actually admitted as minister of the parish.

86. Ibid. vol. 1, Appendix, p. 18. In fact, £1730 6s 5d, or nine-and-a-half years' stipend of Auchterarder, was paid to the Ministers' Widows' Fund: Gordon, *The Life of Archibald Hamilton Charteris*, p. 132 n. 2.

87. Auchterarder Report vol. 1, pp. 145–6 (Mr Bell), 344–7 (Solicitor General).

88. Ibid. vol. 2, p. 20, per Lord President; pp. 45–7, per Lord Gillies; pp. 76–7, per

Lord Justice Clerk; p. 112, per Lord Meadowbank; pp. 131–2, per Lord Mackenzie; pp. 445–9, per Lord Cuninghame; *contra*, pp. 240–52, per Lord Fullerton; pp. 291–3, per Lord Moncreiff; pp. 394–5, per Lord Jeffrey; p. 397, per Lord Cockburn.

89. They referred to the veto of dissents in article 11 of the revised condescendence: ibid. vol. 1, Appendix, p. 21.

90. Statement 5 in the Statement of Facts for the presbytery, quoting the minute of its proceedings: ibid. vol. 1, Appendix, p. 22.

91. Ibid. vol. 2, pp. 252–6, 258, 272–3, per Lord Fullerton; pp. 286–93, and 293–5, per Lord Moncreiff.

92. Ibid. vol. 2, pp. 394–5, per Lord Jeffrey. For the majority, see the passages cited in note 88 above.

93. Macl. & Rob. 220, at pp. 347–9, per Lord Cottenham LC, and pp. 350–1, per Lord Brougham; 6 Cl. & F. 646, at pp. 752–3, per Lord Cottenham LC, and pp. 755–6, per Lord Brougham.

94. For the interlocutor of the Court of Session, see Auchterarder Report vol. 2, pp. 450–1; for the order of the House of Lords affirming that interlocutor, see Macl. & Rob. 220, at p. 351; 6 Cl. & F. 646, at p. 756.

95. Lord Cockburn, *Life of Lord Jeffrey with a Selection from his Correspondence* (Adam & Charles Black, Edinburgh, 1852) vol. 1, p. 386.

96. The hearing in the *Stewarton* case, where the Dean of Faculty spoke over most of three days, is also remarkable to modern eyes for the lack of interruptions from the judges. The speeches of counsel are fully reported in *Stewarton Case. Report of the Pleadings by Patrick Robertson, Esq., Dean of Faculty, and Andrew Rutherfurd Esq., Advocate, in the Process of Suspension and Interdict, William Cuninghame, Esq., and Others, Heritors of the Parish of Stewarton, against the Presbytery of Irvine. June and July 1842. Taken in short-hand by Simon Macgregor* (W. P. Kennedy, Edinburgh, 1842). To judge by the available reports, the hearing in presence in the third *Auchterarder* and *Strathbogie* cases on 24 and 25 January 1843 also seems to have comprised set-piece speeches by the two counsel: *Speech of the Dean of Faculty, in the Court of Session, on the hearing in presence of the whole court* (n. 24 above); *The Scotsman*, 28 January 1843, p. 4; *Caledonian Mercury*, 26 January 1843, p. 2.

97. Looking back, Lord Cockburn rightly saw that, in the first *Auchterarder* case, 'a very large field of historical and other matter was at last all superseded by a single clause in an act, binding and astricting presbyteries to receive and admit qualified persons presented by patrons – this reduces the question to a mere point of statutory construction': Stewarton Report, p. 129.

98. Especially, in the last phase of the *Strathbogie* litigations, just before the Disruption: *Cruickshank v Gordon* (1843) 5 D. 909. See p. 25 and p. 53 n. 261.

99. See, for instance, Auchterarder Report vol. 2, pp. 343–5, per Lord Moncreiff, and pp. 390–1, per Lord Jeffrey. This argument harks back to Dr Chalmers' preference for dealing with the question by the use of the Assembly's judicial powers: Hanna vol. 3, pp. 350–2. See pp. 8 and 20.

100. E.g., Lord Fullerton, Auchterarder Report vol. 2, pp. 270–2; Lord Moncreiff, pp. 344–7; Lord Glenlee, pp. 358–9; Lord Jeffrey, pp. 389–91; Lord Cockburn, pp. 413–14.

101. The Solicitor General was not appearing in his official capacity, but simply as counsel for the presbytery. Until after the Second World War, Law Officers were entitled to accept instructions in cases not involving the Crown and to earn fees for such work.

See J. Ll. J. Edwards, *The Law Officers of the Crown* (Sweet & Maxwell, London, 1964), pp. 98–118. A Law Officer's actions as counsel for other parties did not, of course, bind the Government. Nevertheless, in a case, like the first *Auchterarder* case, which gave rise to issues of importance for the Government, the practice could lead to potential difficulties.

102. Auchterarder Report vol. 1, pp. 385–6. By 'apparitors' Rutherfurd means officials responsible for enforcing the orders of the court.

103. In particular, the jurisdiction issue was treated in great detail, but with increasing impatience on the part of the majority, in the *Culsamond* and *Stewarton* cases.

104. Dr Candlish admitted this in his speech to the 1839 General Assembly: *Report of Speeches of the Rev. Dr Burns, Rev. Robert S. Candlish and Alexander Earle Monteith, Esq., in the General Assembly on Wednesday, May 22, 1839 in the Auchterarder Case* (John Johnstone, Edinburgh, 1839), p. 42.

105. Inglis, p. 579.

106. Even as late as two months before the Disruption, this argument was still in play, but was very firmly rejected by the majority judges, Lord Cuninghame's treatment being particularly trenchant: *Cruickshank v Gordon* (1843) 5 D. 909, at pp. 968–9.

107. Cf. XX, 'The Scotch Church Question: Letter II', *The Times*, 22 May 1843, p. 7.

108. The non-intrusionists' argument is set out very clearly in the speech of Sheriff Monteith in the General Assembly debate on 22 May 1839: *Report of Speeches of the Rev. Dr Burns, Rev. Robert S. Candlish and Alexander Earle Monteith, Esq., in the General Assembly on Wednesday, May 22, 1839 in the Auchterarder Case*, pp. 17–34. The opposing thesis is equally clearly stated in the *Memorial submitted to Her Majesty's Government by a Committee appointed at a Meeting of Ministers, Elders and others, Members of the Church of Scotland, held at Edinburgh, 12th August 1840* (William Blackwood & Sons, Edinburgh and London, 1842), pp. 29–32. The memorial, dated 12 February 1842, was signed by Dr Cook, but was actually composed by John Inglis: S. Halkett, J. Laing, *A Dictionary of the Anonymous and Pseudonymous Literature of Great Britain* (William Paterson, Edinburgh, 1883) vol. 2, p. 1594. See further below, p. 65.

109. *Caledonian Mercury*, 1 March 1838, p. 3.

110. See Auchterarder Report vol. 2. An abbreviated report of the judgments, with some of the supporting material, is to be found in *Earl of Kinnoull v Presbytery of Auchterarder* (1838) 16 D. 661.

111. The majority comprised Lord President Hope, Lord Gillies, Lord Justice Clerk Boyle, Lord Meadowbank, Lord Mackenzie, Lord Medwyn and Lord Cuninghame; the minority comprised Lord Fullerton, Lord Moncreiff, Lord Glenlee, Lord Jeffrey and Lord Cockburn. Lord Gillies gave judgment after the Lord President because, although the Lord Justice Clerk was present at the start of proceedings, he was not feeling well and left the court. He was back in court the following morning when he read his judgment: *Caledonian Mercury*, 1 March 1838, p. 3.

112. Guthrie vol. 2, pp. 9–10.

113. Just how elastic quickly became apparent, e.g. in the *Culsamond* case, *Middleton v Anderson* (1842) 4 D. 957.

114. Auchterarder Report vol. 2, p. 4. See pp. 114–16 below.

115. Ibid. vol. 2, p. 12.

116. (1811) 14 East 1; 104 E.R. 501; see Auchterarder Report vol. 2, pp. 5–6, per Lord President.

117. *Stockdale* v *Hansard* (1837) 7 Car. & P. 731; 172 E.R. 319. See, for example, Auchterarder Report vol. 2, p. 6, per Lord President; pp. 36–7, per Lord Gillies; p. 424, per Lord Cuninghame. The second, fundamental, decision in *Stockdale* v *Hansard* (1839) 9 Ad. & E. 1; 112 E.R. 1112, was given on 31 May 1839, just a fortnight after the critical debate in the General Assembly on the judgment of the House of Lords in the first *Auchterarder* case. Consistently with his stance on the Church courts, Lord Jeffrey considered that the House of Commons, rather than the courts, should determine any disputed question about privilege: undated letter from Jeffrey to Mr Empson, in Lord Cockburn, *Life of Lord Jeffrey with a Selection from his Correspondence* vol. 2, pp. 353–68, with a specific reference to the dispute over jurisdiction with the General Assembly, at pp. 361–2. The *Stockdale* case was clearly very much in the air: in 1842 Andrew Rutherfurd used it as an analogy when defending the way that the presbytery had put its case on jurisdiction in the *Stewarton* case: *Stewarton Case: Report of the Pleadings by Patrick Robertson, Esq., Dean of Faculty, and Andrew Rutherfurd Esq., Advocate*, p. 90; *The Scotsman*, 2 July 1842, p. 3.

118. (1703) 2 Ld Raym. 938. See Auchterarder Report vol. 2, p. 6, per Lord President, and vol. 2, pp. 34–6, per Lord Gillies.

119. Auchterarder Report vol. 2, p. 42 (emphasis in the original).

120. Ibid. vol. 2, p. 380. For a detailed analysis of this important aspect of Lord Jeffrey's influential opinion, see Robertson, pp. 238–46.

121. S, 'Church of Scotland Question' (1840) 24 Law Magazine and Quarterly Review of Jurisprudence 131, at p. 160, referring to the *Stockdale* v *Hansard* case. See n. 117 above. For Lord Cockburn's understanding of Lord Jeffrey's approach, see his *Life of Lord Jeffrey with a Selection from his Correspondence* vol. 1, pp. 390–1.

122. Stewarton Report, p. 72.

123. Ibid., p. 73. See also *Clark* v *Stirling*, Lethendy Report, p. 147, per Lord Medwyn.

124. Wilson, p. 201.

125. Even to his opponent, Dr Bryce, writing after the Disruption, Dr Buchanan was 'one of the most talented and distinguished of the seceding clergy': Bryce vol. 2, p. 391; also vol. 2, p. 145. Dr Buchanan took the lead because Dr Chalmers, who was concentrating on Church Extension matters, had not been a commissioner to the General Assembly since 1833. On his work on Church Extension, see, e.g., Watt, Chapter 11.

126. Buchanan vol. 1, p. 471.

127. Ibid. vol. 1, p. 478.

128. For examples of the judges' language, see pp. 71–4 below.

129. In a debate on a reference from the Presbytery of Auchterarder on 24 May 1838, the day after the big debate on the independence of the Church: *The Scotsman*, 26 May 1838, p. 3.

130. Bryce vol. 1, pp. 90–1. The point was also made, in an article favourable to the non-intrusionists, in *The Times*, 10 May 1839, p. 4.

131. Chalmers, *What ought*, p. 9. This, at least, is the retrospective rationalisation by Chalmers, who was not a member of the Assembly which voted to appeal.

132. See p. 9 above. See also R. Rainy, J. Mackenzie, *Life of William Cunningham, D.D.* (T. Nelson & Sons, London, Edinburgh and New York, 1871), p. 131.

133. *The Times*, 10 May 1839, p. 6. The report records that a number of gentlemen had assembled below the Bar and a considerable number of Scotch Peers attended to hear the outcome of the case.

134. *The Presbytery of Auchterarder* v *Earl of Kinnoull* (1839) Macl. & Rob. 220, at p. 307; 6 Cl. & F. 646, at p. 713.
135. Macl. & Rob. 220, at p. 308; 6 Cl. & F. 646, at p. 714.
136. Macl. & Rob. 220, at pp. 339–40; 6 Cl. & F. 646, at p. 745.
137. Macl. & Rob. 220 at p. 341; 6 Cl. & F. 646, at p. 746. See also *Cruickshank* v *Gordon* (1843) 5 D. 909, at p. 1001, per Lord Mackenzie. For a contrary view, see *Cuninghame* v *Presbytery of Irvine* (1843) Stewarton Report, p. 180, per Lord Jeffrey.
138. Macl. & Rob. 220, at pp. 270–1, per Lord Brougham, and at pp. 321 and 331, per Lord Cottenham LC; 6 Cl. & F. 646, at p. 676–8, per Lord Brougham, and at pp. 726 and 736, per Lord Cottenham LC.
139. Bryce vol. 1, p. 98. Robertson, pp. 257–8, considered that they were contrary to the universal views of the Bench and Bar.
140. 'In city streets, men who had known each other from childhood paused to speak, with eager sympathy upon the subject. In remote country manses, by the farmer's ingle, round the peasant's fireside, Scotland's great concern was the theme of conversation. …': Bayne, p. 121, doubtless with some of the exaggeration to be expected in a highly partisan work.
141. It is as well to remember that the name 'Supreme Court' is not so much a 'cool' symbol of the twenty-first century as a throwback to the nineteenth, when Lord President Hope would declare that 'the House of Lords is the Supreme Court in this country': *Edwards* v *Cruickshank* (1840) 3 D. 282, at p. 308.
142. Cunningham vol. 2, p. 479.
143. Hanna vol. 3, pp. 350–2.
144. Lord President Boyle did not fail to advert to Dr Chalmers' position at this time in *Middleton* v *Anderson* (1842) 4 D. 957, at p. 981.
145. Macfarlane, pp. 63–5: 'Dr Cunningham got round Dr Chalmers' (emphasis in the original); Cunningham vol. 2, p. 479 n. 2. In his not unamusing book Macfarlane, who left the Relief Church for the Established Church in his youth, shows all the zeal of the convert – not to mention a penchant for composing epic similes that could have served as a model for Arnold's *Sohrab and Rustum*.
146. Watt, p. 177, is probably wrong just to take Dr Chalmers' words at face value as excluding any other input.
147. Cunningham vol. 2, pp. 479–80.
148. Ibid., p. 480.
149. Hanna vol. 4, p. 106.
150. Ibid. vol. 4, pp. 109–10. Bayne, p. 124, says that 'all the genius and all the heart of Chalmers glowed and throbbed in his speech on the occasion.'
151. Chalmers, *What ought*, pp. 13–14. For Lord Cockburn's reaction to the debate, see his letter to Andrew Rutherfurd, the Lord Advocate, 23 May 1839: Bell, *Lord Cockburn: Selected Letters*, p. 155, at p. 156.
152. Chalmers, *What ought*, pp. 46–7. The Church should not be deterred from 'the path of consistency and honour' by the predictable clamour of the Tory and Radical press. For Dr Chalmers' own explanation of how his views developed in response to events, see his letter to Andrew Johnston, 2 May 1843: W. Hanna, *A Selection from the Correspondence of the late Thomas Chalmers, D.D., LL.D.* (Thomas Constable & Co., Edinburgh; Hamilton, Adams & Co., London, 1853), pp. 414–15.
153. Hanna vol. 4, p. 106.
154. Watt, p. 180.

155. It is right to recall that, not being a member of the General Assembly in 1838, Dr Chalmers had not himself voted in favour of an appeal.

156. Buchanan vol. 2, p. 53; Bryce vol. 1, pp. 89–90.

157. Bryce vol. 1, p. 90.

158. Cunningham vol. 2, p. 481.

159. Macfarlane, p. 66. He describes the speech, at p. 65, as 'laboured and yet most energetic'.

160. Macfarlane, p. 67†. About a week later, the Rev. James Robertson of Ellon, the thinking man's Moderate, had the impression that, though Dr Chalmers, 'who understands little of the ways of men', still gloried in his triumph, more judicious friends were beginning to feel themselves in rather awkward circumstances: letter to his wife, dated 25 May 1839, reproduced in A. H. Charteris, *Life of the Rev. James Robertson D.D., F.R.S.E.* (William Blackwood & Sons, Edinburgh and London, 1863), p. 79. A trifle optimistic.

161. *Presbytery of Strathbogie* (1840) 2 D. 585, at p. 607.

162. John Inglis in *Memorial submitted to Her Majesty's Government by a Committee appointed at a Meeting of Ministers, Elders and others, Members of the Church of Scotland, held at Edinburgh, 12th August 1840*, p. 18. See, more generally, the discussion at pp. 15–19.

163. Following the death of the Rev. James Martin in May 1834, Candlish became minister of St George's, Edinburgh, where Lord Moncreiff was one of his elders. His speech, late in the evening, marked the beginning of his rise as a Church leader. The scene is well described in Bayne, pp. 127–32. Candlish had been specially asked by Dr Buchanan to take part in the proceedings: Candlish Memorials, pp. 77–9. For his speech, see *Report of Speeches of the Rev. Dr Burns, Rev. Robert S. Candlish and Alexander Earle Monteith, Esq., in the General Assembly on Wednesday, May 22, 1839 in the Auchterarder Case*; Candlish Memorials, pp. 80–5.

164. *Clark v Presbytery of Dunkeld* (1839) Lethendy Report.

165. Lethendy Report, pp. 145–6.

166. For the detail, see Buchanan vol. 2, pp. 80–98; Cunningham vol. 2, pp. 468–9, 477–8, and 486 (putting the various stages of the case into the context of the other events); Bayne, pp. 162–8; Turner, pp. 211–17 with Note B; Hetherington vol. 2, pp. 406–9. The proceedings are fully reported in the Lethendy Report, and, in an abridged form, as *Clark v Stirling* (1839) 1 D. 955.

167. Buchanan vol. 2, pp. 88–90; Rainy, Mackenzie, *Life of William Cunningham*, pp. 123–4; Watt, pp. 186–7.

168. See *Clark v Stirling* (1839) 1 D. 955, at pp. 969–75; Lethendy Report, pp. 21–38.

169. See D. Daube, 'The Defence of Superior Orders in Roman Law' (1956) 72 Law Quarterly Review 494–515, reprinted in D. Cohen and D. Simon (eds), *David Daube: Collected Studies in Roman Law* (Vittorio Klostermann, Frankfurt am Main, 1991), pp. 579–601.

170. Subsequently, in the *Culsamond* case, in the course of the reclaiming motion before the First Division, the court raised the issue of the status of the Commission as a court: *Middleton v Anderson* (1842) 4 D. 957, at pp. 969–72 and 972–3.

171. In the first *Auchterarder* case Lord Fullerton had already expressed sympathy with the members of the presbytery of Auchterarder who were facing a judgment finding them wrong for doing what the superior ecclesiastical courts had required them to do: Auchterarder Report vol. 2 p. 251.

172. Lethendy Report, p. 85.

173. Ibid., p. 184.

174. Ibid., p. 71.

175. A. Dunlop, *An Answer to the Dean of Faculty's 'Letter to the Lord Chancellor'* (1st edition, John Johnstone, Edinburgh, November 1839, 3rd edition, 1840), pp. 118–19; Buchanan vol. 2, pp. 94–7; Brown, *Annals of the Disruption*, pp. 32–3. Many of the leading figures in the Church – such as Guthrie, Cunningham and Candlish – were present in court to support the ministers: Guthrie vol. 2, p. 12.

176. One for the majority of the presbytery, the other by Mr Kessen: Lethendy Report, pp. 207–8.

177. Cockburn Journal vol. 1, pp. 233–4. Cf. a letter from Cockburn to the Lord Advocate, Andrew Rutherfurd, 23 May 1839: Bell, *Lord Cockburn: Selected Letters*, p. 155, at p. 156. He says that in the robing room on 22 May several of the judges tried to persuade the court 'to abstain from calling the Revd Gents to the bar – chiefly because it *provoked* them to be offensive, and so to make bad worse. For which reason (I suppose) Gillies and Meadowbank and all the rest were clear that this was the true course.' In the interest of the authority of the court, the view of the majority was surely correct.

178. Lethendy Report, pp. 211–17. It provoked an anonymous pamphlet, actually written by the Rev. Robert Buchanan: *The Presbyteries of the Church of Scotland Threatened with Imprisonment in the discharge of their official duty in the Address from the Lord President of the Church of Scotland; with an answer to the same in two letters to his Lordship by a Minister of the Church of Scotland* (W. Collins, Glasgow, 1839). Its tone can be gauged from the assertion at p. 30: 'My Lord, I venture to affirm that a doctrine so monstrous was never propounded from the Bench since the days of the Stuarts.'

179. Letter from Cockburn to Andrew Rutherfurd 14 June 1839, Adv. Ms. 9687 f 128 at 129r, National Library of Scotland. His public judgment in his *Journal* vol. 1, p. 234, is rather gentler. Alexander Dunlop thought that the Lord President's manner was kindly: *An Answer to the Dean of Faculty's 'Letter to the Lord Chancellor'*, p. 118. For John Inglis, the Lord President's address was 'solemn and most impressive': Inglis, p. 575.

180. Lethendy Report, p. 216.

181. For the complicated details, see Buchanan vol. 2, pp. 98–140, 225–58, 294–323 and 367–416; Bryce vol. 1, pp. 101–13; Cunningham vol. 2, pp. 486–90 and 496–500; Hetherington vol. 2, pp. 409–15; 417–26, 428–32 and 470–2; Bayne, Chapters XXI and XXII; *Our church heritage; or, The Scottish churches viewed in the light of their history* (Nelson, London, 1875), Chapter IX; Brown, *The National Churches of England, Ireland and Scotland, 1801–1846*, pp. 307–10.

182. For a suggestion that the opposition to Mr Edwards was really based on hostility to his wife among the wives of other ministers in the presbytery, see A. J. Campbell, *Two Centuries of the Church of Scotland 1707–1929* (Alexander Gardner Ltd, Paisley, 1930), p. 246 n. 4.

183. Bryce vol. 1, pp. 115–31.

184. *Edwards v Cruickshank* (1840) 2 D. 1380. For the interdict proceedings, see pp. 77–9 below. For an assessment of the whole situation at about this time, by a legal commentator who is hostile to the Evangelical position, see S, 'The Church of Scotland Question' (1840) 24 Law Magazine and Quarterly Review of Jurisprudence 131, esp. at pp. 162–5.

185. Chalmers, *What ought*, p. 18.
186. *Memorial submitted to Her Majesty's Government by a Committee appointed at a Meeting of Ministers, Elders and others, Members of the Church of Scotland, held at Edinburgh, 12th August 1840*, p. 25.
187. Bryce vol. 2, Chapters III and V and pp. 95–108.
188. *Edwards v Cruickshank* (1840) 3 D. 282.
189. Buchanan vol. 2, pp. 304–22; Brown, *Annals of the Disruption*, pp. 22–4; Henderson, pp. 82–3; Watt, pp. 216–17. Bryce vol. 2, p. 93, by contrast, dismisses the episode in a single sentence.
190. Bryce vol. 2, p. 94.
191. Buchanan vol. 2, pp. 367–408; Bryce vol. 2, pp. 120–66. The presentee, Mr Edwards, was deprived of his licence: Buchanan vol. 2, pp. 408–10.
192. Charteris, *Life of the Rev. James Robertson*, pp. 138 and 143.
193. *Proceedings of the General Assembly of the Church of Scotland 1842*, 30 May 1842, pp. 252–8; Buchanan vol. 2, pp. 429–47 (events surrounding the Commission in August 1841) and p. 523; Bryce vol. 2, pp. 164–5, 225 (August Commission) and 273–5.
194. Brown, *The National Churches of England, Ireland and Scotland, 1801–1846*, p. 308.
195. See *Cruickshank v Gordon* (1843) 5 D. 909, at pp. 913–15. The respondents, who had not appeared, subsequently raised an action of reduction of the decrees pronounced in the suspension proceedings: *Dewar v Cruickshank* (1842) 4 D. 1446.
196. *Cruickshank v Gordon* (1843) 5 D. 909; *Caledonian Mercury* 11 March 1843; Cockburn Journal vol. 2, pp. 6–9. The oral arguments of counsel, which were also intended to cover the third *Auchterarder* case, are reported in *The Scotsman*, 25 January 1843, p. 3, and 28 January, p. 4; *Caledonian Mercury*, 26 January 1843, p. 2. The Dean of Faculty's speech was printed in *Speech of the Dean of Faculty, in the Court of Session* (p. 38 n. 24 above). See also p. 29 n. 229 below. The Court of Session had interdicted the commissioners elected by the minority of the presbytery of Strathbogie from sitting in the General Assembly of 1842: *Majority of Presbytery of Strathbogie v Minority of Presbytery* (1842) 4 D. 1298. The interdict was, in effect, ignored: *Proceedings of the General Assembly of the Church of Scotland 1842*, 27 May 1842, pp. 216–20 and 227.
197. *Edwards v Leith* (1843) 15 Scottish Jurist 375.
198. For the sequel to *Edwards v Leith*, when only fines of £5 were imposed, but the ministers were found liable in expenses, see *Caledonian Mercury*, 27 May 1843, p. 3 (giving the Lord President's remarks); Cockburn Journal vol. 2, pp. 28–9. Two of the minority, the Rev. Harry Leith, Rothiemay, and the Rev. William Duff, Grange, actually remained in the Establishment at the Disruption: McCosh, *The Wheat and the Chaff*, pp. 90–1.
199. For a description of the reaction, from a non-intrusionist standpoint, see Bayne, pp. 200–1.
200. Chalmers, *What ought*, p. 11.
201. Robertson, p. 215 (seeing events from a Moderate standpoint).
202. As reported in *The Scotsman*, 20 December 1839, p. 3, at the time of the ministers' suspension: the *Glasgow Herald* thought that the presbytery should have released itself from the obligation to the law by withdrawing from the Establishment altogether.
203. This was just one of a number of such meetings throughout the country: Hetherington vol. 2, p. 430.

204. He was Sheriff of Perth and then became Solicitor General when Peel came to power in 1841. Subsequently, he was Lord Advocate for three months in 1852, before being appointed to the bench as Lord Anderson and dying the following year: Omond, pp. 161–2. Although not listed in the Session Cases report, when Solicitor General in 1843, he was actually one of the counsel for the seven Strathbogie ministers in their action to have their deposition by the General Assembly set aside: *Cruickshank v Gordon* (1843) 5 D. 909. He did not need to speak after Rutherfurd chose not to develop the argument on jurisdiction: *The Scotsman*, 25 January 1843, p. 3.
205. *The Scotsman*, 5 June 1841, p. 3.
206. *The Scotsman*, 5 June 1841, p. 3.
207. See Disruption Worthies vol. 2, pp. 413–18.
208. By 'the empire', the speaker is referring to the United Kingdom. The usage, current in the period, is not well identified in *The Oxford English Dictionary* s.v. empire, II.5.b.(b). See, for instance, *Ferguson v Earl of Kinnoull* (1842) 1 Bell 662, at p. 733; 9 Cl. & F. 251, at p. 324, where, speaking of certain Acts of Parliament regulating and protecting the rights of patrons, Lord Campbell says 'It is surely for the Supreme Court of this empire to put a construction upon these Acts' – clearly referring to the House of Lords' jurisdiction in the United Kingdom. Similarly, in *Earl of Kinnoull v Ferguson* (the third *Auchterarder* case) 6 December 1842, *The Times*, 20 December 1842, p. 3, the Lord Ordinary (Cuninghame) refers to an argument that the English courts have the right to interpret statutes touching ecclesiastical affairs, 'solely because the King is the head of the church in that part of the empire, while, it is added, that every such right of the Sovereign over the Scottish church was cut off by statute at the Revolution.' When Turner, p. 3, says that the shock of the Disruption 'was felt throughout the empire', he too is referring to the United Kingdom. The same usage is reflected in references to the 'imperial' Parliament or legislature (cf. Stewarton Report, p. 69, per Lord Meadowbank) and to 'imperial' legislation.
209. *The Scotsman*, 5 June 1841, p. 3.
210. No student of psychology will be surprised to note that Mr Monteith had started life as an Episcopalian and had converted to the Church of Scotland under the influence of Dr Chalmers' teaching: Disruption Worthies vol. 2, pp. 415–16.
211. See the report in *The Scotsman*, 5 June 1841, p. 3.
212. Henderson, pp. 91–2.
213. On Dunlop, see p. 66. For Dr Chalmers' view of the line to take, emphasising the spiritual independence issue rather than non-intrusion, see Hanna vol. 4, pp. 280–91; Moncreiff, pp. 101–4. Chalmers was conscious, however, that opponents could represent the claim for spiritual independence as a claim for power for ecclesiastics, rather than for ordinary people: letter of 19 February 1842 to Lord Lorne (the future eighth and first Duke of Argyll), in W. Hanna (ed.), *A Selection from the Correspondence of the late Thomas Chalmers, D.D., LL.D.*, pp. 386–95. In January 1842 the Marquess of Lorne, then aged eighteen, had published anonymously *Letters to the Peers from a Peer's Son, on the Duty and Necessity of an Immediate Legislative Interposition on behalf of the Church of Scotland, as determined by Considerations of Constitutional Law* (William Whyte & Co., Edinburgh, 1842).
214. *Claim Declaration and Protest by the General Assembly of the Church of Scotland* (1842). See Watt, pp. 253–62. Turner, pp. 189–90, makes the valid point that the document was so elaborate and the time for its consideration so short that most of the members of the Assembly who supported it could not possibly have mastered the detail. Of

course, even today, this would be equally true of most MPs and peers and of the legislation they pass.

215. For a hostile commentary see A. Macgeorge, 'The Church in its Relation to the Law and the State', in R. H. Story (ed.), *The Church of Scotland Past and Present* (William Mackenzie, London, n.d., but apparently 1891) vol. IV, p. 1, at pp. 108–15.

216. Letter from Dr Guthrie to his brother, Provost Guthrie: Guthrie vol. 2, p. 44.

217. When Peel formed his Conservative ministry in August 1841, this opened the way for the Tory Lord President Hope to resign, for the Tory Lord Justice Clerk Boyle to become Lord President and for the Tory Dean of Faculty Hope to replace him as Lord Justice Clerk. For Parliament's general attitude to Church matters, see Chadwick, *The Victorian Church* Part I, pp. 222–4; Brown, *The National Churches of England, Ireland, and Scotland, 1801–1846*, Chapter 5.

218. How they could genuinely have entertained any such expectations after the unanimous and straightforward decision of the First Division is, to say the least, a mystery: *Earl of Kinnoull v Ferguson* (1841) 3 D. 778. If even Lord Fullerton could not support its position, the presbytery was doomed.

219. *Ferguson v Earl of Kinnoull* (1842) 1 Bell 662; 9 Cl. & F. 251. The perceived significance of the decision is brought out very clearly in Turner, pp. 291–308.

220. Lord Cuninghame later said that the dictum of Lord Kames, which had been cited in support of that argument, had been 'exploded': *Cruickshank v Gordon* (1843) 5 D. 909, at p. 916. For the modern context, see Sir William Wade, C. Forsyth, *Administrative Law* (9th edition, Oxford University Press, Oxford, 2004), pp. 774–7.

221. Apparently, the idea was first suggested by Dr Chalmers' son-in-law and biographer, Dr William Hanna, in September 1842, after the second *Auchterarder* decision. See the letter of Dr Chalmers to the Rev. John Mackenzie (also a son-in-law) dated 19 September 1842: Hanna vol. 4, pp. 306–7.

222. See the letter dated 21 October 1842 from Dr Guthrie to the Rev. James McCosh reproduced in Guthrie vol. 2, pp. 40–1. Guthrie knew McCosh from the time when they were both ministers in the presbytery of Arbroath: Disruption Worthies vol. 2, p. 343.

223. Letter from Dr Guthrie to Provost Guthrie: Guthrie vol. 2, p. 43.

224. Bryce vol. 1, pp. 310–15; Turner, Chapter XIII; Hanna vol. 4, pp. 309–18, with Appendix D, pp. 551–64. Macfarlane, pp. 110–18, provides a very hostile commentary.

225. Candlish Memorials, pp. 219–59 (notes of the Rev. James Henderson, St Enoch's Church, Glasgow); Arnot, *Life of James Hamilton D.D., F.L.S.*, pp. 210–12; Mrs A. Fleming, *Autobiography of the Rev. William Arnot and Memoir by his daughter, Mrs. A. Fleming* (3rd edition, James Nisbet & Co., London, 1878), pp. 153–8. See Ross, pp. 132–3. Bayne, Chapter XXXI, gives a full account based on Dr Henderson's notes. It is pretty clear that Dr Henderson did not like the interventions by Henry Moncreiff. Forty years later, in a very defensive passage, Moncreiff challenged the accuracy of his record: Moncreiff, pp. 330–3.

226. Candlish Memorials, p. 221.

227. Indeed Dr Chalmers tried to exclude any criticism of patronage: Guthrie vol. 2, p. 46, letter dated 19 November 1842 from Dr Guthrie to Patrick Guthrie.

228. *Ferguson v Earl of Kinnoull* (1842) 1 Bell 662; 9 Cl. & F. 251.

229. Mr Young had already embarked on the third *Auchterarder* case, *Earl of Kinnoull v Ferguson*, 6 December 1842, *The Times*, 20 December 1842, p. 3, judgment of the Lord Ordinary (Cuninghame); Opinions of the consulted judges in *Earl of Kinnoull v*

Ferguson 7 March 1843, Session Papers vol. 388, No. 172, Advocates Library; (1843) 5 D. 1010, judgment of the First Division in accordance with the opinions of the majority of the consulted judges. According to the *Caledonian Mercury*, 11 March 1843, p. 3, having first given judgment in the *Strathbogie* case, the court then dealt with the third *Auchterarder* case. The Lord President simply said, 'All I have to say in this case is that I entirely concur with the opinion of the Lord Justice Clerk.' Lord Mackenzie was of the same opinion, while Lord Fullerton and Lord Jeffrey both agreed in the opinions of the minority of the consulted judges. The court held that the action at the instance of the patron and presentee – concluding for a declarator that the members of the presbytery who were willing to obey the law, though a minority, might effectually take the pursuer on trial, and if found qualified, admit and receive him in the benefice, and for interdict against the interference of the majority – was competent and relevant.

230. Above, pp. 5–6.
231. So *The Glasgow Chronicle*, as reproduced in *The Times*, 25 October 1842, p. 3, commenting on the circular summoning the Convocation.
232. Constitution (Amendment) Act 2002. Lord Nicholls of Birkenhead expressly recognised that this was a legitimate step for the legislature to take, even though he considered it to be profoundly regrettable: *Matthew* v *State of Trinidad and Tobago* [2004] UKPC 33; [2005] 1 A.C. 433, at p. 471, paras 72–3.
233. Hetherington vol. 2, pp. 494–5.
234. Candlish Memorials, p. 243, Dr Candlish.
235. Ibid., pp. 223–4, Dr Guthrie commenting on the argument of Mr Smith.
236. Ibid., pp. 243–4.
237. Ibid., p. 244.
238. As is obvious, for instance, from the tone of J. Begg, A *Violation of the Treaty of Union* (Johnstone, Hunter & Co., Edinburgh, 1871), tracing the present social ills in Scotland to the Church Patronage (Scotland) Act 1711 passed by the 'English' Parliament, which had led to the presbyterian church in Scotland becoming divided and so unable to deal effectively with poverty and education.
239. Some criticism of this account of his stance is to be found in T. Smith, *The Memoirs of James Begg D.D.* (James Gemmell, Edinburgh, 1885, 1888), vol. 1, pp. 411–12.
240. Candlish Memorials, p. 237.
241. Ibid., p. 245. The quotation is from Matthew 10:23: 'But when they persecute you in this city, flee ye into another: for verily I say unto you, Ye shall not have gone over the cities of Israel, till the Son of man be come.' Using the quotation in this context was not a novelty: cf. the letter from Dr Guthrie to Provost Guthrie before the Convocation: Guthrie vol. 2, p. 43.
242. See, however, the subsequent observations of Lord Moncreiff: Stewarton Report pp. 108 and 126–7, and Lord Cockburn, p. 134.
243. Candlish Memorials, pp. 235–6.
244. Fleming, *Autobiography of the Rev. William Arnot*, p. 157.
245. Guthrie vol. 2, pp. 48–50.
246. Beith, *Memories of Disruption Times*, Section II, gives a good idea of what these efforts involved. See also Guthrie vol. 2, pp. 52–3; Rainy, Mackenzie, *Life of William Cunningham D.D.*, pp. 187–9; D. Paton, *The Clergy and the Clearances: the Church and the Highland Clearances 1790–1850* (John Donald, Edinburgh, 2006), pp. 146–51.
247. Bryce vol. 1, pp. 307–9; Turner, pp. 344–9.

248. Guthrie vol. 2, p. 52, letter from Dr Guthrie to his sister, Clementina, dated 26 November 1842.

249. Buchanan vol. 2, pp. 563–71; Bryce vol. 2, pp. 322–4.

250. See pp. 9–10 above.

251. *Cuninghame* v *Presbytery of Irvine* (1843) 5 D. 427; fully reported in the Stewarton Report. Wilson, Chapter VI; Buchanan vol. 2, pp. 553–64; Turner, pp. 339–42; Watt, Chapter 20; Macleod, *Memoir of Norman Macleod D.D.*, pp. 186–7, and 191–7, reproducing a letter dated 18 February 1843 from the Rev. Norman Macleod to the Rev. A. Clerk and another undated letter from him to his sister, Jane. Bryce vol. 2, pp. 352 and 380, mentions the case only *en passant*.

252. Act anent Reunion with Seceders, reproduced in the Stewarton Report, Appendix, pp. iv–v.

253. The Dean addressed the court on 21, 22 and 23 June. Andrew Rutherfurd completed his speech in a single day, 28 June. The speeches of counsel are fully reported in *Stewarton Case. Report of the Pleadings by Patrick Robertson, Esq., Dean of Faculty, and Andrew Rutherfurd Esq., Advocate* (n. 96 above). The projected hearing cast a long shadow beforehand: *Wilson* v *Presbytery of Stranraer* (1842) 4 D. 1294.

254. The offending passages in the presbytery's case were quoted by the Dean in his speech: *Stewarton Case. Report of the Pleadings*, pp. 11–12, and are reprinted in the Stewarton Report, Appendix, p. i.

255. *Stewarton Case. Report of the Pleadings*, pp. 85–88.

256. Ibid., pp. 88–93; *The Scotsman*, 2 July 1842, p. 3. The terms of the minute are reprinted in the Stewarton Report, Appendix, pp. i–iii.

257. See *Report of the Pleadings*, pp. 93–94; interlocutor of 15 July 1842, reproduced in Stewarton Report, Appendix, p. iii.

258. *Report of the Pleadings*, p. 94.

259. See the letter from 'A Churchman', *The Scotsman*, 2 November 1842, p. 3.

260. *The Scotsman*, 26 November 1842, p. 3. Lord Gillies died on Christmas Eve.

261. The following Tuesday, the court began the hearing in presence, before the Whole Court minus the Lord Justice Clerk, in both the third *Auchterarder* case and the Strathbogie ministers' action for reduction of their deposition by the General Assembly. Appearing for the Church, Andrew Rutherfurd acknowledged that the judgments in the *Stewarton* case meant that 'it were now idle and useless to be repeating, to any extent., the general statements formerly and ineffectually made ...': *The Scotsman*, 25 January 1843, p. 3; *Caledonian Mercury*, 26 January 1843, p. 2. The report of his somewhat defeatist submissions suggests that he, at least, realised that the legal position of the Church was now virtually hopeless.

262. See, for example, *Memorial submitted to Her Majesty's Government by a Committee appointed at a Meeting of Ministers, Elders and others, Members of the Church of Scotland, held at Edinburgh, 12th August 1840*, p. 34 (saying, on behalf of the Moderates – before the case had even been argued – that it seemed to be very generally anticipated that the decision would be adverse to the pretensions of the Church).

263. The majority comprised the Lord President, the Lord Justice Clerk, Lord Medwyn, Lord Meadowbank, Lord Murray, Lord Wood, Lord Cuninghame and Lord Mackenzie; the minority comprised Lord Moncreiff, Lord Fullerton, Lord Jeffrey, Lord Cockburn and Lord Ivory.

264. With the departure of Lord Gillies and the arrival of Lord Jeffrey, the disposition of forces in the First Division was now even, with the Lord President and Lord

Mackenzie on the one side, Lord Fullerton and Lord Jeffrey on the other. But the actual decision was given in terms of the opinion of the majority of all the judges: Stewarton Report, p. 184.

265. Some spectators at the hearing thought that they detected a hint that Lord Jeffrey had seen reason to change his mind about the (first) *Auchterarder* case and would not be going any further in supporting the Church's position: *The Scotsman*, 25 January 1843, p. 2; Macfarlane, p. 56*, at p. 57. Significantly or not, that part of his remarks is not fully reproduced in the version revised by him for publication: Stewarton Report, p. 180.

266. Stewarton Report, especially at pp. 52–6.

267. Lord President Boyle, Stewarton Report, p. 143; Lord Justice Clerk Hope, p. 62; Lord Meadowbank, p. 69; Lord Wood, pp. 74–5; Lord Cuninghame, pp. 83–5; *contra*, Lord Moncreiff, pp. 116–17 and 120–1.

268. For example, Lord Medwyn, Stewarton Report, pp. 45–8; Lord Justice Clerk Hope, pp. 60–1; Lord Meadowbank, pp. 68–9; *contra*, Lord Moncreiff, pp. 121–3; Lord Fullerton, p. 172; Lord Cockburn, p. 133. See Wilson, pp. 159–61.

269. Stewarton Report, p. 131.

270. Lord Justice Clerk, Stewarton Report, pp. 57–8; Lord Murray (doubtful), p. 71; Lord Wood, pp. 74–5; Lord Meadowbank, pp. 74–5.

271. Lord Moncreiff, Stewarton Report, pp. 117–19; Lord Fullerton, pp. 170–1. Lord Cockburn puts his points with particular gusto: pp. 130–2.

272. In a speech to the presbytery of Edinburgh on 25 January 1843 about the position of the ministers of *quoad sacra* parishes on the presbytery: *The Scotsman*, 28 January 1843, p. 4.

273. Buchanan vol. 2, pp. 572–82; Bryce vol. 2, pp. 336–8 and 340–52.

274. Charteris, *Life of the Rev. James Robertson*, p. 168. The appeal would have suspended the effect of the Court of Session decision.

275. On 14 June 1843: Rainy, Mackenzie, *Life of William Cunningham, D.D.*, p. 200.

276. Lord Sands, *Dr Archibald Scott of St George's Edinburgh and his Times* (William Blackwood & Sons, Edinburgh and London, 1919), p. 27 n. 1.

277. See, for example, Rainy, Mackenzie, *Life of William Cunningham D.D.*, pp. 200–1.

278. Inglis had foreseen the dilemma of anyone asking for such legislation: Inglis, p. 811.

279. Committee Stage, 26 June 1843, Hansard's Parliamentary Debates, 3rd Series, vol. 70, columns 367–82.

280. Further debate in Committee, 11 July 1843, ibid., columns 906–9; Third Reading debate, 17 July 1843, ibid., columns 1202–6.

281. Ibid., column 1206.

282. Bayne, p. x, Preface to First Edition (1893).

283. *MacMillan v General Assembly of the Free Church of Scotland* (1859) 22 D. 290; (1861) 23 D. 1314; (1862) 24 D. 1282; *MacMillan v Free Church of Scotland* (1864) 2 M. 1444.

284. *Free Church of Scotland v Lord Overtoun* (1904) 7 F. (H.L.) 1; [1904] A.C. 515, discussed at pp. 98–107 below.

285. For instance, the provisions on the appointment of Writers to the Signet as judges of the Court of Session were still-born, but remain on the statute book to this very day.

286. On the other hand, Article XIX of the Treaty was invoked in the English High Court in *R (on the application of Greenpeace) v Secretary of State for Scotland*, unreported, Crown Office transcript 24 May 1995. Popplewell J. held that, by reason of Article

XIX as enacted in the Union with Scotland Act 1706, he had no jurisdiction to entertain an application for the judicial review of a decision by the Secretary of State for Scotland to grant a licence to Shell UK to dispose of an old oil platform in deep water. The same applied to the related decision of the Chief Inspector of the Industrial Pollution Inspectorate in Scotland. The Scottish Office solicitors had been somewhat apprehensive about taking the point and 'going nuclear' by invoking the Act of Union. A cautionary note on Article XIX was sounded in *Tehrani v Secretary of State for the Home Department* [2006] UKHL 47; 2007 S.C. (H.L.) 1, at p. 30, para. 101 and p. 31, para. 105; [2007] 1 A.C. 521, at p. 554, para. 101, and p. 555, para. 105, per Lord Rodger of Earlsferry, who had been Lord Advocate in May 1995.

LECTURE 2

A War and its Warriors

'Open war is now waged between the Church of Scotland and the courts of civil law in that country.' A trifle wordy perhaps, and certainly not to be mistaken for a classic *Sun* headline, but it is nevertheless quite a dramatic opening. Not my own, I hasten to add, but the first words of a pamphlet[1] published in 1841 in an attempt to explain the warfare engulfing the courts and the Established Church in Scotland to bewildered MPs and others in England. Though different in style, it bears some resemblance to a modern newspaper headline after the Government has lost a court case. Old style or new style, the media like to portray the courts as doing battle with the Government or some other powerful body such as the Church.

In some quarters the courts acquire a certain kudos from their supposed role in taking on the executive. In an era when the Whips leave little room for independent action by MPs, it is sometimes argued that the courts are the only effective opposition which can control an arrogant government. For instance, in a leading article in July 2006, *The Independent* said:

> This expanded role for the judiciary is something we should welcome. Judges are becoming a greater influence in checking our elected rulers. As the executive grows increasingly powerful and careless with our civil liberties this can only be a good thing.[2]

Having seen the position from both sides, I would reject the idea that the courts have any such 'expanded role' if it means that they are doing anything more than deciding the issue between the parties in the case according to the law, whether it is ancient common law or, say, the Human Rights Act 1998. After all, judges are just as human as politicians. In judicial review they might err in giving either too much leeway to the decisions of a popular, newly elected government, or too little to those of a government that had been in power for a long time and had run out of public affection.[3] All that unelected judges would, or should, ever be doing is deciding a case between two parties, one of which happens to be the government.

At first sight, one might indeed say that, before the Disruption, all that the Court of Session and the House of Lords were doing was deciding the string of cases involving the Church that were brought before them. Sometimes the pursuer would be a man who had wanted to be a minister but who had been rejected by the presbytery and was now suing it for damages.[4] Sometimes the pursuer would want to stop a rival from being appointed as the minister of a parish.[5] Sometimes the patron and heritors would want to stop the presbytery dividing the parish for which the heritors paid teinds.[6] Or else a minister who had been convicted of theft by his presbytery now sought suspension and reduction of his conviction on the ground that the composition of the presbytery had been unlawful.[7] In the heated atmosphere of the times,[8] as the 1830s gave way to the 1840s, pursuers brought all these and other issues involving the Church before the Court of Session. When the court decided the issue against the presbyteries concerned, its decision could be – and very often was – portrayed as an attack by the judges on the Church. You would readily guess, for instance, that John Hamilton, the pamphleteer who said that open war was being waged between the courts and the Church, was a supporter of the non-intrusionist majority who were at pains to portray the situation in that way.

For their part, the judges who made up the majority in the Court of Session in the various cases were at equal pains to portray themselves as simply performing their traditional role of ensuring that everyone – including any presbytery – complied with the law of the land. So, when Mr Edwards raised an action with a conclusion that the presbytery of Strathbogie should be ordained to admit and receive him as minister of the parish church of Marnoch in Aberdeenshire, and the minority of the presbytery defended the action on the ground that the Court of Session had no jurisdiction to deal with such an essentially spiritual or ecclesiastical matter, the First Division repelled that plea.[9] They stressed that they were only doing what they would do with anyone else who failed to perform his duty. To ram home the point, in words which deserve to be much better known, Lord President Hope took the example of the Crown itself:

> With regard to our jurisdiction, and the jurisdiction of the supreme courts in every civilized country with which I am acquainted, I have no doubt. They have power to compel every person to perform their duty – persons whether single or corporate; and, in our noble constitution, I maintain – though at first sight it may appear to be a startling proposition – the law can compel

the Sovereign himself to do his duty, ay, or restrain him from exceeding his duty. Your Lordships know that the Sovereign never acts by himself, but only through the medium of his ministers or executive servants; and if any duty is refused to be done by any minister in the department over which he presides, or if he exceed his duty to the injury of the subjects, the law gives redress. In England the Court would proceed, according to the nature of the case, by injunction or *mandamus*, or a writ of *quo warranto*. In this country a person would proceed by action or by petition; and, if he was right, a decree would be passed and would be enforced by ordinary process of law. If it be necessary for a man to declare his rights against the Crown, he brings his action against the Officers of State representing the Crown; for there is no officer, be he high or low, civil or ecclesiastical, that the law will not compel to do that duty which the law imposes on him. Your Lordships know that there are some actions which cannot be brought on in this country without the concourse of her Majesty's Advocate, and you will find more than one case in the books where her Majesty's Advocate was called upon to show cause why he refused his concourse; and if he could not show good cause, either they compelled him to give concourse, or they allowed the action to go on without him. It is impossible to suppose that there can be any duty imposed upon any person, single or corporate, which he can refuse to discharge; or, at least, if he refuses, the Court has power to compel him to discharge it.[10]

So far as remedies against the Crown are concerned, the references to English law may paint an unduly rosy picture of the situation in England – if we remember the minefield through which, a century-and-a-half later, the House of Lords had to tiptoe to reach a somewhat similar conclusion in M v *Home Office*.[11] But, for Scots Law, the passage is a classic exposition of the power of the Court of Session to compel the Crown to do its duty, or to restrain the Crown from exceeding its duty. Indeed it is the very fact that, in the Lord President's eyes, the jurisdiction is both startling and well settled that makes it, for him, such a powerful basis for his argument that the presbytery, too, must be subject to the jurisdiction of the court. Unfortunately, the Crown Proceedings Act 1947 appeared to remove part of the court's power over the Crown. Happily, in *Davidson v Scottish Ministers*[12] the House of Lords was able to find a way through the Act and so to restore the power of the Court of Session to a state in which it might almost deserve Lord President Hope's approval.

Why, then, did observers think that there was a war between the courts themselves and the Church?

Today, when a government sustains a series of defeats before the courts, it is generally because those representing some group – say, asylum-seekers or women employees claiming equal pay – are engaged in a sustained campaign against a position which the government, or indeed successive governments, feel obliged to defend. The battle is between the group concerned and the government. But members of the group raise a number of judicial review or similar proceedings in the hope that, if not all at once, at least by stages, the courts will be able to give them the victory over the government that they cannot win by themselves.[13]

On one level, the position was the same in the Disruption cases. They were the product of a struggle between two factions in the Church, the Moderates and the Evangelicals. Instead of confining their struggle to the Church courts, leading members of the Moderate faction quite deliberately chose to take various matters in the dispute to the civil courts. In that way they hoped to win a victory that would inevitably elude them in the Church courts now that the Evangelicals were in the majority in the General Assembly. So the Court of Session had to decide between one party, backed by the Moderates, and another – in practice, a presbytery, which was itself one of the Church courts[14] – backed by the Evangelical majority in the General Assembly. If that had been all that there was to it, then talk of a 'war' between the Court of Session and the Church would have been just the same kind of media hype as we encounter today. In fact, there was actually much more to the dispute.

Today, when the Government or the Scottish Executive lose a case in the Court of Session or elsewhere, they may not like the result, but they accept the authority of the courts of the land and comply with the decision.[15] In an extreme case they may, of course, quite legitimately legislate to reverse it.

The position of the majority party in the Church could not have been more different.[16] They considered[17] that the Church courts had exclusive jurisdiction in ecclesiastical matters and that, consequently, the Court of Session had no jurisdiction at all in those matters. The General Assembly said as much, both in its great debates on spiritual independence and when dealing, as a court, with, say, the Strathbogie ministers. Often, as Lord Fullerton noted,[18] the Church liked to base this position on what he called 'theological dogmas' – and others called 'pompous pratings'.[19] These were to the effect that Christ alone was the Head of the Church, including the Church of Scotland as the Established Church, which was not, therefore, subject to the authority of the State in ecclesiastical matters. Indeed that belief underlay the entire position of the Evangelicals and drove their actions. Before the Court of Session, however, the representatives of the Church were careful not to base their claim to exclusive jurisdiction on that theological belief. Rather, the Solicitor General emphasised[20] that the Church of Scotland, as a national establishment, was dependent on the

State and derived its privileges and immunities from the State. Therefore, it was in a mass of legislation and decisions of the Court of Session from before the Reformation onwards that the legal basis for the exclusive jurisdiction of the Church courts in ecclesiastical matters was to be found.[21] Hence the need for the judges to examine the history of the Church from the time of the Reformation, at least. Hence, also, the interminable judgments, especially of Lord Medwyn and Lord Moncreiff, as they crawl through that history, not year by year but – it often seems – minute by minute.[22]

Even though the claim to exclusive jurisdiction was based on ordinary legal materials, it inevitably meant that the Church, as represented by the majority party, did not simply disagree with the decisions of the Court of Session: it regarded the Court of Session as attacking it – in effect, as invading its territory, attempting 'to break into the precincts of the Church, and to desecrate [its] sanctuary.'[23] Conversely, the Court of Session saw the Church as claiming a right to invade *its* territory and as defying *its* authority. It was this stand-off which gave the dispute its wider constitutional significance for most members of the public.

Writing more than forty years later, when he was the Grand Old Man of the Free Church, Lord Moncreiff's son, Sir Henry Wellwood Moncreiff Bt, suggested – presumably, humorously, though with him it is hard to tell – that the majority judges who failed to uphold the Church's argument on the independence of its courts in ecclesiastical affairs had been infected by an inveterate hereditary disease of English Erastianism which made them unable to see how a church could both be established and yet enjoy spiritual independence.[24] Happily for them, he supposed that the minority judges had been inoculated against this disease by an exposure in early life (that is, during their education in England) to English conceptions. But, in reality, as Sir Henry's own detailed analysis shows, the Church's argument ultimately rested on the idea that the Church derived its powers from God, not from the State – a religious, rather than a legal doctrine.[25] For the Moderates, John Inglis protested against any idea of an 'undefinable, but inherent and indefeasible authority, derived from the Saviour Himself as Head of the Church, in the exercise of which all considerations of expediency and all reverence for civil government must be abandoned and forgotten.'[26]

It was this confrontation over jurisdiction which made talk of a 'war' between the Court of Session and the Church rather more appropriate than in the case of modern disputes between the courts and the executive.

The so-called 'war' went on for more than six years – from the time when Lord Fullerton, as Lord Ordinary, heard the first *Auchterarder* case argued 'at great length' in December 1836 before reporting it to the First Division,[27] until it spluttered to an end with the last gasp of the *Strathbogie* litigations on 26 May 1843, eight days after the Disruption.[28] In the *Culsamond* case[29] in March 1842, Lord President Boyle attempted to dispel any idea of a contest between the Court of Session and the Church:

> As to the childish idea that this court is in collision with, or, by the judicial determinations it is called upon to pronounce, is entering into competition with the General Assembly as to jurisdiction, or is anxious to interfere in such questions as the present, and the many others which have been raised since 1834 …, I shall only say, and I believe I speak the unanimous sentiments of the court, that nothing has been more contrary to its wishes than to have been called upon to adjudicate in any one of them. Let the Church only confine itself to matters that are truly of an ecclesiastical nature … and there will neither be applications made for the protection of the civil power, nor any interference whatever on the part of this court, which can possibly be construed into an attempt to encroach upon the privileges of the Church or any of its courts.

This was a cry from the heart. The Lord President was glad of an occasion to make the point again in February 1843, when the First Division dismissed an action on the ground that the matter was completely within the presbytery's jurisdiction: 'The judgment to be pronounced must satisfy all reasonable men that the Court does not interfere with the Church courts when not imperatively called on to do so.'[30] In their quieter moments even some of the Evangelicals would concede that the judges were only doing their job: the judges' province was 'to give sentence on every question which comes before them; and we must presume that every sentence of theirs rests on their own conscientious views of law and equity.'[31]

Despite the protestations on both sides, the clash over jurisdiction made it look like a war. Moreover, the more enthusiastic and romantic members of the Evangelical party were only too keen to see themselves as heroic figures from Covenanting times:

> We had nought else to do but to pluck the old weapons from the dead men's hands and when the State came down on us in its pride and power, man once more the moss-grown ramparts where our fathers had bled and died. The rust was rubbed from the old swords. …[32]

In truth, some of the language used by the judges did nothing to spread peace. For example, at the start, in the first *Auchterarder* case, Lord Meadowbank dared the General Assembly to do their worst. Referring to the confrontations between Parliament and the English courts over parliamentary privilege, he said:

> No man, nor any body of men, however elevated, have ever yet resisted the law with impunity. We have seen that both Houses of Parliament, the Lords and the Commons of England, having found the arm of the law too powerful for their resistance, were compelled to yield to its omnipotence – and I cannot say that I have much apprehension of all that the General Assembly could do in such a case, under whatever leaders she may think fit to proceed to battle.[33]

Even Lord Fullerton, a star among the minority judges, who supported the Church's position whenever possible, used military language. Dismissing an argument on jurisdiction which was based on the Church courts' lack of any power to enforce their judgments, he said:

> It is true we have artillery strong enough, in the shape of interdicts, and diligence, and fine, and even imprisonment; and the Church courts are now despoiled of the weapons of offensive warfare, once strong enough in their hands. But what is that to the purpose in a question of right? The defensive armour of argument, reason, and justice, at least, are at their command; and I trust those are the arms by which every judicial contest in this court is, and ever will be decided.[34]

The reaction of the prototypical modern judge – whose main duty, many appear to think, is to express dismay if the parties have been remiss enough not to settle their dispute without troubling the courts – may well be to ask whether all these battles, all these judgments and all these legal expenses were really necessary. If it had arisen today, surely, he would suggest, the dispute could have been resolved by the modern miracle of mediation? Happily not. The crucial dispute was about jurisdiction and, for that reason alone, it was unavoidable.

In the first *Auchterarder* case, speaking for the presbytery, but really for the General Assembly, the Solicitor General made this plain. Referring to the Veto Act, he said:

> Whether [the Church] acted wisely or not, is not here the question; nor is this the place to entertain such discussion. She will vindicate her own proceedings to public opinion, she will vindicate her proceedings before the legislature of the State if called upon to do so; but she denies she is under any necessity to defend herself in this court; and the presbytery of Auchterarder will not betray her interest or her rights, by entering into a defence, even before this high tribunal, in a matter as to which, however deep and sincere the respect she feels for your Lordships, she must disclaim its authority.[35]

This was, indeed, the only position which the Church could take since, if its stance was correct and the Church courts had exclusive jurisdiction in ecclesiastical matters, it was its duty to vindicate that jurisdiction by refusing to countenance the jurisdiction of the Court of Session. Either the Church courts had exclusive jurisdiction or they did not. Therefore, for the Church to acquiesce in the jurisdiction of the Court of Session, to any extent, necessarily amounted to abandoning its entire position, that the Church courts alone had jurisdiction.[36] As Dr Chalmers put it, on jurisdiction 'the Church could not, without the surrender of a great and essential principle, recede from her position by a single hair-breadth.'[37] This was why, every time the Church at any level was represented in one of the long series of cases before the Court of Session, its counsel had to renew the battle over jurisdiction.[38] It was not an issue that could be settled by an adjustment of the parties' positions. Indeed the majority party in the Church quite often tried to avoid any suggestion that they recognised the authority of the Court of Session by simply not defending actions brought against the representatives of the Church. A decision in undefended proceedings did not count as a *res judicata* and so did not prevent the Church from re-opening the point if it arose subsequently.[39]

Although the original *casus belli* was the Veto Act, this was a minor matter compared with the question of jurisdiction – or, as the Church called it, the 'spiritual independence' of the Church from the dictates of the State courts in ecclesiastical matters. Dr Chalmers described the veto as 'a mere bagatelle and dust in the balance' by comparison with the spiritual independence of the Church.[40] When the Church's Claim of Right was being drafted for presentation to Parliament in the spring of 1842, Chalmers insisted that the emphasis must be on spiritual independence, rather than on the Veto Act, since he thought that the complexities of the dispute about that Act would make little impression outside Scotland.[41] But it seems clear that everyone realised that, if the Veto Act were challenged, the question of the respective jurisdictions of the civil and ecclesiastical courts would immediately arise. Indeed, in its defences as originally drafted in the first *Auchterarder* case, the presbytery mentioned that, in certain circumstances, it might have been its duty to the court 'to have respectfully declined your Lordships' jurisdiction.'[42] After the position changed when the pursuers revised their condescendence, the first plea-in-law for the presbytery was indeed to the effect that the Church courts had exclusive jurisdiction.[43] Writing in March 1835, when the Auchterarder dispute was still going through the Church courts, Lord Cockburn referred to doubts which Lord Advocate Jeffrey had expressed in a letter to him in 1833 and added, 'The collision on which

Jeffrey speculates between the civil and ecclesiastical courts was always foreseen, and is now about to take place.'[44]

The dispute began in the Church courts – the presbytery, the synod and the General Assembly. These courts – in particular, the General Assembly – were familiar territory to a circle of advocates who would regularly appear there as counsel for parties to a dispute, even though, unfortunately, their clerical clients were notoriously bad payers.[45] But, in addition, many of the most active non-clerical members of the General Assembly were advocates and other lawyers. Both the Evangelicals and the Moderates could count a number of advocates among their most devoted supporters. So, when the struggle over the Veto Act moved from the General Assembly to the Court of Session, it was really continued by many of the people who had already been fighting one another in the General Assembly. The difference was that they were now acting as advocates in the civil court. What was probably inevitable, but is certainly more surprising to modern eyes, is that many of the judges who were called upon to decide the case in the Court of Session had also been involved previously with the issue, whether in the General Assembly or as Law Officers.

First, the advocates. In the first two *Auchterarder* cases, and in the *Lethendy* and *Strathbogie* cases, on the Moderate side, we have the Dean of the Faculty of Advocates, John Hope, who had been the Tory Solicitor General for Scotland until 1830, when the Whigs came to power and Henry Cockburn succeeded him.[46] There was more than a suspicion that the Dean was, in effect, the mastermind behind the action by the Earl of Kinnoull and Mr Young. Certainly, he was an implacable opponent of the Veto Act. Not only had he spoken and voted against it in the 1834 General Assembly, but, as already noted,[47] he had also had his dissent and the reasons for it specially recorded. In the court vacation of 1839, after the House of Lords had delivered its judgment in the first *Auchterarder* case, the Dean published a repetitious and highly contentious pamphlet, running to some 290 closely printed pages, in the guise of *A Letter to the Lord Chancellor*.[48] If Lord Chancellor Cottenham had bothered to open his letter, he would have found the Dean trampling over the whole subject and hammering away, yet again, at the Evangelicals' case. Curiously enough, shortly before he went on the bench as Lord Justice Clerk in October 1841, the Dean was criticised by his own side for entering into secret, but unsuccessful, negotiations with the Evangelicals' Dr Candlish in an attempt to resolve the whole dispute.[49] On the afternoon of the Disruption – the climax of the drama which he had done so much to produce – there Lord Hope was in St Andrew's Church, watching events from a place close to the Lord High Commissioner.[50]

With the Dean in the first *Auchterarder* case was Robert Whigham,[51] also already very much a veteran of the fight against the veto. A member of the General Assembly since 1817, he regularly spoke on the Moderate side in debates, not least on the subject of patronage and the Veto Act. In April 1834 he had told the House of Commons Committee on Patronage that in his view the existing system of patronage worked well and that he knew of no possible alternative scheme that did not appear 'to be so very dangerous to the establishment of the Church of Scotland, patronage being one of the connecting links between the two ranks of society.'[52]

Also appearing from time to time on the Moderate side – for instance, driving through the snowy wastes of Aberdeenshire 'to a scene of un-paralleled ecclesiastical desolation' when Mr Edwards was inducted into the parish of Marnoch in January 1841 – we find none other than young John Inglis.[53] At first sight, not so much the future Lord President, perhaps, as the dutiful son of the late Dr John Inglis, the leading Moderate and advocate of church establishment[54] who had died in January 1834, just as the patronage issue was hotting up. In 1839 the son published two articles in *Blackwood's Magazine*[55] on 'The Present Position of the Church of Scotland'. In them he set out the Moderate case in the plain style that, many years later, was to be the hallmark of his judgments as Lord President. He pleaded, in particular, for 'an end to mystification' on the legal position of the Church. He was also the draftsman of the memorial, signed by Dr Cook, denouncing the non-intrusionists' position, which the Moderate party presented to Peel's government in February 1842.[56]

The publication of the memorial led to a dramatic episode when the leading Evangelical, the Rev. William Cunningham, was reported as having said, in a speech in Belfast, that Inglis' *Blackwood's* articles were 'characterised by the same gross ignorance and reckless mendacity which characterises this memorial.' When this came to their notice, both Cook and Inglis threatened to sue Cunningham for libel. Indeed, on 24 March Inglis commenced proceedings for damages of £1,000 in the Court of Session. Cunningham then completely withdrew the allegations and, less than a week later, Inglis dropped his action.[57] Perhaps nothing, his sanctimonious biographer tells us,[58] rejoiced Lord President Inglis' heart in his declining years so much as the part he had taken in vindicating the position of the Kirk as an establishment.

If there was no lack of commitment on the part of the counsel for the Moderates, much the same can be said of the Evangelical side. Naturally, once the General Assembly had decided to back the Presbytery of Auchterarder, it was to be expected that the Procurator of the Church, Robert Bell, would enter the lists. As legal adviser to the whole of the

General Assembly, the Procurator did not make stridently partisan speeches. And indeed he did not ultimately leave the Established Church at the time of the Disruption but continued in his post as Procurator. Nevertheless, he must have been sympathetic to the supporters of the Veto Act, for he was very much involved with the family of Lord Moncreiff who had moved its adoption. His daughter, Isabella, was married to Lord Moncreiff's third son, James – who appeared for the Evangelicals in many of the cases and was eventually to become Lord Justice Clerk Moncreiff.[59] Indeed, Mr Bell being a widower, the couple lived with him.[60]

Number two for the presbytery in the first *Auchterarder* case was the Solicitor General, Andrew Rutherfurd, who was to become a fixture in the Evangelicals' legal team. He was the son of a minister of St Giles'[61] and an intimate friend of Lord Cockburn. His later speeches in Parliament and elsewhere show that he, too, was sympathetic to the non-intrusionists, though anxious lest their supporters should overstep the mark.[62] At the Disruption, he joined the Free Church.[63]

Last but not least in the team comes Alexander Dunlop, who would certainly have kept his seniors up to the mark. He is the Dunlop who achieved a certain immortality among Scots lawyers by giving his name to one of the series of reports of Court of Session cases. More importantly, he was the leading and ubiquitous legal figure on the non-intrusionist side of the fight. Tireless and ascetic, if there was a pamphlet to be composed, or a motion to be proposed, or a resolution to be drafted, or a speech to be made, Dunlop was your man.[64] Brevity was not, I fear, one of his virtues: his *Answer to the Dean of Faculty's 'Letter to the Lord Chancellor'* ran to 198 pages, and his heavy hand lies behind many of the Church's wordy pronouncements. Having burned his professional boats over the Disruption, he was lucky enough to marry money in the shape of the daughter of a West India merchant, 'as Free as he is'.[65] He changed his name to Murray Dunlop and ended up as a respected Liberal MP.

Given all this background, it is not surprising that counsel's speeches in the first *Auchterarder* case mention their previous involvement before the case came to court. For instance, at one point Mr Whigham refers to 'Some of my friends who have taken a part in the discussion elsewhere' – alluding to speeches by the Procurator and Mr Dunlop in the General Assembly.[66] The Procurator returns the compliment by mentioning part of Mr Whigham's evidence to the House of Commons Committee and his speech in the General Assembly of 1834.[67] Occasionally – and improperly, by modern standards at least – counsel let slip their own personal opinion on the issues before the court. For example, early on in his address,[68] the Procurator says that he would belie his own opinion if he admitted any jurisdiction in the Court of Session to control the Church courts.[69] No rebuke comes from the judges. They were probably too familiar with the personal views of all of the counsel for this breach of good practice – if it was one – to be of any real significance.

More importantly, perhaps, the counsel and parties in the case must have been only too well aware of the views of many of the judges.

Take the Dean's father, Lord President Hope, and his colleague, Lord Justice Clerk Boyle.[70] When Mr Whigham was giving his evidence against the veto to the House of Commons Committee in 1834, he was actually asked if it was a matter of notoriety that the two heads of the Court were of the same view as him as to the veto.[71] Their attitudes were indeed scarcely a state secret.

In Church circles Lord President Hope was remembered – and not with affection – for a supposedly Erastian speech on the relationship between the Church and the State which he had made in the General Assembly in 1826[72] when successfully opposing proposed Church legislation to prevent parish ministers from holding University chairs. The Lord President had not scrupled to say that such an Act would be *ultra vires* and, if the Church sought to invoke the assistance of the civil courts to enforce it, this

> must necessarily bring the question of competency before the civil court, which has, and which must have power to keep all other jurisdictions within the bounds of their legal powers, and thus a most unpleasant collision would arise between the civil and ecclesiastical authorities.[73]

The Lord President went on to trawl through the statutes relating to the Church. In particular, he observed that the Act 1579 c. 69 signified in the most distinct terms, both to the Church and to the people, that 'the Kirk had no power and no jurisdiction, but what it derived from the authority of the legislature.'[74]

The Lord President was answered on this occasion by none other than Mr James Moncreiff, who in due course was to become Lord Moncreiff. He, too, adopted a line that was to find an echo in his judgment in the first *Auchterarder* case. He accepted that the establishment depended for its existence on the provisions of the system of government derived from the will of the people:

> But it is quite another thing to say that all the powers of this Church, established under such a government, are derived solely from the express enactments of Acts of Parliament, in which particular things are committed to the Church – or that the measure of these powers is to be restrained within the limits of such express civil enactments. This would be, in other words, to say that the Church courts may, indeed, have certain powers as a

part of the civil government; but that, as the judicatories of the ecclesiastical establishment properly considered, and independent of any special statutes, they have no power at all.[75]

In reality, the two lines of thought that were to run through the Disruption cases are already discernible in these speeches of Lord President Hope and James Moncreiff in 1826.

In the General Assembly of 1832 Lord Justice Clerk Boyle spoke in the debate on the overtures on calls. Some of the overtures were to the effect that, before any presentee could be settled, he should have a concurrence of the majority of heads of families. The Lord Justice Clerk declared that 'In this there would be an open violation of the rights of patrons.'[76] On this occasion he had the misfortune to have his speech analysed in a maiden speech by the Rev. James Begg[77] which so pleased the Moderator, Dr Chalmers, that for an instant he clapped his hands with delight.[78] In 1833, in the debate on Chalmers' precursor to the Veto Act, the Lord Justice Clerk[79] went out of his way to express his 'most unqualified dissent' from Lord Moncreiff's exposition of one particular point of law.[80] He went on to say that he believed, in conscience, that conferring a power of veto 'would be destructive to the National Church'.[81] The following year, like the Lord President, the Lord Justice Clerk voted against Lord Moncreiff's Veto Act.[82]

One does not know quite where to begin with Lord Moncreiff. The son of a revered leader of the Evangelical party in the Church, Sir Henry (Harry) Moncreiff,[83] he was plainly a popular figure among the Evangelicals in the General Assembly. Leaving aside his speech in the debate in the General Assembly in 1826,[84] Lord Moncreiff's views on the expediency of legislation along the lines of the Veto Act were on public record from his contributions to debates in the Assembly and from his evidence to the Commons Committee in 1834.[85] In 1833 he had been one of the people who influenced Dr Chalmers, against his better judgment, to support the idea of a Veto Act. He had moved the Act in the General Assembly of 1834 and had moved the rejection of Mr Young's appeal in the Assembly of 1835.[86] Quite a track record.

Alongside Lord Moncreiff sat two close friends whose position on the veto was also well known. As Lord Advocate, Jeffrey had appeared to support the idea of a veto and, along with Lord Brougham, he had discussed Lord Moncreiff's evidence on patronage before he gave it to the Commons committee.[87] Similarly, as Solicitor General, Lord Cockburn had been favourably disposed to the idea of a veto and had been party to persuading Dr Chalmers that a Veto Act would be valid and was therefore the best way forward.[88] In 1834 he supported the Veto Act.[89]

The Lord President, the Lord Justice Clerk and Lord Moncreiff had been active members of the General Assembly throughout much of their adult lives, when the lines of battle were drawn between the Evangelicals and Moderates. So too had Lord Gillies[90] and Lord Meadowbank,[91] both on the Moderate side. As advocates, used to speaking in public and familiar with the law and the workings of courts, the judges would have been very much at home in the General Assembly, whether as a forum for debate, as a legislature or as a court. They had not seen any need to abandon their membership of the Assembly once they had gone on the bench – nor to withdraw from the more controversial aspects of its deliberations. So they argued and voted – and, no doubt, plotted and schemed – on the hot issues of the day. Indeed Lord Moncreiff had still been doing battle with Mr Whigham in the 1837 General Assembly, just six months before the Court of Session heard the first *Auchterarder* case.[92] But, eventually, due to the Disruption controversy, all the judges felt compelled to give up sitting in the Assembly, 'partly by the insolence of understrappers in their own profession, and partly by the unhappy agitations and violence which [had] ensued.'[93] Lord Moncreiff was very much alive to the delicacy of his position as a judge when giving evidence to the Commons Committee on Patronage about the power of the General Assembly to pass a measure like the Veto Act.[94] By contrast, it does not seem to have occurred to him that he would be in an even more delicate situation if he were to move the adoption of the Veto Act itself, well knowing that it was likely to be challenged in the Court of Session.[95] When that eventuality arose, there he was, judging the validity of his very own Act.[96]

Despite the judges' known previous involvement in the veto issue, there was no motion that any of them should not sit on the first *Auchterarder* case. The doctrine of declinature *ratione suspecti iudicis* was, of course, a well established part of the common law of Scotland, though the recognised reasons for declining appear to have been quite circumscribed.[97] We do not know whether counsel on either side ever contemplated making a motion for any of the judges to withdraw. I would guess not. After all, there was little to choose between the two sides. If the Lord President, Lord Justice Clerk and Lord Meadowbank had to step down, what about Lords Moncreiff, Jeffrey and Cockburn? If you actually supposed that the judges would decide on the basis of their previous utterances and in breach of their judicial oath, then, in order to get rid of the likely supporters on the other side, you would have to risk losing one or more of your own likely supporters. And, again on that questionable supposition, you might have reckoned that your best hope of success lay in your supporters winning over one or more of the uncommitted judges. In such a situation a declinature motion would have been a very doubtful tactic.

In any event, I suspect that any such motion would have failed. Even today, in a small jurisdiction such as Scotland, it quite often happens that a judge has some, more or less remote, involvement with a case that comes before him. All the more so, in the confined milieu of Edinburgh in those days 'where everyone knew everyone else and much of their business besides.'[98] A supposed reason for a judge not to sit might therefore be fairly easy to concoct. But it is the judge's duty to sit, unless, as a matter of law, he cannot properly do so. The fact that it is a matter of duty is important since, strange to relate, judges might otherwise seek to excuse themselves in order to get out of a long or potentially controversial case. In the Disruption cases, it would have been particularly important to ensure that, if possible, all the judges took their fair share of the inevitable burden of work and of public criticism and contributed to making any decision by the court as authoritative as possible.

Despite being anything but an impartial observer,[99] Lord Cockburn – who was in a position to know – considered that all the judges had acted conscientiously.[100] Which is exactly what one would expect. That said, it is hard to suppose that judges with so obvious a previous involvement in the veto question would be able to sit today.[101] This is one respect in which I believe the cases would have been handled differently nowadays. Indeed, the issue of declinature would rarely arise in that form, since modern ideas prevent judges from pursuing any but the most innocuous outside activities. Since the *Pinochet* case[102] the judges have, if anything, become even more cautious.

Holding office as Lord Advocate and taking part in debates in Parliament was once the accepted route to high judicial office in Scotland. We have now reached the position where it actually risks becoming a disqualification from taking a full part in the work of the court. For instance, in 2001, as one of three judges in an Extra Division, Lord Hardie interpreted a provision in the Scotland Act on which, as Lord Advocate, he had spoken for the Government when the Bill was before the House of Lords. In reality, his position was little different from that of Lord Jeffrey or Lord Cockburn in the first *Auchterarder* case. Yet, in the particular circumstances, in *Davidson* v *Scottish Ministers (No 2)*,[103] the House of Lords held that, because of Lord Hardie's prior involvement, the decision of the Extra Division must be set aside on the ground of apparent bias. In a subsequent case,[104] Baroness Hale of Richmond and I urged caution in going too far down that line. I was conscious, of course, of my previous role as Lord Advocate and of the implications for holders of that office or any similar office, if they were to continue to be eligible for appointment to the Bench. As a former Law Commissioner, Baroness Hale was equally conscious of the role that she and other judges who had been commissioners had played in developing policy and framing reforming legislation on a whole range of topics. If you were not careful, you would make it impossible for judges to decide cases in those very areas of the law where their previous experience might mean that they would have a potentially informed contribution to make.[105]

While the judges with a previous involvement in the veto issue did not feel obliged to stand down, they might have been expected to be particularly careful about the way in which they formulated their judgments. Today, even where no question of a conflict of interest arises, judges in any high-profile constitutional case are aware that every word in their judgment will go round the world on the internet and will be scrutinised and analysed by all kinds of experts. They choose their language with particular care. It is perhaps worth remembering that, when the Disruption cases began, the modern series of Court of Session reports had been going for only about fifteen years. Like previous reports, many of the early reports in the series were very brief and were really intended as an adjunct to the Session Papers. It was not so long, indeed, since the work of the Court of Session had been conducted almost entirely in writing, with the decisions of the judges having to be worked out from their interlocutors.[106] So it was a comparative novelty for the judges to have to reckon with their reasons being fully reported, far less being reported – as happened in four of the cases[107] – in special volumes which went on sale to the general public. The judges of those days may therefore have been less aware that, in choosing their language, they needed to bear in mind its possible impact on those outside the court room.[108]

Whatever the reasons, it is pretty clear that, even at the outset and before their patience was sorely tried, the judges sometimes used language which caused real offence and so made their judgments even less palatable to the losing side. For instance, in the first *Auchterarder* case, when dismissing any argument against the Court's jurisdiction based on the doctrine of Christ's Headship of the Church, Lord President Hope accepted what was said about the position of the Church of England and added: "But that our Saviour is the Head of the Kirk of Scotland in any *temporal* or *legislative* or *judicial* sense, is a position which I can dignify by no other name than absurdity.'[109]

Even if the law was right, the Lord President's language was offensive and provocative.[110] It was also gratuitously so, since the Solicitor General had made it quite clear that he was not basing his argument on the theological proposition of the Headship of Christ, but on statutes and case law.[111] In the General Assembly later that year, Dr Buchanan was reported[112] as saying that

> He would undertake to say that language so extraordinary had never before been heard in the Court of Session; and he would add, with the utmost deference, that he believed more serious damage to the interests and well-being of the National Establishments in general, and of ours in particular, had arisen from such sentiments, coming from such a high quarter, than all the hostilities of their enemies during the controversy which had existed for six years, had been able to accomplish (hear, hear).

When he came to write up the events of those times, Dr Buchanan contented himself with the milder comment that the Lord President spoke 'with less perhaps of decorum than of dogmatism.'[113] At the very least, the use of such language can only have served as a reminder that the Lord President might not be bringing an entirely fresh mind to the question.

Similarly, in November 1842, the Lord Ordinary, Lord Cuninghame, was probably less than wise to describe the position of the General Assembly in the *Strathbogie* dispute as involving a 'preposterous – if not a blasphemous – abuse of language.'[114] At the hearing of the reclaiming motion (appeal), Andrew Rutherfurd concluded his address by describing Lord Cuninghame's remark as 'an imputation quite intolerable to the parties and of the injustice of which, on their part, he did complain, and of which he trusted that they would hear no more.'[115] Two months later, in the third *Auchterarder* case,[116] just before the Disruption, Lord Justice Clerk Hope said of one particular aspect of the defenders' case that 'to lawyers this matter is very plain' and 'to every man of common sense it will be equally plain' but that 'in the extraordinary notions advocated by the defenders (giving them full credit for sincerity)', the point would be lost sight of.[117]

To modern eyes, it is surprising enough that the Lord Justice Clerk felt able to give any opinion at all in a case that was just an extension of the two earlier cases in which he had represented the same pursuers against the same defenders.[118] But the practice then was different. Shortly after his elevation to the bench, Lord Justice Clerk Hope had found himself sitting in a case where he had previously acted as counsel. The Court unanimously concurred in holding that 'no ground thence arose for his declining himself.' Lord Meadowbank recalled that, on the promotion of Lord President Blair of Avontoun in 1808, 'it had been ruled by the whole Judges that his having been counsel in most of the cases which were about to be advised was no disqualification in reference to his judging in those cases.'[119] Nevertheless, the circumstances in the third *Auchterarder* action surely called for peculiar restraint, rather than exuberance, from the Lord Justice Clerk in describing the defenders' position. Meanwhile, the pursuers' position was causing equal pain to Lord Cockburn. He betrayed his feelings when he ended his short opinion in a sentence of which John McEnroe might have been proud: 'My only difficulty is in believing that the pursuers are serious.'[120]

In the House of Lords, if anything, Lord Brougham did even worse. Amazingly, in the first *Auchterarder* appeal, which could not have been more important, he actually departed from what he said was his usual practice of writing down his judgment[121] and delivered an extempore speech of more than three hours. Today the speeches of the Law Lords are all written in advance and are adopted by their authors, without being read out, in a special sitting of the House at which, usually, the only members present are the Law Lords and a bishop. By contrast, Lord Brougham was delivering a speech in circumstances where 'a number of gentlemen' had assembled below the bar and various Scottish peers were present to hear the outcome.[122] In the normal way, he would almost certainly be rather more conscious of the effect of his words on his audience in the House than on those who would eventually read a shorthand report of his speech. This may help to explain how he felt able to compare the right of a congregation to call their new minister with the formal presentation of the Sovereign to the people for their approval at a coronation. It was 'a decent and convenient solemnity', but their rejection would have 'no more weight than the recalcitration of the champion's horse in Westminster Hall during the festival attending the great solemnity.'[123] The deliberate equiparation of what many in the Church regarded as a vital part of the procedure leading to the solemn rite of ordination with a piece of empty ceremonial involving a horse at a banquet may have seemed a good idea to Lord Brougham at the time.[124] But the inevitable effect of such language was to reinforce the impression among the non-intrusionists that the judges had failed to appreciate the significance of their case. It certainly did nothing to assist the Moderates.

A twentieth-century critic, broadly sympathetic to the position of the Evangelicals, described Lord Brougham's reasons as 'a mixture of irritating irrelevancies, fancied analogies, non-existent cases, wrapped up in a mush of sentiment and threats.'[125] Lord President Boyle, on the other hand, described both speeches in the House of Lords as 'luminous'.[126] But the truth is that there was a significant difference between the two speeches. Even at the time, some, at least, of the Evangelicals could see it: addressing the Court of Session on behalf of the Church in 1843, Andrew Rutherfurd referred to the Lord Chancellor's 'well-considered and admirable speech'.[127] Happily, also, the same modern critic, who criticised Lord Brougham so strongly, accepted that Lord Cottenham's speech was 'quite on another plane' from Lord Brougham's. He had obviously taken care to marshal his arguments and to express them as clearly as possible.[128] Which is, simply, the least that can be expected of a judge deciding any case, far less one of such enormous importance.

I suspect that judges today would be more conscious of the impact of their comments outside the courtroom and so more circumspect in their language. It is easier, of course, to choose calm and appropriate language when you yourself feel calm and at ease. From the very outset, however, the old judges must have felt that both they and their court were under siege. Not only had they been dragged into a bitter dispute between two rival factions in the Church, but the predominant party in the Church was refusing to recognise their jurisdiction while its counsel were issuing threats about what would happen if the judges found against it.

One way counsel made the point, in suitably coded language, was as part of the argument on jurisdiction: the court would be stepping outside its jurisdiction if it pronounced an order to which it could not give effect. So, in the first *Auchterarder* case, the Procurator, Robert Bell, submitted on behalf of the Church that, whatever might be the judges' opinion as to the propriety of what the Church had done in enacting the Veto Act,

> I trust you will never submit to hazard the dignity of this court, by pro-
> nouncing a judgment which you cannot enforce; and which, for any thing
> you can know, may be contemned by the party against whom it is proposed
> to direct it.[129]

When it came to his turn, Solicitor General Rutherfurd declared:

> [A] court of law will not duly consult its own dignity, and will not much
> exercise the respect due to its proceedings, especially when engaging in a
> collision of jurisdictions, such as that which unquestionably exists here, if it
> do not calculate beforehand, and see the way, clearly, to the final extrication
> of the case by the constitutional assertion of its power.[130]

Having listed a number of remedies which, he claimed – wrongly, as it turned out – the court could never contemplate granting, the Solicitor General ended with two rhetorical questions:

> Is this a state of things in which the Supreme Court of the country should
> legally engage? Is this a conflict and collision between high constitutional
> authorities, to which a wise man would commit himself without seeing his
> course clearly and distinctly to the end?[131]

Just to make sure that the judges kept the point in mind when deliberating on their decision, the Solicitor General returned to the theme at the very end of his speech:

> It is impossible to look without deep concernment to the possible conflict of jurisdiction which may ensue, and to the consequences which may be the result of that conflict to the interest of the Church, and of the State, as well as to the interest of the more immediate parties, who will be placed in a state of the most painful and inextricable embarrassment, from the impossibility of giving effect to your decree, if it should be pronounced in favour of the pursuers, without incurring the censure of their ecclesiastical superiors – a consequence the most painful and intolerable.[132]

How, then, was the court supposed to react when all these hypothetical complications were pointed out? What weight could the judges properly give to them?

While carefully describing their stance as unattractively as possible, Lord Brougham simply pretended that, somehow or other, counsel had completely misrepresented the position of the Evangelical ministers, who would actually be the last people on earth to resist the judgments of the Court of Session and House of Lords:

> I have declared my inviolable respect for the kirk and General Assembly, but any want of respect that I could show towards them, any irreverence, any mockery of them, any slander that I could bring against them, any attempt to revile them, or to hold them up to hatred and to scorn, would be a mere jest compared to the attempts that are made by some who take an opposite view of the case, and who, without meaning, God knows, any more than I do, any the least disrespect, think they are taking the best means for establishing their privilege by holding out indications that the Assembly will pursue its own course; that the Assembly will disregard the authority of the law; that an assembly of Christian ministers will be parties to the fomenting of discords; that the last thing the ministers of peace are mindful to promote is the peace of the church of Christ committed to their care; and that the only thing they now think of is the victory of them, the churchmen, the pastors of Christ's flock, over the judges, over the supreme judges of the land, and over the law of the land itself – a victory to be won by setting up acts of their own, which they have not title to pass, against Acts of King, Lords and Commons, the statute law of the realm.
>
> My Lords, I defend the Assembly against the arguments and the threats of their advocates. I protest on the part of the Assembly, as a body of Christian men, of whom the bulk are Christian ministers, against the imputation thus thrown out against them by this course of defending them, and I say that my hopes of them, my confident expectations of what will be their conduct, are wholly the reverse of those prospects thus held out; that

it was an injudicious line of argument on their behalf, an argument which I am morally certain would be repudiated and spurned by the Assembly itself. My Lords, that Assembly will do its duty, will show its veneration for the established authority of the law, will rest satisfied with having entered its protest and indicated upon its records its own opinions; but will, with the inferior judicature, the presbytery, render a willing and respectful obedience to the law of the land as pronounced by the Court of Session, and as affirmed by your Lordships.[133]

Magnificent stuff, but utterly unhelpful because untrue: 'Lord Brougham, notwithstanding his big talk, knows better.'[134]

Of course, if the extreme consequences of granting a declarator convinced the judges that the Court of Session could not have jurisdiction to do so, then they would dismiss the action and their problems would be at an end. But if – as the majority actually thought – the court had jurisdiction, then the judges had no option but to exercise that jurisdiction and, depending on their view of the merits, to grant the decree of declarator which the pursuers sought. As the House of Lords recalled in the *Tehrani* case,[135] unless a plea of *forum non conveniens* is made out, a court is duty-bound to exercise its jurisdiction if a party calls on it to do so and there is a live issue to be decided.[136] This is the judicial equivalent of the cab-rank rule for counsel: a court cannot pick and choose, but is bound to consider the case that is put in front of it and to give judgment according to the view that it reaches.

To do anything else would be a dereliction of the judge's office, as Lord Brougham pointed out:

> If it were just as clear that the judgment we are about to give would be resisted, as I know it to be demonstrably certain that it will be cheerfully obeyed, still it is the office of your Lordships to pronounce your opinion upon the question of law brought before you; and you would betray your duty most grossly if you were to suffer yourselves to be diverted from pursuing the course of your duty by any fear of other persons still more scandalously betraying their duty both as ministers and as subjects, and still more flagrantly violating the law.[137]

Likewise, a judge cannot decline to grant a remedy to which the pursuer is entitled just because the defender points to various potentially awkward consequences that may ensue if the pursuer later asks for more. That would be too like applying Cornford's Principle of the Wedge, 'that you should not act justly now for fear of raising expectations which you are afraid you will not have the courage to satisfy.'[138] I suspect that Cardinal Newman's words of submission, 'One step enough for me', are, in general, a sound guide for judges. It is hard enough to get that one step right without trying to foresee the implications of all the other steps that may or may not follow, depending on events over which the judge will usually have no control whatever. But, as Lord Cockburn pointed out, without himself being able to resolve the dilemma for the majority, such a course is potentially hazardous:

> The defenders endeavour to alarm us, by shewing how they may set our judgment at defiance; and the pursuers try to allay the alarm by assuring us that the Church will speedily yield. This is a matter which concerns the court more deeply than some of your Lordships seem to be aware. No doubt it is our duty to declare the law, and the duty of all to obey it. I cannot doubt that the Church will obey it, both from inclination and necessity. But it is also the duty of a Supreme Court to avoid every collision, through which it cannot see its way. Its dignity must necessarily be put in jeopardy by its exposing itself to a conflict in which it cannot explain how it is to prevail. This, I fear, is the position in which this court is about to place itself. It is about to enter upon an untried voyage without a compass or a star. From the moment that a judgment shall be pronounced in favour of the pursuers, the civil and the ecclesiastical authorities *are* in a state of legal collision. Yet it is disclosed that no one, either at the bar or on the bench, can tell us what is to come next.[139]

The position would have been difficult enough for the court if the point had arisen in only one case, say, the first *Auchterarder* case. But that was very far from so. According to official figures supplied to the House of Commons, as at June 1842, there were no fewer than twenty-five separate actions on patronage pending before the Court of Session, though many of them involved the same parties.[140] There were another thirteen cases arising out of the dispute over *quoad sacra* parishes, where essentially the same jurisdiction issue arose.[141] Some of the second group of actions were particularly unmeritorious since they concerned ministers who had been found guilty of theft or immorality by their presbytery and now sought to challenge that decision, not on its merits, but on the ground that the presbytery should not have included ministers of *quoad sacra* parishes.[142] Again, it would not have been so bad if the pursuers in all these different actions had wanted nothing more than the declarator sought by the pursuers in the original *Auchterarder* case. But, as the Solicitor General had anticipated, fairly soon their demands escalated and the judges were forced to confront exactly the kinds of questions which he had foreseen.

Some of these demands did indeed turn out badly for the court.[143] In particular, when, in December 1839, the Commission of Assembly suspended the seven Moderate ministers in the presbytery of Strathbogie who had defied the commands of the General Assembly, prominent Evangelical ministers were despatched to take over their duties in the parishes.[144] Moderate critics accused them of gallivanting in other ministers' parishes while leaving their own flocks untended.[145] The suspended ministers went to the Court of Session and asked the court to suspend their suspension and, in the meantime, to interdict the Evangelical ministers from preaching in the churches, churchyards or schools in their parishes. The respondents did not lodge answers and the court granted the interim interdicts.[146] Since all the property concerned was admittedly subject to the civil law, the Evangelical ministers obeyed the interdicts and betook themselves, instead, to the wintry market places and open fields.[147] A couple of months later, in February 1840, still with no answers from the respondents, the Court of Session granted an unopposed decree of suspension of the ministers' suspension and, in addition, granted the interdicts to their full extent so as, in effect, to prevent the Evangelical ministers from doing anything at all in the parishes. When, in May, the General Assembly took the same line as the Commission, the Court of Session followed the same two-stage procedure, first pronouncing limited interim interdicts[148] and later following them up with perpetual interdicts to the full extent.[149]

Strictly speaking, of course, the court was merely giving practical backing to its decree reinstating the Strathbogie ministers, which should have freed them from interference in their parishes by other ministers.[150] But there seems to have been a widespread view[151] that, though unopposed, these interdicts were a step too far: they were open to being represented as stopping ministers of the Established Church from preaching the gospel in the Strathbogie parishes when any chartist or infidel was free to spread his message there.[152] In the hope of martyrdom at the hands of overbearing judges, the very high-profile Evangelical ministers concerned took a delight in publicly trampling the interdicts underfoot and in preaching in defiance of them.[153] '[T]he haughs and holms of Bogie rang with such eloquence as they had never heard since they emerged from the primeval sea.'[154] Dr Guthrie exclaimed: 'What madmen these ministers were to crave and serve this interdict! It is the best pocket-pistol I ever carried.' He hoped that the Strathbogie ministers would complain of the breaches to the court – while adding quickly that 'it were wrong to court the personal glory' of any suffering in prison.[155] To their opponents, the Evangelical ministers were deliberately defying the law 'and all the while roaring for sympathy as if they were innocents.'[156] They were cheated of their crowns of martyrdom, however, since the petitioners never brought proceedings for breach. While this was, undoubtedly, a wise exercise of discretion on their part, it left the Court of Session looking foolish and impotent. A famous cartoon of the time, with the title of 'The Reel of Bogie',[157] portrays Lord President Hope brandishing a sword, while various ministers, including Dr Chalmers and Dr Candlish, whirl round furiously to the delight of the opponents of the Established Church. Like many modern politicians, Dr Chalmers was vain enough to be pleased with his portrayal and liked to show the cartoon to his students.[158]

As they said, so far from being the masters of events, the judges of the Court of Session were really only reacting to the cases which came before them and to the submissions which were made to them. By sustaining the jurisdiction of the civil court in the first *Auchterarder* case, the Court of Session and the House of Lords had opened a door for the Moderates. The Moderates did not hesitate to use it to press home their advantage – not with any desire to embarrass the Court of Session, but because they saw it as a way to inflict damage on their opponents. If they could not defeat the Evangelicals in the General Assembly, the Moderates could certainly tie them up in decrees, damages and expenses,[159] while, every time the Evangelicals defended themselves, they forced the majority of the court to repeat that very view on jurisdiction which was anathema to them.

To an outsider, it might indeed have looked as if, through the stream of decisions, the court was pursuing a preconceived plan of attack on the Evangelical majority in the Church. Similarly, today, when the House of Lords takes decisions against the Government, first, say, on the detention of the Belmarsh detainees[160] and then, say, on the admissibility of evidence extracted by torture,[161] it is easy for some sections of the media to portray the House as pursuing a predetermined line which shows too little understanding of the need for the Government to be able to take firm action to deal with terrorists. Looking at the same decisions, others in the media may praise the House for pursuing a course of vindicating the human rights of terrorist suspects in the face of the allegedly illiberal policy of the Government. The truth is more mundane. The House considers these questions only because they have been raised by the parties and the points of law are of general public importance. When the cases arise, while the judges must have regard to previous decisions and all the various human rights and other arguments, they reach their own individual judgments on them. The House has no predetermined strategy of any kind. The outcome of the case on the exclusion of evidence obtained by torture illustrates the point. All seven Law Lords held that evidence obtained by torture should be excluded, but the House divided very sharply on the formulation of the test to be applied. It is noteworthy that the three in the minority were actually the most senior judges, Lords Bingham, Nicholls and Hoffmann, who would, one imagines, have set the predetermined policy, if one had existed. In truth, however, there was no such policy. On the contrary, no one knew the outcome until all the speeches were in.

In much the same way, I am sure the old Court of Session judges were following no predetermined agenda. But, after their decision in the first *Auchterarder* case had been confirmed by the House of Lords, the line was set. In the later cases the judges rarely changed sides – and then only because one of the minority judges was unable to escape the binding effect of a previous decision.[162] Even so, their judgments are no mere formalities: on the contrary, they are formulated for the occasion and display the hallmarks of their individual authors. Indeed, the judgments are all more personal in tone and structure than Court of Session judgments today. Moreover, as year succeeds year and still the cases come, the pertinacity of the judges is remarkable. The Episcopalian Lord Medwyn's enthusiasm for researching the by-ways of ecclesiastical history only seems to increase.[163] How his brother judges must have dreaded having to wade through his latest discoveries. ... Moreover, when you have read your way through the Lord President and two other judges in the First Division pounding away, yet again, at the Church's defences, you know, as they knew, that there, sitting off to one side, will be the clever and learned Lord Fullerton – 'Fully' to his friends[164] and very much a judges' judge – waiting for his turn. He too does not tire; he too never gives up. Though only too well aware that he is yet again in a minority and that what he says cannot affect the outcome, he constantly refines and refurbishes his arguments. It is a performance to be savoured.[165]

Of course, we can wonder at some of the judges sitting in these cases, given their previous involvement in the issues. Of course, by modern standards, their judgments often seem impossibly long. Of course, we can criticise some of the language that they used. Of course, we can debate their reasoning or question their dicta. Of course, in hindsight, not all of their decisions were wise. But never forget: the Disruption cases represent the most sustained challenge to its authority which the Court of Session has ever faced. In that crisis for the court, the integrity of the judges was unquestionable and the intellectual level of many of their judgments was enviably high. Above all, we can only admire the way the judges, whether in the majority or minority, refused to be swayed by the pressures on the court. Criticise them we may, but, if ever a similar challenge presents itself, we shall have every reason to be proud if the judges of the Court of Session acquit themselves as well as their predecessors in those far-off days.

NOTES

1. J. Hamilton, *A Remonstrance respectfully addressed to the Members of the Legislature and others in relation to the Scottish Church Question* (Bell & Bradfute, Edinburgh; Ridgway & Son, J. Nisbet & Co., L. & G. Seeley, London, 1841), p. 1. Hamilton was qualified as an advocate and, along with his friend Alexander Dunlop, acted as a highly influential backroom adviser of the non-intrusionist party: Disruption Worthies vol. 1, pp. 295–300. Unlike most non-intrusionist activists, such as Dunlop, Hamilton was a strong Conservative in politics: Rainy, Mackenzie, *Life of William Cunningham*, p. 139.
2. 5 July 2006.
3. I am not aware of any statistical evidence to show that this actually happens, however.
4. *Ferguson v Earl of Kinnoull* (1842) 1 Bell 662; 9 Cl. & F. 251.
5. *Clark v Presbytery of Dunkeld* (1839) Lethendy Report.
6. *Cuninghame v Presbytery of Irvine* (1843) Stewarton Report.
7. *Livingstone v Proudfoot* (1849) 6 Bell 469. In the light of the *Stewarton* case, the problem was that the presbytery included ministers of *quoad sacra* parishes. See also *Campbell v Presbytery of Kintyre* (1843) 5 D. 657, at p. 663, where the pursuer founded on the fact that the General Assembly and its Commission contained *quoad sacra* ministers and there had been a slight involvement of the Commission ('the disease with which these bodies were infected being contagious' was Lord Jeffrey's sardonic summary of the pursuer's argument).
8. Both Lord Cockburn and Lord Fullerton thought that the scheme for *quoad sacra* parishes would not have been questioned in quiet times: Stewarton Report, pp. 133 and 172, respectively.
9. *Edwards v Cruickshank* (1840) 3 D. 282.
10. (1840) 3 D. 282, at p. 306.
11. [1994] 1 A.C. 377.
12. [2005] UKHL 74; 2006 S.C. (H.L.) 41.
13. The same approach can be adopted by companies: 'Skilled corporate litigators think ahead like pool players: they argue for their clients on narrow grounds hoping for incremental victories that turn into much bigger ones later': R. Dworkin, 'The Supreme Court Phalanx', *New York Review of Books*, 27 September 2007.
14. In the third *Auchterarder* case, *Earl of Kinnoull v Ferguson*, 6 December 1842, *The Times*, 20 December 1842, p. 3, the Lord Ordinary (Cuninghame) emphasised that the Church courts appeared as parties in the Court of Session. Often, the presbytery was split and the Church supported the Evangelical faction.
15. Hence, for example, the need for Parliament to restrict the availability of interdicts and orders for specific performance in private law proceedings against the Crown: section 21(1) of the Crown Proceedings Act 1947. The assumption is that, otherwise, the Crown would have to comply with such orders – which might be obtained as of right – however inconvenient they might be.
16. Cunningham vol. 2, p. 472.
17. In practice, the majority of the General Assembly determined its stance – when exercising a deliberative rather than a judicial function.
18. *Middleton v Anderson* (1842) 4 D. 957, at p. 1029.
19. XX, 'The Scotch Church Question: Letter II', *The Times*, 22 May 1843, p. 7.
20. Lord Mackenzie makes specific reference to this in *Middleton v Anderson* (1842)

4 D. 957, at p. 1010; Taylor Innes, *The Law of Creeds in Scotland*, p. 73 n. 3. In his speech in the hearing in presence in the *Strathbogie* case, Rutherfurd stressed that 'nothing was claimed by the Church which statute did not give. If he had at any period been compelled to state otherwise, he could not have appeared at the bar to maintain so preposterous a doctrine': *Caledonian Mercury*, 26 January 1843, p. 2.

21. Auchterarder Report vol. 1, p. 348; similarly, in the last stages of the war, Rutherfurd emphasised the point in his remarks on the *Strathbogie* case in the hearing in presence on 24 January 1843: *The Scotsman*, 25 January 1843, p. 3.

22. The position was, of course, taken to be the same in the *Stewarton* case: see, for instance, Stewarton Report, p. 53, per Lord Justice Clerk Hope; p. 133, per Lord Cockburn; p. 138, per Lord President Boyle; p. 160, per Lord Mackenzie; and p. 164, per Lord Fullerton.

23. Sheriff Monteith, 4 June 1841, as reported in *The Scotsman*, 5 June 1841, p. 3. The report gives 'his' sanctuary, but the word must have been 'its' or 'her'.

24. Moncreiff, p. 170. Why Sir Henry, whose mother was English and related to various Anglican clergymen (including Sir Henry's brother, George), should himself have escaped the hereditary disease he does not explain.

25. Moncreiff, pp. 179–81. Although he suggests that the law of Christ must ultimately prevail, he recognises that, if there is an irreconcilable difference, there remains no room for a scriptural connection between a particular church and the State.

26. Inglis, p. 576.

27. Interlocutor of 21 December 1836: House of Lords Appeal Papers, p. 38, Advocates Library.

28. *Caledonian Mercury*, 27 May 1843, p. 3; Cockburn Journal vol. 2, pp. 28–9, the sequel to *Edwards v Leith* (1843) 15 Scottish Jurist 375.

29. *Middleton v Anderson* (1842) 4 D. 957, at p. 988.

30. *Campbell v Presbytery of Kintyre* (1843) 5 D. 657, at p. 664. See also the Lord Ordinary (Cuninghame) in the third *Auchterarder* case, *Earl of Kinnoull v Ferguson*, 6 December 1842, *The Times*, 20 December 1842, p. 3: 'There was nothing ultroneous on the part of this Court in any process instituted before them, or in any judgment pronounced by them. These proceedings were not created or sought by them. It was established in the previous branches of the Auchterarder case, that the Church, in the supposed exercise of their legislative powers, enacted some time ago new laws, affecting the rights of patrons and presentees, whereby they altered the law of the land as it stood on the statute book, and had been in force for ages; while they, at the same time, inflicted severe and illegal sentences on their brethren who refused to join them. The parties aggrieved applied to this court for redress and protection, and the judges were bound by their oaths to take cognizance of their cases, and to decide them according to law.'

31. Chalmers, *What ought*, p. 12.

32. Guthrie vol. 2, p. 13, reproducing words from a pamphlet that Dr Guthrie published in 1859. At the time of the first *Auchterarder* decision, the bicentenary of the Glasgow General Assembly of 1638, which 'crumpled up acts of parliament as if they were waste paper' and excommunicated the bishops, only served to encourage these sentiments: Cunningham vol. 2, pp. 474 and 478; Bryce vol. 1, pp. 81–2, referring to 'demi-theatrical exhibitions'. Interestingly enough, the weapons of Covenanting times were to reappear in 1900 on the walls of the inaugural meeting of the United Free Church in the Waverley Market: C. G. McCrie, *The Church of Scotland: Her Divisions and Re-Unions* (Macniven & Wallace, Edinburgh, 1901), p. 324.

33. Auchterarder Report vol. 2, p. 113.
34. *Middleton v Anderson* (1842) 4 D. 957, at p. 1025. Lord Fullerton seems to be rejecting the kind of argument on the superiority of the civil courts advanced in Inglis, pp. 574–5. Inglis was himself junior counsel for the suspenders. Lord Jeffrey thought that Lord Fullerton's was '*by far* the best speech in the case, the other three being, as I think, singularly poor; and Mackenzie's especially a show of elaboration strangely tainted with injudicial prejudice and passion.' But he had some doubts about the way that Lord Ivory and Lord Fullerton distinguished *Presbytery of Strathbogie* (1840) 2 D. 585: Letter of Lord Jeffrey to Lord Cockburn, 7 April 1842, Adv. Ms. 9.1.11, f. 1075, National Library of Scotland.
35. Auchterarder Report vol. 1, p. 408. The passage was quoted by Lord Gillies in the *Culsamond* case to show the very argument which was decisively rejected in the *Auchterarder* case: *Middleton v Anderson* (1842) 4 D. 957, at p. 1001.
36. The point of view of the majority party in the Church is particularly clearly explained in the *Memorial addressed to the Members of Her Majesty's Government by Robert Gordon D.D., Moderator of the General Assembly of the Church of Scotland, and others, Commissioners appointed by the Church* (September 1841), pp. 20–4.
37. Chalmers, *What ought*, p. 19.
38. Maintaining the Church's position became increasingly difficult, of course, as ruling after ruling was handed down against it. By the time of the hearing in presence in the third *Auchterarder* and *Strathbogie* cases on 24 January 1843, counsel for the Church, Mr Rutherfurd, was really reduced to going through the motions: *The Scotsman*, 25 January 1843, p. 3; *Caledonian Mercury*, 26 January 1843, p. 2.
39. *Memorial addressed to the Members of Her Majesty's Government*, pp. 22–3. A decree in absence does not count as *res judicata*: there must have been a decree *in foro contentioso*. See J. A. Maclaren, *Court of Session Practice* (W. Green, Edinburgh, 1916), pp. 396 and 1089; *Esso Petroleum Co. v Law* 1956 S.C. 33.
40. In his speech in the Commission of Assembly, 11 December 1839: Bryce vol. 1, p. 121. See also Chalmers, *What ought*, p. 19.
41. Hanna vol. 4, p. 284; Watt, p. 243. See also p. 50 n. 213.
42. Auchterarder Report vol. 1, Appendix, p. 17.
43. Ibid. vol. 1, Appendix, p. 26.
44. Comment on the letter from Jeffrey to Cockburn, 24 February 1833, Adv. Ms. 9.1.9, f. 577 at f. 578v, National Library of Scotland. See also Cockburn Journal vol. 1, pp. 60–1, entry for 7 June 1834.
45. J. Crabb Watt, *John Inglis* (Green & Sons, Edinburgh, 1893), p. 58.
46. His role is painted in the blackest terms by Bayne, pp. 153–7.
47. See p. 9 above.
48. *A Letter to the Lord Chancellor on the Claims of the Church of Scotland in regard to its Jurisdiction and the Proposed Changes in its Polity* (William Whyte & Co., Edinburgh; John Murray, London, 1839). The first edition was published shortly after the end of the Commission of Assembly in August 1839: Hanna vol. 4, p. 135.
49. Ironically, the sticking point seems to have been the attitude of the Strathbogie ministers who, having followed the Dean's advice in obeying the orders of the Court of Session, refused to compromise their position to help his negotiations: Bryce vol. 2, pp. 201–9.
50. G. B. Ryley, *A Historical Retrospect and Memorial of the Disruption* (Archibald Constable & Co., London, 1893), pp. 301–2.
51. The Dean and Mr Whigham were the Moderates' team in many of the litigations,

including the *Daviot* case, *Mackintosh v Rose* (1839) 2 D. 253, where they pressed home the victory that had been won in the first *Auchterarder* case.

52. *Minutes of Evidence taken before the Select Committee on Church Patronage, Scotland,* 21 April 1834, p. 423, Question 2783, and p. 428, Question 2796.

53. See Crabb Watt, *John Inglis*, p. 69. The author gives a useful account of some of the litigations in which Inglis was involved, at pp. 65–72.

54. He was the author of *A Vindication of Ecclesiastical Establishments* (W. Blackwood, Edinburgh, 1834).

55. Inglis' argument, in Inglis, pp. 574–5, on the superiority of the jurisdiction of the Court of Session, which had powers to execute its judgment, did not impress Alexander Dunlop: *Answer to the Dean of Faculty's 'Letter to the Lord Chancellor on the claims of the Church of Scotland in regard to its jurisdiction, and the proposed changes in its polity'* (John Johnstone, Edinburgh, 1840), p. 89*. Nor did it fare much better with Lord Fullerton in the *Culsamond* case: *Middleton v Anderson* (1842) 4 D. 957, at p. 1025.

56. *Memorial submitted to Her Majesty's Government by a Committee appointed at a Meeting of Ministers, Elders and others, Members of the Church of Scotland, held at Edinburgh, 12th August 1840.*

57. *The Scotsman*, 2 April 1842, p. 3; Rainy, Mackenzie, *Life of William Cunningham*, pp. 169–70; Omond, pp. 204–5. Curiously enough, Crabb Watt makes no mention of the articles or the resulting controversy. Forty years later, Inglis was, of course, to return to the Scottish courts as a litigant when, as Lord President, he fought and won *Shotts Iron Co. v Inglis* (1882) 9 R. (H.L.) 78.

58. Crabb Watt, *John Inglis*, p. 74, concluding a horrendous purple passage on General Assemblies.

59. For the Lord Justice Clerk's connection by marriage with Mr J. B. Balfour, later Lord President Blair Balfour (Lord Kinross), see p. 126 n. 70.

60. Omond, p. 154 n 1. They were still living with Bell, long after the Disruption, when Moncreiff was Lord Advocate. Cf. *Index Juridicus: The Scottish Law List and Legal Directory for 1852* (Adam & Charles Black, Edinburgh, D. Robertson, Glasgow and Stevens & Norton, London) pp. 148 and 157. Like his father and elder brother, James Moncreiff, who appeared in many of the litigations on the non-intrusionist side, joined the Free Church at the Disruption, although he did not leave the Establishment immediately and spoke in the Church of Scotland Assembly after the split had occurred. His father, Lord Moncreiff, was actually in London in May 1843. He had gone there with his wife who was seriously ill: Lord Cockburn, *Circuit Journeys*, entry for 20 April 1843. She died in London on 28 May: Sir Francis J. Grant, *The Faculty of Advocates in Scotland 1532–1943 with Genealogical Notes* (1943), p. 153. Henry Moncreiff went to join his parents in London immediately after the Disruption and adhered to the Free Church on his return to Scotland in June, as did Lord Moncreiff. See Moncreiff, p. 332.

61. Omond, pp. 47–9. His father was Dr Greenfield, but the family changed their name to Rutherfurd in 1799.

62. Ibid., pp. 76–7 and 78.

63. As a master of conveyancing, Rutherfurd, along with Alexander Dunlop, was involved in drawing up the Model Trust Deed on which much of the property of the Free Church was held: Free Church Appeals, p. 519; A. Taylor Innes, 'The Creed Crisis in Scotland' (1904–5) 3 Hibbert Journal 217, at p. 224 n. 1.

64. See the descriptions in Bayne, pp. 231–2, and Buchanan vol. 2, p. 515.
65. Cockburn to Jeffrey, 10 May 1843: Bell, *Lord Cockburn: Selected Letters*, p. 186 at p. 188.
66. Auchterarder Report vol. 1, p. 57.
67. Ibid., p. 135.
68. Ibid., p. 94.
69. The rhetorical closing passage in the speech of the Dean of Faculty in the third *Auchterarder* case, some of which is quoted at p. 4 above, is an astonishing example of the same phenomenon: *Speech of the Dean of Faculty, in the Court of Session*, pp. 12–13; *The Scotsman*, 28 January 1843, p. 4.
70. The Lord Justice Clerk's daughter, Elizabeth, was married to the Lord President's third son, the Dean's younger brother, James Hope WS: Sir James Balfour Paul (ed.), *The Scots Peerage* vol. IV (David Douglas, Edinburgh, 1907), p. 212.
71. Evidence, 21 April 1834, Question 2941.
72. The Lord President seems to have entered the General Assembly for the first time as a commissioner from the presbytery of Annan in 1795, the year before his colleague, the Lord Justice Clerk, began his General Assembly career: *The Acts of the General Assembly of the Church of Scotland, Begun at Edinburgh, the 21st Day of May 1795, and concluded the 26th Day of the said Month and Year*, p. 14.
73. *Report of the debate in the General Assembly of the Church of Scotland on the overtures anent the Union of Offices, May, 1826* (John Lindsay & Co., Edinburgh, 1826), p. 42. See, for instance, Moncreiff, pp. 32–42. Both the Lord Justice Clerk and Lord Meadowbank voted on the same side as the Lord President in the ensuing vote. The Lord President was alluding to this occasion when he said, in his judgment in the first *Auchterarder* case, that some years previously he had had occasion to consider, with great care and attention, the powers of the Church in its relation to the State: Auchterarder Report vol. 2, p. 2.
74. *Report of the debate in the General Assembly of the Church of Scotland on the overtures anent the Union of Offices, May, 1826*, p. 49.
75. Ibid., p. 117.
76. Conveniently reproduced in Smith, *The Memoirs of James Begg, D.D.*, vol. 1, pp. 232–5, at p. 233.
77. Ibid., pp. 235–43. The section dealing with the Lord Justice Clerk is at p. 237.
78. Ibid., p. 244, quoting a newspaper.
79. He was famous, or notorious, for a speech denouncing the idea of Home Mission, on the ground that it might be dangerous to the peace of the realm, in his first General Assembly in 1796: ibid., vol. 1, p. 232 n. 1. David Boyle was a commissioner from the presbytery of Irvine: *The Acts of the General Assembly of the Church of Scotland, Convened at Edinburgh, the 19th Day of May 1796* (Edinburgh, 1796), p. 15.
80. S. MacGregor, *Report of the Debate in the General Assembly of the Church of Scotland on the Overtures anent Calls, May 23, 1833* (John Hamilton, Edinburgh; W. R. M'Phun, Glasgow; Lewis Smith, Aberdeen; Simpkin & Marshall, London, 1833), p. 140.
81. Ibid., p. 143.
82. Cunningham, vol. 2, pp. 458–60; J. Hope, *A Letter to the Lord Chancellor*, p. 55. When things went wrong, Lord Justice Clerk Boyle could not help pointing out that he had told the Evangelical party so: *Clark v Stirling*, Lethendy Report, p. 72.
83. In both the first *Auchterarder* case and the *Stewarton* case, Lord Moncreiff had to endure having Sir Henry's views cast up to him by the majority judges. See, for

example, Auchterarder Report vol. 2, pp. 3–4, per Lord President Hope; p. 52, per Lord Gillies; p. 74, per Lord Justice Clerk Boyle; pp. 278–81, per Lord Moncreiff, and p. 407, per Lord Cockburn; Stewarton Report, p. 47, per Lord Medwyn; p. 59, per Lord Justice Clerk Hope; and p. 149, per Lord President Boyle; pp. 121–2, per Lord Moncreiff, and p. 133, per Lord Cockburn.

84. See pp. 67–8 above.
85. See p. 9 above.
86. See pp. 8–9 and 11 above.
87. See p. 9 above.
88. The day before the debate in the General Assembly in 1834, Cockburn wrote to Jeffrey that 'We are confident of carrying the veto tomorrow …': Bell, *Selected Letters*, p. 134, at p. 135.
89. Moncreiff, pp. 243–4. See also p. 9 above.
90. Auchterarder Report vol. 2, p. 51.
91. Ibid., p. 79, recording that he had retired from the Assembly before it took up the patronage issue, but had spoken in opposition to the Veto Act in the Edinburgh Presbytery.
92. *Report of the Proceedings of the General Assembly of the Church of Scotland 1837* (The Church Review and Scottish Ecclesiastical Magazine, June 1837) *passim*.
93. P. Forbes, *Considerations on the Constitution of the Church of Scotland* (William Blackwood & Sons, Edinburgh, 1841), p. 28.
94. Minutes of Evidence taken before the Select Committee on Church Patronage, Scotland, 26 March 1834, Lord Moncreiff's second preliminary observation; also 27 March 1834, Question 1343. See further Auchterarder Report vol. 2, pp. 275–6.
95. Lord Cuninghame referred to the situation in which he was called on to determine the validity of the Veto Act which his learned brother, Lord Moncreiff, had warmly supported in the General Assembly: Auchterarder Report vol. 2 pp. 437–8.
96. Interestingly enough, a critic of Lord Moncreiff's advocacy of the Veto Act foresaw, not that he would feel bound to defend it if it were challenged in court, but that he would be driven to disown the position he had adopted in the Assembly: Mentor [Alexander Fleming DD of Neilston], *A Letter to the Honourable Lord Moncreiff respecting two Acts of the General Assembly of 1834* … (W. Hunter, Edinburgh, 1835), p. 2. In that, at least, the author was very much mistaken.
97. For a characteristically clear account of the law in this period, see J. M'Glashan, *Practical Notes on the Jurisdiction and Forms of Process in Civil Causes of the Sheriff Courts of Scotland* (2nd edition, Thomas Clark, Edinburgh, 1842), paras 290–8.
98. A. Stewart, 'The Session Papers in the Advocates Library', in H. Macqueen (ed.), *Miscellany IV* (Stair Society, Edinburgh, 2002), p. 199, at p. 220, citing a case from 1780 in which Lord Covington admitted that he knew the defender well 'but in this case he must give an oppinion [sic] against him.'
99. For a full discussion of Lord Cockburn's attitude to the Church, see I. F. Maciver, 'Cockburn and the Church', in A. Bell (ed.), *Lord Cockburn: a Bicentenary Commemoration, 1779–1979* (Scottish Academic Press, Edinburgh, 1979), pp. 68–103.
100. Cockburn Journal vol. 2, pp. 40–1, entry for 8 June 1843.
101. For the attitude as late as 1904, however, see p. 100 below.
102. *R. v Bow Street Metropolitan Stipendiary Magistrate, Ex pte Pinochet Ugarte (No 2)* [2000] 1 A.C. 119.
103. [2004] UKHL 34; 2005 1 S.C. (H.L.) 7. For an analysis of the approach in

the modern cases, see S. Styles, 'Judicial Opinions and Judicial Impartiality' 2007 Juridical Review 293–314.

104. *R (Al–Hasan)* v *Secretary of State for the Home Department* [2005] UKHL 13; [2005] 1 W.L.R. 688.

105. I did not sit in *Kearney* v *H. M. Advocate* [2005] UKPC D1; 2006 S.C. (P.C.) 1 because I had actually been responsible for the appointment of Mr Macdonald QC as a temporary judge. In his judgment, however, Lord Hope of Craighead made extensive reference to his own part in setting up the very system which was under challenge: 2006 S.C. (P.C.) 1 at pp. 11–13, paras 30–5.

106. Stewart, 'The Session Papers in the Advocates Library', in *Miscellany IV*, pp. 199–200, with references.

107. The *Auchterarder, Lethendy, Culsamond* and *Stewarton* cases. The Stewarton Report was published on 25 February 1843, just a little over a month after the decision: *The Scotsman*, 25 February 1843, p. 1.

108. On judges' language, see, generally, Lord Rodger of Earlsferry, 'The Form and Language of Judicial Opinions' (2002) 118 Law Quarterly Review 226–47 and the literature cited there. The reference, at p. 232, to Lord Lyndhurst LC, should, of course, be to Lord Cottenham LC.

109. Auchterarder Report vol. 2, p. 10 (emphasis in the original).

110. The passage is singled out, for instance, in N. L. Walker, *Chapters from the History of the Free Church of Scotland* (Oliphant Anderson & Ferrier, Edinburgh and London, 1895), pp. 12–13. In *Cruickshank* v *Gordon* (1843) 5 D. 909, at p. 1000, Lord President Boyle envisaged a hypothetical case in which the Court would suspend and reduce a decree of the General Assembly deposing Lord President Hope from his office as an elder 'on the mere ground that his opinions, formerly delivered from this chair in certain causes, amounted to a denial of the sacred Headship of the Church, and a violation of its constitution ...'.

111. See pp. 59–60 above and p. 110 below.

112. In the debate on spiritual independence on 23 May 1838, *The Scotsman*, 26 May 1838, p. 2.

113. Buchanan vol. 1, p. 460.

114. *Cruickshank* v *Gordon* (1843) 5 D. 909, at p. 917. Particular exception was taken to Lord Cuninghame's implied comparison of the Church to an incorporation of tailors. See the remark in the submissions of Andrew Rutherfurd in the hearing in presence on 24 January 1843: *The Scotsman*, 25 January 1843, p. 3; *Caledonian Mercury*, 26 January 1843, p. 2. Lord Cuninghame (Cockburn's successor as Solicitor General) stands out among the Whig judges as a determined supporter of the majority position on the court. Not surprisingly, therefore, perhaps, Lord Jeffrey referred to 'the crude prejudices of Cuninghame': Letter to Lord Cockburn, 5 February 1842, Adv. Ms. 9.1.11, f. 1045.

115. *Caledonian Mercury*, 26 January 1843, p. 2.

116. *Earl of Kinnoull* v *Ferguson*, 6 December 1842, *The Times*, 20 December 1842, p. 3 (Outer House); (1843) 5 D. 1010 (First Division). On the Outer House decision of Lord Cuninghame, see Charteris, *Life of the Rev. James Robertson*, pp. 162–4; on the decision of the First Division, see Mr Robertson's letter to his wife dated 14 March 1843, reproduced ibid., p. 164.

117. Opinions of the Consulted Judges in *Earl of Kinnoull* v *Ferguson*, 7 March 1843, Session Papers vol. 388, No. 172, Advocates Library.

118. The Lord Justice Clerk distinguished between the third *Auchterarder* case and the *Strathbogie* litigation. He had already recused himself in a satellite action in the *Strathbogie* litigation in June 1842: *Dewar v Cruickshank* (1842) 4 D. 1446, at p. 1451. Similarly, he did not attend the hearing in presence in January 1843 because it was to cover not only the third *Auchterarder* case but the *Strathbogie* case too: *The Scotsman*, 25 January 1843, p. 3. The Lord President simply announced that the Lord Justice Clerk 'had some time ago, from reasons which it was now needless to detail, signified his wish to be relieved from judging in the Strathbogie case': *Caledonian Mercury*, 26 January 1843, p. 2. Possibly, the reasons related to the problems surrounding his attempt to reach a compromise with Dr Candlish, which had foundered on the opposition of the Strathbogie ministers. See p. 64 n. 49 above. So far as the third *Auchterarder* case was concerned, his absence from the oral argument turned out not to matter, since Andrew Rutherfurd chose not to add anything to the written statement of the defenders' position.

119. *King v King* (1841) 4 D. 124, at p. 127*. Lord Meadowbank was Lord President Blair's son-in-law.

120. Opinions of the Consulted Judges in *Earl of Kinnoull v Ferguson* 7 March 1843. See also p. 29 n. 229 above.

121. *Presbytery of Auchterarder v Earl of Kinnoull* (1839) Macl. & Rob. 220, at pp. 284 and 350–1; 6 Cl. & F. 646, at pp. 690–1 and 755–6.

122. *The Times*, 10 May 1839, p. 6.

123. Macl. & Rob. 220, at p. 304; 6 Cl. & F. 646, at p. 710.

124. The analogy of the call with the presentation of the sovereign to the people at the coronation appears to have been suggested by the Attorney General in argument for the pursuers: Macl. & Rob. 220, at p. 304; 6 Cl. & F. 646, at p. 710.

125. Watt, pp. 174–5.

126. *Middleton v Anderson* (1842) 4 D. 957, at p. 985.

127. As narrated by his opponent, the Dean of Faculty: *Speech of the Dean of Faculty, in the Court of Session*, p. 6. *The Scotsman*, 25 January 1843, p. 3, records Rutherfurd as referring to 'the Lord Chancellor, in his well considered opinion'; the *Caledonian Mercury*, 26 January 1843, p. 2, has 'his very powerful and well considered argument.'

128. Watt, p. 175. Lord Mackay – admittedly, not perhaps an ideal critic of judicial style – spoke of the Lord Chancellor's 'great speech': *Ballantyne v Presbytery of Wigtown* 1936 S.C. 625, at pp. 683 and 688.

129. Auchterarder Report vol. 1, pp. 124–5; also pp. 101–2.

130. Ibid., p. 390.

131. Ibid., p. 391.

132. Ibid., p. 408.

133. *Presbytery of Auchterarder v Earl of Kinnoull* (1839) Macl. & Rob. 220, at pp. 313–15; 6 Cl. & F. 646, at pp. 719–20. See also Macl. & Rob. 220, at pp. 250–1; 6 Cl. & F. 646, at pp. 656–8.

134. *The Times*, 10 May 1839, p. 4.

135. *Tehrani v Secretary of State for the Home Department* [2006] UKHL 47; 2007 S.C. (H.L.) 1, at p. 16, para. 54; [2007] 1 A.C. 521, at p. 539, para. 54, per Lord Hope of Craighead; 2007 S.C. (H.L.) 1, at p. 31, para. 106; [2007] 1 A.C. 521, at pp. 555–6, para. 106, per Lord Rodger of Earlsferry. See also the remarks of the Lord Ordinary (Cuninghame) in the third *Auchterarder* case quoted above at p. 82 n. 30.

136. Lord President Hope had made precisely this point in urging the General Assembly

not to court conflict with the civil law in the debate on the union of offices in 1826: 'When [such questions] come before us, we have no choice, we cannot refuse to entertain them ...': *Report of the debate in the General Assembly of the Church of Scotland on the overtures anent the Union of Offices, May, 1826*, p. 42.

137. Macl. & Rob. 220, at p. 251; 6 Cl. & F. 646, at pp. 657–8. See also, for instance, the remarks to the same effect of Lord Corehouse: Auchterarder Report vol. 2, pp. 217–18.

138. F. M. Cornford, *Microcosmographia Academica* (Bowes & Bowes, Cambridge, 1908), Chapter VII.

139. Auchterarder Report vol. 2 p. 417.

140. *A Return to show the Number of Causes, with the Date of the Commencement of each, which are at present pending in the Court of Session, respecting the Exercise of Patronage in the Church of Scotland ...*, House of Commons, 7 June 1842.

141. See p. 57 above.

142. These actions were not, of course, any part of the campaign being waged by the Moderate leaders: the pursuers were simply jumping on the bandwagon.

143. See the general comments of Turner, pp. 201–11.

144. Evangelical ministers were also despatched to parishes throughout the country to counteract the accounts in the press. See Beith, *Memories of Disruption Times*, pp. 35–40.

145. Bryce vol. 1, p. 138; Macfarlane, pp. 98–9.

146. *Presbytery of Strathbogie* (1839) 2 D. 258.

147. Buchanan vol. 2, p. 132; Guthrie vol. 2, pp. 16–21. Bryce paints a rather different picture of the reception of the Evangelical ministers in the 'Dead Sea': Bryce vol. 1, pp. 131–3 and 137–8. See also Macfarlane, pp. 99–102. Even Dr Begg, who describes great enthusiasm in the area for his preaching, admits that he met stout resistance at Turriff and Ellon (the home patch of the Rev. James Robertson): Smith, *The Memoirs of James Begg D.D.*, vol. 1, pp. 361–5, especially at pp. 361–3. For an apparently quieter sojourn in the area in the summer of 1840, see Fleming, *Autobiography of the Rev. William Arnot*, pp. 143–7, letter of 27 August 1840 from the Rev. William Arnot to the Rev. John Mackail.

148. *Cruickshank* (1840) 2 D. 1047.

149. *Cruickshank* (1840) 2 D. 1380.

150. So Bryce vol. 1, pp. 133–7.

151. See, for example, Charteris, *Life of the Rev. James Robertson*, pp. 153–60.

152. Buchanan vol. 2, pp. 134–6; Guthrie vol. 2, pp 16–17.

153. Brown, *Annals of the Disruption*, pp. 34–42; Guthrie vol. 2, pp. 17–19; Smith, *The Memoirs of James Begg D.D.*, vol. 1, pp. 330 and 369–70;

154. Bayne, pp. 176–7 (not ironic).

155. Letter to Mrs Guthrie, 20 February 1840, reproduced in Guthrie vol. 2, pp. 18–21, at p. 21.

156. XX, 'The Scotch Church Question: Letter II'. *The Times*, 22 May 1843, p. 7.

157. Apparently prompted by remarks of Dr Chalmers in the Spring meeting of the Commission of Assembly in 1840: Rainy, Mackenzie, *Life of William Cunningham*, pp. 145–8. The cartoon was a lithograph from a drawing by Benjamin William Crombie (1803–47).

158. Cunningham vol. 2, p. 508 n. 2.

159. So, in more colourful language, Chalmers, *What ought*, pp. 11–12.

160. A v *Secretary of State for the Home Department* [2004] UKHL 56; [2005] 2 A.C. 68.
161. A v *Secretary of State for the Home Department (No 2)* [2005] UKHL 71; [2006] 2 A.C. 221.
162. For example, Lord Fullerton in *Clark* v *Stirling* (1841) 3 D. 722, at p. 739. In the *Lethendy* case Lord Cockburn, basing himself on the decision of the House of Lords in the first *Auchterarder* appeal, considered that the Court of Session was warranted in interfering: Lethendy Report, pp. 79–84. In the *Stewarton* case, he said he had come to doubt that view and that, in any event, he was certain that he had expressed himself far too strongly: Stewarton Report, p. 134.
163. For some, the mere fact that Lord Medwyn was an Episcopalian was sufficient to invalidate his judgments. In doing a headcount of the judges in the first *Auchterarder* case, Bayne, p. 104, remarks: 'If we believe, as we certainly may, that an Episcopalian was more or less disqualified to decide upon a thoroughly Presbyterian question. ...'
164. He and Lord Cockburn were fast friends. Moreover, their wives were sisters and 'Uncle Cockburn' was a popular figure in the Fullerton household: Lord Strathclyde, *Lord Fullerton* (W. Hodge & Co. Edinburgh and Glasgow, 1921), p. 18. For some further biographical information on Lord Fullerton see 'Events of the Quarter' (1854) 20 Law Magazine and Quarterly Review of Jurisprudence (n.s.) pp. 176–8.
165. For an assessment of his excellence as a judge, see A. Ure (later Lord President Strathclyde), 'Lord Fullerton: Lawyer and Judge' (1901) 13 Juridical Review 379–98.

LECTURE 3

The Long Shadow of the Disruption

In 1994 the Church of Scotland Board of National Mission appointed the Rev. Helen Percy to the position of associate minister in a parish with such an impossibly long name that the editor of Session Cases wisely just describes it as being 'in Angus'.[1] The Board can little have thought that, by appointing her, they were starting a process that was eventually to take the Church of Scotland on its first foray into the House of Lords since 1842. Given the result, several more generations may rise and fall before the Church ventures there again. What matters for present purposes is not so much that the Church lost but why it lost. It advanced an argument that the civil courts, including the House of Lords, had no jurisdiction to entertain the case – and it lost that argument.

The basic facts are straightforward. Ms Percy was unmarried. In 1997, during her tenure of the office of associate minister, an allegation of improper sexual conduct was made against her. Although her first reaction was to resign her post, she subsequently took legal advice and decided to withdraw her resignation. The Board of National Mission agreed to reinstate her, but suspended her on full pay pending an investigation by the presbytery of Angus into the complaint against her. Some months later, after a process of mediation, the presbytery accepted her offer to demit her status as a minister. Then, in February 1998, Ms Percy applied to an employment tribunal, complaining of unfair dismissal and of sex discrimination, contrary to section 6 of the Sex Discrimination Act 1975. In particular, she complained that 'similar action' had not been taken against male ministers who had had extra-marital sexual relationships. She had therefore been treated differently on the ground of her gender, and that amounted to sex discrimination under section 6. She did not specify what she meant by 'similar action' but appears to have been referring to the initiation of a trial by libel by the presbytery and her suspension on full pay by the Board.[2]

In her application to the employment tribunal Ms Percy named the

Church of Scotland as the respondent, but the notice of appearance was entered in the name of the Church of Scotland Board of National Mission. In that notice the Board submitted that, by virtue of the Church of Scotland Act 1921, the matters raised by the appellant fell outside the jurisdiction of the employment tribunal, as a civil court, and that her application was accordingly incompetent. They also denied that Ms Percy was an employee.

When the case on sex discrimination reached the First Division of the Court of Session, the Procurator of the Church persuaded us that Ms Percy was not properly to be regarded as an employee under a contract of employment, in line with a presumption that there was no intention to create contractual relations in the case of ministers and priests.[3] So she had not been working under 'a contract' and the Sex Discrimination Act did not apply.[4] I confess that I was glad to decide the case on that basis and to be relieved of the need to deal with the Church's first argument, that the matter did not fall within the jurisdiction of the civil courts.

Although Ms Percy was no longer a minister, after the decision of the First Division, the General Assembly appointed a legally qualified Special Commission, chaired by a sheriff, to hear her complaint of sex discrimination. It had power to award her compensation if the complaint was established. Eventually, however, the commission dismissed the complaint for want of prosecution.[5]

Ms Percy then reverted to her civil proceedings and appealed the decision of the First Division to the House of Lords. By a majority, their Lordships reversed the First Division.[6] Lord Hoffmann dissenting, they first held that the parties had indeed entered into a contract under which Ms Percy was to provide services to the Church and that this was a contract 'personally to execute any work or labours' for the purposes of section 82(1) of the Sex Discrimination Act.[7] This meant that the House needed to address the argument that Ms Percy's complaint fell within the category of 'matters spiritual', which were excluded from the jurisdiction of the civil courts by the Church of Scotland Act 1921. It is fair to say that, against the background of the European directive,[8] their Lordships appeared to have little difficulty in rejecting that submission and in affirming the jurisdiction of the employment tribunal. In fact, the case was settled and so it did not return to the tribunal: without admitting liability, the Church paid Ms Percy £10,000 as compensation and a further £10,000 by way of legal expenses repayable to the Scottish Legal Aid Board.[9]

The week after the decision of the House of Lords, I asked Lord Hope, if, that weekend, hordes of rioters had been despatched by Church HQ at 121 George Street in Edinburgh to break his windows. He assured me that his windows were intact and that all had been quiet. He had been door-stepped by reporters and photographers outside his house? Again, no sign of them. Indeed, the case, including the decision of the House, attracted only comparatively little attention in the media – and then only because of the element of sex.

The decision of the House of Lords appears to have prompted no comment at all in the ordinary British legal journals and there seem to be only two discussions of the jurisdiction point.[10] Yet, in former times, the decision would have been regarded as being of major constitutional importance, dealing, as it does, with the relationship between the civil courts of the State and the courts of the Church of Scotland which are recognised by the State.

To put the point another way, if Lord Moncreiff or any of the other early Victorian judges had been alive today, they would immediately have spotted that the *Percy* case raised that self-same vexed question of the spiritual independence of the Church of Scotland which first divided the Court of Session and then split the Church and Scottish society at the Disruption in 1843. Interestingly enough, the words 'spiritual independence' do not feature in any of the speeches in the *Percy* case. Moreover, although the Procurator referred to the Disruption in her argument for the Church, there is no mention of that event or of any of the cases which preceded it. The whole issue is treated – and, in a very real sense, rightly treated – as turning on the terms of the Church of Scotland Act 1921.

The contrast between the close attention which people throughout Scotland paid to every twist and turn of the Disruption cases and the almost complete lack of interest shown in the *Percy* case is striking. It tells us quite a lot about our society today. Very obviously, it reflects the decline in interest in organised religion and, more particularly – or, perhaps, in consequence – the decline in interest in questions of ecclesiastical governance. In an age of indifference and of ecumenical co-operation in a multicultural country with a significant Muslim population, debates over the spiritual independence of the Church of Scotland may seem irrelevant – or, at the very least, much too arcane for a sound-bite generation. On a wider view, the only civil cases in the Scottish courts to attract any real attention from the media in recent years have related to prisoners – slopping-out and votes come to mind – or Tommy Sheridan's reputation. Prisoners always make good copy and any opportunity to talk or write about sex is too tempting to miss. Even so, in both cases the reporting was superficial. By contrast, in the nineteenth century full reports of the judgments in four of the Disruption cases were published and there were 782 'distinct pamphlets on this one subject printed during these years, circulated by thousands, and falling like snowflakes all over the land.'[11] Clearly, at that time, a significant number of people throughout Scotland – a lot of them, presumably, ministers[12] – were prepared to devote both time and money to following the serious and complex issues in detail. Nevertheless, even then, speaking in London after the Disruption, Dr Cunningham complained that 'the newspaper press in general gave to the world no more of the subject than what might be called the gossip and the scandal of it.'[13]

Given the almost complete lack of interest in the *Percy* case, it may seem perverse in the extreme to spend time on it. But I happen to believe that the case does matter. For one thing, questions about the place of religion in our public life are far from unimportant. More particularly, *Percy* marks a significant development in an area of the law which many people hoped had been settled once for all when Parliament passed the Church of Scotland Act 1921. That Act was intended to put an end to a kind of religious dispute that had been the very stuff of Scottish history. Indeed, at the time of the Disruption cases, the point was often made that, by contrast with England where the key historical struggles seemed to have been for political liberty, in Scotland the key struggles had been, not even for religious liberty in a broad sense, but for the liberty to have a presbyterian form of church government. One such comment is found in Henry Moncreiff's *Letter to Lord Melbourne*:

> It has been well remarked, that while the English were laying the foundations of a free civil constitution, the attention of the Scotch was engrossed by their earnest struggles for the maintenance and preservation of their ecclesiastical liberties.[14]

There is considerable force in the point. In part at least, it helps to explain the relatively slight role which the law is regarded as playing in the wider history of Scotland.

One of the things for which the Romans are most famous is their law. Even today, some of us believe that the Roman jurists have never been equalled, far less surpassed, in their skill in handling complex legal questions. But we find very little sign that their non-lawyer contemporaries regarded the jurists' achievement as remarkable or looked with pride or affection on the law as one of the glories of Rome. For the most part, Roman lawyers were '*ungeliebt*' – 'unloved', as a German scholar recently described them.[15]

Arguably, English law enjoys an altogether different place in the life and history of England. Of course, modern English lawyers are pretty *ungeliebt* too, the law's delays are infamous and the courts of Chancery have never shaken off the caricature in *Bleak House*. But even that caricature is now softened by association with the fogs and larger-than-life characters which Dickens has made our idea of nineteenth-century London. Go back to Chaucer's *Canterbury Tales* in the fourteenth century and you find quite an affectionate portrayal of the Serjeant at Law, already freighted with his books of cases from the time of William the Conqueror onwards.[16] Five hundred years after Chaucer, Tennyson described England as a country

> Where Freedom slowly broadens down
> From precedent to precedent.[17]

The ordinary reader is assumed to know what precedents are and to appreciate how freedom might be thought to broaden down from one precedent to another. In our times Lord Denning saw the law as bound up with the history, and indeed with the literature and poetry, of England. As he recounted it at least, the history of the common law was synonymous with the history of liberty in England and in English-speaking lands beyond the seas.[18] This belief shaped not only his judgments but his public persona and helped to make his views and his picture of the law familiar to many members of the public.

The attitude of Scottish people to their law seems to me to be closer to the Roman than to the English attitude. In Scotland too, of course, the public have no love for lawyers. Thanks in part to Stevenson's caricature in *Weir of Hermiston*, Lord Braxfield is remembered for his harsh conduct of the Court of Justiciary, rather than for his mastery of our feudal land law – a system which did, actually, help to shape the towns and cities of Scotland. That feudal law, which has a strong claim to being the real intellectual achievement of the Scottish judges, was unceremoniously binned by the Scottish Parliament – unmourned even by its supposed acolytes, the Professors of Conveyancing. If pride in our inheritance from Roman law even exists, it can only be among a relatively few lawyers, and certainly not among the population as a whole. No Lord Denning has woven Scots law into the history or literature and poetry of Scotland, and we tend to take our landmark constitutional cases from English law, quite properly integrating them into our history as part of Britain and the Empire.

Against that background, with the decline in interest in the religious struggles which were so much a feature of Scottish life in the past, it is not surprising that the Scots law relating to those religious matters is not generally seen as having played a part in shaping life in Scotland today. So the Disruption cases have faded from the public memory. But, even after the First World War, the effect of those decisions was still powerful enough for Parliament to intervene to deal with it by passing the Church of

Scotland Act 1921, the Act with which the House had to grapple in the *Percy* case.[19] A sketch of some of the events in the eighty years between the Disruption and the 1921 Act may help to put it in context.

When Dr Chalmers delivered his opening address to the first General Assembly of the new Free Church in May 1843, he declared:

> In a word, we hold that every part and every function of a commonwealth should be leavened with Christianity, and that every functionary from the highest to the lowest, should, in their respective spheres, do all that in them lies to countenance and uphold it. That is to say, though we quit the Establishment, we go out on the Establishment principle – we quit a vitiated Establishment, but would rejoice in returning to a pure one. To express it otherwise, we are the advocates for a national recognition and national support of religion – and we are not Voluntaries.[20]

The Scotsman described the address as a 'strange farrago' and exclaimed, in particular, at the difference between Dr Chalmers' acts and these words.[21] In one sense, his abandonment of the Established Church was indeed astonishing. He had always been passionate in his belief that the only way to achieve religious and social progress in Scotland was through a national church, endowed by the State, with its ministers serving all the needs of the people in its parishes throughout the length and breadth of the land.[22] This declaration was presumably Dr Chalmers' way of reconciling his former with his present, very different, position.[23]

Certainly, his audience would have been in sympathy with this characterisation of their position on establishment. While inside the Establishment, they had for years been fighting off the incursions of the Voluntary churches. Now to be classed with those Voluntaries as 'dissenters' would have been the last thing that this, socially very respectable, audience would have wanted.[24] 'Many of the dowagers of both sexes would have gone into hysterics had it been proposed to them off-hand to become Dissenters, and still more shocking, Voluntary Dissenters.'[25] The Free Church 'did not for a moment think of itself as a body of Seceders or Dissenters.'[26] A week after the Disruption, *The Scotsman* commented on how 'a taint of vulgarity', as it put it, attached to every class of dissenter except Episcopalians,[27] and observed how peculiarly gratifying all those present at the Free Church Assembly had found the announcement that the Marquis of Breadalbane had adhered to the new church.[28] Far better, then, from every point of view, for those in the new church to see themselves as the true heirs of the Established Church.[29] But, if Dr Chalmers' words would have been welcome to his audience, because the Free Church circulated his address in an appeal for funds, they were also to have enormous repercussions long after his death in 1847, at a time when the idea of establishment had lost its grip on most members of the Free Church.

Thanks to the organisational skills of Dr Chalmers, the new Free Church found itself in amazingly good financial heart.[30] Critics might scoff at the unrelenting drive for 'voluntary' contributions to its funds,[31] but the results were there for all to see. Churches were built, ministers paid, schools erected, mission stations manned and, before the decade was out, a new settlement had been planted on the South Island of New Zealand at what was to become Dunedin.[32] Gold was discovered in the area and the settlement prospered so that, by the 1870s, a university had been established, with handsome stone buildings, very much in the Scottish style. The link with the Free Church is commemorated in the name of the nearby Port Chalmers.

To begin with, many Free Church leaders seem to have believed that the existing Church of Scotland would collapse and that the Free Church would indeed become the Established Church on its terms, as Dr Chalmers had hoped might happen.[33] But the Church of Scotland survived the initial shock of the Disruption, then went on a vigorous recruiting drive for new ministers to man the vacant parishes[34] and, slowly but surely, over the next twenty years it revived. The hostility which had marked relations between the Evangelicals and the Moderates in the pre-Disruption Church of Scotland replicated itself in the relations between the Free Church and the Established Church.[35] In the early years at least, the hostility was often even more pronounced.

Even though the Established Church recovered, its position in the life of Scotland had been weakened. Society was becoming more secular.[36] In 1845, the Poor Relief (Scotland) Amendment Act transferred responsibility for the relief of poverty from the Church to the State. This was the very antithesis of the kind of system favoured by Dr Chalmers. Even more significantly perhaps, after many attempts at reform, in 1872 the Episcopalian Lord Advocate, George Young, managed to get Parliament to pass the Education (Scotland) Act. Previously, through its presbyteries, the Church had been responsible for schools and schoolmasters,[37] but there was general agreement that the system had become unsatisfactory. The 1872 Act transferred that responsibility to local Boards, with provision being made for religious instruction to be given to children whose parents did not object. In these ways, the practical significance of the establishment of the Church in the everyday life of Scotland was reduced.

As the years went by,[38] it dawned on many in the Free Church that they were never going to be the Established Church. Nor would any government ever again endow the Established Church. A new model for the relations between the Church and the State would have to be developed to meet the needs of a liberal, pluralist society.[39] In any event, as the history of the Free Church seemed to proclaim, a church could have a national reach without being supported by the State. This suggested to them that, after all, establishment was no part of God's plan for the Church. So, on the one hand, the Free Church should campaign against the vitiated establishment of the Church of Scotland,[40] and, on the other, it should try to unite with churches, such as the United Presbyterian Church, which were similar in doctrine, save that they had always rejected the idea of establishment. This became the dominant view in the Free Church under its powerful leader, Principal Robert Rainy.

Not all were convinced. A minority, known as the 'constitutionalists' and led for many years by Dr James Begg, clung tenaciously to the view that, as Dr Chalmers had declared in that first General Assembly, the establishment of the Church by the State was one of the central tenets of the Free Church.[41] They saw the majority's abandonment of the establishment principle as just one of a number of departures from the purity of the belief and practice of the Free Church at the time of the Disruption.[42] Indeed, some felt so strongly about one particular departure from the standards of the Church in the Declaratory Act of 1892 that, the following year, in what was sometimes called 'the Second Disruption', they left the Free Church to set up the Free Presbyterian Church.[43]

Eventually, however, Principal Rainy carried the day[44] and, on 31 October 1900, the Free Church united with the United Presbyterian Church to form the United Free Church. Despite the impressive processions on the day, the great congregation of about 10,000 in the Waverley Market, and the stream of congratulations,[45] never in actual fact can any church have had a less auspicious beginning. Within three weeks, the tiny constitutionalist minority in the Free Church still opposed to the union – some 24 ministers out of 1100 – announced that legal proceedings would be taken.[46] On 14 December they began their Court of Session action against the United Free Church to claim the church property.[47] In reality, the opposing positions were held so firmly as to admit of no compromise.[48] If the pursuers' funds held out, a long contest lay in prospect.[49]

The pursuers claimed that those who had gone into the United Free Church had departed from the original doctrines of the Free Church not only on the principle of establishment[50] but also – when the case reached the House of Lords[51] – on predestination and the Atonement.[52] By doing so, they had forfeited their right to all the vast property built up by the Free Church and held on trust for a church which adhered to its original central and unchangeable beliefs. So all the church buildings, the Assembly Hall, the colleges and the mission stations, plus all the Church's investments, were still on trust, they said, not for the new United Free Church, but for the old Free Church and its few remaining ministers and members.

On the other side, the United Free Church argued that it was entitled to all the property. Despite Dr Chalmers' declaration in his opening address to the first General Assembly,[53] establishment had never been a defining tenet of the Free Church. The Free Church had accordingly been entitled to unite with a church which had always rejected establishment. There had, the United Frees said in the House of Lords, been no change in doctrine on predestination and the Atonement.[54]

Since much of the dispute thus turned on the position of the Free Church when it came into existence at the Disruption, counsel for both parties referred to the Disruption cases and to the Claim of Right in order to try to show on what points of principle the Evangelical party who founded the Free Church had taken their stand.[55]

Counsel for the United Free Church also argued that, even if there had been changes in the position of the Free Church on establishment or on predestination and the Atonement, the Church had been empowered to make them without forfeiting its property.[56] In planning their tactics, members of the United Free team differed as to whether it was preferable to give prominence to the argument that there had been no real change in the Church's position or to their argument that, in any event, the Church had been free to change.[57] In the end, however, the question whether the Free Church enjoyed this freedom to change without losing its property was an important issue in the appeals.[58]

The Lord Ordinary and the Second Division had no hesitation in rejecting the submissions of the Free Church minority.[59] The pursuers had indeed anticipated this, since it was thought that judges in the Court of Session would be very conscious that a decision stripping the new, and potentially powerful, United Free Church of its assets would produce a convulsion, not just for that church, but for much of Scottish society. The judges in Scotland would be reluctant to pronounce a judgment which would have that effect. The judges in the House of Lords, insulated to some extent at least from these considerations, might look at the case more objectively and apply what the Free Church minority saw as the powerful authority in their favour in the decision of Lord Eldon in the *Craigdallie* case.[60] From the outset the pursuers planned their strategy accordingly, selecting Lord Low as Lord Ordinary for his likely care[61] and the Second Division for the reclaiming motion[62] because any decision against the pursuers was likely to be couched in extreme terms which would provide a good stepping-off point for any appeal to the House of Lords.[63]

The House of Lords heard the appeals twice.[64] Lord Shand, who had been one of the judges at the first hearing,[65] died before judgment could be given. There were powerful rumours to the effect that he had prepared a speech in favour of dismissing the appeal[66] and, some years later, Lady Shand confirmed that he had indeed 'written a most careful draft of a possible judgment just before his last illness.'[67] On the other hand, at the first hearing Lord Chancellor Halsbury had appeared to be in favour of the appellants:[68] indeed, reports of his attitude on the very first day of that hearing had greatly alarmed Dr Rainy, back in Edinburgh.[69]

The Lord Chancellor invited Lord President Kinross[70] to sit in the new hearing. On Tuesday, 7 June 1904 he duly caught the night train to London, with a view to taking his place among the Law Lords when the hearing started on the Thursday.[71] But, the previous week, *The Times* had published a letter from the Rev. John Sinclair, the Church of Scotland parish minister of Kinloch Rannoch, pointing out that, in the run-up to the union, the (bland[72]) Procurator of the Free Church, Mr Guthrie QC, had consulted Mr Balfour QC (now Lord Kinross) as to 'whether there would be any risk of the United Church not being able to retain the property of the Free Church.' Mr Balfour had replied that 'there was no risk whatever.'[73] Dean Asher, Mr Haldane and Mr Guthrie, who were privy to Lord Kinross's advice to their side on the very issue in the case, were to remain members of the appellants' legal team in the new hearing.[74] Presumably after discussing the position with the Lord Chancellor on the Wednesday, Lord Kinross came to the view that he should indeed excuse himself, for fear he might be supposed prejudiced 'by former opinions he had entertained' on the subject.[75] So, having attended the Lord Mayor's Banquet for His Majesty's Judges on the Wednesday evening,[76] a doubtless somewhat disappointed Lord President was back on the train to Edinburgh on the Thursday when, in Westminster, the second hearing was getting under way.[77] The only Scottish judge among the seven at that hearing was Lord Robertson.[78]

The fact that Lord Kinross felt compelled to stand down suggests that, by 1904, rather stricter standards on conflicts of interest were being applied than in Disruption times. On the other hand, since he actually set off for the hearing, he cannot have been persuaded initially that he needed to excuse himself. That would not have been an isolated view: *The Scots Law Times* indicated that, 'in legal circles', the suggestion in Mr Sinclair's letter that Lord Kinross should not sit would meet with no support.[79]

The new hearing of the appeal, which took place, of course, in the great empty chamber of the House of Lords, did not attract much public interest.[80] The general audience was never more than about twenty or thirty – but the Archbishop of Canterbury was on the bishops' bench for a good deal of the time.[81] Apart from him, seven elderly gentlemen sat on the benches, paying close attention to the arguments, except when they appeared to fall asleep.[82] About a dozen lawyers were at the bar of the House, 'huddled in a pen', with their back-up teams having to stand nearby. The House sat from ten till four, with only one half-hour break,[83] but occasionally the proceedings were adjourned because of the demands of other public business.[84] By contrast with the hearing of the first *Auchterarder* case in the Court of Session back in 1837, when there were almost no questions or interruptions from the bench, in the House of Lords in 1904 there was a dialogue between counsel and the judges. The questioning was dominated by the Lord Chancellor, Lord Davey and Lord James of Hereford. To United Free Church observers, the Lord Chancellor was 'almost derisively' against them and jeered at their case.[85] Certainly, he and others of the judges harried counsel for the United Frees on various matters, especially on the extent of the freedom they claimed for the Church to alter its doctrines – could the Church, for instance, adopt Roman Catholic doctrines?[86] One eye-witness records that Lord Robertson sat perfectly still throughout the hearing;[87] another referred to his 'vigilant reticence';[88] a third described him sitting 'in grim and smiling silence'.[89] As in the first hearing,[90] Lord Macnaghten and Lord Lindley said hardly a word. In the cloakroom during the hearing, Dr Rainy commented, 'This is very dry and very dreigh.'[91]

Unfortunately, space does not permit a general examination of the arguments of counsel.[92] I confine myself to the speech of Mr Haldane, who was second in the United Free team led by Dean of Faculty Asher ('clever and versatile if not deep'[93]). On 5 May 1899, Haldane had given an emphatic opinion to the effect that there would be no risk of the new church not being entitled to the property of the Free Church – even suggesting that, if anything went wrong in the Court of Session, the House of Lords would put it right.[94] In September of the same year, in a speech in Inverness, Haldane had staked 'his reputation as a lawyer' that 'in the constitution of the Free Church there was from the beginning to the end nothing that pledges that church, or binds that church, with the principle of an establishment.'[95]

Haldane's practice was largely in the Privy Council and the House of Lords. Indeed, given any opportunity or none, he would deliver you a speech on the appellate tribunals of the Empire.[96] He tells us that he knew the judges in the House of Lords and Privy Council so well that he could follow the working of their individual minds.[97] Actually, it is usually more important for the judges to be able to follow the working of counsel's mind – a point which Haldane singularly overlooked in his address in the *Free Church* case. His failure to communicate his arguments on predestination and the Atonement, in particular, makes his speech a textbook study in the art of bad appellate advocacy.

In theory, Haldane must have seemed the ideal person to deal with the matter.[98] He came from a family that was steeped in Scottish theology. When suffering religious doubts at the age of seventeen, he had gone to Göttingen University for a few months to study philosophy and theology. Throughout his life he had lectured and written on metaphysics. Haldane tells us[99] that, in consultation before the *Free Church* case, he had not been impressed by the theologians who had been summoned to support counsel. They did not strike him as being as fully possessed of the subject as their predecessors in the great days of theology in Scotland. His sense of his own superior knowledge of the topic was to prove his undoing before the House of Lords. Success would have depended on explaining theological distinctions between Calvinism and Arminianism which were not just fine, but invisible or incomprehensible to those unfamiliar with the subject. Sometimes the skill of an advocate lies in making something that is actually simple appear complicated. But here Haldane's task was to make what was actually complicated appear simple. A perceptive member of the United Free team spotted a tendency in him to be doctrinaire, and added: 'I hope he won't waste his time on "Arminianism" – ten minutes should polish off that business.'[100] If only. ... Instead, he went into it in great detail and baffled his listeners, except for Lord Halsbury who fancied himself as having some knowledge of the subject and was determined to pursue his own line anyway.[101]

We have a sketch by an admirer of Haldane, Sir Edmund Gosse, who witnessed the scene and naïvely took his polished serenity in the face of the judges' bewilderment as a sure sign of his intellectual superiority. In Sir Edmund's eyes, he was 'making a very fine performance' and 'turning the whole thing into a supplement of his own *Pathway to Reality*.'[102] 'Whether or not it was war,' remarked a member of the United Free team, 'it was philosophically magnificent.'[103] The trouble was, precisely, that it was not war.

Any sensible onlooker[104] would have seen that Haldane was doing his case no good at all when, for example, Lord James of Hereford said 'With the greatest deference, I have not the slightest idea how that last answer of yours answers what I have put to you.'[105] Worse is to come. Next morning,[106] Haldane reads into his argument a tract of material from a Professor Taylor's *Elements of Metaphysics*,[107] followed by a passage from

Ethical Studies by Mr F. H. Bradley of Merton College, Oxford.[108] Then, as the crowning delight for their Lordships, Haldane announces that he has himself translated a few sentences from page 414 of the German edition of *Die Menschliche Freiheit* by Professor Vatke,[109] a Professor of Theology at the University of Berlin, which he would venture to read to them.[110] I shall spare you, as Haldane did not spare their Lordships, such things as 'the speculative conception of nature within the moments of the idea. ...' Having completed his reading, he reassures their Lordships that he does not ask them to follow these things out – in other words, 'it doesn't really matter if you can't understand what I've been reading.' This patronising comment makes quoting the passage a waste of time. Haldane is soon referring to Mr Balfour's book on *Foundations of Belief*.[111] Then he gives Lord Alverstone a child's guide to what is meant by antinomy. The 'jovial old whig',[112] Lord James of Hereford, must have spoken for all the judges when he interrupted Haldane, who had just mentioned 'the first thinkers' in the subject, to say, 'The first thing is to understand you – I hope I have tried my best, but I cannot say I have succeeded very well so far.'[113] Not long after, Lord James gave up: 'I never knew how incapable I was of understanding these things until I heard your argument.'[114] Haldane's clever and clear-sighted sister was watching from the gallery above. It is kinder not to imagine what she must have made of his performance.[115]

The House gave judgment on Bank Holiday Monday, 1 August 1904. Despite the holiday, more people had gathered to hear the judgment than to hear any judgment for many years.[116] Lords Macnaghten and Lindley dissenting,[117] the House allowed the appeal.[118] The delivery of the speeches was interrupted by the formalities for signifying Royal Assent to a number of Acts.[119] All of their Lordships except the Lord Chancellor, who gave his readers some Greek with a Latin translation, ducked the question on predestination and the Atonement[120] and concentrated on the establishment question.[121] There was little law in their decision. In effect, not least because of the address by Dr Chalmers to the first General Assembly, the majority held that, as a matter of fact, adherence to the principle of establishment had been a defining tenet, which the Free Church had not been free to discard without forfeiting its property in terms of the *Craigdallie* decision.[122]

Although it was said that Principal Rainy, who was present below the Bar in the House, had been stunned by the decision, according to one admirer, 'there was no ruffle on his brow, no cloud on that placid face.'[123] We are told that, when the proceedings ended, addressing his close colleague, Carnegie Simpson, his first words were simply, 'Well, Carnegie, what do you think of it?' He was walking about in the lobby with his splendid serenity and as smiling and happy as ever.[124] Haldane came up and they walked out together.[125] Was it, I wonder, in part a consciousness of the failure of both his over-confident initial opinion and his impenetrable speech that made Haldane immediately say to Rainy that he would contribute £1,000 to a fund to support the United Free Church?[126] Certainly, at least one of Rainy's supporters might have thought so. Referring to Haldane, he said that part of the responsibility for the decision against the United Frees 'must be allotted to that able man's singular lack of judgment.'[127]

The Edinburgh correspondent of *The Times* reported[128] that the possibility of a successful outcome to the appeal had been too remote ever to be seriously discussed and that the decision had come home to Scotland with striking suddenness. In Glasgow and the west of Scotland also, it had caused a profound sensation. Hundreds of thousands of people had been rendered churchless and several hundreds of ministers would share their exile,[129] while the four or five thousand people in the Free Church would now find themselves heirs to hundreds of churches and to millions in cash and securities.[130] The decision was widely denounced – for instance, as having 'left for centuries a stain on the annals of the Supreme Court of the realm.'[131]

Once the initial shock was over, it was realised on all sides that something would have to be done. Some breathing space was afforded by the fact that the Inner House of the Court of Session had to apply the judgment of the House of Lords and this could not be done until the court sittings resumed in October.[132] While insisting on occupying the Assembly Hall and New College,[133] the Free Church victors recognised that they could not possibly administer, far less make use of, all the property. In their view, they should keep as much of the property as would be proportionate to their needs and the remainder should fall to the Crown.[134] On the very theory of the judgment of the House of Lords, even if, *per impossibile*, they had been so minded, the victorious Free Church minority could not simply have come to an arrangement to transfer the surplus property to the United Free Church. To do so would have been to commit precisely the same breach of trust as the majority had committed by entering into the United Free Church.

The United Free Church and its sympathisers exerted themselves to bring its plight to the attention of the public, the Government and politicians generally.[135] Eventually, the Government decided to set up a Royal Commission.[136] In April 1905 it reported that a power should be created to allocate the property. The result was the Churches (Scotland) Act 1905, which established a Commission with the necessary power.

Working under the chairmanship of Lord Elgin, the Commission eventually carried out its task in a way that the Free Church minority, somewhat reluctantly, found acceptable.[137]

Although *The Times* correspondent stressed that the decision of the House of Lords could not have been foreseen, that can hardly have been so. The atmosphere of the hearing would have told you a lot, and indeed the London correspondent of the *Scottish Law Review*, writing at the end of June, had heard that the general drift of the proceedings would suggest that the appeal would be allowed.[138] The Free Church supporters had also been encouraged: for them there was little doubt which side had emerged most successfully from the final argument.[139] On the other side, Taylor Innes, too, had thought that the hearing was going in favour of the Free Church[140] and Principal Rainy himself was well aware that the United Frees were losing.[141] On the train back to Edinburgh after the hearing, he already 'foresaw the Church spoiled of her goods, turmoil, chaos, suffering.'[142] After the decision had been announced, he acknowledged that the outcome was 'by no means unexpected.'[143]

On the other hand, portraying the decision as having been unforeseeable in advance of the legal proceedings was essential for the United Free leaders if they were to enlist the sympathy of the public and of politicians. Any idea that Principal Rainy and his supporters had run a known risk and lost would put things in a very different light.[144] Yet, as was quickly pointed out in *The Scotsman*, that was the reality.[145]

In March 1897 Taylor Innes had alerted Rainy to the possible problems over the property of the Free Church in the event of a union.[146] Rainy raised the matter with the Procurator, Mr Guthrie, who informally consulted Mr J. B. Balfour. Balfour indicated that the Church could not abandon its view on establishment without risking its right to its property.[147] Indeed he startled Guthrie and Rainy by saying that there was a chance that the Church would lose all its property, including that held under the Model Trust Deed (which Taylor Innes had thought safe). Despite this, Rainy was determined to go on.[148]

The potential problems can have come as no real surprise to Rainy. He was well aware that the property position in the event of a union had been investigated by both sides in 1873 when a union with the United Presbyterian Church had been under active consideration for some years.[149] The proposal was bitterly opposed by Dr Begg and others, partly on the ground that it would entail an abandonment of the establishment principle. In that connection, in the spring of 1873 he and his supporters prepared an elaborate memorial, on the constitution of the Free Church and its significance for the determination of the rights to the property of the Church, for the opinion of various counsel.[150] The counsel included the Solicitor General, Mr Rutherford Clark (later Lord Rutherford Clark), and Mr J. B. Balfour.[151] Among the answers returned by them was the following: 'We are of opinion that the Church has no power by a majority, however large, to alter its constitution in any essential or fundamental point, which, as we have stated, we consider the Establishment principle to be.'[152] The other opinions were to similar effect.[153]

On the afternoon of 20 May 1873, two days before the Free Church General Assembly opened, leading members of the Church who were in favour of union with the United Presbyterians – including a now frail Dr Candlish and Dr Rainy himself – also consulted the same Mr Rutherford Clark and Mr Balfour, along with the young Taylor Innes. The consultation was short and, at Candlish's insistence, there was no written memorial and only a verbal opinion, 'leaving no documentary trace'.[154] Nevertheless, Clark had 'no doubt that the doctrine of establishment was part of [the Free Church] constitution.'[155] When Dr Begg's memorial and opinions were published in September 1874,[156] Taylor Innes and Rainy discussed whether Clark and Balfour might have been over-influenced by that elaborate memorial.[157] Shortly after the Assembly in 1873, and again the following year, Taylor Innes shrewdly suggested that the Free Church should deliberately introduce changes in order to show that it could, but his advice was not acted upon.[158]

In 1899, with the principle of the proposed union due to be discussed at the General Assembly, Dr Rainy and other leaders of the Free Church were persuaded to obtain formal legal advice on the property question. The counsel were, of course, made aware of the opinions taken a quarter of a century before.[159]

First, after a 'conversational consultation', with Rainy putting the questions, on 14 March Dean of Faculty Asher returned an opinion that was anything but encouraging and warned that 'establishment was an original tenet or principle of the Free Church' and so there were potentially grave risks for the property.[160] Nevertheless, it was decided to go ahead and to recommend union. The Church then turned to Mr Haldane and, in May, shortly before the Free Church General Assembly, he gave his emphatic opinion that all would be well.[161]

Lastly, in August 1899, the Church sought the opinion of Mr Balfour, the future Lord President Kinross and the sole survivor of the counsel who had advised in 1873.[162] Mr Balfour remained of the view that establishment was one of the original tenets of the Church, but 'raised hopefully the important point of that body having the right to modify those tenets'[163] and, presumably on that basis, concluded – contrary to his earlier opinions

– that 'there was no risk whatever'.[164] One can only suppose that he would have said, in the immortal words of Bramwell B during oral argument in *Andrews v Styrap*, 'The matter does not appear to me now as it appears to have appeared to me then.'[165] The explanation – which was indeed put forward at the time – may be that Balfour changed his mind because the facts as set out in the memorial for his opinion were stated more fully, and rather differently from the way they had been presented in 1873.[166] Who knows what Lord Kinross would have held if he had sat on the appeal? That must remain a minor 'What if?' of legal history.

After the judgment, the Free Church did not fail to emphasise this general background. In the memorandum which its Law and Advisory Committee issued on 17 August, they referred to the opinions of counsel and commented that 'parties who, knowing that there is a risk, deliberately accept it, have no claim to sympathy, on the profession that they are taken by surprise when the issue goes against them.'[167]

Another complaint which the United Free Church side made against the decision of the House of Lords was that it represented an attack on the spiritual independence of the Free Church. In other words, the House of Lords was interfering with the right of the Free Church to formulate its beliefs. But, as was also quickly pointed out, this appeal to spiritual independence was scarcely justified. The House of Lords did not say that the Free Church was not free to reformulate its beliefs: all it said was that, if it did, the church could not keep property which was held on trust for a church professing its original beliefs. More fundamentally perhaps, spiritual independence, as it was understood before the Disruption, had nothing to do with property.[168] The Evangelical party had always recognised that, so far as property was concerned, it fell to be regulated by the civil courts.[169] On that approach, the dispute in the *Free Church* case fell squarely within the jurisdiction of the civil courts.[170] Unfurling the banner of spiritual independence could therefore be presented as an attempt on the part of the United Free Church to distract attention from the true, more 'sordid', nature of the dispute.[171]

If nothing else, the decision of the House of Lords sent out the clearest possible warning to any church, whose constitution was not regulated by statute, of the dangers that lurked in any purported change in its central tenets. Unless it could be shown that the church in question had the power to make a change by some appropriate mechanism, the *Free Church* case indicated that its right to its property would be called into question. Not surprisingly, therefore, in 1905 the General Assembly of the United Free Church passed a declaration on the spiritual independence of the Church.[172] The following year this was turned into an Act,[173] which referred to the Free Church appeals and confirmed the power of the new church to make alterations in doctrine.

The problem that had been confronting the Church of Scotland for some time was different. It arose precisely because the Church was regulated in part by statute. For some years, the Church had been discussing the possibility of changing the formula by which ministers and elders subscribed to the Confession of Faith. But the Church had been advised by counsel that the old Scots Act 1693 c. 22 prevented it from making the change.[174] Therefore amending legislation would be necessary. It had seemed unlikely that the Conservative Government would wish to provide the necessary time in its legislative programme for such a measure which would, in any event, have been liable to meet with opposition, especially among Liberal MPs. So, when it became clear in August 1904 that legislation was going to be needed to sort out the problems caused by the judgment of the House of Lords in the *Free Church* case,[175] the leaders of the Church of Scotland immediately seized on this unexpected opportunity. A clause was inserted in the Churches (Scotland) Bill which, when enacted, put the power of the Church of Scotland to adopt a new formula of subscription beyond legal challenge.[176]

The creation of the United Free Church had been a major step forward in producing unity among the presbyterian churches outside the Establishment. But the much larger prize would be for the Church of Scotland itself to join with the United Free Church. If this could be brought about, the Church of Scotland would include the successors of most of the ministers and congregations who had left at the time of the Disruption. The position of the Church of Scotland would be strengthened. This was thought to be particularly desirable at a time when the Church seemed to be losing influence, not least because of the rise of the Roman Catholic Church, especially as a result of immigration from Ireland to the West of Scotland.[177] Nothing could be done, of course, until the chaos in the affairs of the United Free Church had been sorted out. But the predicament of the United Frees had struck a chord with many in the Established Church. When the United Free Church was eventually able to look around itself, the Church of Scotland suggested that the two churches should explore the possibilities of union. In 1909 the United Free Church agreed.[178]

The negotiations covered a variety of topics.[179] One was the form of establishment after any union, since, having fought off a determined campaign for its disestablishment,[180] the Church of Scotland naturally insisted that establishment – in one sense its defining characteristic – should be maintained in some form. While the United Presbyterian strand in the United Free Church was opposed to establishment in principle, for the most part, the real question was the terms of any future establishment. Those would have to be determined. A related problem is the one that matters for present purposes: the spiritual independence of any united church from the dictates of the civil courts.[181]

So far as the Established Church was concerned, there had been no recurrence of hostilities with the courts since 1843. In *Wight v Presbytery of Dunkeld*,[182] in an act of filial piety, the Free Church Lord Justice Clerk Moncreiff had taken the opportunity to play down what he called 'inconsiderate dicta' which had been 'thrown out' in earlier cases – by which he clearly meant the Disruption cases. Other post-Disruption decisions had indeed suggested that, in practice, the Court of Session would not readily interfere. '[O]stentatious obsequiousness' was one observer's plausible description of the attitude of the Court of Session to the Established Church after the Disruption.[183] Nevertheless, the decisions of the House of Lords in the *Auchterarder* cases stood, and they represented the law, so far as the Church of Scotland was concerned. The Church did not, of course, consider that those decisions meant that she lacked the necessary degree of spiritual independence. But, so long as the position remained as laid down in the Disruption cases, the United Free Church would never enter a union with the Church of Scotland since it would mean being subjected to the very legal régime from which the forefathers of the Free Church element in its midst had departed, at great cost to themselves, at the Disruption.

All these matters were discussed by a joint conference of representatives of both churches. Partly due to an interruption during the First World War, its work stretched out over a period of years.[184] In the end, the Church of Scotland was quite happy to have a new comprehensive declaration of its spiritual freedom.[185] The upshot was the Church of Scotland Act 1921,[186] one of whose main aims was, precisely, to secure the spiritual independence of the Church of Scotland – and hence of any united church. This was done by drawing up a series of painstakingly worded articles which were said to be declaratory of the constitution of the Church of Scotland in matters spiritual, and by putting those articles into the schedule to the 1921 Act. Section 4 of the Act provided that it was to come into force on a date after the articles had been adopted by an Act of the General Assembly of the Church of Scotland with the consent of a majority of the presbyteries of the Church. In other words, the articles would first have been made fully binding on the Church by the operation of the Barrier Act. These steps were duly carried out and only then was the 1921 Act brought into force by the Church of Scotland Order 1926.[187]

Section 1 of the 1921 Act provides that the Declaratory Articles in the schedule are lawful articles and that 'the constitution of the Church of Scotland in matters spiritual is as therein set forth.' In *Percy v Board of National Mission* Lord Nicholls of Birkenhead commented that the expression 'matters spiritual' is not defined.[188] In one sense that is so. But Parliament must have regarded all the matters in the schedule as 'matters spiritual', since the whole point of the schedule is to set out the constitution of the Church in such matters. In other words, what the Act does is to substitute this new constitution of the Church of Scotland in matters spiritual for the old constitution as it had been shaped by the decisions of the Court of Session and the House of Lords in the Disruption cases.[189] Parliament was doing in 1921 what it had refused to do when asked in 1840–3.

This is confirmed when we see the terms of section 3 of the Act. It provides that, subject to the matters dealt with in the Declaratory Articles being recognised as 'matters spiritual', nothing in the Act is to affect or prejudice the jurisdiction of the 'civil courts' in relation to any matter of a 'civil nature'. The language is redolent of the Disruption cases. So all the matters in the Declaratory Articles are to be regarded as matters spiritual and the implication is that, to this extent, the Articles are to affect or prejudice the jurisdiction of the civil courts. In short, the civil courts' jurisdiction is excluded in the case of the matters spiritual in the articles.

On turning to Article IV, we immediately recognise the theological doctrine of the Headship of Christ. The article provides that the Church receives from Lord Jesus Christ alone 'the right and power, subject to no civil authority, to legislate and to adjudicate finally in all matters of doctrine, worship, government and discipline in the Church, including the right to determine all questions concerning membership and office in the Church. ...' So, by enacting section 1 and Article IV, Parliament gave statutory effect to the position which Solicitor General Rutherfurd had quite deliberately not advanced on behalf of the Church in the first *Auchterarder* case – and which Lord President Hope had been able to dignify by no other name than 'absurdity'.[190] Somewhat ironically, it is by the authority of the legislature of the State that legal effect is given to the Church's position, that it receives its right and power to legislate and adjudicate finally in the specified matters, not from the State, but from Christ alone. The final words of Article IV seem intended, in part at least, to address this point by insisting that, by its legislation, the State does nothing more than recognise the position of the Church. Whatever the possible ironies, such legislation was, of course, the only way to obliterate the law, to precisely the opposite effect, which had been laid down by the courts in the Disruption cases.

The effect of all this seems to be that, by virtue of the 1921 Act, the Church of Scotland was to be given a constitution of the kind which the Evangelical party had always claimed was its historic constitution as secured by the Act of Union. They considered that, under that historic constitution, the Church had enjoyed a spiritual independence which was destroyed by the courts in the Disruption cases. They carried that view with them into the Free Church and from there into the United Free Church. The hope and intention behind the 1921 Act was that, once the constitution in the schedule was given legal effect, the United Free Church would be satisfied that the spiritual independence of the Church of Scotland was now secure. The ministers and members of the United Free Church would therefore lose none of their highly prized spiritual independence if they went into a union with the Church of Scotland.

There was a further problem which, it had always been recognised, the Church of Scotland would need to sort out before there could be any union with the United Frees. An Act of Parliament would be needed in order to transfer the ecclesiastical property and endowments from the State to the Church of Scotland so as to put an end to the situation where, say, the right of a minister to occupy the manse could give rise to questions of civil law, thus giving an opening to the civil courts to exercise their jurisdiction. In addition, the system of teinds, which was regulated by the (civil) Teind Court, would need to be ended.[191] The proposed legislation was strongly resisted by landowners whose interests were affected – in particular, by having to pay a lump sum to redeem the teinds. They saw no reason why they should, in effect, be asked to make a financial sacrifice in order to facilitate union between the two churches.[192] In the end, however, the Church of Scotland (Property and Endowments) Act 1925 was passed.

The two Acts had the desired effect. The final negotiations for union were now able to proceed[193] and, with the exception of a small group in the United Free Church,[194] the two churches eventually united on 2 October 1929.[195]

In practice, the 1921 Act was certainly used to good effect in those cases – mostly unreported – where ministers tried to challenge the decisions of Church of Scotland courts before the Court of Session. Citing the Act, the court would hold that it had no jurisdiction.[196] That put a speedy end to the proceedings. *Percy* has changed things, but it may be some time before we can tell how far-reaching the change is.

It is important to remember that Ms Percy was not complaining that she had suffered sex discrimination in the general run of her employment with the Church. Her complaint was that, by being suspended by the Board of National Mission and subjected to judicial proceedings before her presbytery, she was being treated differently from male ministers in a similar position. At first sight it would seem that a presbytery which adjudicates on the conduct of a minister is either adjudicating on a matter of government or discipline in the church, or else is determining a question concerning office in the church, in terms of Article IV. The same would apply to accepting a minister's demission of her status in the course of such proceedings. The same would also apply to suspending an associate minister's appointment on disciplinary grounds. In that event, in terms of Article IV, the Church's adjudication or determination would be final. To put the matter in another way, the Church would have exclusive jurisdiction in this matter spiritual. Any encroachment by the civil court on to the area of those decisions would once more threaten the spiritual independence of the Church.

I have little doubt that this is how those who framed the 1921 Act would have intended it to work. They would have thought that Ms Percy's only remedy for any unfairness in the proceedings of the presbytery or the actions of the Board, such as sex discrimination – an impossible idea, of course, with the all-male ministry and eldership back in 1921 when the Act was passed – lay in an appeal to the General Assembly, whose decision would be final.[197] In principle, today, one would expect the General Assembly to make sure that Church courts and other bodies avoided any sexual discrimination in their proceedings. But Baroness Hale records that in *Percy* the Church conceded that it did not provide internal remedies which met the requirements of the Equal Treatment Directive.[198] She concluded that the civil law must therefore do so.

In effect, the judges are saying that, since the actions of the Board and the Church court, the presbytery, in disciplining Ms Percy allegedly caused her an injury for which the civil court, in the shape of the employment tribunal, provides a remedy under the civil law, she must be able to claim that remedy from the tribunal. That is not, in substance, very different from the approach of the Court of Session and the House of Lords in the *Auchterarder* cases. The action of the Church court, the presbytery, in refusing to take Mr Young on trial had allegedly caused him and his patron an injury for which the civil court, in the shape of the Court of Session, provided a remedy under the civil law. Therefore, they must be able to claim that remedy from the court. As these cases show, the simple fact is that a civil court will be reluctant to accept that it cannot deal with what it sees as an allegation of a substantial wrong. Like the House of Lords and the majority of the Court of Session in the *Auchterarder* cases, their Lordships in *Percy* were satisfied that they were not interfering in any matters spiritual. In the light of history, it would not be surprising if some in the Church thought otherwise.[199]

The Equal Treatment Directive played a significant part in Lord Hope's reasoning, but not, so far as I can see, in the reasoning of Lord Nicholls.[200] Presumably, he just concluded that section 6 of the Sex Discrimination Act had impliedly repealed section 1 of the 1921 Act and Article IV in the schedule, to the extent necessary to make section 6 effective in these circumstances. Lord Hope, on the other hand, invoked the court's obligation under *Marleasing*[201] to interpret national law, so far as possible, to achieve the result pursued by the Directive – here, equal treatment of men and women.[202] The Church accepted that its procedures could not provide an adequate remedy for the purposes of the Directive. Using the *Marleasing* approach, Lord Hope considered that Article IV of the Declaratory Articles could be interpreted in such a way as to avoid leaving this gap in the protection which national law was required to provide. He held that the Article was 'sufficiently broadly worded' for him to be able to hold that the exercise of the exclusive jurisdiction in matters spiritual did not extend to a claim of unlawful sex discrimination.[203] In its first real trial, the 1921 Act thus proved to be anything but *ein' feste Burg*, a sure fortress, for the Church.

Much of the reasoning of the House of Lords in the *Percy* case is posited on the view that, as an associate minister, Ms Percy was working under 'a contract personally to execute any work or labour.'[204] Arguably, the position of parish ministers is different and so that reasoning would not apply. This remains to be seen. Although Ms Percy had named the Church of Scotland as the respondent to her application to the employment tribunal, as already mentioned,[205] the notice of appearance was entered in the name of the Board of National Mission. So Lord Hope confined his consideration to the Board's actions in the performance of what he had found to be their contract with Ms Percy as an associate minister.[206] Those actions were plainly of a disciplinary nature. But, in reality, the main thrust of Ms Percy's complaint was directed at the actions of the Presbytery of Angus, to which, like any other minister in the district, she was subject in matters of discipline. In any event, it would be hard to isolate the actions of the Board from the parallel actions of the presbytery. In substance, therefore, the *Percy* decision shows that, despite the 1921 Act, the civil court is ready to involve itself in actions taken by the Church to discipline a minister where that involvement is necessary to give effect to the Sex Discrimination Act and the Equal Treatment Directive. Perhaps, as Taylor Innes said of the Disruption cases, 'What has really been settled is the general relation of the Church of Scotland to the British

Parliament and to its legislation in Church matters.'[207] Or perhaps what has been settled is the general relation of the Church to the European Community and its legislation.

We have come full circle – we are back discussing the very kind of jurisdictional question which arose in the Disruption cases. It is as good a point as any at which to take stock.

It is tempting to ask: Who was right in the Disruption cases? The majority or the minority judges? The partisan literature is overwhelmingly in favour of the minority – not surprisingly, since most of it was written by Free Church authors. On the other hand, the author of the chapter on Church and State in Story's late Victorian *magnum opus* on the Church of Scotland is magisterially dismissive of the Free Church position.[208] More significantly perhaps, given that he was devoted to the Free Church, Taylor Innes wrote:

> I have never been able to join in the condemnation launched against the Judges who laid down this solid mass of our existing law. I believe that they dealt with a great constitutional question, which was forced upon them, and that they did so with immense deliberation as well as firmness, and that all the decisions from first to last depended upon that one principle of subjection and subordination, which, whether true or not, has never since been even called in question.[209]

Like Professor Lyall,[210] I prefer to leave the question open. After all, it does not admit of a single straightforward answer. An authority on the history of the Reformation or on events in the seventeenth and eighteenth centuries might prefer the historical expositions of Lord Moncreiff to those of Lord Medwyn or vice versa. But that would still not really decide whether the general approach of the majority or minority judges to the immediate issues before the court was to be preferred – far less, whether the decision in any particular case was appropriate.

As is often the case, some of the arguments used by the judges do not look altogether convincing. For example, when Lord President Hope said in the first *Auchterarder* case 'that in every civilized country, there *must* be some court or other judicature, by which every other court of judicature may be compelled to do their duty, or kept within the bounds of their duty,'[211] this was really just assertion.[212] As the minority judges did not tire of pointing out, it did not actually seem to be true of Scotland, where the Court of Exchequer and the Court of Justiciary appeared to be co-ordinate courts, each, like the Court of Session, supreme in its own realm. The Lord President would have been hard pushed indeed to concoct a scenario in which the Court of Session would pronounce an interlocutor ordering the

Court of Justiciary to do its duty. The best that Lord Justice Clerk Hope could come up with was a situation where the Court of Justiciary admitted someone to the office of Lord Justice Clerk who did not have the Queen's grant of appointment.[213]

On the other hand, the Lord President had not just dreamed up this position for purposes of the first *Auchterarder* case. There was significant support for it in at least two previous decisions concerning schoolmasters. The first was *The Heritors of Corstorphine v Ramsay* – a decision in which Lord President Hope himself had presided more than a quarter of a century earlier.[214] In dismissing a libel against a schoolmaster relating to alleged fraud, the Edinburgh presbytery had taken account of the Criminal Procedure Act 1701 c. 6, which barred further criminal proceedings against the minister in the circumstances. There was no right of appeal from the presbytery to a higher Church court. In a bill of advocation, the heritors complained that, by taking account of the 1701 Act, the presbytery had proceeded on a ground of which it was not competent to judge and the Court of Session could intervene to correct this excess of power. On behalf of the schoolmaster, Mr James Moncreiff – the future Lord Moncreiff of the Veto Act – submitted that the libel was an ecclesiastical libel and the Court of Session had no jurisdiction. There is a striking similarity between counsel's submissions and the submissions in the first *Auchterarder* case.[215] The Court of Session held that it had jurisdiction. Lord President Hope said:

> It is no solution of this question to say that this is an ecclesiastical libel. It is so; but the presbytery must go on with it, and not go beyond their powers in judging of it. It is very true that the 43d of the King gave the exclusive jurisdiction as to schoolmasters to presbyteries alone. But that jurisdiction is exclusive only where they act in matters committed to them. But if they refuse to act at all, or go beyond their powers, they may be controlled by this court.[216]

In 1829 that decision had been followed by the House of Lords in *Campbell of Kilberry v Brown*,[217] upholding a similar decision of the First Division. Again, the case concerned the presbytery's deposition, not of a minister, but of a parochial schoolmaster, for neglect of duty. Lord Chancellor Lyndhurst rejected the argument that the Court of Session had no power of review in an ecclesiastical matter and said:

> But I apprehend that (particularly from the circumstance of the appeal being taken away) a jurisdiction is given in this case to the Court of Session, not to review the judgment on the merits, but to take care that the Court of Presbytery shall keep within the line of its duty, and conform to the

provisions of the Act of Parliament. There is in the Court of Session in Scotland, that superintending authority over inferior jurisdictions, which is requisite in all countries, for the purpose of confining those inferior jurisdictions within the bounds of their duty. ... Now, in this particular case, the power of final judgment is given to the presbytery, under certain limitations and certain restrictions. The party is to be served with the libel – the necessary proof is to be taken – and unless the inferior tribunal pursue the course pointed out by the Act of Parliament, they have no authority to proceed to judgment; and if, without pursuing the course pointed out, they do proceed to a judgment, in that case all their proceedings will be so inconsistent with the authority with which they are invested, that the superintending authority of the Court of Session may be interposed for the purpose of setting aside those proceedings.[218]

Of course, the circumstances in that case were distinguishable from those in the first *Auchterarder* case. It could be said, for instance, that the appointment or deprivation of a schoolmaster was not intrinsically a matter of ecclesiastical discipline or order.[219] Moreover, Parliament had taken away the schoolmasters' right of appeal to the higher Church courts, while ministers still had that right of appeal. Nevertheless, the House of Lords had indeed spoken of a superintending authority being 'requisite in all countries'. The Lord Chancellor had also affirmed the jurisdiction of the Court of Session to review the decision of a presbytery, an ecclesiastical court, in the purported performance of a duty imposed by an Act of Parliament.[220] Even Alexander Dunlop had not rejected that view before he became carried away with championing spiritual independence in the years before the Disruption.[221]

Judges in the minority argued that, as a court, the General Assembly of the Church of Scotland was comparable to the Court of Justiciary. If the civil Court of Session did not interfere with judgments of the criminal Court of Justiciary, it shouldn't interfere with those of the ecclesiastical General Assembly.[222] As a matter of pure logic, that is compelling – even though the real question may have been whether, in relation to the particular duty of the presbytery under the relevant legislation, the Church courts were indeed supreme.[223] But the majority judges were right to see that the General Assembly was not really like the Court of Justiciary. Its composition changed from year to year; most of the members were not legally qualified; it was often swayed by rhetoric or wit or emotion, rather than by precise reasoning. An advocate member, Graham Bell, commented in 1838 that he had 'sat in the Assembly for the last three days, putting to himself the question from hour to hour, whether he was in a legislative assembly or in a court; and he must admit that he had been compelled to answer that, if he was in a court, it was certainly not in a court of justice.'[224] So scrutiny of the decisions of the General Assembly by the Court of Session was actually rather different from scrutiny of the decisions of the Court of Justiciary.

Lord Jeffrey could reply that the argument proved too much: if you took that line, you should not respect any of the decisions of the Church courts, and yet the majority judges were happy to respect any decision on purely spiritual matters.[225] Again, a good logical point, but it does not actually alter the basic fact that the General Assembly is a very different animal from the Court of Justiciary and one which looked, at the time, as if it might need some controlling. Lord Mackenzie made the contrast in vivid terms in the *Stewarton* case. Having referred to the Court of Justiciary and the Exchequer Court and having suggested that in practice jurisdictional problems did not arise, he continued:

> They are, like this court, merely judicial bodies, determining, on actions brought, the interests of others. And the judges of these courts are all removeable in a mode pointed out by the constitution. They never could, or did, pretend to be any thing but the mere servants of the State, *i.e.* of King and Parliament. But the Church is a body of quite a different kind. It has always pretended to certain powers by divine right, subject, within its province, to no human control. It claims, and with modification enjoys, a *quasi* oligarchic constitution, its office-bearers being appointed not without its concurrence, and removeable by itself; and it has always struggled to get this power entirely into its own hands, excluding the State altogether. It is not a merely judicial power, determining the interests of others, but always studying and urging its own. Look at the present state of the Church. Is the General Assembly altogether like an ordinary court of justice, deciding between litigants, whom it regards with indifference, and judging its own jurisdiction with equal indifference? When I ask the question, I am not censuring the Assembly at all. I am only doubting their similarity with a mere court of justice.[226]

As Lord Mackenzie was pointing out, the General Assembly was – and is – very different from the Court of Justiciary. Although at one time the Court of Session and the Court of Justiciary exercised extensive powers of legislation by Act of Sederunt and Act of Adjournal, by this period those powers were, in practice, much reduced. The courts were, to all intents and purposes, simply courts. But the General Assembly was not just a court: it was also a legislature and a forum for deliberating on the affairs of the Church. Attitudes formed in its deliberative or legislative functions could easily be carried over into its judicial function. It was this combination of the claim to legislate in a way which did in practice impinge on civil rights with a claim to adjudicate finally on the validity, interpretation and application of its legislation, that made it a unique body.[227] To many people these claims were not only unique: they were potentially alarming in the hands of zealous churchmen. What might future majorities in the Assembly not claim to do?[228]

People became alarmed, for example, in August 1840 when Dr Candlish conceded that the Evangelical party might be said to have taken their original decision to pass the Veto Act under a mistaken apprehension of the civil law,[229] but continued:

> But we were under no mistake in regard to the law of Christ. We thought the law of the land allowed – we were sure that the law of Christ required – us to decide as we did decide. And whatsoever the law of the land may now be found, or may be made, to say, the law of Christ is not changed – the law of Christ requires that we abide still by our decision. The question, should this man be pastor of Christ's flock in this parish, has already been settled, according to the mind of Christ.

Dr Candlish was claiming that he, and those for whom he spoke, actually knew the mind of Christ on the question of the Veto Act and on whether someone should be admitted as a pastor. Remember: the Act was a piece of Assembly legislation which had not even been thought of ten years before and which Dr Chalmers still considered should be repealed.[230] Yet, here we have Dr Candlish saying that the law of Christ had required the Assembly to decide to pass the Act and that the law of Christ also required that they abide by that decision. Just in case anyone wondered, he declares that they are under no mistake with regard to the law of Christ.

To many this appeared to be a papal assertion of infallibility.[231] At all events, a General Assembly which acted on the basis that it could say that its legislation was an infallible enactment of the law of Christ looked potentially dangerous. It would be doubly so, if there were no outside body to control it.

Claims of this kind cost the Evangelical party public sympathy. They liked to stress the appeal of the Veto Act and of Evangelical thinking to those whom Dean of Faculty Hope described as 'the lower orders among the members of the Establishment',[232] particularly those whom the Rev. Henry Moncreiff referred to as 'peasants'.[233] In the words of Dr Chalmers, 'evangelical theology is also the popular theology.'[234] But, curiously enough, with all their Whig credentials, the Evangelicals found themselves on the wrong side of the democratic argument. This was an age of Reform, when established churches, church taxes, State endowment of churches and so on were under attack. At such a time, making wild assertions about the powers of the General Assembly was not likely to attract widespread support among the poorer classes, or indeed among those who were generally in favour of change in society. In the words of one not unsympathetic critic,[235] the Church 'began by demanding a popular right, but it ended by demanding a clerical right, which, at will, could have scattered the popular to the winds.' Somehow, the Evangelicals' claim, that they were only asserting the right for the clergy in order to use it for the benefit of the people,[236] failed to carry conviction. On the other side, interference with the civil right of patronage and defiance of the courts of the land alienated the more conservative members of society who might otherwise have been natural supporters of the Church, especially in uncertain times. Understandably too, most members of Parliament found it impossible to side with the Church when it would not respect the decisions of the civil courts.

In a strange way, the old Tory judges – Lord President Hope and Lord Justice Clerk Boyle – read the spirit of the times more accurately. Whether they were right or wrong in their interpretation of what had happened at the time of the Reformation and afterwards was not really the point. Lord Cockburn saw that: all these historical excursuses could not really decide the issue, he said, since much of the material dated from a time when the Church was making claims to obtrude 'its intolerance both into all public affairs, and into every asylum of private life' which no one would have acknowledged now.[237] What mattered was whether the Church courts, including the General Assembly, should be free from control in the conditions of the 1830s and 1840s. On that, the judicial instinct of the majority may well have been correct. In other words, they may well have been right to sense that, in the new climate of the times, it was not acceptable for the Established Church to be outside the control of the civil courts if it was going to assert an unfettered right to adopt measures such as the Veto Act which affected civil rights. Significantly, when the Evangelical party appealed to Parliament, for the most part the Whigs were as opposed to their stance as Peel's Conservatives. There is, perhaps, more than a hint of these problems to come in Lord Jeffrey's gloomy comment to Lord Cockburn in April 1838:

> [The Church] has allowed the interested flatteries of a faction to lead it into a belief that in good earnest it is sacrosanct and the only thing in short for which Government and Society are established. This is a course that has been run before – but the time is gone bye when it could prosper and the end will be that no party in the state will submit to its exactions, and, having lost all hold on the affections of the people it will be pulled down amidst their shouts and laughter. Sic vaticinor, et fiat.[238]

The obvious self-sacrifice of the ministers who left the Church at the Disruption, which Jeffrey so much admired,[239] may have helped postpone some of the effects which he foresaw, for a time at least.

There I must bring these lectures to a close, even though I have only scratched the surface of the topic. For instance, I have not followed the travels of the non-intrusion *corps diplomatique*[240] back and forth to London to lobby ministers and others – all in vain.[241] The wider political context, both in Scotland and in England, is important and relevant and I have said next to nothing about it. The parallels with the developments in the Church of England, with the rise of the Oxford Movement,[242] are also significant, not least in explaining the stance of the Government and Parliament towards requests from the Evanglical party in the Church of Scotland for recognition of its spiritual independence. Even *The Tablet*, newly founded in 1840, followed the disputes leading to the Disruption with interest, since it could see the importance of spiritual independence for the Roman Catholic Church. So far as the law is concerned, I have not been able, for example, to look at Lord Medwyn's theory of Church and State, which so fascinated Harold Laski,[243] or at Lord Jeffrey's theory of the scope of the Court of Session's power of review. Nor have we opened the box of delights which awaits those with a proper taste for the competency of pure declarators, the scope of defences to interim interdicts, the reconciling of overlapping jurisdictions and much, much more besides. I shall be more than happy, however, if I encourage anyone, whether judge, practitioner, student or non-lawyer, to open the Disruption cases which have, for too long, remained closed and neglected.

NOTES

1. *Percy v Board of National Mission of the Church of Scotland* [2005] UKHL 73; 2006 S.C. (H.L.) 1; [2006] 2 A.C. 28.
2. 2006 S.C. (H.L.) 1, at p. 13, para. 48; [2006] 2 A.C. 28, at p.45, para. 48, per Lord Hoffmann. That assumption is confirmed by the fact that, in the proceedings before the Special Commission set up by the General Assembly, Ms Percy claimed that 'a man in her position would not have been suspended, would not have been the subject of a preliminary inquiry' and would not have been advised by 'three men appointed by the Church' to demit status and resign her appointment as an associate minister. See the Report of the Special Commission, *Reports to the General Assembly 2004* (Church of Scotland, Edinburgh, 2004), pp. 34/1–34/13.
3. 2001 S.C. 757. The applicant did not proceed further with her claim for unfair dismissal.
4. See section 82(1) of the Sex Discrimination Act 1975.
5. Opinion of the Special Commission dated 20 October 2003, reprinted as Appendix 3 to their Report: *Reports to the General Assembly 2004*, at pp. 34/10–34/13.

6. 2006 S.C. (H.L.) 1; [2006] 2 A.C. 28.
7. On this aspect of the decision, see *The New Testament Church of God v Rev. Sylvester Stewart* [2007] EWCA 1004.
8. Equal Treatment Directive 76/207.
9. Section 2.2 of the Report of the Legal Questions Committee, *Reports to the General Assembly 2007* (Church of Scotland, Edinburgh, 2007), p. 6.4/4.
10. F. Cramner, S. Peterson, 'Employment, Sex Discrimination and the Churches: The Percy Case' (2006) 8 Ecclesiastical Law Journal 392 and M. Maclean, F. Cranmer, S. Peterson, 'Recent Developments in Church–State Relations in Scotland' (unpublished).
11. Guthrie vol. 2, p. 27. The number is derived from Buchanan vol. 1, p. 3*.
12. The full report of the first *Auchterarder* case in the Court of Session was published on 26 May 1838, the last day of the General Assembly, just three days after the big debate relating to the decision. See the advertisement in *The Scotsman*, 26 May 1838, p. 3.
13. *The Times*, 29 June 1843, reporting his speech at a meeting the previous day. The meeting shows the Free Church speakers consorting with, and buttering up, dissenters in England.
14. The Rev. Henry Moncreiff, *A Letter to Lord Melbourne* (John Johnstone, Edinburgh; J. Nisbet & Co., London, 1840), p. 41. See also Mackinnon, *Some Chapters in Scottish Church History*, Preface.
15. D. Liebs, 'Der ungeliebte Jurist in der römischen Welt' (2006) 123 Zeitschrift der Savigny Stiftung für Rechtsgeschichte (Romanistische Abteilung) 1–18. See also D. Nörr, *Rechtskritik in der römischen Antike* (Verlag der Bayerischen Akademie der Wissenschaften, Munich, 1974), especially Chapter VI.
16. Prologue, lines 325–6.
17. From the third verse of 'You ask me, why, tho' ill at ease', first published in A. Tennyson, *Poems* (E. Moxon, London, 1833). It was a Northern Irish judge, Lord Carswell, who quoted these lines in *A v Home Secretary (No 2)* [2005] UKHL 71; [2006] 2 A.C. 221, at p. 300, para. 152. One might wonder, of course, exactly how much of Britain Tennyson was including in 'England'. He also refers to 'That codeless myriad of precedent' in 'Aylmer's Field', first published in Alfred, Baron Tennyson, *Enoch Arden, etc.* (E. Moxon & Co., London, 1864).
18. See, for instance, in addition to his judgments, his Hamlyn lectures – Sir Alfred Denning, *Freedom under the Law* (Stevens & Sons, London, 1949) – and Lord Denning, *Landmarks in the Law* (Butterworths, London, 1984) and *Leaves from my Library: An English Anthology* (Butterworths, London, 1986).
19. A deputation of the Church of Scotland met the Prime Minister, Lloyd George, and two sons of the Free Church manse, the Leader of the Opposition, Bonar Law, and the Scottish Secretary, Robert Munro, to discuss the prospective legislation at a breakfast meeting at 10 Downing Street on 20 March 1920. See C. L. Rawlins (ed.), *The Diaries of William Paterson* (Faith and Life Books, Edinburgh, 1987), at pp. 273–4.
20. *Proceedings of the General Assembly of the Free Church of Scotland at Edinburgh, May 1843*, p. 20.
21. *The Scotsman*, 20 May 1843, p. 2.
22. See, in particular, S. J. Brown, *Thomas Chalmers and the Godly Commonwealth in Scotland* (Oxford University Press, Oxford, 1982).
23. In fact, he was forced to qualify his position shortly afterwards – a fact that was not brought to the attention of the House of Lords. See p. 99 n. 54 below.

24. The *Caledonian Mercury*, 20 May 1843, p. 3, referred to 'the sensitive apprehensions this distinguished Divine seemed to entertain, about being confounded with the general body of Dissenters.' The editorial writer surmised that the speech had contained certain references and a certain tone 'which would not have been exactly adopted by Dr Candlish or Dr Cunningham.'

25. J. G., 'A Word to Dissenters', *The Scotsman*, 27 May 1843, p. 4.

26. Walker, *Chapters from the History of the Free Church of Scotland*, p. 40.

27. Chapter XLV of Brown, *Annals of the Disruption*, which, tellingly, is devoted to the social standing of Free Church ministers, reverses the point by saying that dissent had never stood in a position of social inferiority in Scotland to the same extent as in England, 'owing, perhaps to the fact that with us the Episcopalian clergy and laity are Dissenters.' Omond, himself the son of a Free Church minister, remarks that, after the Disruption, 'the clergy and the laity were of the same social standing as those who remained in the Established Church': Omond, p. 94. For an analysis of the social composition of Free Church congregations in different parts of Scotland, see P. L. M. Hillis, 'The Sociology of the Disruption', in Brown and Fry (eds), *Scotland in the Age of the Disruption*, pp. 44–62. On the north of Scotland, see Paton, *The Clergy and the Clearances*, pp. 152–60.

28. 27 May 1843, p. 2. The hostile editor had been caught out by the large number of ministers who left the Established Church on a matter of principle.

29. 'Many who have joined the ranks of the Free Church cannot persuade themselves that they have descended to those of *Seceders* and *Dissenters*; and no great disposition has been shown by them to fraternise, on anything like terms of equality, with their new associates …': Bryce vol. 2, pp. 386–7.

30. The acceptance of money from slave-owning circles in the American South caused a major crisis, however. See, e.g., G. Shepperson, 'Thomas Chalmers, the Free Church of Scotland, and the South' (1951) 17 Journal of Southern History 517–37, with references.

31. Macfarlane, pp. 153–64.

32. Brown, *Annals of the Disruption*, pp. 569–71. A circular, entitled 'Scheme of the Colony of the Free Church of Scotland at Otago in New Zealand', was issued by the Lay Association of the Free Church of Scotland for Promoting the Settlement of a Scotch Colony at Otago, New Zealand, in 1845. Among the members were well-known legal Free Church veterans of the Disruption struggle such as Sheriff Speirs, Sheriff Monteith and Mr John Hamilton, Advocate. (Peter Skegg showed me his copy of the circular in Dunedin and kindly sent me a scanned copy.) For a wider view of the position in the colonies, see B. C. Murison, 'The Disruption and the Colonies of Scottish Settlement', in Brown and Fry (eds), *Scotland in the Age of the Disruption*, pp. 135–50.

33. Writing in 1859, Turner, p. 9, refers to 'the conviction entertained by many, that even yet the triumph of the party was but a few years delayed, that the temporary structures about to be erected for the outgoing congregations would more than outlive their brief secession, to be followed by a triumphant restoration …'.

34. Bryce vol. 2, p. 385. Brown, *Annals of the Disruption*, p. 560, paints an amusing picture of the colonial ministers who adhered to the Establishment 'in hot haste' and 'left their Canadian congregations, and started across the sea eager to have a share of the spoil.'

35. Bryce vol. 2, pp. 385–90, but also pp. 414–17; Omond, pp. 94–5.

36. For the general background, see O. Chadwick, *The Secularization of the European Mind in the Nineteenth Century* (Cambridge University Press, Cambridge, 1975).

37. After the Disruption, the Free Church had made a big effort to set up its own schools – thereby weakening the position of the Established Church in the field of education and so also weakening its claim to be recognised as the national church. See Hutchison, *A Political History of Scotland 1832–1924*, pp. 72–3. But its policy on education soon split the Free Church in a way that was to have lasting effects. See D. J. Withrington, 'Adrift among the Reefs of Conflicting Ideals: Education and the Free Church, 1843–55', in Brown and Fry (eds), *Scotland in the Age of the Disruption*, pp. 79–97.

38. For a full account, see Ross, Chapter III; also J. L. MacLeod, *The Second Disruption: The Free Church in Victorian Scotland and the Origins of the Free Presbyterian Church* (Tuckwell Press, East Linton, 2000) and Fry, *Patronage and Principle*, pp. 51–8.

39. Ross, pp. 147–53.

40. The somewhat curious reason for the majority in the Free Church coming to adopt that position is explained in Ross, pp. 119–21.

41. Ross, pp. 139–47.

42. Ross, Chapter VI; Life of Rainy vol. 1, Chapter VII.

43. For the background and reasons, see MacLeod, *The Second Disruption* and *History of the Free Presbyterian Church of Scotland* (Glasgow, 1933, reprinted, 1965), especially Chapters V–VII.

44. For the way that a lawyer, and hitherto ardent constitutionalist, reconciled himself to the union, see J. Buchan, *Andrew Jameson Lord Ardwall* (William Blackwood & Sons, Edinburgh and London, 1913), pp. 106–14. In reproducing his speech to the General Assembly of 1899, Buchan tactfully deletes the indication which Sheriff Jameson actually gave that the property question was likely to be resolved in favour of the majority: *Proceedings and Debates of the General Assembly of the Free Church of Scotland, held at Edinburgh, May 1899* (Macniven & Wallace, Edinburgh; James Nisbet & Co., London, 1899), pp. 172–3, quoted in Ross, Chapter I n. 151 at p. 313. In the immediate aftermath of the disaster of 1 August 1904, Jameson suggested that the union should be rescinded and that the former Frees among the United Frees should rejoin the Frees: R. L. Orr, *Lord Guthrie: a Memoir* (Hodder & Stoughton, London, 1923), p. 141. That idea was swiftly rejected at the special Commission held on 10 August: Taylor Innes, 3 Hibbert Journal 217, at pp. 232–4. John Buchan was himself the son of a Free Church minister. By the time he wrote the biography of Lord Ardwall, he was a member of the United Free Church. On unification in 1929, he became a member of the Church of Scotland.

45. Life of Rainy vol. 2, pp. 247–54 and pp. 260–1; H. Morrison, *Manual of the Church Question in Scotland* (Keith & Co., Edinburgh, 1905), pp. 12–16. The Free Church naturally saw the day's events rather differently: Cameron, pp. 41–9.

46. Morrison, *Manual of the Church Question in Scotland*, p. 19.

47. *Bannatyne v United Free Church of Scotland* (1902) 4 F. 1083. The United Free Church itself raised proceedings for possession of a manse: *United Free Church of Scotland v M'Iver* (1902) 4 F. 1117. This was a way of ensuring that the Model Trust Deed, under which most congregational property was held, was brought into the picture: Life of Rainy vol. 2, pp. 264–5. To some extent the move backfired since it allowed the United Free Church to be portrayed as harshly driving out a long-serving minister from his home. See further p. 100 n. 64.

48. This was seen at the time, when the Lord Provost of Glasgow was asked to try to bring the two sides together: Life of Rainy vol. 2, pp. 309–10. For the compromise proffered at a late stage by the United Free Church, see p. 100 n. 68.

49. On the financing of the litigations for the Free Church minority, see Stewart and Cameron, pp. 189–90, and Cameron, p. 86.

50. Appellants' Case, in Free Church Appeals, pp. 89–98; Ross, pp. 55–72 and 136–53.

51. Free Church Appeals, p. 487.

52. Only hinted at in the Appellants' Case, in Free Church Appeals, p. 98; Ross, pp. 73–81 and 166–223.

53. See p. 96. Although it was recognised in 1843 that Dr Chalmers was but one man, the perception was that 'he is the man of the movement' and, moreover, that, in his address to the General Assembly, 'he spoke as the mouthpiece of the party': J. G., 'A Word to Dissenters', The Scotsman, 27 May 1843, p. 4.

54. Some, at least, of the criticism of the judgments of the majority on establishment was based on pronouncements by the leaders of the Free Church which were never put before the House of Lords. See, for instance, H. Macpherson, The Scottish Church Crisis (Hodder & Stoughton, London, 1904), pp. 7–30; Taylor Innes, 3 Hibbert Journal 217, at p. 228 n. 1. It may be that the United Free Church legal team underestimated the difficulties and did not include enough of the material, which might have gone some way to counter the famous passage from Dr Chalmers' address to the first General Assembly.

55. Free Church Appeals, pp. 209–23 (Johnston KC); 346–60 and 386–96 (Dean Asher).

56. Respondents' Case, in Free Church Appeals, pp. 130–2; denied by the Appellants in their Case, in Free Church Appeals, pp. 98–105; Ross, pp. 82–103, 194–216 and Chapter VI.

57. Dr Rainy preferred not to emphasise the Church's freedom to change, while Taylor Innes was of the opposite view: Taylor Innes, pp. 236–7. Dean Asher put considerable emphasis on the freedom of the Church to change – perhaps being influenced by the advice of Mr Balfour given in August 1899, shortly before he became Lord President. See pp. 106–7.

58. So, rightly, Ross, p. 82.

59. Bannatyne v United Free Church of Scotland (1902) 4 F. 1083; United Free Church of Scotland v M'Iver (1902) 4 F. 1117. The decision of the Second Division was printed in a separate report: The Church Union Case: Judgment of the Court of Session 4th July 1902. Opinions revised by their Lordships (William Blackwood & Sons, Edinburgh and London, 1902), with a brief introduction by Taylor Innes. Curiously, in Thomas Shaw (First Lord Craigmyle): a Monograph by his Son (Nicholson & Watson, London, 1937), p. 46, it is said that Shaw, a member of the United Presbyterian Church, was not only prominent in the negotiations for union, but was also the leading counsel for the United Free Church in the Court of Session. In fact, Dean of Faculty Asher was the leader in the Court of Session and Shaw was not instructed. It was not 'by some blunder never adequately explained' that he was not instructed in the House of Lords. In effect, those who had been advising the leaders of the Free Church before the union, Asher, Haldane and Guthrie, represented the United Free Church in the litigation.

60. Craigdallie v Aikman (1813) 5 Paton 719; (1820) 6 Paton 618. See Taylor Innes, The Law of Creeds in Scotland, pp. 222–36.

61. On the proceedings before him and his judgment, see Stewart and Cameron, pp. 157–70.

62. On the proceedings in the Second Division, see Stewart and Cameron, pp. 171–89. This was essentially the notoriously impatient and slapdash Second Division whose exploits were so bravely exposed in N. J. D. Kennedy, 'The Second Division's Progress' (1896) 8 Juridical Review 268. The composition of the Division changed shortly after the Free Church case finished. Lord Trayner resigned at the end of 1904, Lord Moncreiff three weeks later and Lord Young in May 1905. The Free Church hero of the litigation, Mr Johnston KC, succeeded Lord Young on the bench and soon had to decline to deal with the after-effects of his triumph: *Free Church of Scotland v M'Rae* (1905) 7 F. 686. For Lord Young's attitude to his own judgment, see the account of his conversation with Taylor Innes in Taylor Innes, p. 234 n.1.

63. Stewart and Cameron, pp. 152–3. This was no *ex post facto* rationalisation: the point was made in a circular asking for funds to finance the appeal to the House of Lords: Cameron, p. 86. *The Scotsman*, 2 August 1904, p. 4, commented that the judges in the House of Lords had gone into the heart of the case, had probed it to its depths, had faced the facts unflinchingly and had not been deterred from pronouncing what law and justice had to say from fear lest the ecclesiastical heavens should fall: 'It has been common subject of comment that as much could not be said of the judgments upset by yesterday's findings. That of the Lord Ordinary, whatever may be thought of its law, was indeed a careful, thoughtful, and reasoned deliverance. But of the weight and value of the dicta that issued from the majority of the members of the Second Division who had the case in their hands, perhaps the less said the better.' The reference to the majority must be an allusion to the absence of Lord Moncreiff due to illness. See Life of Rainy vol. 2, p. 307. He was a grandson of Lord Moncreiff of Disruption times, a son of Lord Justice Clerk Moncreiff, and the brother-in-law of Lord President Kinross. On account of this relationship the Lord President declined jurisdiction in an appeal by him against a decision of the Sheriff of Chancery: (1904) 12 Scots Law Times (News) 38.

64. The decision after the second hearing is reported in Session Cases as *Free Church of Scotland v Lord Overtoun* (1904) 7 F. (H.L.) 1. This appeal was conjoined with an appeal in *Macalister v Young*. The decisions of the House of Lords in the two appeals are also reported as *Free Church of Scotland v Lord Overtoun* [1904] A.C. 515. The Appeal Cases report is superior since it gives the gist of the argument and also reproduces many of the relevant documents. In addition, there were two editions of the judges' speeches produced for sale to the general public: A. McNeill, *The Free Church Case* (William Hodge & Co., Edinburgh, 1904) and A. Taylor Innes, *Free Church Union Case, judgment of the House of Lords, 1st August 1904, revised by their Lordships* (Blackwood, Edinburgh, 1904). But the appeals are best studied in the verbatim report by Orr, *The Free Church of Scotland Appeals 1903–4* ('Free Church Appeals'). *Macalister v Young* was a case brought by pursuers, claiming to be the United Free trustees of the former Free Buccleuch and Greyfriars Church in Edinburgh, for possession of the church. It was treated as a test case for congregational property held under the Model Trust Deed. At the first hearing, the appeal in the *Macalister* case was argued separately at the end: *The Scotsman*, 8 December 1903, p. 7. But, contrary to the thinking of Taylor Innes, pp. 239–40, counsel for the United Frees came to the view that the outcome would follow the decision in the main appeal and so, at the second hearing, there was no separate consideration of this case and the

argument was withdrawn: Free Church Appeals, pp. 337–8. Doubtless, counsel based this assessment on their feeling about the way the argument had gone in the first hearing. Taylor Innes set out the (impressive) argument on the Model Trust Deed which he favoured in 3 Hibbert Journal 217, at pp. 222–5.

65. The arguments in the first hearing are not reproduced in the reports, but they were extensively reported in *The Scotsman*, 27 November 1903, p. 7; 28 November, p. 11; 2 December, p. 10; 5 December, p. 7; and 8 December, p. 7. Counsel for the appellants were Johnston KC and Christie; for the respondents the Dean of Faculty (Asher KC), Haldane KC, Guthrie KC (a son of Dr Guthrie of Disruption times) and Orr. A little of the atmosphere of the hearing comes through in Orr, *Lord Guthrie*, pp. 137–9, and in the letter from Principal Rainy to Dr Ross Taylor reproduced in Life of Rainy vol. 2, pp. 311–12. As late as the evening of 26 November, it was still not settled whether Guthrie or Haldane should make the second speech for the United Free Church. Possibly because Guthrie was less confident than Haldane about the soundness of their case, the choice eventually fell on Haldane: Orr, *Lord Guthrie*, pp. 137–8.

66. Rainy's impression from the hearing was that Lord Shand had seemed to be for the United Frees: Life of Rainy vol. 2, p. 312. Stewart and Cameron, p. 173, only just manage to avoid attributing Lord Shand's death to an intervention of Divine Providence in favour of the Free Church minority.

67. Taylor Innes, p. 234 n. 1, at p. 236. The clear implication is that the draft was favourable to the United Frees. This would have been consistent with Lord Shand's view, expressed in a conversation as far back as 1876, that the Free Church had considerable freedom to change its view on what were to be regarded as fundamentals: Taylor Innes, p. 234 n. 1, at pp. 235–6.

68. Because of the way the first hearing had gone, during the General Assembly of the United Free Church in May 1904, shortly before the second hearing of the appeal was due to start, an offer of a compromise settlement on the basis of a lump-sum payment of £50,000 was made. It was ignored by the Free Church side. See Life of Rainy vol. 2, pp. 313–15; Stewart and Cameron, pp. 195–200. Taylor Innes and some others had favoured making an offer of settlement based on a numerically proportional share of the property, but this suggestion had not attracted support within the United Free Church: Taylor Innes, 3 Hibbert Journal 217, at p. 234 n. 1; Taylor Innes, pp. 237–9.

69. Taylor Innes, pp. 235–7.

70. Lord Kinross was the son of an Established Church minister. Having been widowed in 1872, five years later he married Eliza, the second daughter of (the Free Church) Lord Justice Clerk Moncreiff and the sister of the Second Division judge, Lord Moncreiff.

71. *The Scotsman*, 8 June 1904, p. 8.

72. G. M. Reith, *Reminiscences of the United Free Church General Assembly (1900–1929)* (The Moray Press, Edinburgh and London, 1933), p. 17.

73. Letter from John Sinclair, dated 24 May 1904, *The Times*, 2 June 1904, p. 4, reprinted in (1904) 12 Scots Law Times (News) 31–2. The Procurator, Mr Guthrie, had described the advice in these terms in the Free Church General Assembly debate on 31 May 1900: *Proceedings and Debates of the General Assembly of the Free Church of Scotland, held at Edinburgh, May 1900* (Macniven & Wallace, Edinburgh; James Nisbet & Co., London, 1900), p. 161. See further pp. 106–7.

74. The only change in the representation was that Mr Salvesen KC, who had been instructed in the Court of Session but omitted at the first hearing in the House of Lords, was restored to the appellants' team. Lord Salvesen's biographer does not

explain why this happened: H. F. Andorsen, *Memoirs of Lord Salvesen* (W. & R. Chambers, London and Edinburgh, 1949), pp. 66–7. His omission may have been to save costs.

75. As explained by the Lord Chancellor at the start of the hearing: Free Church Appeals, p. 173. A curious feature of the first hearing was that there was an even number of judges (six): the Lord Chancellor, Lords McNaghten, Shand, Davey, Robertson and Lindley. The rumour was that they were divided 3–3, presumably with the Lord Chancellor, Lord Davey and Lord Robertson being in favour of allowing the appeal, the rest being against. On that footing the appeal would have been dismissed. If the House had pronounced judgment after Lord Shand's death, however, there would have been a majority in favour of allowing the appeal. So it was decided to hold a fresh hearing. Curiously, however, the Lord Chancellor's original intention was to add three new judges, Lords Alverstone, James of Hereford and Kinross, to the surviving five, so as once again to produce an even number (eight). It was only because Lord Kinross stood down that, at the second hearing, the House comprised the more usual, odd, number of judges (seven).

76. *The Scotsman*, 9 June 1904, p. 6.

77. *The Scotsman*, 10 June 1904, p. 4. Lord Kinross died the following year without ever sitting judicially in the House of Lords, but he had sat in the Privy Council at the end of April and beginning of May 1904. See, for example, *Smith v Macarthur* [1904] A.C. 389 and *Newfoundland Steam Whaling Co. Ltd v Government of Newfoundland* [1904] A.C. 399. Cf. (1904) 12 Scots Law Times (News) 3.

78. It was noticed at the time that Lord Kinnear and Lord Moncreiff, both peers, would have been eligible, but neither had been asked to sit. So far as the last-minute problem is concerned, replacing Lord Kinross with either of them in time for the start of the hearing would have been, at best, problematical.

79. (1904) 12 Scots Law Times (News) 30. *The Scotsman*, 10 June 1904, p. 4, approved of Lord Kinross's decision. See the interesting note in (1904) 16 Juridical Review 205–6 referring to *Hall v Hall* (1891) 18 R. 690, where Lord Low's name appears both as counsel for the second party and, at p. 697, as one of the consulted judges. As counsel, he had signed the minute of debate. See also pp. 69–71 and 72–3.

80. 'Notes from London' (1904) 20 Scottish Law Review 182; McNeill, *The Free Church Case*, p. vi. The arguments were, however, reported extensively in *The Scotsman*, 10 June 1904, p. 7; 17 June, p. 6; 18 June, p. 10; and 24 June, p. 6.

81. Cairns, pp. 227 and 230, letters from Dr MacEwen of 10 and 14 June 1904. He was a former United Presbyterian member of the United Free team, the other non-legal members being Dr Rainy and Dr Archibald Henderson: Cameron, p. 103.

82. Letters from Dr MacEwen to his wife, dated 10 and 11 June 1904: Cairns, pp. 227–8. Dr MacEwen actually told his wife that their Lordships fell asleep. *Quod raro accidit.*

83. Ibid., pp. 226–7, letters of Dr MacEwen to his wife dated 9 and 10 June 1904. See also ibid., p. 228, letter of 11 June.

84. Ibid., p. 226, letter of Dr MacEwen to his wife, dated 9 June 1904; Free Church Appeals, pp. 308 and 405.

85. Cairns, pp. 227 and 231, letters from Dr MacEwen of 10 and 16 June 1904. By contrast, a Free Church observer 'greatly admired the way in which the Lord Chancellor held in hand counsel for both sides ...': Cameron, p. 87.

86. Free Church Appeals, pp. 374–5, 410, 459 and 471–7 (the Dean); 53, 529–32, 544–6 (Haldane).

87. Diary of Sir Edmund Gosse, 21 June 1904, as reproduced in R. F. V. Heuston, *The Lives of the Lord Chancellors* (Clarendon Press, Oxford, 1964), pp. 195–6. Almost certainly, Lord Robertson had already made up his mind after the first hearing. Sheriff Guthrie's impression after the first day of the first hearing had been that 'Robertson wants to be against us if he possibly can': letter of 26 November 1903 to Mrs Guthrie, reproduced in Orr, *Lord Guthrie*, p. 137. After the first day of the second hearing, 9 June 1904, Dr MacEwen wrote to his wife that the Lord Chancellor and Lord Robertson were palpably against them, Lord Davey mainly so; Lords Lindley and Macnaghten were in their favour and so the case would turn on the views of Lords James and Alverstone: Cairns, p. 226.

88. Life of Rainy vol. 2, p. 322.

89. Dr MacEwen in his letter to his wife, 11 June 1904: Cairns, pp. 228–9. A brilliant description.

90. Life of Rainy vol. 2, p. 312.

91. Cameron, p. 87.

92. In the Free Church Appeals volume, the speeches of counsel for the appellants (Johnston KC and Salvesen KC) occupy roughly 164 pages, plus 11 pages of reply by Mr Johnston, while the speeches of counsel for the respondents (the Dean of Faculty [Asher KC] and Haldane KC) take approximately 213 pages. The substance of Johnston's speech is denounced by Carnegie Simpson, Principal Rainy's henchman and biographer: Life of Rainy vol. 2, pp. 316–21. In a letter to his wife dated 10 June 1904, Dr MacEwen reported that Johnston had been as effective as he could have been – although there was a good deal of misrepresentation: Cairns, p. 227.

93. Letter of Dr MacEwen to his wife, 11 June 1904: Cairns, p. 229.

94. Life of Rainy, p. 227; R. B. Haldane, *An Autobiography* (Hodder & Stoughton, London, 1929), p. 76.

95. Stewart and Cameron, p. 205. See, however, Haldane's retort in a speech in East Lothian: *The Scotsman*, 13 October 1904, p. 7. See also p. 106.

96. E.g., R. B. Haldane, 'The Appellate Courts of the Empire' (1900) 12 Juridical Review 1, reprinted in R. B. Haldane, *Education and Empire: Addresses on Certain Topics of the Day* (John Murray, London, 1902), p. 131 (an address to the Scots Law Society, with Lord President Balfour presiding, on 8 January 1900: (1900) 7 Scots Law Times (News) 139); Viscount Haldane, 'The Work for the Empire of the Judicial Committee of the Privy Council' (1921) 1 Cambridge Law Journal 143 (an address to the University Law Society on 18 November 1921); Viscount Haldane, 'The Judicial Committee of the Privy Council' (1923), reprinted in R. B. Haldane, *Selected Essays and Addresses* (John Murray, London, 1928), pp. 218–37.

97. Haldane, *An Autobiography*, p. 52. Accepted uncritically by Heuston, *The Lives of the Lord Chancellors*, pp. 189–90.

98. Note, however, that at the first hearing the Dean and Haldane both favoured Guthrie making the second speech for the United Frees: Orr, *Lord Guthrie*, pp. 137–8.

99. Haldane, *An Autobiography*, p. 76.

100. Letter from Dr MacEwen dated 11 June 1904: Cairns, p. 229.

101. At the first hearing Haldane's argument does not seem to have been so elaborate and he did not, apparently, encounter so many problems with the judges: *The Scotsman* 5 December 1903, p. 7, and 8 December 1903, p. 7.

102. Diary, 21 June 1904, as reproduced in Heuston, *The Lives of the Lord Chancellors*, pp. 195–6. The reference is to R. B. Haldane, *The Pathway to Reality: Stage the First: being*

the Gifford lectures delivered in the University of St Andrews in the Session 1902–1903
(John Murray, London, 1903) and *The Pathway to Reality: Stage the Second: being the Gifford lectures delivered in the University of St Andrews in the Session 1903–1904* (John Murray, London, 1904).

103. Life of Rainy, vol. 2, p. 322.

104. Not least the astute Free Church team: Stewart and Cameron, pp. 207–8.

105. Afternoon of 20 June 1904, Free Church Appeals, p. 486. 'Haldane did not begin very effectively this afternoon': Letter of Dr MacEwen to his wife dated 20 June 1904: Cairns, p. 232.

106. 21 June 1904, Free Church Appeals, pp. 493–4. The date of Sir Edmund's diary entry would suggest that this was the session that he was describing.

107. A. E. Taylor, *Elements of Metaphysics* (Methuen & Co., London, 1903).

108. F. H. Bradley, *Ethical Studies* (Henry S. King & Co., London, 1876).

109. W. Vatke, *Die menschliche Freiheit in ihrem Verhältniss zur Sünde und zur göttlichen Gnade wissenschaftlich dargestellt* (G. Bethge, Berlin, 1841), i.e. 'Human Freedom in its Relationship to Sin and to the Mercy of God scientifically described'.

110. Free Church Appeals, p. 494.

111. A. J. Balfour, *The Foundations of Belief, being Notes Introductory to the Study of Theology* (Longman, Green & Co., London, 1895).

112. R. F. V. Heuston, 'Judicial Prosopography' (1986) 102 Law Quarterly Review 90, at p. 104.

113. Free Church Appeals, p. 495. See also Haldane, *An Autobiography*, p. 77. But the sense that Haldane is failing to communicate runs right through the report of his speech and the interventions of the judges.

114. Free Church Appeals, p. 502. Although Dr MacEwen thought that Haldane's metaphysics might read as overdone and 'so it was in a way', he also thought that it had brought over Lord Alverstone: 'Indeed, things look a little brighter, not much': Letter dated 21 June 1904: Cairns, p. 233. In hindsight, at least, not his most perceptive comment.

115. Elizabeth S. Haldane, *From One Century to Another* (Alexander Maclehose & Co., London, 1937), pp. 211–13. As she records, sitting in the gallery opposite was Lady Frances Balfour, the formidable Churchwoman, biographer of Lord Balfour of Burleigh, and daughter of the eighth and first Duke of Argyll who, as Marquis of Lorne, had supported the non-intrusionist position in the events leading to the Disruption. See George Douglas Eighth Duke of Argyll, *Autobiography and Memoirs* (edited by the Dowager Duchess of Argyll, John Murray, London, 1906) vol. I, Chapter VIII.

116. *The Times*, 2 August 1904, p. 11. The order was drafted by Lord Robertson: Taylor Innes, pp. 243–4.

117. The result, including the majority, had leaked out: Life of Rainy vol. 2, p. 327. Lord Davey apparently told Dr Rainy that he had originally written an opinion in favour of the United Frees, but became convinced that it was not sound in law: ibid. vol. 2, p. 334. Taken as a whole, Simpson's account gives some impression of the atmosphere in the House when the speeches were being delivered and of the manner of their delivery: ibid. vol. 2, pp. 327–43.

118. On the decision, see N. J. D. Kennedy, 'The Free Church Cases' (1904) 12 Scots Law Times (News) 75–7 (hostile, despite the fact that – as Cameron, pp. 82–3, notes – the House was reversing the Second Division whose performance in other cases he

had so much criticised); J. R. Christie, 'The Free Church Cases' 12 Scots Law Times (News) 77–80 and 84–8 (favourable, by the junior counsel for the Free Church) and C. N. Johnston (Lord Sands), 'The "Obiter" of the Free Church Case' (1904) 12 Scots Law Times (News) 122–3 (by the Procurator of the Church of Scotland). There is a brief editorial at 12 Scots Law Times (News) 73. See also A. T[aylor] I[nnes], 'Church Law and Trust Law' (1904) 16 Juridical Review 314–16 (mixed); A. Taylor Innes, 'The Creed Crisis in Scotland' (1904–5) 3 Hibbert Journal 217–36 (critical, but mainly on the Model Trust Deed point, which was not pressed by counsel); J. Ferguson, 'The Scottish Church Case' (1904) 16 Juridical Review 347–60 (balanced); M. Williamson, 'The Free Church Case' (1904) 20 Law Quarterly Review 415–26 (balanced). The most interesting legal critique of the decision is to be found in F. C. Lowell, 'The Free Church of Scotland Case' (1906) 6 Columbia Law Review 137–60. The criticism is based, however, on a wholly different approach to the working of trust law in these circumstances and really presupposes (at p. 145) that the House should not have applied the *Craigdallie* case. That is, of course, a legitimate point of view for an academic writer to take, but *Craigdallie* had long been regarded as settling the law on the point in Scotland.

119. *Journals of the House of Lords* 1 August 1904, pp. 298–302.
120. The Lord Chancellor's disquisition on the subject was much criticised, but even Dean Asher had clearly found the point very difficult. See Life of Rainy vol. 2, pp. 329–33. For contemporary criticism, see also Macpherson, *The Scottish Church Crisis*, pp. 7–30.
121. For the reaction of the United Free supporters to the disposal of this point, see Life of Rainy vol. 2, pp. 344–51.
122. *Craigdallie* v *Aikman* (1813) 5 Paton 719; (1820) 6 Paton 618.
123. D. G. Mitchell, *Life of Robert Rainy, D.D.* (John J. Rae, Glasgow, n.d. [1907]), pp. 206–7.
124. G. F. Barbour, *The Life of Alexander Whyte D.D.* (Hodder & Stoughton, London, Toronto and New York, 1923), p 443, quoting a speech by Whyte.
125. Life of Rainy vol. 2, pp. 351–2.
126. Haldane, *An Autobiography*, p. 75.
127. R. Mackintosh, *Principal Rainy: A Biographical Study* (Andrew Melrose, London, 1907), Appendix, p. 134. Referring to Haldane and the judges, he says, at pp. 132–3: 'Bluff Englishmen do not like to have acrobatic feats forced upon their minds. They thought it jugglery when he explained, very fully, that opposite statements may, and indeed must, both be true. He frightened them, but he persisted; and then he irritated them. All this made them less than ever likely to listen to his evidence. The plainest bit of common-sense, from him, was suspected as a new mystification.' John Buchan thought that 'there cannot have been many cases where the Bench received less assistance from the Bar'. He singled out Haldane's philosophical argument 'based upon familiar Hegelian formulas' for criticism and observed that 'Lord Haldane's masculine intelligence dealt harshly with Mr Haldane's metaphysics.' See J. Buchan, 'The Judicial Temperament', in J. Buchan, *Homilies and Recreations* (Thomas Nelson & Sons, London, 1926), p. 207, at pp. 228–9, reprinted in (1999) 73 The Australian Law Journal 260, at p. 268. The essay is omitted from the third edition of *Homilies and Recreations* published in 1939.
128. *The Times*, 2 August 1904, p. 8.
129. A suitably pathetic account of the practical effects of the judgment is to be found in Life of Rainy vol. 2, pp. 473–6 – a pale imitation, however, of Brown's *Annals of the Disruption*.

130. For United Free criticism of the judgment as unnecessarily causing a great national scandal, see Life of Rainy vol. 2, pp. 354–8. On the reaction of Lord Chief Justice Alverstone to the furore, see The Right Hon. Viscount Alverstone, *Recollections of Bar and Bench* (Edward Arnold, London, 1914), pp. 263–4, with the comments of Lord Shaw of Dunfermline, *Letters to Isabel* (Cassell & Co., London, 1921), pp. 190–2, and *Thomas Shaw (First Lord Craigmyle): a Monograph by his Son*, pp. 47–8. As Lord Shaw points out, Lord Alverstone's account is astonishing in that he appears to be unaware that the United Presbyterian Church, so far from being a party, had been absorbed into the United Free Church and was not involved in any way in the proceedings. For Lord Davey's idea of what should be done, see the letter from X to *The Times*, 26 September 1904, p. 8. The correspondent was actually Taylor Innes: Taylor Innes, p. 244; Life of Rainy vol. 2, pp. 381–2.

131. See Cameron, p. 91 and further, at pp. 93–6.

132. On 18 October 1904 the proceedings before the Second Division of the Court of Session on the petitions to apply the judgment of the House of Lords were unusually lively and protracted, the aim of the United Frees being to delay in the hope that Parliament would come to the rescue. See Life of Rainy vol. 2, pp. 383–4. On that occasion the court made avizandum on the question of whether to send the case to the Summar Roll for debate. See *The Scotsman*, 19 October 1904, p. 9. On Saturday, 22 October the Division, Lord Young dissenting, decided that the case should not be sent to the Summar Roll since the court's function in applying the judgment of the House was purely ministerial. The court granted the prayer of the petition: *The Scotsman*, 24 October 1904, p. 10. On this stage in the dispute, see Cameron, Chapter VII.

133. The Free Church brought interdict proceedings against Principal Rainy and others to prevent the United Free Church from using the college. The case first came before the Lord Ordinary on the Bills (Lord Pearson) in a hearing at his residence on the evening of 18 October 1904 after the Second Division had made avizandum, earlier that day, on the petition to apply the judgment of the House of Lords. On that occasion he refused interim interdict and ordered answers: *The Times*, 19 October 1904, p. 8; *The Scotsman*, 19 October 1904, p. 10. After an opposed hearing, on 27 October, he granted interim interdict: *General Assembly of the Free Church v Rainy* (1904) 12 Scots Law Times 387. For a case concerning the use of the church at Strathpeffer, which, it was argued, was not within the very terms of the judgment of the House of Lords, see *General Assembly of the Free Church of Scotland v Johnston* (1905) 7 F. 517.

134. Morrison, *Manual of the Church Question in Scotland*, pp. 37–87; Stewart and Cameron, pp. 267–8, 283–4 and 293–4. Morrison's *Manual* contains an extraordinary amount of detailed information about the property in dispute.

135. See, in particular, Life of Rainy vol. 2, Chapter 26; also Haldane, *An Autobiography*, p. 75; Lord Shaw of Dunfermline, *Letters to Isabel*, pp. 182–90, trying – as always, unsuccessfully – 'to keep [himself] out of all this story'. See also *Thomas Shaw (First Lord Craigmyle): a Monograph by his Son*, pp. 47–50.

136. Life of Rainy vol. 2, pp. 393–7, 407–10, and 413–17. A second Commission under Sir John Cheyne dealt with the temporary arrangements needed to deal with the immediate problems facing congregations: Life of Rainy vol. 2, pp. 410–13.

137. For a one-sided account of the Commission and its elaborate proceedings, see Stewart and Cameron, Chapters XIII–XV; Cameron, Chapter IX.

138. 20 Scottish Law Review 182.

139. Stewart and Cameron, p. 208.

140. Cameron, p. 87.

141. Cairns, p. 232, letter of Dr MacEwen to his wife, 17 June 1904.

142. Orr, *Lord Guthrie*, p. 137. In letters at the time he tended to indicate that all might not be lost: Life of Rainy vol. 2, pp. 325–6.

143. *The Scotsman*, 2 August 1904, p. 4.

144. So, surely correctly, Stewart and Cameron, pp. 245–7. As already mentioned, Guthrie, the legal adviser of the Free Church before the Union, had been very conscious of the risks: Orr, *Lord Guthrie*, p. 136.

145. E.g., by *The Scotsman*, 5 August 1904, p. 8: 'The leaders of the Free Church [i.e. Principal Rainy, etc.] know that a few years ago legal opinions were given against the Union. Apparently these are all accounted as of no importance. Yet the then leaders of the Free Church must have known of them, and must have been certain that the resolution to carry out the Union was not unchallengeable.' *The Scotsman* had long been hostile to Rainy.

146. Taylor Innes, p. 227; Life of Rainy vol. 2, p. 213.

147. Life of Rainy, p. 213.

148. Taylor Innes, p. 228 and pp. 229–30.

149. In fact, it was called off at the General Assembly of that year. For the prolonged struggle, see Ross, pp. 14–27; Life of Rainy vol. 1, Chapter VII.

150. J. Begg, *Memorial with the Opinions of Eminent Counsel in regard to the Constitution of the Free Church of Scotland* (Johnstone, Hunter & Co., Edinburgh, 1874), pp. 101–234. In 1873, a proposal was put before the Free Church for mutual recognition of certain ministries. Dr Begg saw this proposal as posing essentially the same threat as the Union proposal, but eventually the two sides were reconciled. In that connection, Begg prepared a memorial for the opinion of the Solicitor General, William Watson (Lord Watson), but it was not published: ibid., p. VI.

151. Their opinion for Dr Begg, at pp. 246–54, does not bear a specific date in 1873, whereas the two other opinions were dated in April 1873. By 28 April, however, the supporters of union had heard that the anti-unionists had the opinion of *inter alios* Clark and Balfour, 'favourable in some sense or other': N. L. Walker, *David Maclagan F.R.S.E.* (T. Nelson & Sons, London, Edinburgh and New York, 1884), p. 102, reproducing Maclagan's journal entry for that date.

152. Begg, *Memorial*, p. 247.

153. Begg, *Memorial*: opinion of John Millar (Lord Craighill), pp. 234–5, and of Edward Gordon (Lord Gordon), p. 238. Excerpts from Millar's opinion were reproduced in a letter from Vindex, *The Scotsman*, 10 August 1904, p. 10.

154. Taylor Innes, pp. 205–6; see also Life of Rainy vol. 1, pp. 188–94.

155. Walker, *Donald Maclagan*, pp. 107–8, Maclagan's journal entry dated 20 May 1873. Counsel did not consider that the proposal on mutual recognition involved any question on establishment and thought that opponents of the plan would find it most difficult to raise any question as to the Church property. Maclagan's journal shows that Carnegie Simpson was wrong to say that the question of establishment was not raised with counsel: Life of Rainy vol. 1, at p. 194.

156. See *The Scotsman*, 22 September 1874, p. 4, and 26 September, p. 4, and McCrie, *The Church of Scotland: Her Divisions and Re-Unions*, p. 258 n. 1.

157. Taylor Innes, pp. 212–13.

158. Taylor Innes, pp. 210–13.

159. Begg's book had been sent along with the memorial to Haldane and Balfour: Orr, *Lord*

Guthrie, p. 145. The British Library copy comes from the library of Viscount Haldane.

160. Life of Rainy, pp. 226–7; Taylor Innes, p. 230–1. Taylor Innes hints that there was some difficulty in getting agreement that Asher should be consulted. Asher was not asked about the property held under the Model Trust Deed.

161. Life of Rainy, p. 227. See p. 101.

162. As he explained to the Assembly in May 1900, the Procurator had deliberately consulted Balfour because he was the only survivor among the counsel consulted in 1873: *Proceedings and Reports of the General Assembly of the Free Church of Scotland 1900*, p. 161

163. Taylor Innes, p. 232.

164. Life of Rainy, pp. 227–8; Stewart and Cameron, p. 101; cf. also Ne Obliviscaris, 'The Appeal to Caesar', *The Scotsman*, 4 August 1904, p. 5.

165. (1872) 26 L.T. (N. S.) 704, at p. 706.

166. Letter of 26 August 1904 from Guthrie to Mr John Nicholson reproduced in Orr, *Lord Guthrie*, pp. 144–5.

167. *The Scotsman*, 18 August 1904, p. 5.

168. Indeed, if this had not been so, the attitude of that most stout of all defenders of spiritual independence, Dr Begg, in obtaining and publishing the opinions of counsel on the property question, would have been incomprehensible.

169. See, in particular, pp. 14–15 above. As explained at pp. 26–7, the Claim of Right departed from this position, to some extent.

170. *The Scotsman*, 10 August 1904, p. 6.

171. Stewart and Cameron, pp. 257–60.

172. Life of Rainy vol. 2, pp. 423–40; Taylor Innes, pp. 242–6.

173. 1906 Act I.

174. See Lord Sands, *Dr Archibald Scott*, Chapter 9. The opinion had been given in 1900 by Dean of Faculty Asher QC, Professor (later Sir John) Rankine QC and Mr Constable. Part of the opinion is reproduced in Taylor Innes, *The Law of Creeds in Scotland*, pp. 137–40.

175. The proposed Bill raised an issue of principle since it involved Parliament passing an Act to reverse, with retroactive effect, the decision of the House of Lords and, in large measure, to hand victory to the losing party. Such legislation is, of course, not unknown, but it is rare. See, for example, section 3 of the Compensation Act 2006, reversing, for victims of mesothelioma, the effect of the decision of the House of Lords in *Barker* v *Corus UK Ltd* [2006] UKHL 20; [2006] 2 A.C. 572. In 1905 Lord Robertson's protest against the legislation attracted no support: Second Reading Debate, 31 July 1905, The Parliamentary Debates, 4th Series, vol. 150, columns 849–58.

176. The clause became section 5 of the Churches (Scotland) Act 1905. On the steps by which the Act was eventually passed, see Life of Rainy vol. 2, Chapter 28. The idea of taking advantage of the situation occurred to figures in the Church of Scotland within a few days of the judgment: Lord Sands, *Dr Archibald Scott*, pp. 130–4. The various steps by which section 5 was eventually secured are very fully discussed in chapter 10 of the same work. See also Lady Frances Balfour, A *Memoir of Lord Balfour of Burleigh K.T.* (Hodder & Stoughton, London, 1925), pp. 147–50. For the Free Church perspective on this move, see Stewart and Cameron, pp. 302–4. The Free Presbyterian view was that the section was 'skilfully though not creditably engineered by astute ecclesiastics': Synod's Statement of Differences between the Free Presby-

terian Church and the other Presbyterian Churches in Scotland, reprinted as Appendix III in *History of the Free Presbyterian Church of Scotland*, pp. 228–52, at p. 229.

177. The social background to the move for reunification is well described in Henderson, pp. 135–42.

178. D. M. Murray, *Rebuilding the Kirk: Presbyterian Reunion in Scotland 1909–1929* (T. & T. Clark, Edinburgh, 2000), pp. 32–4.

179. See R. Sjölinder, *Presbyterian Reunion in Scotland 1907–1921* (T. & T. Clark, Edinburgh, 1962); D. M. Murray, *Freedom to Reform: The 'Articles Declaratory' of the Church of Scotland 1921* (T. & T. Clark, Edinburgh, 1993).

180. For an account of those days, see, for instance, Lady Frances Balfour, *Life and Letters of the Reverend James Macgregor D.D.* (Hodder & Stoughton, London, 1912), Chapter XIV.

181. Sjölinder, *Presbyterian Reunion*, especially pp. 182–5, 290–6 and 363–7.

182. (1870) 8 M. 921, at p. 925.

183. Bayne, p. 218. For a survey of the decisions, by an author with very different sympathies, see Macgeorge, in Story (ed.), *The Church of Scotland Past and Present* vol. IV, pp. 104–7.

184. The public interest in the topic can be gauged by the packed hall and the special editions of the newspapers which were run off to give the latest news of the debate in the 1912 General Assembly: Balfour, *A Memoir of Lord Balfour of Burleigh K.T.*, p. 152.

185. This was not the first attempt to deal with the matter. For instance, in 1886, as part of his campaign against the disestablishment of the Church of Scotland, Mr R. B. Finlay, MP – the future Lord Chancellor, Viscount Finlay – introduced a Bill to declare the Constitution of the Church of Scotland. Similar bills were introduced in three sessions down to 1896. The aim was to identify 'matters spiritual' and to declare that the Church courts had the sole and exclusive right to regulate, determine and decide all such matters within the Church, with the procedure, regulations and decisions of the Church courts on these matters not being subject to any manner of review by any court of civil jurisdiction.

186. On the Act, see Lyall, *Of Presbyters and Kings: Church and State in the Law of Scotland*, Chapter V.

187. S.I. 1926 No. 841, which came into force on 28 June 1926.

188. 2006 S.C. (H.L.) 1, at p. 12, para. 40; [2006] 2 A.C. 28, at p. 43, para. 40.

189. So, in effect, Lord Justice Clerk Aitchison in *Ballantyne v Presbytery of Wigtown* 1936 S.C. 625, at p. 654, rejecting the view that the Act 'did nothing to recognise the wider claims of the Church ... to legislate and adjudicate finally in all matters of doctrine, worship, government and discipline, as matters that lay peculiarly within its own province.'

190. Auchterarder Report vol. 2, p. 10. See pp. 71–2 above.

191. In fact, however, because the reform took place gradually as charges fell vacant, even fifty years later, the Teind Judge – the second most junior Lord Ordinary – still sat briefly every few weeks to deal with routine motions.

192. Murray, *Rebuilding the Kirk*, Chapter 5. Haldane, by now Viscount Haldane, turned up again, this time chairing the departmental Committee on the Property and Endowments of the Church of Scotland, which was set up in April 1922 to explore the problems. It reported in April 1923. He carried the matter forward when he was Lord Chancellor in the short-lived Labour Government of 1924.

193. The United Free Church obtained the opinion of H. P. Macmillan KC (the future Lord Macmillan and a son of the Free Church manse) and Oswald Dykes on whether the United Free Church would carry its whole rights and property into a union on the proposed basis. Counsel confirmed that it would: Memorial for the Law Committee of the United Free Church of Scotland for Opinion of Counsel, printed as an Appendix to the Report on the Conference with the Church of Scotland, in *Reports to the General Assembly of the United Free Church of Scotland 1928*, pp. 13–31.

194. Their position, and their unhappiness at the way that they were treated, can be seen in J. Barr, *The United Free Church of Scotland* (Allenson & Co. Ltd, London, 1934), especially Chapters XV and XVI.

195. Murray, *Rebuilding the Kirk*, pp. 1–2, contains a brief description of the day's events.

196. Lord Osborne considered that position in more detail in *Logan v Presbytery of Dumbarton* 1995 S.L.T. 1228.

197. This formulation deliberately omits the now defunct intermediate appeal to the synod.

198. 2006 S.C. (H.L.) 1, at p. 40, para. 152; [2006] 2 A.C. 28, at p. 75, para. 152. There is no indication of the reasons why the special commission procedure was thought not to meet the requirements of the Directive.

199. Lord Justice Clerk Aitchison long ago warned that 'If past history affords any guidance for the future, such an interference could not be other than calamitous': *Ballantyne v Presbytery of Wigtown* 1936 S.C. 625, at p. 658.

200. 2006 S.C. (H.L.) 1, at p. 12, paras 40–1; [2006] 2 A.C. 28, at pp. 43–4, paras 40–1.

201. *Marleasing SA v La Comercial Internacional de Alimentación SA* C–106/89 [1990] E.C.R. I–4135.

202. 2006 S.C. (H.L.) 1, at p. 32, para. 124, and pp. 33–4, paras 130–3; [2006] 2 A.C. 28, at pp. 65–6, para. 124, and pp. 67–8, paras 130–3.

203. It might be said that the more broadly the Article is worded, the greater the extent of the exclusive jurisdiction of the Church.

204. Section 82(1) of the Sex Discrimination Act 1975.

205. Above, p. 92.

206. 2006 S.C. (H.L.) 1, at p. 30, para. 118; [2006] 2 A.C. 28, at p. 63, para. 118.

207. A. Taylor Innes, *Church and State: A Historical Handbook* (2nd edition., T. & T. Clark, Edinburgh, 1890), p. 226 n. 1 at p. 227.

208. A. Macgeorge, in Story, *The Church of Scotland Past and Present* vol. IV, p. 1, at pp. 76–104.

209. A. Taylor Innes, *Mr. Finlay's Bill and the Law of 1843* (Macniven & Wallace, Edinburgh, 1886), p. 34, quoted by Macgeorge in Story, *The Church of Scotland Past and Present* vol. IV, p. 1, at p. 120.

210. *Of Presbyters and Kings: Church and State in the Law of Scotland*, pp. 48–9.

211. Auchterarder Report vol. 2, p. 4. See also *Presbytery of Strathbogie* (1840) 2 D. 585, at p. 606. See p. 16 above.

212. See, for instance, the powerful passage in the dissenting judgment of Lord Moncreiff in the *Stewarton* case: Stewarton Report, pp. 123–7; also *Cruickshank v Gordon* (1843) 5 D. 909, at pp. 971–3, per Lord Ivory (dissenting).

213. *Cuninghame v Presbytery of Irvine* (1843) Stewarton Report, p. 62. See the comments of Lord Moncreiff: Stewarton Report, p. 125. In *Middleton v Anderson* (1842) 4 D. 957, at p. 1010, Lord Gillies was reduced to imagining 'cases that can never happen.' Which is as good a way as any of describing the situation envisaged by Lord

Justice Clerk Hope. In the first *Auchterarder* case Lord Corehouse was more cautious, not going further than indicating that damages would be available in his rather more complex hypothetical situation: Auchterarder Report vol. 2, pp. 235–6.

214. 10 March 1812, 16 Faculty Collection 544.

215. E.g., 'It has been said that there must be a sovereign jurisdiction in every country to which, as controlling all inferior judicatories, a right of appeal must lie': 16 Faculty Collection 544, at p. 546. In the *Stewarton* case, referring to the *Corstorphine* case, Lord President Boyle commented that 'the exclusive jurisdiction of the Church courts was strenuously, though unsuccessfully maintained, in a most able and elaborate argument by one of your Lordships' number in the other Division, in which almost the whole authorities referred to in the present case were brought to bear upon the question': Stewarton Report, p. 142.

216. 16 Faculty Collection 544 at p. 549.

217. (1829) 3 W. & S. 441.

218. 3 W. & S. 441, at p. 448.

219. Auchterarder Report vol. 2, p. 250, per Lord Fullerton. Lord Gillies made the point that, when the presbytery failed to perform a ministerial duty, there was really no exercise of judgment to appeal to the higher ecclesiastical courts, ending with the General Assembly: Auchterarder Report vol. 2, p. 43.

220. See, for instance, Auchterarder Report vol. 2, p. 76, per Lord Justice Clerk Boyle, and pp. 447–8, per Lord Cuninghame; Stewarton Report, p. 142, per Lord President Boyle.

221. For the evolution of his thinking, compare A. Dunlop, *Law of Patronage and Settlement of Parochial Ministers* (William Blackwood, Edinburgh, T. Cadell, London, 1833), Chapter VIII, especially paras 296–305, and A. Dunlop, *Parochial Law* (2nd edition, William Blackwood, Edinburgh, T. Cadell, London, 1835), Chapter VIII, paras 296–304, with A. Dunlop, *Parochial Law* (third edition, William Blackwood & Sons, Edinburgh and London, 1841), Chapter VIII, especially paras 297–305.

222. The question of the relationship of the Court of Session and the Justiciary Court is argued with great sophistication in the judgment of Lord Jeffrey in the first *Auchterarder* case: Auchterarder Report vol. 2, pp. 363–4 and 373–7. See also Lord Cockburn: Auchterarder Report vol. 2, p. 409. For an analysis of Lord Jeffrey's position, see Robertson, pp. 238–46.

223. Robertson, pp. 239–40.

224. Intervention in the abortive proceedings on 26 May 1838 relating to the Rev. Robert Young's protest against the Presbytery of Auchterarder: *The Scotsman*, 30 May 1838, p. 3. For the proceedings, bordering on farce, see Buchanan vol. 1, pp. 486–90; Bryce vol. 1, pp. 68–72.

225. Stewarton Report, p. 179. The argument was criticised at the time on the not wholly convincing ground that it ignored the role of the ever changing juries in preventing the Justiciary Court from persisting in an erroneous course: *The Scotsman*, 25 January 1843, p. 2.

226. Stewarton Report, p. 162.

227. Indeed in the first *Auchterarder* case Lord Moncreiff emphasised that 'the General Assembly is a body of quite another character from any court which has merely the powers of a court of justice. It not only can decide judicially the cases which come before it, but it has power *to pass laws*, from time to time, on all the subjects which belong to *its own jurisdiction* and *that of the presbyteries*; and to deny this is, with

submission, to remove one of the essential foundations of the constitution': Auchterarder Report vol. 2, p. 345 (emphasis as in the original).

228. XX, 'The Scotch Church Question: Letter II', *The Times*, 22 May 1843, p. 7.
229. R. S. Candlish, *Tracts on the Intrusion of Ministers No IX* (J. Johnstone, Edinburgh,
10 August 1840), pp. 3–4.
230. See p. 21 above.
231. Macfarlane, p. 92.
232. *A Letter to the Lord Chancellor*, pp. 35–9, referring, in particular, to populist passages
in Dr Chalmers' speech on the Veto Act in the General Assembly of 1839.
233. *A Letter to Lord Melbourne*, p. 139: 'It is impossible not to sympathise with a Scottish
peasant, when, with regret, but at the same time, with firmness, he turns his steps away
from the parish church where his fathers worshipped, and resorts to the dissenting
meeting-house, where the word of life is faithfully and earnestly preached. There are
many such peasants in our land. ...' Dr Bryce too spoke of Scotland's 'pious and
religious peasantry': Bryce vol. 2, p. 418. The rural population was seen as pious by
comparison with the unchurched urban masses whom Dr Chalmers aimed to reach
through his Church Extension schemes.
234. Chalmers, *What ought*, p. 25 and, more generally, pp. 25–7.
235. Turner, p. 5 – one of the Forty Thieves.
236. Chalmers, *What ought*, p. 26.
237. Stewarton Report, pp. 128–9.
238. Letter of Lord Jeffrey to Lord Cockburn, 12 April 1838, Adv. Ms. 9.1.10 f. 952, at
f. 957. The text, as copied out by Lord Cockburn's daughter, Jane, gives 'fiat': 'Thus I
foretell. And let it come to pass.' But it may be that Lord Jeffrey, whose writing was
notoriously difficult to read, wrote 'fiet'. That would be more consistent with him just
predicting future events, without wanting them to come to pass: 'Thus I foretell. And
it will come to pass.'
239. Hanna vol. 4, p. 339. The accuracy of the report of this famous, and supposedly
private, remark is presumably confirmed by Lord Cockburn's allusion to it: *Life of Lord
Jeffrey with a Selection from his Correspondence* vol. 1, p. 391.
240. So described by Macfarlane, p. 83.
241. The impossibly complicated negotiations and setbacks are elegantly summarised by
Henderson, pp. 86–91. See also, Brown, *The National Churches of England, Ireland,
and Scotland, 1801–1846*, pp. 303–4 and 355–6.
242. Chadwick, *The Victorian Church* Part I, Chapter III.
243. H. J. Laski, 'The Political Theory of the Disruption' (1916) American Political
Science Review 437, reprinted as H. J. Laski, *Studies in the Problem of Sovereignty* (Yale
University Press, New Haven; Oxford University Press, London, 1917), Chapter II.

Index

The notes references are to the page on which the note is printed.

Teaching the Teachers

The History of
Jordanhill College of Education
1828–1993

Edited by
MARGARET M. HARRISON
and
WILLIS B. MARKER

FOREWORD BY JAMES McCALL

JOHN DONALD PUBLISHERS LTD
EDINBURGH

In memory of
HENRY PEART WOOD
1908-94

Principal of Jordanhill College
from 1949-71
'a wise and enlightened leader'

ISBN 0 85976 436 2

British Library Cataloguing in Publication Data
A catalogue record for this book is
available from the British Library

Typeset by WestKey Limited, Falmouth, Cornwall
Printed and bound in Great Britain by Bell & Bain Ltd, Glasgow.

Contents

Foreword by James McCall
Dean of the Faculty of Education

The merger of Jordanhill College of Education with the University of Strathclyde on 1 April 1993 to form its Faculty of Education marked the end of a significant period in the development and delivery of teacher education and indeed of other courses of professional education in Scotland. For over 70 years the twin copper clad towers of Jordanhill College have been prominent physical landmarks in the west of Glasgow and throughout the same period the name Jordanhill has become synonymous with developments in professional education and training, initially of teachers but in later years also for other professions, and it is therefore fitting that this history should be published at this time.

The authors of the various chapters of this volume, all of whom are either current or former members of staff, trace the history of Jordanhill from its origins in 1828 in the Drygate in Glasgow, to its present position as one of the major providers of initial and continuing professional education in the UK, and offer insights into the impact its staff and students have had on national and international developments.

This however is not simply a history of an institution, rather it is a history of developments in education and training for a range of professions— teaching, social work, speech therapy, community education, physical education and sport. It is set in the context of a particular institution, its staff and its students and shows how they not only reacted to changes in the requirements imposed by society and government, but also contributed to and shaped developments in theory and practice at home and abroad. As the authors clearly demonstrate, many of the issues which confronted our predecessors are still with us today: questions of supply and demand ; of quality; of the relationship between theory and practice in professional education; of partnerships between higher education institutions and those in the professions they serve; of resource constraints; of increasing accountability; of individual professional autonomy and collective responsibility.

Readers of this volume who are already familiar with some of the history and work of Jordanhill College, its staff and its alumni, will find much to broaden their understanding through the contextualisation of developments in both the chronological and thematic sections of this history. For those who come relatively fresh to the work of the college this book provides carefully researched material against which they can compare their own experiences and make their own evaluations as to the impact of Jordanhill.

The motto of Jordanhill College as granted in the Court of Arms by The Lord Lyon King of Arms was *Ut Et Alios Instruam*, 'in order that I may instruct others'. This book and the ongoing work of the Faculty of Education continue that noble activity.

Glasgow, 1996   *James McCall*

Editorial Preface

Jordanhill College, throughout its long history, has been best known as the major provider of teacher education in Scotland (hence the title of this book), but in more recent years it has also played a prominent part in the education of social workers, community educators and speech thereapists. Now that it is no longer a separate institution, we felt that it should not fade into oblivion without that history being recorded. The writing of such a history has its pitfalls. If it is done by 'insiders' it may become simply a celebration of the institution's achievements. Or, in order to commemorate the many people who have contributed to its work, it may become a catalogue of names and dates. We have tried to avoid these pitfalls and to produce a reasoned history of Jordanhill within its educational and political context. Some may say that critical comments are too muted. Others may regret that people who gave sterling service to the college receive little or no mention. We recognise that this is so, but constraints of space make it inevitable.

The history has been planned in two parts. The first six chapters give an overview of the college's history from the founding of the Glasgow Normal Seminary to the merger with the University of Strathclyde. Chapters 7–16 deal in greater detail with particular aspects of that history. This means that there is some overlap between the two parts as significant events have to be mentioned in both.

We wish to record our thanks to our colleagues on the Editorial Board, Dr Peter Hillis and Professor Douglas Weir, and to our contributors. Also to the library staff at Jordanhill, particularly Anne Blair and Anne McGunnigle, and to the many others who helped by providing information or by being interviewed. For financial assistance we are grateful to the University of Strathclyde and to the Retired Staff Association of Jordanhill. Acknowledgement is due to Miss Margaret Patton for permission to reproduce the photograph of her father, to the University of Aberdeen for allowing us to reproduce the photograph of Miss Milligan and to Brian Lochrin and Neil McLennan for the modern photographs of college events and activities. The remaining illustrations are taken from the Jordanhill Archive collection.

Glasgow, 1996

Margaret Harrison
Willis B. Marker

Timeline

1973 BEd in Speech Pathology and
       Therapeutics
1974 Opening of Wood Building
1975 BEd in PE and Human Movement
       (CNAA)
1976 Student sit in   1977 Campaign against college closures
1981 Takeover of Hamilton College   1981 Closure of Hamilton, Callendar
                                                     Park and Craiglockhart Colleges
1983 End of secondary BEd   1983 SED Action Plan
1984 BEd degree for primary teachers   1984 All-graduate entry to primary
                                                     teaching
1986 Last intake to SSPE   1986 Introduction of Standard Grades
                                                     STEAC report
1987 BTechEd and BEd in Music
1991 BA in Community Education
1992 BA in Social Work   1992 SHEFC – end of binary line
1993 Merger with Strathclyde University

Abbreviations

ALCES	Association of Lecturers in Colleges of Education in Scotland
AST	Association of Speech Therapists
AUPE	Associateship in Upper Primary Education
BSST	British Society of Speech Therapists
CAST	Curriculum Advice and Support Team
CCC	Consultative Committee on the Curriculum
CCETSW	Central Council for the Education and Training of Social Workers
CEC	Central Executive Committee (of the NCTT)
CI	Central Institution
CNAA	Council for National Academic Awards
COSLA	Convention of Scottish Local Authorities
CST	College of Speech Therapists
CP	Committee of Principals
CQSW	Certificate of Qualification in Social Work
EIS	Educational Institute of Scotland
FTE	Full time equivalent
GPC	Glasgow Provincial Committee for the Training of Teachers
GSST	Glasgow School of Speech Therapy
GTC	General Teaching Council for Scotland
HMI	Her Majesty's Inspector
HMCI	Her Majesty's Chief Inspector
HMSCI	Her Majesty's Senior Chief Inspector
IVPC	Internal Validation Procedures Committee
JBG	Jordanhill Board of Governors
JBS	Jordanhill Board of Studies
JCCES	Joint Committee of Colleges of Education in Scotland
NCTT	National Committee for the Training of Teachers
NCITT	National Committee for the Inservice Training of Teachers
NICCET	National Inter-college Committee on Educational Technology
PGCE	Postgraduate Certificate in Education
ROSLA	Raising of the school leaving age

SCEEB	Scottish Certificate of Education Examining Board
SCES	Select Committee on Education and Science
SCET	Scottish Council for Educational Technology
STEAC	Scottish Tertiary Education Advisory Council
SCOSDE	Scottish Committee for Staff Development in Education
SCOTCAT	Scottish credit accumulation and transfer scheme
SCOVACT	Scottish Council for the Validation of Courses for Teachers
SCTT	Scottish Council for the Training of Teachers
SED	Scottish Education Department
SOED	Scottish Office Education department (from 1991)
SAFIS	School and agency focused inservice (from 1987)
SFEU	Scottish Further Education Unit
SFE	School of Further Education
SFIS	School focused inservice
SLT	Speech and language therapy
SSFE	Scottish School of Further Education (from 1989)
SSPE	Scottish School of Physical Education
UVP	Unified vocational preparation

1

David Stow

Glenda White

When, in 1894, Glasgow University introduced its first MA course in education, listed among the set books was *The training system of education* by David Stow. On the face of it this is quite astonishing. By then the original book was more than 60 years old: even the 11th edition, published in 1859, must have seemed out of date to end-of-the-century students. Its author, dead for 30 years, had been a silk merchant all his life, having gone out to work straight from school. Apart from his early experiences as a Sabbath school teacher he had never taught regularly. A couple of marble busts, the ubiquitous portrait, the name of a college of further education, a plaque on the house where he was born and a faculty building: these appear to be all that have survived from a lifetime's service to education. Except, that is, for his books.

Yet the pedagogy described in his books, and exemplified in the infant and juvenile schools and two teacher training colleges established during Stow's lifetime, influenced generations of teachers and their pupils. Children from the infant schools were taken the length and breadth of Scotland to demonstrate the efficacy of their education and the prospectus produced to establish the first infant school in the Drygate became the paradigm for similar schools in other parts of the country. As early as 1838, the Marquis of Lansdowne reported to a Parliamentary Select Committee that 'all the improvements in education worth mentioning which had appeared in England of late years could easily be traced to the Glasgow Normal Seminary'.[1] During the period 1845–1886, the Dundas Vale Normal Seminary trained 3,181 teachers including 447 from the Wesleyan Church. Many of these went to the colonies, taking the principles enshrined in *The training system* with them. During the same period 3,274 teachers were trained at the Free Church Seminary in Cowcaddens Street.[2] One of the rectors of the Glasgow Normal Seminary became principal of a normal college in America. *The training system* itself ran to 11 editions in 25 years. Thus, although the full extent of Stow's influence has never been fully researched, his books were clearly a persuasive vehicle for conveying his ideas to a wide audience.

David Stow was born in Paisley on 17 May 1793. A plaque in Stow Street, named after land owned by the family, was erected a century later to mark his birth. His family appears to have been well established and prosperous: William, his father, became the town magistrate. His mother, Agnes, was a major influence on his life, particularly in religious and moral matters. He had at least four sisters and possibly two brothers. He attended Paisley Grammar School, receiving an education which he later compared disparagingly with his own pedagogical approach. In 1811, at the age of 18, Stow joined his brother in law in business in Glasgow, six years later becoming a partner in the firm of Wilson, Stow and Company. It was this expanding silk firm, first merchandising and later manufacturing, that financed Stow's educational ventures over the next 40 years. He married twice. Both wives, and two sons and a daughter predeceased him.

Sabbath schools

In his early twenties Stow became acutely aware of the effects of the unremitting poverty afflicting the children of his city. He had taken lodgings south of the River Clyde and since he worked in Argyle Street he spent most of his days in and around the Saltmarket. Here he witnessed the calamitous effects of the poor living and working conditions associated with the beginnings of the industrial revolution. Although the death rate from disease was high, the birth rate was rising: in 1821, 48% of the population was under 20 years.[3] In addition, soldiers returning from the Napoleonic wars swelled an influx of Highlanders and Irish seeking employment in the city. Stow's local parish consisted of overcrowded, insanitary, disease-ridden tenements, inhabited by a poorly paid and often unemployed population. Traditional family values had been disrupted and crime was rife.

In 1815, Dr Thomas Chalmers arrived from Anstruther to become the minister, first of the Tron Church and then of St John's Parish in the Gallowgate. David Stow became one of his elders and so began a friendship which deeply influenced his social conscience and which, in turn, was the inspiration for much of his educational work. Although Chalmers quickly instituted a better organised form of poor relief, Stow came to realise that what the poor needed was a basic education in literacy, numeracy, hygiene, religious and moral values and, above all, the restoration of their self respect. Since many of the young people were working all week in local mills and factories, Stow rented a room in the Saltmarket for half a crown a week and opened a Sabbath School.

During the next ten years it was these 'unruly children' whose 'tricks and Sabbath pranks might fill a volume'[4] who taught Stow a philosophy and methodology that was to be the basis of *The training system*. He learned how to keep control of too many children with no resources and no clear idea of what to teach, how to differentiate between children of differing ages and attainment, how to get to know the children and their family backgrounds, and how to nurture each child's dignity and self worth. 'Thus', wrote Stow, 'the germs of the leading features and peculiarities of the system were worked out for seven years at least, before I attempted, or at least effected, their introduction into a Model and Normal school on weekdays'.[5]

He continued as a Sabbath school teacher at least until 1838. Altogether, he founded seven local societies which maintained 37 schools. His greatest satisfaction lay in training youngsters from his own Sabbath school to establish and teach in others. His first group, acting like 'a hive of bees'[6], founded 15 schools with 350 children in one district alone. If Stow had achieved nothing else, he might be remembered for this. 'From that squalid lane', says Fraser, his first biographer, 'processes were instituted which affected the history of thousands, and changed for generations the character of a town district'.[7]

The first infant school in the Drygate
By 1824, however, Stow recognised that although Sabbath schools made an important contribution to the education of the poor, not least in teaching people to read, their overall effect was very limited. Of necessity, the curriculum was narrow; the children were tired; the two hours of moral teaching were quickly undone by six days surrounded by vice; and the older pupils, in particular, had already acquired intractably hostile attitudes to authority. By contrast, full time education removed children from their environment for the greater part of the day and provided more opportunities for developing positive relationships. Moreover, Stow believed that children aged between two and six were more susceptible to both moral and educational influences. Full time attendance at an infant school was clearly the answer, but the cost was prohibitive.

The Glasgow Infant School Society was formed in 1827. The main aim was to provide an infant school for children aged two to six years,

> with the view of imbuing their opening minds with the knowledge of religious truth, of training them up in habits of obedience and good order and of giving them such elementary instruction, as may prepare them for entering with advantage into Parochial and other schools.[8]

This last point is interesting, since it makes clear that the Society's original aim was to feed children into the established educational system. In fact, juvenile and industrial schools were provided in turn, as the children taught in the infant school grew older. The annual report of 1829 also makes it clear that the Society intended to influence other educational institutions.

Their own infant school would be a 'model school' which others, recognising its worth, could copy. The Glasgow Society would furnish apparatus at cost price, advise on the erection and maintenance of a school, and even offer financial assistance.

The Society issued a 'Prospectus' stating the aims of infant education, and describing the benefits and teaching methods employed in infant schools. Although some public discussion ensued, it was not enough to raise the substantial funds required for the purchase of a property. Consequently, a cottage in the Drygate was leased for a period of seven years. It is generally concluded that the school opened on 23 April 1828. Mr and Mrs David Caughie were recruited as teachers and Samuel Wilderspin, an agent of the London Infant School Society, was hired for the first month to train them. By the end of this period, the children were ready for a public examination. In a magnificent publicity stunt the children, neat and scrubbed, were taken to the Gaelic Chapel in Hope Street in carts decorated with greenery. Crowds lined the streets and a thousand people attended. They were enchanted with the children's appearance, behaviour and knowledge. The spontaneity of the children's replies to questions was refreshingly honest and original. One boy, asked to explain the meaning of the terms 'suspended' and 'supported' took out a piece of string weighted with a button which he first hung to show 'suspended' and then held on the palm of his hand to indicate 'supported'. The response of the public to this delightful spectacle was warm and immediate. The Glasgow Infant School Society was launched.

Having accomplished the establishment of a Model Infant School in the Drygate, and created an enthusiasm which led to the foundation of five infant schools in Glasgow alone, with many more throughout Scotland, the Glasgow Infant School Society continued to operate on a smaller scale until 1834, by which time the Glasgow Education Association, a similar, but probably separate, society was established. The new Society's aims were formulated, and a committee constituted. An advertisement to this effect was placed in the *Glasgow Herald* on 11 April 1834 and this marks the official beginning of the Society. The first president of the Association was J.C. Colquhoun, MP for Dunbartonshire. On 2 October 1834, Colquhoun chaired a meeting of the Glasgow Education Association on the subject of 'extending the Parochial Schools in Scotland'. It was addressed to the 'Friends of Education and of our Religious Institutes in Glasgow'. Stow was involved on both counts. He could not but decry the paucity of educational provision in the city and any public meeting or society which aimed to improve the situation attracted his support. Another patron was George Lewis, whose well known pamphlet, *Scotland: a half educated nation*[9], was first issued under the auspices of the Society.

The formation of the Educational Society and Stow's involvement with it, marks a turning point in his career. Although the Society adopted the Drygate School as its Model Infant School, its overt aim was the training of teachers rather than the teaching of children. Stow always held an affection for young children and argued that the training of teachers should begin and end with practice in the teaching of infants, when the 'final polish' to their training was added. Nevertheless, his attention and financial resources were now directed towards students rather than the infants he had served so well.

The beginnings of teacher training
In the appendix to *Granny and Leezie*[10] Stow, referring to the opening day of the Infant school in the Drygate, wrote:

> Two teachers on the same day were enrolled as Normal students,[11] with a view to two schools in Glasgow, in the process of being erected in neighbouring parishes, to be conducted on the same system.

This reference to teacher training is confirmed in the second annual report of the Glasgow Infant School Society, 1830: 'During the course of the year, our teacher (Mr Caughie) has given instruction in the Art of Infant Tuition to several individuals, some of whom are now employed in different parts of Scotland as Infant School Teachers'.[12]

Although we do not know what form this training took, it seems reasonable to regard it as the beginning of organised teacher training in Scotland—a view endorsed by Rusk[13] and by the centenary celebrations in 1928. However, the originality of training teachers attached to an infant school must not be overstated. Stow himself had brought in Samuel Wilderspin to train the Caughies and many visitors had attended Robert Owen's infant school in New Lanark. Indeed, from 1815 to 1828 there was a lively debate throughout the UK about infant schools, their rationale, administration and methodology, and contacts among such influential men as Robert Owen and James Buchanan, the teacher in the New Lanark school, Wilderspin, Stow, Lancaster, Bell and Pestalozzi may be surmised. There was such a noticeable similarity among the various institutions that it seems likely that they were all based on commonly held beliefs and procedures.

Nevertheless it was important that Stow established the principle that teachers should be trained. Caughie's apparent success in training teachers in the Model Infant School in the Saltmarket then convinced the Glasgow Educational Society to adopt the school as part of their envisaged system of teacher training:

Here had been trained almost all the teachers of Infant Schools at present in Scotland, now between 40 and 50 in number, and it was the knowledge of its previous success as a training school, under the charge of its experienced teachers, that induced the Society, at once to give the preference to this school, and to adopt it as part of their Normal Seminary for the professional training of Schoolmasters. The idea of the Society was that every young man desirous of the benefits of the Society's Model Schools should pass a certain period in the Infant School, in order to be thoroughly initiated into the system of Bible lessons—lessons in natural history, elliptical and interrogatory methods, mutual responses, etc.—and afterwards to pass into the Juvenile Model School; on his dismissal from which he would receive from the Society a certificate of qualification. This was the first step towards a Normal Seminary.[14]

Just 18 months after this speech, in November 1836, the foundation stone was laid for the first Normal Seminary in Britain, the precursor of Jordanhill College of Education. The costly and ambitious building in Dundas Vale, opened on 31 October 1837, could accommodate 1000 children and up to 100 students in three model schools: an infant school, a juvenile school and a female school of industry. In all, there were 16 classrooms, a students' hall and five playrooms. Students, both men and women, were lodged in recommended accommodation nearby and followed just such a pattern of teacher training as that described above. They spent part of their eight hour day in study and part in observing model lessons conducted by their tutors. This was followed by the dreaded 'crit' lessons when the students' own performances were subjected to criticism by their peers and masters. Most students could afford to stay only for the minimum course of six months, although some managed the year's course recommended by the Society. The low salaries offered by Scottish schools both dissuaded students from studying longer and encouraged them, once trained, to take up posts in England, where rates of pay were substantially higher.

The interest aroused by the foundation of the Glasgow Normal Seminary, and its influence throughout the world, was substantial. The Select Committee on Education of the Poorer Classes in 1838 took evidence from Dr James Kay[15] (later Sir James Kay Shuttleworth) on the Glasgow Seminary, in formulating a policy for teacher training in England. 15 teachers were trained and sent out to New South Wales and Van Diemen's Land in 1837, at the instigation of John Dunmore Lang.[16] One of those teachers later described his training at Glasgow in evidence to a government commission on education in Australia.[17] Many more teachers were sent out to the colonies, including Nova Scotia[18] and Cape Breton[19], and the system was publicised in America by Alex Dallas Bache[20] and George Combe.[21]

The post of Rector had excited the interest of Thomas Carlyle,

It is likely that they will want, as Jane says, a Chalmers-and-Welsh kind of character; in which case: *va ben, felice notte.* If otherwise, and they ... had the heart, I am the man for them. Perhaps my name is so heterodox in that circle, I shall not hear at all.[22]

History does not record with what emotions the managers received this application.

The Normal Seminary was plagued by problems almost from its inception. The first Rector, Mr McCrie, having spent seven or eight months visiting normal schools in France and Germany, died of typhus before the Seminary opened. A government inspection in 1841 reported that only 55 students were enrolled, placing an inevitable burden on maintenance costs. In addition, the capital costs had not been paid off. At the time, the offer of state aid in the form of £5,000 towards capital costs and £500 per annum towards maintenance, in exchange for transfer of management to the Church of Scotland, must have appeared very reasonable. It can be envisaged how much of the remaining debts, many owed to local tradesmen, were paid from the profits of Stow's expanding silk firm. Only a few years later, the Disruption of the Church of Scotland robbed him of the college which many regard as the pinnacle of his educational achievement.

Towards a theory of education

Stow's conception of the education of young children was not original. The justification for his place in the history of education lies in his evolution of a coherent educational philosophy, worked out in practical detail, which others could emulate. Four fundamental tenets underlie this philosophy.

Firstly, one of Stow's most significant insights was that, whatever the social consequences of the industrial revolution, there was no going back, and any rational system of education must focus on the peculiar problems of urban society. In order to make appropriate provision for the large numbers of children requiring education, given the limited resources available, Stow classified town populations into 'wealthy', 'sinking', 'sunken' and 'uprising' classes. The wealthy could make arrangements for the education of their own children. Similarly, the 'uprising class' were already making use of the few facilities available, sending their children to 'model schools' or to private academies. Of the 'sunken class', consisting of the 'openly vicious, the wandering, the neglected, also beggars, thieves and the abandoned', Stow despaired. He noted, ironically, that the greatest provision was already made for this class in the form of prisons, penitentiaries, and asylums. Stow therefore argued that 'the sinking class ought to be the objects of our most intense interest'.[23] Without positive discrimination, the sinking class would enlarge the ranks of the sunken.

But even concentrating resources on this one group was expensive. City parishes would have to provide not one but several schools, each with a teacher and school house. The financial burden would fall initially on the parish concerned, but those in the areas most needing schools were also the least able to provide funds. In the absence of state funding, the wealthy had to be persuaded to contribute. Stow marshalled several arguments to persuade them to contribute to working class education. He emphasised the advantages of keeping children off the streets; of training them to be responsible members of the community with respect for personal and state property; of preparing a generation of factory workers conditioned to habits of punctuality, regular attendance, hard work and honesty; of producing a literate electorate necessary for enlightened democracy; of politically controlling the population through moral training; and of releasing the mothers to work in the mills and factories without anxiety over their children.

Although he advanced utilitarian reasons, Stow's own motivation, strengthened by evangelical zeal, was the moral regeneration of society. The intellectual aspirations of rich and poor might differ, but their moral instruction must be equal, and society was responsible for the moral welfare of all its members. Charitable contributions alone could not cope with the disaster of the cities. Stow argued forcibly that the state must intervene. After pointed references to the cost of prisons and penitentiaries; to the 20 millions spent on the emancipation of slaves and to the 40 millions squandered at Waterloo, he concluded on a contemporary note: 'We must, however strange, talk as familiarly of millions for education as we were wont to do for war ...'[24]

Stow's second main tenet was that education must take place within the social context of the family and the community. His arguments centred around the twin concepts of 'assistance' and 'interference'. Where parents were making adequate provision for their children's education, the school should seek to assist but never supersede them. However, where parents provided for the physical needs of their children, but abdicated responsibility for their intellectual and moral growth, then society was bound to interfere:

> Allowed to go unprotected in the midst of crowded streets by the carelessness of parents, or locked up in dreary solitude during their necessary absence at work, the accidents to which children were exposed, the vicious habits they contracted, and the state of squalid wretchedness in which they grew up, loudly called for interference.[25]

Stow continued: 'The command 'train' is of course addressed to parents and what they cannot accomplish personally they are bound to 'do by proxy'.'[26] Nevertheless, Stow was against removing children from their parents and placing them in asylums 'thus breaking up every family tie'.[27] Even the ineffectual family was of paramount importance to the child, and to the formation of his links with society.

Thirdly, Stow contended that education must result in a change of behaviour. His definition of education as 'training',[28] not 'teaching', referred to the method by which children acquired intellectual or physical skills and moral habits. 'Teaching' was a didactic process involving instruction and occasionally demonstration, where the child remained the passive recipient of the teacher's knowledge or the text book's information. 'Training', on the other hand, involved active participation in one's own learning. The child was led to deduce knowledge from given information, to practise skills and to acquire moral habits through natural situations and events: 'Education consists not in the mere amount of knowledge communicated, but in the due exercise of all the faculties whereby the pupil acquires the power of educating himself'.[29]

In a closely reasoned argument, Stow suggested that in physical exercise the concept of training the child had always been obvious. Children were not merely told or instructed in the skill but actually put it into practice. Stow extended this argument to the field of intellectual and moral growth. In training the intellect, Stow drew the teaching material initially from the child's need to understand, and therefore master, his environment. The coal on the fire, the wood used for furniture, the wool and cotton in the children's clothes were all suitable topics for oral lessons. The intellectual advantages were two-fold: the curriculum was relevant to the child and therefore stimulating; and the child could be trained to use his own powers of observation, analysis, deduction and previous experience to create his own learning. Children learned how to learn, a process which laid the foundations of lifelong education.

Stow argued that the method was just as successful in the field of moral education, since there was ample first hand experience on which the teacher could build. The teacher observed the children in the playground, 'the uncovered classroom', and used the incidents as a basis for moral training. Thus children learned respect for the property of others by not picking the blackcurrants in the playground; they learned honesty by admitting to misdeeds; and they learned social justice by sitting in judgment on their peers' behaviour. Teachers were encouraged to follow the children into the playground, 'the microcosm of their little world', noting those who were active, quiet, leaders, followers, generous, kindly or bullying. Not only did this provide a context for teaching, it gave an insight into the individual natures of the children when not restrained by unnatural circumstances. Similarly, children were worthy of respect by the teacher, and should neither be bribed by rewards and prizes, nor bullied by punishments, especially corporal punishment. Neither should children be encouraged to compete with one another by ranking, or awarding class places.

The training system

It is somewhat unfortunate that Stow should also use the term 'training' in its more commonly accepted sense, to mean the instruction in his system both for those who provided schools and those who taught in them. For his fourth contribution to a theory of education was the provision of specific and detailed instructions for those who wished to emulate his system. He specified the size and height of school buildings, allowing for an atmosphere of airiness and light, a central fireplace for warmth in winter, room for marching and physical exercises, teaching posts for the display of visual aids to groups, and a raised gallery for class instruction and oral work. Details included provision for an area to hang outdoor clothes, a smaller room for the instruction of older and more experienced pupils and, particularly, an extensive playground with a garden. The playground should be open for an hour after the school closed in winter, or at dusk in summer. Schools should be provided for separate age groups (by contrast with the all-age parish schools) including infant schools (two to six years), juvenile schools (six to twelve years) and industrial schools (12–15 years). Stow also recommended that parents should make some financial contribution, to avoid the taint of charity and to inculcate a sense of responsibility for their children's upbringing. He advocated coeducation on the grounds that the boys intellectually elevated the girls and the girls morally elevated the boys, although he admitted cases where the reverse was true!

He included examples of timetables to be followed, advocating equal amounts of time to be spent in the playground and in as the classroom, and the intermingling of physical exercises with oral training, 'to let off steam'. Despite his emphasis on Biblical and moral training, his curriculum was mainly secular and considerable in its scope. An analysis of the examples of lessons given in *The training system* and the *Glasgow Infant School magazine* indicates that science, natural history, geography, history, mechanics, arithmetic, marching, singing and poetry at least were taught. Resources to support this curriculum were also suggested; sets of apparatus were available from the Glasgow Educational Society and instructions for making wooden bricks, hoops and swinging poles were given. Beyond the resources of the school, however, lay those of the community. The children of the model schools were frequently taken on walks around their district, to the nearby countryside, to gardens and museums, thus gaining first hand experience.

Stow brought both humour and humanity to the teaching of young children. In a witty and readable book, *Granny and Leezie*,[30] he describes the eventual conversion of the grandmother whose 'oes' (grandchildren) are attending the model infant school. 'In my young days', she argues 'we sat hale three hours at a time in the schule, and durstna turn the side o' our head a' the time, for fear o' the taws whistling past our lugs'.[31] Perhaps her oft quoted criticism aptly conveys both the atmosphere of the model infant school and of David Stow's contribution to children's education: 'The schule canna be the right sort when they hae sae muckle fun'.[32] Such a book deserves a place on every training course for teachers!

Notes and references

1 Select Committee on Education of the Poorer Classes 1838. Minute of evidence 5 March 1838.
2 Houseman, R.E. *David Stow, his life and work 1793–1864*. Unpublished MEd thesis. University of Manchester, 1938, p.181.
3 Smout, T.C. *A history of the Scottish people 1560–1830*. London: Fontana/Collins, 1969, p.245.
4 Stow, D. *The training system*. 10th ed. London: Longman, 1854, p.54.
5 *Ibid.*, p.57.
6 Fraser, W. *Memoir of the life of David Stow*. London: Nisbet, 1868, p.65.
7 *Ibid.*, p.62.
8 Glasgow Infant School Society. First annual report, 1829, p.1.
9 Lewis, G. *Scotland: a half educated nation, both in the quantity and quality of her educational institutions*. Glasgow: Collins, 1834.
10 Stow, D. *Granny and Leezie: a Scottish dialogue: Grandmother's visit to the first Infant training school*. 6th ed. London: Longman, 1860.
11 ie Following the 'norm' or 'rule'. The term originated in Prussia and was used throughout Europe.
12 Rusk, R.R. *The training of teachers in Scotland*. Edinburgh: EIS, 1928, p.12.
13 *Ibid.*, p.39.
14 Speech by Mr Lewis of the Glasgow Educational Society, quoted in the *Glasgow Herald* 22 May 1835, and in Rusk, R. *op.cit.*, p.50.
15 Select Committee on Education of the Poorer Classes 1838. Minute of evidence by J.P. Kay MD 5 March 1838, pp.39–41.
16 Undertaking by schoolmasters selected by the Glasgow Normal Seminary for New South Wales and Van Diemen's Land, 20 June 1837, with covering letters by David Stow ... Published in *Historic records of Australia*, series 1, vol.14, p.5.
17 Lowe Committee on Education. Evidence by Peter Steel 9 July 1844. *Volumes and proceedings of the Legislative Council of New South Wales, 1844*, vol.11, pp.519–524.
18 Harvey, D.C. The origin of our Normal School [Nova Scotia]. *Journal of education*, September 1937, pp.566–573.
19 Johnston, H.H. *The contribution of the Scottish teachers to early Cape Breton education*. Dalhousie University, 1973. Unpublished thesis.

20 Bache, A.D. *Report on education in Europe.* Philadelphia: Bailey, 1839, pp.159–166, 178–9, 656–7.
21 Combe, G. *Notes on the United States of North America during a phrenological visit in 1838–39–40.* Edinburgh, 1841. vol.III, Appendix II, pp.443–450. Description of the Normal Seminary of Glasgow by R. Cunningham, Rector. 23 November 1840.
22 Carlyle, T. Letter to his brother John, February 1835. National Library of Scotland, MS 523.28.
23 Stow, D. *The training system.* 1854, p.90.
24 Stow, D. *National education.* London: Hatchard, 1847, p.67.
25 Glasgow Infant School Society. First annual report, 1829, p.9.
26 Stow, D. *The training system.* 1854, p.37.
27 *Ibid.*, p.92.
28 From the Biblical dictum 'Train up a child in the way he should go and when he is old he will not depart from it.' Proverbs 22, verse 6.
29 Stow, D. *The training system.* 1854, p.14.
30 Stow, D. *Granny and Leezie.* 1860.
31 *Ibid.*, p.8.
32 *Ibid.*, p.6.

2

The Church College Period, 1843–1904

Peter Hillis

Introduction

Early in the morning of 18 May 1843 onlookers began to fill the galleries of St Andrew's Church in Edinburgh in order to view the opening of the General Assembly of the Church of Scotland. Many more people waited outside the church in anticipation of an event which was to prove crucial in Scottish history. In the early afternoon the commissioners to the General Assembly entered the church, soon followed by the Royal Commissioner. After an opening prayer proceedings were interrupted when the retiring Moderator rose and told the Assembly that there had been an infringement so great that the General Assembly could not be constituted. In place of the normal reading out of the roll of new commissioners the Moderator read a protest against the attacks made by Parliament and the courts against the Scottish Church. These attacks made it impossible for those who believed in the spiritual independence of the Scottish Church to remain within the Established Church of Scotland. The Moderator laid the protest on the table, bowed to the Royal Commissioner and moved to the door of the church, followed by the Evangelical leaders including Thomas Chalmers. Row after row of commissioners joined the procession until the left, or Evangelical, side of the church was almost empty. The procession made its way to Tanfield Hall, where the commissioners and over 450 ministers signed the Deed of Demission marking their secession from the Church of Scotland. A rival national church, the Free Church of Scotland, had been founded.[1]

Almost two years later, on 8 May 1845, David Stow 'stood for the last time in splendid Normal College'[2] ready to lead a procession from the seminary. He was joined by the directors, 50 students, 700 pupils and every teacher, with the exception of the master of music. The procession, headed by David Stow and Nathaniel Stevenson, a director, threaded 'its course through a multitude lining the streets'[3] as it made its way to a new location in the Cowcaddens area of Glasgow. Temporary accommodation was provided in 'long canvas-covered tents, with a saw-dust floor and with rough benches...'[4] Drawing parallels with events in Edinburgh in 1843 the *Glasgow Herald* labelled the secession from the Church of Scotland Normal

Seminary as the 'Disruption of the Glasgow Normal Seminary'.[5] This large scale withdrawal of directors, staff and students from the Church of Scotland Seminary marked the founding of the Free Church of Scotland Normal Seminary in Glasgow. Its name was later changed to the Free Church Training College and then to the United Free Church Training College, resulting from the merger of the Free Church and United Presbyterian Church, which created the United Free Church in 1900. Although the Church of Scotland Normal Seminary was again fully operational by the late 1840s, the division between both colleges continued until 1905, when they were united under secular control.

The founding of the Free Church Normal Seminary was one example illustrating the widespread impact on Scottish life of the Disruption. The consequences for education have been evaluated in a recent essay by Donald Withrington,[6] while Marjorie Cruickshank's *History of the training of teachers in Scotland*[7] provides a comprehensive account of the Glasgow Church of Scotland and Free Church Training Colleges. This chapter will, therefore, focus on three main areas of each training college. Section 1 will analyse the motives which lay behind the schism in the Glasgow Normal Seminary, in an attempt to explain the delay of two years from the Disruption of 1843 until the secession from the Church of Scotland Seminary in 1845. Section 1 also provides a socioeconomic profile for directors and office bearers belonging to the Established and Free Churches in Glasgow. In an attempt to test some previous assumptions concerning the background of Scottish teachers section 2 analyses students attending the training colleges, with specific reference to age, religious affiliation, social class and county of birth. This section will help to answer the question recently posed by Donald Withrington: 'but where did the Free Church get all its teachers from?'[8] The final section describes and evaluates the curriculum and training provided by the training colleges.

Formation and management of the Free Church and Church of Scotland Training Colleges
The Free Church of Scotland, as befitted its full title, attempted to match the provision made for education by the Church of Scotland. By 1849 over £40,000 had been raised to build 500 schools, with a further £3,500 a year set aside for teachers' salaries.[9] Consequently, it might appear as if the secession from the Glasgow Normal Seminary was part of this wider effort to create a rival establishment to the Church of Scotland. Within the Glasgow Educational Society the majority of directors joined the Free Church but evidence suggests that they were prepared to continue working with the Church of Scotland in the joint provision of teacher training. This offer to cooperate coincided with protracted negotiations between the

Glasgow Society, the Privy Council and the General Assembly over debt incurred on the Normal Seminary. Consequently, it took over two years from the Disruption of 1843 until July 1845 for the foundation stone of the Free Church Normal Seminary to be laid.[10]

Opposition to a joint venture came from the Church of Scotland, whose Assembly insisted that only members of the Established Church could serve as members of staff in the Normal Seminary.[11] Article IV in the Constitution and Regulation of the Glasgow Educational Society stated that, 'All persons, of whatever religious denomination, desirous of being professionally trained as school masters, shall be admissible to the benefits of the Society's Normal Seminary.'[12] Despite the considerable degree of ill feeling between many adherents of the Free Church and Church of Scotland, with terms such as 'dumb dog' and 'stinking moderates' used to describe those who supported the establishment,[13] attempts were made to maintain the non-sectarian provision for teacher training. In a letter dated 21 September 1843 David Stow wrote to James Kay Shuttleworth, Permanent Secretary to the Privy Council's Special Committee on Education, that:

> We are now no better off in this respect with the present established Church Comt. which is in reality an Edinb. Comt. but the new ingredient of the Free Church adds to the difficulty for out of eight who guarantee the debt seven have joined the Free Church and only one teacher remains in the Establishment. All are willing to continue and labor together but the Established Church Comt. threatens to discharge every individual not of the Establishment the moment the Deed is signed.[14]

Stow and six other directors of the Normal Seminary were guarantors for the debt on the building. In March 1841 James Buchanan, treasurer to the Society, informed Stow that the deficit stood at £7,100 but there was 'no demand for immediate payment, provided the interest could be regularly paid...'[15] However, by 1844 the debt had risen to £10,677,[16] which placed added urgency on meeting the conditions placed on a £5,000 grant from the Privy Council. These conditions involved the transfer of the Normal Seminary to the General Assembly of the Church of Scotland, who would match the grant of £5,000 in order to liquidate the debt. Negotiations and attempts to raise £5,000 continued until 1845, so delaying any secession from the Normal Seminary. In 1845 the debt was liquidated and the Normal Seminary 'passed into the possession of the Established Church'[17] who refused to allow adherents of the Free Church to serve as members of staff. David Stow, a majority of directors, pupils and staff left the Dundas Vale Seminary to form the Free Church Training College in a building later called Stow College (no relation to the later further education college of that name).

In June 1845 a Committee of Management was appointed for the Free Church College. This committee comprised nine ministers and ten lay directors, many of whom had served on the committee of the Glasgow Educational Society. Most of its business was taken up by discussions over finance.[18] Prominent among the lay directors were those members who dominated the Kirk Sessions and Deacons Courts of the Free Church, namely, the 'new shoots' of the middle class who had prospered from Glasgow's economic growth.[19] One example was Nathaniel Stevenson, co-leader of the procession from the Normal Seminary in May 1845. Born in 1787, Stevenson began his career in 1803 working for James Dunlop & Sons, owners of a cotton spinning mill in Calton. In 1812 he became a partner in Oswald Stevenson & Company, cotton yarn agents, a firm which continued in existence until 1853. In addition to being treasurer for the Free Church Training College, Stevenson helped in the founding of the 'Infant School System of the Young Men's Christian Association and the City Mission'.[20] Nathaniel Stevenson's progress up the social scale can be seen in a move of residence from 3 Hope Street in 1828[21] to the then west end suburb of 4 Woodside Crescent in 1850.[22]

Similar profiles can be established for many other directors of the Free Church Training College, such as Alexander Wingate, partner in the firm of Black & Wingate, manufacturers and printers in 9 Royal Exchange Square and John Blackie, founder of Blackie & Sons, publishers.[23] It is interesting to note that Blackie published the early editions of David Stow's *The training system* despite the presence of another publisher, William Collins, on the Committee of Management.

The Church of Scotland Training College was also managed by a committee which in 1876 comprised eight ministers and seven lay members.[24] If 'new shoots' describes middle class members of the Free Church then the term 'deep roots' can be applied to their Church of Scotland counterparts, including many of those responsible for the training college. James Alexander Campbell came from a well established middle class background. Born in April 1825, he was the son of Sir James Campbell, Lord Provost of Glasgow 1840–43 and partner in the firm of J & W Campbell, warehousemen, 39 Ingram Street.[25] Sir James Campbell owned the 4,000 acre estate of Stracathro in Brechin, to which James Alexander Campbell succeeded in the 1880s.[26] James Alexander entered the family business but in 1880 became Conservative MP for Glasgow and Aberdeen Universities.[27] His brother, Sir Henry Campbell-Bannerman, had different political loyalties. In addition to his work for the Church of Scotland Training College, James Alexander Campbell was a member of the Privy Council, Deputy Lieutenant for Lanark and Forfar, and LL.D of Glasgow University.[28]

Other lay directors of the Training College in the 1870s and 1880s were: John Neilson Cuthbertson, chemical broker, chairman of Glasgow School Board in 1885 and Knighted in 1887[29]; Daniel Forbes, partner in the firm of Moncrieff Paterson, Forbes & Barr, writers, 45 West George Street; James King, merchant[30]; Andrew Laughlen, civil engineer; Montgomery Paterson, manufacturing chemist of the Whitevale Chemical Works; David Wallace, iron merchant and partner in William Baird & Company, coal and iron masters, Gartsherrie, Blair, Eglinton, Lugar, Muirkirk and Portland Works.[31] In 1876 Wallace lived at Lochwood House, Coatbridge.[32] It was possible for aspirant members of the middle class to assume positions of responsibility within the Church of Scotland Training College. Nonetheless, the general trend was that the lay directors of both colleges were drawn from those sections of the middle class who dominated the respective denomination. The course of events surrounding the formation of the Free Church Training College indicated that it was not always 'excessive Free Church zeal'[33] which led to secessions from the Church of Scotland. In the provision of teacher education some prominent members of the Free Church were prepared to continue working with the Church of Scotland. Opposition to any such cooperation came from the establishment, although both colleges remained surprisingly non-sectarian in their recruitment of students.

The student body
The normal method of entry to both training colleges was through the pupil teacher system, whereby future teachers were indentured at the age of 13 to serve a five-year apprenticeship with a teacher. At the end of this period of training they sat an examination, and if successful were expected to proceed to the two-year course at training college. Scholarships were offered to all successful applicants at open examination but pupil teachers were more successful than other applicants,[34] especially those from rural and Gaelic speaking areas.[35] One consequence of the pupil teacher system was that, as shown in Table 1, most students attending the training colleges were in their late teens, and according to some commentators possessed an inadequate education. In his evidence to the 1866 Argyll Commission into Scottish education, Simon Laurie, secretary to the Education Committee of the Church of Scotland, commented that the system of training teachers had 'lowered their qualifications generally for the special work of Scotch parochial schools... in respect of the small attention which is paid to Latin and Greek.'[36]

Both colleges were financially supported by the state through grants from the Privy Council and the government, while Queen's scholarships and studentships covered student costs at college. Colleges also received a block

TABLE 1

AGE PROFILE OF STUDENTS ATTENDING THE CHURCH OF SCOTLAND
TRAINING COLLEGE, GLASGOW, 1864–1866(i) AND THE FREE CHURCH
TRAINING COLLEGE, GLASGOW, 1855, 1865 AND 1872(ii)

| Age | Church Of Scotland College | | Free Church College | |
	Female students	Male students	Female students (excl.1855)(iii)	Male students
16–18	20	8	19	18
19–21	80	92	90	113
22–24	6	2	8	16
25–35	0	1	3	16
Non recorded	0	0	3	2
Totals:	106	103	123	165

(i) Register of students attending the Glasgow Established Church Training College 1864–1866, Jordanhill Archives. This is the only extant register to give detailed information on students.
(ii) Glasgow Free Church of Scotland Training College register of students 1855–1873, Jordanhill Archives.
(iii) Age was not recorded for 1855.

grant, £500 in 1846, if the church contributed a matching sum. From 1853 lecturers were paid a bonus of £100 per annum if they passed an examination in one of history, geography, physical science and applied science. These sources of income were important to the success of the Free Church College, in particular, which had to meet the substantial costs of the new building in the Cowcaddens. In March 1846 it was reported to the Committee of Management that there was 'a deficiency in funds of nearly Three Thousand Pounds',[37] a deficit which had risen to £3491 by June of the same year.[38] Consequently, the committee 'unanimously agreed to apply to Government for a grant in aid of the Institution',[39] to which the Privy Council responded with a grant of £3,000.[40]

With a system of grants partly determined by the number of students, satisfactory levels of recruitment were important. This partly explains why both colleges were prepared to accept students from a wide range of denominational and religious backgrounds. Table 2 analyses this pattern of adherence, which in one case allowed a Roman Catholic to attend the Free Church College. At a meeting of the Committee of Management in February 1872 the Rector:

brought under the notice of the Committee the case of Lizzie Morgan, a Roman Catholic who had taken the admission examination with the view of attending the school and had passed high enough to entitle her to a scholarship. It was unanimously agreed to grant her scholarship on the usual conditions.[41]

TABLE 2

DENOMINATIONAL ADHERENCE OF STUDENTS ATTENDING THE CHURCH OF SCOTLAND TRAINING COLLEGE, GLASGOW, 1864–1866(i) AND THE FREE CHURCH TRAINING COLLEGE, GLASGOW, 1855, 1864 AND 1872(ii)

Denominational Adherence of Students	*Church of Scotland College 1864–1866*	*Free Church College 1855, 1864, 1872*
Church of Scotland	136	14
Free Church of Scotland	17	229
Baptist	2	1
Church of England	1	–
Congregational	1	–
Episcopalian	3	1
Evangelical Union	1	2
Glassite	–	1
Independent	4	2
Irish Presbyterian	–	1
Old Scotch Independent	1	–
Reformed Presbyterian	6	5
Roman Catholic	–	1
Unitarian	–	1
United Presbyterian	34	51
Wesleyan Methodist	–	6
Unrecorded	3	3
Totals:	209	318

(i)Register of students attending the Glasgow Established Church Training College, 1864–1866, Jordanhill Archives.
(ii)Glasgow Free Church Training College register of students 1855–1873, Jordanhill Archives.

Table 2 underestimates the early importance to the Free Church College of students from the Wesleyan Methodists. Out of 36 students in 1845, 23 'are paid for by the Wesleyan Body',[42] a vital source of revenue in the early years of the institution. It is also interesting to note that the Free Church College was more successful in attracting United Presbyterian students, which suggests that both denominations were sharing resources before formal union in 1900.

Teaching the Teachers

TABLE 3

COUNTY OF BIRTH AND OF FIRST TEACHING APPOINTMENT OF STUDENTS
ATTENDING CHURCH OF SCOTLAND TRAINING COLLEGE, 1849–51 AND
1864–66 (i) AND FREE CHURCH COLLEGE 1855 AND 1872 (ii)

County	Number of students County of birth		Number of students First appointment	
	C of S 1849–51 & 1864–66	FC 1855–72	C of S 1864–65(iii)	FC 1855–72(iv)
Aberdeen	1	6	2	1
Argyll and Bute	22	20	1	6
Angus	–	–	–	1
Ayr	49	37	19	6
Banff	4	1	2	–
Caithness	–	3	–	–
Clackmannan	–	2	1	1
Dunbarton	17	8	8	3
Dumfries	18	3	2	1
East Lothian	1	–	–	1
Fife	5	2	–	–
Forfar	1	10	1	–
Inverness	3	9	–	3
Kincardine	–	8	1	2
Kirkcudbright	5	4	–	–
Lanark	84	55	41	21
Midlothian	5	3	6	–
Moray	1	5	–	–
Nairn	–	1	–	–
Orkney	–	1	–	1
Perth	11	15	4	–
Renfrew	24	5	7	9
Ross and Cromarty	1	7	1	4
Roxburgh	3	–	3	–
Selkirk	1	–	–	–
Stirling	14	3	4	2
Sutherland	1	1	–	–
Wigtown	5	2	2	–
England	5	5	8	13
India	–	1	–	–
Ireland	4	1	–	2
Wales	1	–	–	1
New Zealand	–	–	–	1
East India	1	–	–	–
USA	1	–	–	–

TABLE 3 CONTINUED

County	Number of students County of birth C of S		Number of students First appointment	
	1849–51 & 1864–66	FC 1855–72	C of S 1864–65(iii)	FC 1855–72(iv)
Re-entered (ii)	–	–	–	119
Private teaching	–	–	–	2
Emigrated	–	–	3	–
Died	–	–	1	5
Married	–	–	3	–
Left course due to ill health	–	–	1	1
Unrecorded or county not identified	5	3	21	9
Left teaching/Non-completion of course	–	–	2	6
Totals:	291	221	144	221

(i) Report of the Church of Scotland Education Committee 1851, and Register of students attending the Glasgow Established Church Training College 1864–1866, Jordanhill Archives.

(ii) Free Church of Scotland Training College. Register of students 1855–72. Jordanhill Archives.

(iii) The 1851 report of the Church of Scotland Education Committee did not record the counties in which students gained their first teaching posts. It is not possible to identify where those students who enrolled in 1866 obtained their first teaching post. Most students in the year group would have re-entered in 1867 for the second year of the course, but there is no extant register of students after 1866.

(iv) In any given year approximately one half of the year group re-entered for the second year of the two year course.

The Free Church College also, unusually for that time, trained a student from Japan, Tadashi Nishimura, in 1878–80.[43] Nishimura was one of six students sent abroad to be trained as teachers, at the instigation of Henry Dyer, who had been recruited by the Japanese government to establish engineering education in that country. Dyer was a highly talented young academic from the Glasgow and West of Scotland Technical College, precursor of the University of Strathclyde, and an adherent of the Free Church. Of the six students, three went to America, one each to Germany and France and the other to the Glasgow Free Church Training College.

The non-sectarian constitution of the Glasgow Educational Society continued to be reflected in both training colleges, reinforced by the financial imperatives of student recruitment. The widespread pattern of religious adherence suggests that both colleges recruited students beyond their immediate geographic area. This is confirmed in Table 3 which analyses students' county of birth and county of first teaching appointment.

Reflecting the strength of the Free Church in the highlands[44] its Glasgow College attracted a higher proportion of students, 16.7%, than the Church of Scotland College, 9.2%, from the highland area.[45] Noticeable in Table 3 is the widespread geographic area covered in the recruitment of students despite the concentration on Ayrshire, Lanarkshire and Renfrewshire. Nonetheless, Table 3 would create a misleading impression if it was assumed that students returned to their county of birth for their first teaching appointment. In 1872 only eight male students and three female students in the Free Church College were employed in their county of birth.[46] A similar pattern was evident in the Church of Scotland, as illustrated by William Torrie from Islay, who obtained his first teaching post in Lochwinnoch in 1866.[47] The example of William Torrie taken alongside the more general picture shown in Table 3 suggests that the highland and rural lowland areas were at a double disadvantage in staffing their schools. As previously noted it was more difficult for pupil teachers from these areas successfully to pass the scholarship examinations, so placing an added financial handicap on attendance at training college. Moreover, there was a net outflow of newly qualified teachers from the highland and lowland rural areas into the urban areas, with the enticements of greater job opportunities and, in many schools, higher salaries.

In a student body drawn from both rural and urban areas it might be expected that a wide range of parental occupations would be represented in the training colleges. Some commentators have mentioned the narrow social backgrounds of male students, who were 'usually sons of labourers', while female students were the 'daughters of shopkeepers and clerks'.[48] Other analyses have claimed that students were 'mainly of good working or middle class stock'.[49] It was not possible to compare Free Church and Church of Scotland students, since the Free Church register of students did not record parental occupations. Table 4 shows the social composition of students attending the Church of Scotland Training College, but any conclusions should be seen as tentative. 14 students were recorded as sons or daughters of farmers but no indication was given as to their status in relation to size of farm or tenancy arrangements. Several students came from merchant families but from such descriptions as 'grain merchant' and 'wine and spirit merchant' it was not possible to ascertain the scale of the business. Despite these qualifications some initial conclusions can be drawn.

In the Church of Scotland Training College students were recruited across a broader range of the social spectrum than suggested by the previous quotations, although the majority were classed as related to skilled trades-men. Teaching offered relatively secure employment prospects compared to traditional crafts threatened by mechanisation and the cyclical downturns

TABLE 4

PARENTAL SOCIAL BACKGROUND OF STUDENTS ATTENDING THE CHURCH OF
SCOTLAND TRAINING COLLEGE, GLASGOW, 1864–1866(i)

Parental social background	Female students	Male students
Landed and professional	34 (31.1%)	11 (10.6%)
Public servants	11 (10.3%)	11 (10.6%)
Small merchant tradesmen	13 (12.2%)	11 (10.6%)
Skilled tradesmen	30 (28.3%)	48 (46.6%)
Farm and related workers/ unskilled	15 (14.1%)	22 (21.3%)
Others (dead, father abroad, unspecified)	3 (2.8%)	0 (0%)
Totals:	106	103

(i) Register of students attending the Glasgow Established Church Training College,
1864–66, Jordanhill Archives.

of the British economy. Furthermore, a career in education was seen as 'respectable', an important ambition for many skilled workers.[50] Most male students were from a skilled or unskilled background but a significant proportion, 31%, came from middle class families. Perhaps the most significant trend illustrated in Table 4 relates to female students, of whom almost one-third came from landed and professional families, with the equivalent ratio being one-tenth for male students. With limited opportunities for education and a career, teacher training was seen by many women 'as their only chance'[51] to escape from domesticated middle class life. Nevertheless, while at college the female student studied a markedly different curriculum from her male colleague.

The curriculum

Throughout the Church College period the curriculum of one college was 'practically the curriculum of the other'[52] and, with the exception of the 1860s, steadily expanded to meet the growing number of subjects taught in elementary and secondary schools. In the 1840s the student day, which began at 6.00 am and finished at 10.30 pm, consisted of five hours of instruction in the 3Rs, grammar, syntax, English composition, geography and religious knowledge. This was followed by two and a half hours teaching, with the remaining time devoted to observation and recording. Moreover, there was a weekly lecture in pedagogy and the public criticism lesson given to pupils in the normal seminaries in front of fellow students, the Rector and many of the staff.[53]

A period of contraction was forced on the colleges when the Privy Council issued the Revised Code of 1863. This reduced the financial subsidy, which forced the colleges to reduce the range of subjects and concentrate on reading, writing and arithmetic. Examination results in these subjects determined a school's income from the government. Under the 'payment by results' system, colleges were paid retrospectively for the students they had trained, once those students had completed their two years' probation in an inspected school. Those who took private situations, emigrated, or female students who married, without completing their probation period, represented a loss of income and every attempt was made by the colleges to recover their costs from the students themselves. Many a prospective bridegroom was requested to pay for his fiancee's teacher training![54]

In February 1864 the Free Church College was forced to make some staff redundant[55] but this did not prevent the steady accumulation of debt, which by 1867 had risen to £214.[56] The situation became so serious that the college was only saved from closure by a large public subscription in 1873.[57] However, the expansion of education brought about by the 1872 Education (Scotland) Act forced the government to expand the supply of teachers and increase the grants given to the colleges. Extra staff were recruited and more subjects added to the timetable. Moreover, by 1877 the student regime had become somewhat more relaxed, starting at 8.30 am instead of 6.00 am, with 'ten minutes space... given for relaxation at the end of each hour, and a quarter of an hour for lunch at twelve'.[58] The timetable for first year male and female students by then included science subjects for men, with domestic economy and needlework for women. This reflected the different subjects studied by boy and girl pupils in schools.

These differences between male and female students continued into the 20th century despite a continued growth in the number of subjects. Some subjects could be studied concurrently at Glasgow University in an attempt to raise the academic standards of training college students. This reflected a growing debate in the 19th century over the academic versus professional training of teachers. As noted above, Simon Laurie criticised the low academic standards of pupil teachers in comparison to university graduates who had entered teaching without passing through the training colleges. Similar criticisms were made by James Knight, Head Master of St James's School in Glasgow, who commented that 'on the side of scholarship the system had failed since pupil teachers simply reflected the scholarship of their master, and water cannot rise above the level of its source. When the master was highly educated his pupils were the same, and per contra.' In an even more critical vein Knight continued:

> The testimony of pupil teachers... who have passed through the Training
> College is absolutely unanimous; the two years spent there were a waste of

TABLE 5

GLASGOW CHURCH OF SCOTLAND NORMAL SCHOOL
TIMETABLE OF TRAINING DEPARTMENT 1877[59]

	9–10	10–11	11–12	12–1	1–2	2–3	3–4
Drill at 8.30 am Twice a Week			FIRST YEAR'S MALES				
Mon	Mr Robertson Grammar, School Management Dictation	Mr Dixon Arithmetic, Mathematics	Mr Stevenson History, Geography	Mr Robertson Latin	Mr Stevenson Religious Knowledge, Reading Composition	Mr Dixon Magnetism & Electricity	Mr Forsyth Drawing
Tues	"	Psychology	"	Mr Stevenson Latin and History	Geology	Mr Moodie Music	"
Wed.	"	Arithmetic Mathematics	"	Mr Robertson Latin	Religious Knowledge	Mr Dixon Magnetism & Electricity	"
			The Rector	Mr Stevenson	Reading		
Thurs	"	Psychology	Greek, half an hour.	Latin and Geography	Composition Geology	Mr Dixon Music	"
			The Rector	Mr Robertson			
Fri.	"	Arithmetic Mathematics	Greek, half an hour.	Latin	Religious Knowledge Reading, Composition	Mr Dixon Magnetism & Electricity	"

GLASGOW CHURCH OF SCOTLAND NORMAL SCHOOL
TIMETABLE OF TRAINING DEPARTMENT 1877

	9–10	10–1 1	11–12	12–1	1–2	2–3	3–4
			FIRST YEAR'S FEMALES				
Mon	Mr Stevenson History, Geography etc.	Mr Robertson Grammar, Composition, School Management	Mr Dixon Arithmetic	Miss Foulis Domestic Economy Needlework	Mr Robertson Religious Knowledge, Dictation Reading	French	Mr Forsyth Drawing
Tues	"	"	"	"	French	Mr Moodie Music	"
Wed	"	"	"	"	Mr Robertson Religious Knowledge Dictation	French	"
Thurs.	"	"	"	"	French	Mr Moodie Music	"
Fri.	"	"	"	"	Mr Robertson Religious Knowledge Dictation	Mr Robertson Botany	"

time... while the very mention of School Management as a subject exacts a smile, if not ribald laughter. Others, less severe, praise the Normals for giving a welcome rest after the hard work of apprenticeship... One good thing the Normals have done, they have sent up their best students to the University...[60]

Nonetheless, Knight did acknowledge, perhaps in self contradiction, that the method of teacher training 'produced men and women who were excellent teachers'.[61] A similar conclusion was reached by D. R. Fearon, an inspector of schools from England, who gave evidence on the Scottish system to the Taunton Commission into secondary education in England. Although Fearon did not differentiate between graduates and pupil teachers he reported that teachers 'come to the work better prepared on the whole, and better qualified than the ordinary teachers of middle schools...in England'.[62]

There is some evidence to suggest that a number of students shared the concerns expressed by Laurie and Knight over the quality of teacher training provided by the colleges. In the *Dundas Vale monthly*, student magazine of the Church of Scotland Training College, several articles recommended reform of the training system. In 1899 it was suggested that pupil teachers should spend longer in secondary school 'and thereafter enter the Training College and the University; the former for the acquisition of the art of education, the latter for the continuation of their own studies'. The author did not agree with the suggestion made by Professor Henry Jones of Glasgow University that 'the practical training for the teaching profession... would be sufficiently guaranteed by some practice in a public school, at the close of a University career in arts...' The *Dundas Vale monthly* countered: 'Practical training, if it is to be efficient and thorough, must be undertaken, in an institution set apart for the purpose—in other words, in a Training College.'[63]

Many other comments and reports were equally supportive. Committee of Management members regularly inspected their college and recorded their overall impressions. 'I have been much pleased with the work of the different classes I have inspected' wrote the Reverend Dr Leishman in 1853 after visiting the Church of Scotland College.[64] Educationists from other countries came to observe the training system, as in 1852 when Miss Chessen of the Home and Colonial Training Schools, and Henry Barnard, Superintendent of Common Schools in Connecticut visited the Church of Scotland College.[65] Both colleges were annually inspected by Her Majesty's Inspectors of Schools, whose reports were invariably favourable. In 1898 the inspection of the United Free Church College 'found everything in perfect working order'[66] while in 1876 Her Majesty's Inspector had been happy to report 'in favourable terms regarding...the general working arrangements' of the Church of Scotland College.[67] In the following year the Rector's annual report claimed that the institution was 'in a very prosperous condition.'[68] A note of caution is required for this latter claim, since the Committee of Management minutes for the same year tell a different story of continuing student unrest over the withholding by the

Rector of student bursaries. In June 1877 'crackers were thrown in several classes'[69] and in July 'The students as a body absented themselves from their classes and in a tumultuous and disorderly manner met in the staircase and lobby...'[70] The Rector was found to be largely at fault and he was dismissed, after which relations between staff and students improved, as witnessed in the wide range of activities and clubs including reunion dinners, picnics, a Literary Association, Rambling Club, Football Club and Golf Club.[71]

Despite the efforts made by the colleges to expand their curriculum and run concurrent programmes with Glasgow University, the churches found it increasingly difficult to meet the demand for teachers brought about by the continued growth of elementary and secondary schools. The churches could not find the necessary resources for specialist rooms, gymnasia and well-equipped practising schools.[72] Furthermore, in an increasingly secular century[73] demands were made, even from within the colleges, 'to put an end' to ecclesiastical influence over teacher training.[74] Consequently, in 1905 control over the colleges passed from the churches to the state through the establishment of Provincial Committees for the Training of Teachers. The Church College period was at an end.

Conclusion

Given the close bonds between church and education it was perhaps inevitable that the history of the Free Church and Church of Scotland Training Colleges mirrored religious developments between 1843 and 1905. The secession from the Glasgow Normal Seminary resulted from a major religious schism within the Church of Scotland, while reunion under state control in 1905 illustrated the gradual reduction in the influence of the church over Scottish life. In the introduction to this chapter the question was posed, 'but where did the Free Church get all its teachers from?' This analysis has shown that the colleges recruited students from a wide range of social and religious backgrounds. However, their core support in both managers and students, came from those social classes and areas of Scotland where each church was strongest. The scholastic qualifications of students attracted persistent criticism, but during the 1860s when the state reduced its financial provision, the colleges continued to train teachers funded to a large extent by the churches and their supporters. In response to critical comments, both colleges attempted to raise the academic standards of their students by encouraging attendance at university classes. Few, if any, contemporaries criticised the teaching skills of students. The debate over academic versus professional training continued into the 20th century and will arguably always exercise those involved in teacher training.

Notes and references

1 See Brown, S. and Fry, M. (eds.). *Scotland in the age of Disruption*. Edinburgh University Press, 1993, pp.vii-viii for a fuller account of these events.

2 Fraser, W. *Memoir of the life of David Stow*. London: Nisbet, 1868, p.177.

3 *Ibid.*, p.179.

4 *Ibid.*, p.177.

5 *Glasgow Herald*, 12 May 1845. A more detailed account was given in the *Scottish Guardian*, 9 May 1845.

6 Withrington, D. *Adrift among the reefs of conflicting ideals? education and the Free Church, 1843–1855* in Brown, S. and Fry, M. (eds.). *op.cit.*

7 Cruickshank, M. *History of the training of teachers in Scotland*. University of London Press, 1970.

8 Withrington, D. *op.cit.*

9 Cruickshank, M. *op.cit.*, p.51.

10 Glasgow Free Church Normal Seminary. Minutes, 10 July 1845. Jordanhill Archives.

11 Scotland, J. *The history of Scottish education*, vol.1. University of London Press, 1969, p.314.

12 Glasgow Educational Society. Constitution and regulations. Jordanhill Archives.

13 Macleod, R. Ministerearan an arian? a profile of nineteenth century Hebridean moderates. *Transactions of the Gaelic society of Inverness*, Lii, 1980–2, pp.243–269.

14 Letter from D. Stow to J.P. Kay Shuttleworth, 21 September 1843. Copy in Jordanhill Archives.

15 Letter from J. Buchanan to D. Stow, 30 March 1841. Copy in Jordanhill Archives.

16 Report of the Education Committee of the Church of Scotland, 1844.

17 *Glasgow Herald*, 12 May 1845.

18 Glasgow Free Church Normal Seminary. Minutes, 11 June 1845.

19 See Hillis, P.L.M. Presbyterianism and social class in mid-nineteenth century Glasgow: a study of nine churches. *Journal of ecclesiastical history*, 32:1, January 1981. For a similar conclusion in Aberdeen see MacLaren, A.A. *Religion and social class: the Disruption years in Aberdeen*. London: Routledge, 1974, chapter 5.

20 See *Memoirs and portraits of one hundred Glasgow men*. Glasgow, 1886, vol.2, chapter LXXXV, pp.291–294 for a profile of Nathaniel Stevenson.

21 *Glasgow Post Office Directory* 1828.

22 *Ibid.*, 1850.

23 The other members of the committee were Hugh Logan, Allan Buchanan, Henry Dunlop, James Buchanan and Hugh Brown.

24 Glasgow Church of Scotland Training College. Minutes, 14 November 1876. There is only one extant volume of minutes (1875–77) for this committee. Jordanhill Archives.

25 An account of a testimonial dinner for Sir James Campbell appeared in the *Glasgow Herald*, 16 May 1845.

26 Profile of James Alexander Campbell, unidentified newspaper cutting. Mitchell Library.

27 *Glasgow and Lanarkshire Illustrated*. Hamilton Herald, 1903, p.5. Mitchell Library.

28 *Ibid*.

29 A profile of Sir John Neilson Cuthbertson appeared in the magazine of the Church of Scotland Training College, *Dundas Vale monthly*, February 1905. Jordanhill Archives.

30 Glasgow Church of Scotland Training College. Minutes, 30 April 1877. James King could not be positively identified in the *Post Office directories*.

31 *Glasgow Post Office directory*, 1865.

32 *Ibid*., 1876.

33 Fraser, W. *op.cit.*, p.177.

34 Scotland, J. *op.cit.*, vol.2, p.326.

35 For a discussion on these issues see Cruickshank, M. *op.cit.*, pp.107–111.

36 First report of the Commissioners on Schools In Scotland, 1865–1867, vol.XVII p.120.

37 Glasgow Free Church Normal Seminary. Minutes, 11 March 1846.

38 *Ibid*., 9 June 1846.

39 *Ibid*., 18 August 1847.

40 *Ibid*., 4 January 1848.

41 *Ibid*., 5 February 1872.

42 *Ibid*., 1 December 1845.

43 Letters from Munefumi Hirata to the Librarian, Jordanhill College, 28 January and 10 February 1988. Jordanhill Archives.

44 See for example Hunter, J. *The making of the crofting community*. Edinburgh: J. Donald, 1976, p.96 and Hillis, P.L.M. *The sociology of the Disruption* in Brown, S. and Fry, M. (eds.). *op.cit.*

45 In this example the highland area is taken to include Argyll and Bute, Inverness, Ross and Cromarty, and Sutherland.

46 Glasgow Free Church Training College Register of students 1855–1872, Jordanhill Archives.

47 Register of students attending the Glasgow Established Church Training College, 1864–1866, p.111, Jordanhill Archives.

48 Cruickshank, M. *op.cit.*, p.61.

49 Scotland, J. *op.cit.*, vol.1. p.316.

50 Tholfsen, J.R. The artisan and the culture of early Victorian Birmingham. *University of Birmingham historical journal*, 4, 1954, pp.146–166.

51 *Ibid*., p.327.

52 Editorial entitled 'The Training College'. *Dundas Vale monthly*, October 1904.

53 Cruickshank, M. *op.cit.*, pp.48–49.

54 *Ibid*., p.75.

55 Glasgow Free Church Training College. Minutes, 8 February 1864.

56 *Ibid*., 25 March 1867.

57 *Ibid*., 7 March 1873 for a full list of subscribers.

58 Report of the Church of Scotland Education Committee, 1877.

59 *Ibid.*
60 Knight, J. The training of teachers in Scotland. *Proceedings of the Royal Philosophical Society of Glasgow*, 1901–02.
61 *Ibid.*
62 Report of the Commission of Inquiry Into Education, vol.VI, 1868, p.47. (Argyll Commission).
63 Crookes, F.M. The training system: a criticism and a suggestion. *Dundas Vale monthly*, November 1899.
64 Glasgow Church of Scotland Training College. Committee visiting book, 1849–1853. Jordanhill Archives.
65 Glasgow Church of Scotland Training College. Visitors book June and July 1852. Jordanhill Archives.
66 Glasgow Free Church Training College. Minutes, 15 June 1898.
67 Glasgow Church of Scotland Training College. Minutes, 15 November 1876.
68 Report of the Church of Scotland Education Committee, 1877.
69 Glasgow Church of Scotland Training College. Minutes, 16 June 1877.
70 *Ibid.*, 25 June 1877.
71 *Dundas Vale monthly* in October 1899, November 1899 and May 1900 carried accounts of these activities.
72 Cruickshank, M. *op.cit.*, p.135.
73 The point is discussed in Brown, C. *The social history of religion in Scotland since 1730*. London: Methuen, 1987, chapter 7.
74 Editorial entitled 'The training colleges'. *Dundas Vale monthly*, October 1904.

3

The College Under The Glasgow Provincial Committee For The Training of Teachers

Willis Marker

At the turn of the century, there were two almost completely separate school systems. For working class or lower middle class children, there were the elementary schools run either by the School Boards or by the churches. The Board Schools were nominally non-denominational, but in practice they were Presbyterian. The church schools were mainly Roman Catholic and, to a lesser extent, Episcopalian. For the better off there were various types of secondary school: endowed schools, private venture schools and higher class schools (the old burgh schools which had been transferred to the School Boards). Scholarships and bursaries provided a narrow bridge between the two, over which few could pass.

Despite these limitations, secondary education was growing in importance. The gradual march towards universal elementary education after 1872 inevitably created a demand for something more. From 1888 the Leaving Certificate gave the schools a goal to work towards and in 1892 Secondary Committees were established throughout Scotland to promote developments. One consequence was to add to the administrative confusion. Another was to increase the demand for secondary teachers. With the raising of the school leaving age to 14 in 1901 it became more doubtful whether the teacher training system was adequate to meet those demands.

Teacher training c1900

Arrangements for teacher training were as confusing as those for the schools. Training might be provided by the schools themselves to pupil teachers, who could then qualify by passing the certificate examination; or by one of the church training colleges to which some of the pupil teachers would progress. The universities might also be involved. Since 1873, they had provided academic courses enabling college students to study for a degree concurrently with their teacher training. They had, however, been debarred from professional training until the 1895 Code created a new category of 'Queen's students', whose professional training was organised by Local

Committees in which the universities had a dominant voice.[1] In Glasgow there were four institutions involved in teacher training: the two Presbyterian church colleges, the Roman Catholic college and the university. Unlike the universities at Aberdeen and St Andrews, however, Glasgow was a late and rather reluctant participant. It had never created a Chair of Education and had delayed setting up a Local Committee until 1903.

These arrangements were clearly inadequate. The church colleges, even with university help through the Local Committees, could not expand to meet the growing demand for secondary teachers. The system was ripe for reform. One possibility might have been to move towards the model adopted in England, where university departments of education trained secondary teachers and training colleges, run either by churches or local authorities, trained primary. SED policy was quite different. By this time, the Protestant churches in Scotland were willing to give up their role in teacher training. For SED, local authority colleges were not an alternative, nor was it prepared to see the training of secondary teachers in the hands of universities over which it had no control, and which it believed to have little interest in, or capacity for, teacher training. So the SED agenda was to rationalise teacher training and to bring it under its own centralised control, but this purpose, it felt, was best left partly concealed.

Therefore, when the Committee of Council Minute (January 1905) set up four Provincial Committees based on the notional provinces of the four ancient Scottish universities 'to enlarge and improve existing facilities for the training of teachers', the rhetoric of the preamble spoke of the need to ensure 'that training shall be brought into as close connection with the University organisations as the attainments of the students upon entering admit of'.[2] The new committees were given powers to provide both initial and inservice training, for which they were to receive a government grant, and to take over the existing church colleges. The Local Committees were disbanded and the grants hitherto paid to them transferred to the Provincial Committees. The Provincial Committees had to operate within a tight framework of control by the Department. SED provided the finances, approved the courses and inspected the training centres. Hardly had the Provincial Committees been set up before SED was encouraging them to form a Joint Committee. This held its first meeting in March 1907 and at once began to make recommendations for standardising the system across Scotland.[3] The Glasgow Committee was none too happy about this, expressing the view that 'the Joint Committee is merely a voluntary association existing only for convenience and having no statutory authority',[4] but the pressure towards centralisation remained.

It was within this framework that, on 15 November 1905, the Glasgow Provincial Committee (GPC) for the Training of Teachers held its first meeting. It was a large body: 33 members, heavily weighted towards representatives of the School Boards. Nominally, the churches were marginalised—only allowed co-opted membership. In practice, church influence remained strong through the School Board representatives: ten of the members attending the first meeting were clergy.[5] The new committee was faced with a number of pressing problems. Training was being carried on in five different buildings—the university, Church Street School (Partick), Queen Margaret College (Hillhead), Dundas Vale and Stow College—most of which, according to the Director, were 'entirely unsuitable for the purposes in view'.[6] Right from the start it was recognised that the long term solution was the building of a new college and demonstration school. In the meantime, the committee had to make the best of split-site working, while trying to create a unified staff for what was now one institution.

Initially the former staff of the two church colleges and some of the employees of the Local Committee were transferred to the new centre. The first Director of Studies (Principal) was Donald Macleod, Rector of Hamilton Academy, and the Rectors of the two Church Colleges, T.M. Morrison and A.M. Williams, were appointed joint Rectors under him. The remainder of the staff were then reorganised on a departmental basis, with one lecturer in charge of each subject. Whatever bruised egos there may have been were possibly soothed by the advantages of greater specialisation and the improved salaries the GPC was able to offer, because amalgamation produced economies of scale: increased numbers of students were taught by the same number of staff. On average in the pre-1914 years, there were just over 50 staff for between 1,000 and 1,200 students—a ratio of about 20:1. 70% of the staff were male, about 75% of whom were graduates. As some of the female staff were teaching subjects like needlework and cookery, the proportion of female graduates was nearer 50%.

One important element of their work was largely determined for them. In 1906 the SED followed up the 1905 Minute with a new set of Regulations which, with minor changes, provided the framework for teacher training for the next 60 years. The pupil teacher system was to be phased out, and in future primary teachers were to be trained for at least two years at a college, to which they might gain access by one of two routes: either by completing a course for the Junior Student Certificate or by taking the Higher Leaving Certificate, followed by six months of practical training. Having arrived at college either by these routes or from universities or central institutions, students were trained in three categories, set out in Chapters III, V and VI of the Regulations. Chapter III students were those preparing for the General Certificate, whose purpose was 'to secure a sufficient supply of well-equipped teachers for the ordinary public (ie elementary) schools of the country'. They might be ordinary graduates taking a one-year course, but mostly they came straight from school or from a Junior Student Centre and followed either a two-year or a three-year course; the latter allowed them to take a number of university classes concurrently. Together they made up the bulk of the student population: 1293 out of 1461 in 1908–9. The small group of Chapter V students were honours graduates taking a one-year course to qualify as 'teachers of higher subjects' in intermediate or secondary schools. Chapter VI students were diplomates of central institutions, who also took a one-year course to qualify as 'teachers of special subjects', ie in art, domestic economy, physical training or technical subjects.

Article 55 of the Regulations also gave the Provincial Committee responsibility for 'the further instruction of teachers in actual service'. So inservice classes, offered either in the evenings or during the summer vacation, became a regular feature of its work. Although there were some general interest classes, the staple fare from the 1920s to the late 1950s was the provision of classes for teachers seeking to improve their qualifications, whether endorsements for needlework or drawing under Article 37(b), as an infant mistress under Article 51, as a teacher of an additional secondary subject under Article 39, or as a teacher of the mentally and physically handicapped. These classes gave the college an assured place in inservice work and a firm base from which to expand when curriculum change demanded.

Meanwhile one of the first tasks for the staff at the new training centre was to revise the curriculum within the tight constraints of the Regulations, which laid down that all curricula had to be approved by SED and, in Article 22, that the professional subjects to be taught were personal and school hygiene, psychology, logic, ethics, education, and the methods and practice of teaching. In the two and three-year courses for the General Certificate, these professional studies were combined with general education taught either in the centre or at the university. The two-year students had to take English, phonetics, mathematics and methods, nature study, singing and religious instruction. They also normally took two additional subjects (educational handwork, drawing and applied design, physical training or singing) or one supplementary subject (eg needlework or cookery), and had the option of taking a language.[7] Compared to the curriculum of the church colleges, this represented a swing away from the classics and towards a common curriculum for men and women. The result was a very heavy timetable. Over the two years the timetabled hours in the 1912–13 Prospectus were:

	Year one	Year two
Professional subjects	150	180
Methods & practice	120	150
General subjects	330	250
Additional/supplementary	120	120
Religious instruction	40	40

In addition, those taking the optional language did 90 hours in both years. What was the rationale for this? According to Macleod the new curriculum tilted the balance from general towards professional education because

> if education is to be regarded as a profession, it must concern itself first of all with the study of the professional subjects…The movement in the direction of professional training is not a new thing; it has been in process for many years. The old Regulations brought the movement up to the educational Rubicon; the new Regulations have brought it across it—while still in front lies the unrealised ideal of an educational science and an educational profession.[8]

So, right from the start, the staff of the centre were vexed by the still-unresolved problems of how teaching might come to be regarded as a profession and, if so, whether it could lay claim to a distinctive body of knowledge.

What do we know about the students for whom this curriculum was designed? Unlike the church college records analysed by Hillis, the records of the GPC do not provide information about the age distribution, social background or religious affiliations of the students. However, they do record where they came from and where they took up their first appointments.[9] In this respect, the situation had greatly changed. The opening of colleges at Aberdeen and Dundee meant that the Glasgow Centre now drew its students almost exclusively from west central Scotland, as it has continued to do so. About 80% of them came from within Glasgow, Lanarkshire, Renfrewshire, Dunbartonshire, Ayrshire and Argyll, and returned there to take up their first teaching post. Predominantly they were women taking the two-year course for the General Certificate.

TABLE 1
NUMBERS OF STUDENTS TAKING THE GENERAL CERTIFICATE: 1906–14

Year	Men	Women	Men (Univ)	Women (Univ)	Total
1907–8	303	906	234	280	1209
1908–9	312	981	242	314	1293
1909–10	310	885	223	232	1195
1910–11	288	871	169	159	1159
1911–12	231	829	123	84	1060
1912–13	241	797	105	60	1088
1913–14	257	779	113	63	1016

So the proportion of women students was constant at around 75%, but the proportion taking university classes, which had peaked at 77% for men and 32% for women in 1908–9, had fallen by 1913–14 to 44% for men and only 8% for women.[10]

This fall in the proportion of university students was partly due to the University Arts Ordinance of 1908, which introduced a three-term year and consequently, through the greater demands of the university timetable, made it more difficult to take college and university courses concurrently. More important was the determination of SED to weaken the university connection. One of the first steps taken by the Joint Committee of the colleges had been to set up a sub-committee to plan a four-year concurrent course in conjunction with the universities, which would have produced qualified graduate teachers—an ideal not to be realised for nearly 80 years. Even while it was deliberating, Sir John Struthers (Secretary of the SED) made clear to the Joint Committee the SED view that professional training should be the exclusive preserve of the colleges.

> In so far as Prospectuses issued by the Committee give prominence to the MA degree Course, they proceed on a wrong principle ...The functions of the university and of the Provincial Committees should be regarded as entirely distinct. The University lays down conditions for graduation: it is for the Provincial Committee to determine what constitutes an efficient training for the Public School Teachers. The relations of the two authorities would be more satisfactory in proportion as each confined itself to its proper sphere.[11]

So, when the Joint Committee finally presented its scheme, the SED rejected it and insisted that all professional training should be undertaken by the colleges. While allowing a three-year concurrent course to continue, it limited to five the number of university classes which could be taken. The GPC protested strongly about this, as it left teachers with the burden of taking two extra classes in their own time in order to graduate, and made the three year course less attractive, hence the fall in numbers already noted. The SED brushed its objections aside, stating bluntly that it was not prepared to sanction more than five university classes within the three-year course and that 'in the circumstances the Department feel that it would be idle to embark upon a prolonged discussion'.[12]

In its attempts to improve the quality of training, the Glasgow Centre was hampered by its scattered and unsuitable buildings. The Sites Committee looked at about a dozen possibilities and, by January 1911, had narrowed them down to four: Woodend (ie Jordanhill), Woodcroft, North Kelvinside and Dundas Vale. On the merits of these the senior staff were split into two camps. Some favoured a central site, like Dundas Vale, because of its convenience for teaching practice and its nearness to the university, but the Director argued strongly for Woodend as a cheaper and potentially more beneficial site.

In respect of sanitary conditions, quietness and environment, the Woodend site easily comes first... The factor of environment is also one of great significance, especially in the case of the best type of student. At the student stage, when character and habit are in the making, suggestions from without, ethical and aesthetic, exercise a formative power which it would be unwise indeed to overlook. Environment is the half of destiny; and it is difficult to believe that a student living for three or four years in such an environment... as can be created at Woodend would not look back on his College with the same pride, loyalty and affection that the public school boy of the best kind bestows upon his old school.[13]

An interesting passage in two respects: it refers only to men, the minority of the students; and it illustrates the public school ideal infiltrating the supposedly more egalitarian Scottish system.

Whether the committee was more swayed by arguments about cost or character, Macleod's views carried the day. In July 1911, the GPC recommended the purchase of the Jordanhill estate at a cost of £425 an acre. SED was not convinced that such a large site was necessary, but eventually accepted that it was reasonable if the plans included a hostel as well as the college and demonstration school. Six local firms of architects were invited to compete for the contract. Interestingly, one of these was Honeyman, Keppie and Mackintosh, and there is a record of Charles Rennie Mackintosh representing the firm at a meeting with the GPC in July 1913.[14] Unfortunately, he was at that time severing his connection with the firm and the college was not destined to be a product of his brilliant imagination. The winning design for the college was that of H & D Barclay, at an estimated cost of £74,000. Although the SED provisionally accepted this in October 1913, arguments about costs rumbled on over the winter and it was not until summer 1914 that work was begun on the site.

The war then began to have drastic effects on the work of the centre. As more and more men enlisted or later were conscripted, student numbers fell. By 1916–17, there were only 799 taking the General Certificate, of whom 767 were women, as were all 25 Chapter V students. 17 of the male staff enlisted but, with student numbers lower, there was little pressure to appoint new staff. As a result, the staff re-emerged after the war little changed in personnel (one can only speculate on the effects of their war-time experiences). In 1920–21, of the 46 full time officers of the centre, 35 had been appointed before 1914 and about half of those were former staff of the two church colleges.

The most visible effects of the war were on the new college buildings. Progress was delayed by increased costs and by shortages of manpower and materials. When the buildings were nearing completion in 1919, the military authorities requisitioned them; first the Admiralty as a hostel for shipyard workers and then the War Office as a temporary military hospital. However, in December 1919, the War Office formally handed them back to the GPC, and teacher training began at Jordanhill in September 1921. Work still remained to be done on the buildings and the first students had to pick their way through the mud and clutter of a building site to attend lectures. Eventually the building, described as one of the most spacious and commodious buildings of its kind in the world,[15] was officially opened on 3 November 1922.

The interwar years
The move from the old premises to this splendid new building can be seen as a symbol of the high hopes with which the interwar years began. The 1918 Education (Scotland) Act had proposed to raise the school leaving age to 15, had given powers for the provision of nursery and continuation schools and had reshaped the administration of education. It abolished School Boards and gave the responsibility for administering primary and secondary education to ad hoc authorities in the 33 counties and 5 burghs. As the providers of maintenance grants to student teachers, as contributors to the costs of training and as their employers once the students were trained, the new authorities had a strong interest in teacher training. This was recognised in 1920 by the creation of a National Committee for the Training of Teachers (NCTT), which was given general responsibility for the finances of the colleges, for their buildings and staffing, student numbers and courses.[16] The NCTT, however, was a large and unwieldy body, which met formally only once a year. The real work was done by the Central Executive Committee (CEC) and its officers. The Provincial Committees were left with little to do except the care and maintenance of buildings. At all three levels, Provincial Committee, CEC and NCTT, clerical influence remained strong.[17]

From the vantage point of the SED, these changes offered a measure of decentralisation, even though the Department retained final control of finance and policy. From the point of view of individual colleges, the reduced role of the Provincial Committees meant that the system was more centralised rather than less. The CEC exercised detailed control over almost every aspect of college work. It laid down salary scales, appointed staff (to its service not to individual colleges, though in practice staff were not usually moved), approved courses and financial estimates.

The writ of the CEC did not extend into the field of educational ideas. In the postwar years, these began to be influenced by Dewey, Montessori, Freud and the psychoanalysts. These were the years of the founding of the New Education Fellowship in which William Boyd, a part time member of staff from 1910–1923, played a prominent part. 'Probably at no time in their history', one HMCI wrote of the colleges in 1922, 'has the spirit of enquiry and experiment been so active'.[18] How far this spirit penetrated into day to day work is doubtful. The college had to operate within constraints which exerted strong pressures for continuity rather than change: the tight financial control exercised by the CEC; the slow turnover of staff; supervision by the inspectorate and the straitjacket of the Regulations. In comparison with the last 30 years, the general picture of the interwar years is one of stability, almost of stagnation. It is perhaps symptomatic of this that, between the official opening in 1922 and Kerr's retiral as Director in 1949, the only reference to the college in the *Glasgow Herald* is to the unveiling of the War Memorial in 1924.[19]

Throughout the period, the college had to operate within a very tight budget. As part of the postwar retrenchment (the so-called 'Geddes axe'), the annual outlay on training (as opposed to buildings) was cut from £52k in 1920–21 to £38k in the following year. After that it crept slowly upwards but did not reach £50k again until 1936–37. Within that tight budget, the CEC controlled even the most trivial items of expenditure; for example, the purchase of five boot lockers for £2–15, a set of specimen jars for £3 and a sewing machine for £7–1–9.[20] Moreover, whatever new ideas the war had encouraged, the staff who took over the new college building were those of the prewar era. Macleod had retired as Director in 1918, to be succeeded by Hugh McCallum, himself a member of staff since 1906. Of the 45 full time members of the teaching staff in 1920–21, 33 had been appointed before 1914 and 15 of those (33% of the staff), including 10 of the Principal Lecturers, had been on the staff of the church colleges before 1906. Between the wars, the average turnover of staff was 2.5 a year, ie about 5% of staff. In 1938–39, 13 of the 1920–21 staff were still in post and 10 of those had been appointed before 1914. One small improvement was in the proportion of female staff, which averaged 40% between the wars compared to 30% before.

The freedom of staff to innovate was restricted by supervision exercised by SED and the Inspectorate. The college prospectus had to be approved by SED. The Inspectorate had the right to attend college classes and, in effect, to give the lecturers a 'crit'. They also expected to check the college's teaching marks by visiting a cross-section of the students on teaching practice. This scrutiny of staff continued into the 1950s and was often resented, as Gordon Rae (Principal Lecturer in Geography) described:

> During my first year I was visited by the HMI, Dr John Gilbert. I had applied for the Inspectorate and had been on the short leet, but he had got the job. He came with the Assistant Secretary, Alan Rodger, who was a civil servant,

and he sat at at the back of my class and gave me a crit. ... After that Dr
Gilbert came to my Saturday morning classes once a year and sat at the back.
I was furious because professionally and in our careers we had been brought
up together.[21]

Another strong pressure for continuity came from the Regulations. These
had not changed, and so the college prospectus for 1921–22 was identical
with that of 1911–12, except for minor changes in the allocation of hours
to subjects. Although the basic framework remained until 1965, some
changes did take place between 1919 and 1939 and, as has so often been
the case with teacher training, the key factor in these changes was teacher
supply.

For a short time after the war, there were fears that there would be a
shortage of teachers needed to implement the provisions of the 1918 Act
for raising the school leaving age and for continuation classes.[22] These fears
were soon dissipated. Demand for teachers decreased because the act was
not implemented, because the 'Geddes axe' led to cutbacks in staffing and
because the birthrate was falling. Meanwhile, supply improved as the new
national salary scales made teaching more attractive financially and wastage
rates dropped as fewer women left to get married. By 1923 fears of shortage
were already being replaced by fears of unemployment. In January 1928
the SED was noting that two thirds of the graduates who had qualified
under Chapter III in 1926–27 were still without a post,[23] and over the next
few years the situation worsened further. The CEC's response was to impose
quotas on the number of students entering the colleges from 1928 onwards.
However, the futility of training for unemployment meant that the number
of applicants, particularly of women graduates, fell off to such an extent
that by 1936 the CEC could report that 'there is no longer any need for
precise schemes of limitations of entrants'.[24]

Improved supply provided opportunities, as it did later in the 1970s and
1980s, to raise the level of entry requirements and to lengthen the period
of initial training. The 1924 Regulations ended the Junior Studentships[25]
and made it a requirement 'that all students entering on a course of training
for the General Certificate must hold the Leaving Certificate... and that all
male entrants must hold in addition a University Degree'.[26] This discrimination between men and women was justified partly on the grounds that it
would not have been possible to recruit enough graduate women to staff
the schools; but also because of genuine doubts whether an Ordinary Degree
followed by the Chapter III course was the best preparation for primary
teaching.[26] The 1931 Regulations extended the course for non-graduate
women from two to three years.

If the year 1931 brought some disappointment, it also brought a most valuable addition to the college's work. In 1930 the CEC decided that, with the growing demand for male physical education teachers and the extension of the course from two to three years, it would be better to train men and women PE teachers separately. So Dr MacKenzie (the Principal of Dunfermline College) was transferred to Jordanhill along with two of his staff (Punchard and Rosser) and in October 1931 the first male PE students began their course.

These changes affected the composition of the student body more than student numbers, which increased modestly for a few years after the war, reaching a peak of 1233 in 1925–26. Then the combined effects of the quotas and of unemployment led to a falling off; so that in the 1930s numbers fluctuated within the range of 915 (1932–33) and 1044 (1931–32). Within those totals, however, the proportion of graduates increased from 51% in 1924–25 to 72% ten years later. So, in the 1930s, the college came closer to what many people in Scotland regarded as the ideal situation: one in which general education was provided by the universities and central institutions and the college provided only professional training.[27] The changes also affected the balance between the sexes to the detriment of women. In the early 1920s they represented beween 75% and 80% of the students, as they had done before the war. Then the proportion declined and between 1930 and 1939 averaged little over 60%. The main reason was the dramatic fall in the number of women graduates taking the course for the General Certificate. In 1928–29, this course attracted 122 men and 226 women; ten years later the number of men was roughly the same at 116, but the number of women had fallen to 87.

Restrictions on student numbers, fear of unemployment and financial stringency had other effects. Restricted numbers meant that there was little need for further buildings. A new gymnasium had to be built when the SSPE came, and another hostel (Douglas House) was opened in 1933.[28] Fear of unemployment meant that nearly all the honours graduates took the course for the General Certificate as well as the Chapter V course.[29] The consequent pressure must have made it difficult for them to take much part in college social life, even had they wished to do so. More seriously, it affected relationships between students and staff because so much depended on the teaching mark.

> The written examinations didn't worry us but the teaching mark did because Glasgow paid more highly than the counties. But to teach in Glasgow you had to have a VG. The range of marks went from Fair to Excellent in labels and each label had a mark. But the tutors put a numerical mark on your diary and this often caused trouble ... This was an area of great anxiety thoughout our course.[30]

One difficulty about describing this period is that relatively little is known about most of the people. Throughout its history, the college recruited staff who had been successful teachers or who were competent academics, but not quite good enough to secure university posts. Neither source was likely to yield the intellectual giants who give lustre to the annals of certain universities. So, however well staff did their work, little trace of it remains; often nothing more than obituaries and farewell tributes. Between 1919 and 1940, the college had two Directors of Studies, neither of whom has left any great mark. McCallum (1919–24) is now a shadowy figure. Reading between the lines of his obituary,[31] Burnett (1924–40) seems to have been an extremely conscientious administrator who overburdened himself to the point where his health suffered and he died in harness. Along with David Kennedy Fraser, he was one of the founders of the Atholl Preparatory School in Milngavie.

Two of the most popular lecturers appear to have been Shepherd Dawson, Head of Psychology, who was sufficiently well regarded to be made President of the Psychological section of the British Association, and Robert R. Rusk, Head of Education. Rusk was Director of the Scottish Council for Research in Education for 30 years and the author of the *History of teacher training in Scotland* published in 1928 to mark the centenary of teacher training. He also wrote a number of scholarly, though derivative, works on education. He was able to do all this because life in college was not very demanding. There was little administration, the same lectures could be given year after year, thus leaving ample time for writing and for a regular afternoon round of golf.[32] Perhaps the only people with reputations which went beyond the west of Scotland were Frank Punchard for his work with the Lingiad, Anne McAllister, the founder of the Glasgow School of Speech Therapy, Jean Milligan, joint founder and inspiration of the Royal Scottish Country Dance Society[33] and George Pratt Insh, the historian.

The war years and their aftermath, 1939–49

With the outbreak of war in 1939 whatever limited thoughts there may have been about educational development had to be put aside. Student numbers fell as the men went away to military service. By 1943–44 the student population had fallen by about one third to its lowest point of 626, 92% of whom were women. Even with these reduced numbers the college was overcrowded, because accommodation had to be shared with the staff and pupils of the College School, requisitioned for military use from 1940–44. As a result memories of the war are not about education but about hardships shared: the queues for food, nightly fire watching done by staff and students, the Clydebank blitz, which spared the college other than minor damage to doors and windows, 246 of which had to be replaced.[34]

There was even a legend that the *Luftwaffe* used the twin towers of Jordanhill to line up their approach to Clydebank.

The end of the war ushered in a period of strain. Provision for teacher education had to be rapidly expanded to meet the pent-up demands of the demobilised exservicemen and to provide the extra teachers for the raising of the school leaving age in 1947. The solution in England and Wales was to open a number of emergency colleges, but SED decided that there was enough spare capacity in the Scottish system to absorb the extra numbers. Jordanhill thus found itself having to cope with a student population which more than doubled in three years: from 733 in 1944–45 to 1,647 in 1947–48. That population changed not only in size but in character. The proportion of men shot up to nearly 40%, most of whom were exservicemen on one of the shortened courses allowed for by the emergency training scheme. This created an administrative problem:

> There were times when the only person who knew exactly who was in the college was myself [Wood] as Principal Master of Methods, because I had to place them in schools. The college office was in a high degree of chaos, because the servicemen were allowed to have a two-term course for the graduates and they could come in at any time.[35]

A more serious problem was the attitude of some of the older members of staff, who found it difficult to adapt their methods to mature exservice students impatient with some of their rigid and authoritarian ways. In these difficult times the college was helped to pull through by a number of factors. One was the humane and helpful personality of the Principal, William Kerr,[36] in his dealings with the students—'the man for the hour', Moffett called him. Another was the administrative skill of Wood. A third was the influx of 41 new members of staff in 1946,[37] often exservicemen themselves, who were much more in tune with this new type of student.

The beginnings of change, 1949–59
By 1949, when Kerr retired, he had seen the college through the stresses and strains of the immediate postwar period. Wood, his successor, was a very different personality. Fundamentally a man of great warmth, superficially he often appeared withdrawn and aloof. A good listener, he preferred to speak briefly and to the point. The college quip about him was that he never used two words when none would do. However, when he did speak, his words carried great weight, both within Jordanhill and in the wider educational scene in Scotland, because he came to be recognised as someone who saw clearly to the core of any issue and judged it wisely. Unlike some administrators, he both thought deeply and cared deeply about education.

Along with Sir Godfrey Thomson, he ranks as one of the two outstanding figures of this century in Scottish teacher education. Unusually for a college principal, Wood was both an Englishman and a scientist. Born in Northumberland, he came to Jordanhill from a post in the Education Department of Manchester University. As a result, he had the advantage of seeing the college in a wider perspective,[38] and he did not entirely like what he saw.

The Scottish system was ahead of the English in insisting on three years' training for primary teachers and on degrees or diplomas for all male teachers. Against this were set the limitations imposed by the internal organisation of the college and by the attitudes of the staff.

> I came here from Manchester University, which was a very liberal institution, and I was shocked by Jordanhill. It was all set and everybody's status was fixed. The Heads of Department were the bosses. Nobody uttered anything in a meeting... The other thing that was staggering was the worship of the universities. I'd been on a university staff for seven years and I'd never met anything like it. The teachers couldn't think past the university and neither could the staff of the college. There was this graduate/non-graduate tension in the college all the time.[39]

Over the next ten years, Wood endeavoured both to loosen some of those rigidities and to bring the college curriculum more into line with postwar needs. Neither of these tasks was easy, but there were factors which encouraged change. People were looking for a new start in almost every aspect of public life. One sign of this unwillingness to accept the old order was that Janet Gallie wrote to the GPC in 1948 on behalf of women members of staff, asking that those college positions currently reserved for men should be open to women.[40] The GPC passed on the request to the CEC 'for favourable consideration', but the all-male CEC decided to take no action. In teacher education, the Advisory Council on Education in Scotland had produced a report in 1946 urging reform, generally thought to have been written by McClelland,[41] and so the CEC, which he dominated, encouraged experimentation by the colleges in the 1950s. Powerful constraints remained: externally, the need for approval by the CEC and SED; internally, the conservative attitudes of those staff thirled to the academic tradition and the entrenched powers of the Heads of Department, who believed that, within the hours allocated to their subject, they should determine what was taught and how.

Within such constraints, progress could only be slow and partial, but a number of interesting experiments were initiated, paralleled by those in other colleges.[42] Within the General Certificate course, a special course was devised for graduates wishing to teach in junior secondary schools, taught partly by practising teachers. Arrangements were made for students taking the Rural Course to have four weeks' teaching practice in rural schools in Kirkcudbrightshire. The three-year diploma course was revised by reducing the number of subjects studied in the first two years and giving the students a choice of two main subjects in the third year, one from a group of academic subjects and the other from practical and aesthetic.[43] This change significantly affected the largest group of students, whereas the decision to centralise full time courses for technical teachers at Jordanhill affected one of the smallest[44]; but in it, and the subsequent decision to appoint Mason as Principal Lecturer in Further Education in 1957, lay the seeds of the Scottish School of Further Education. Such experiments helped to give an impetus to research, which began to play a more noticeable, if still very minor part, in college activities.[45] In so far as these changes began the slow process of moving away from lectures towards more discussion and investigation, they made greater demands on the college library which it was ill-equipped to meet within the confines of the old library accommodation. By the end of the 1950s this was a matter of general concern throughout the college system and nowhere more so than at Jordanhill.[46]

While encouraging these developments internally, Wood was able to ease the external constraints in two respects: the procedures for appointing staff, and inspection. Until 1956, staff were appointed by the whole Provincial Committee, a system which led to 'an enormous amount of fiddling and canvassing for friends of so-and-so'.[47] As a result, Heads of Department received new staff whom they had played no part in selecting and might even never have seen. Wood persuaded the GPC to delegate appointments to a small Chairman's Committee, which made the appointments much more professional, although Heads of Department were still not involved except through informal discussions with the Principal. Then, in the following year, Brunton, recently appointed as HMSCI, made a deal with Wood and Inglis [Principal of Moray House] to end formal inspection of the colleges:

> Early on he [Brunton] came to Jordanhill to speak to me and then he went to Moray House to see Inglis. He said he wanted our help with his ideas for curriculum development. Inglis and I talked him into giving up formal inspection of the colleges in return for our help.[48]

This, however, was a purely informal agreement. The SED did not give up its right to inspect the colleges. It simply chose not to exercise it for the time being and so, when circumstances changed, it was able to exercise it again. However, the assumption at the time was that inspection would never happen again, as Brunton's concession was part of a general move to raise the status of the colleges by giving them more independence within a reformed national system.

While discussions were taking place about this new system, the pressing problem for the college was the one which was to dominate the next 20 years: teacher shortage and the need for expansion. Once the postwar bulge was over, the number of students fell back to 1389 (1952–53). From there it began to climb again to 1953 in 1958–59, against the background of a rising birthrate.[49] The SED was slow to react. Although the Kerr Building was opened in 1958 to house technical subjects and craftwork, this did little to ease the pressure on the main building, where the problem of overcrowding became more and more acute. In November 1958 Wood submitted a report to the GPC, which highlighted the problems of shortage of accommodation for staff and students:

> The students are required to work harder than ten years ago (for the equivalent number of students, the issue of books from the library has doubled in that time) but they are disturbed by bustle, lack of quiet and space. They stand in queues for food and for lavatories, and in free periods and lunch hours they have difficulty finding anywhere to sit, since common rooms and reading rooms are too small and the library seats only 60.

As a result, Brunton and Rodger (the Assistant Secretary responsible for teacher training) came to the college in February 1959, saw the situation for themselves and acknowledged that remedies had to be found. So began the process of planning a new range of permanent buildings.

Notes and references
 1 Bell, R.E. The Scottish universities and educational studies <u>in</u> Thomas, J.B. (ed.). *British universities and teacher education*. London: Falmer Press, 1990.
 2 GPC minutes, 1905–6, Appendix II.
 3 *Ibid*. Meeting of the Joint Committee of the Provincial Committees, 9 February 1907.
 4 *Ibid*., 30 May 1909.
 5 *Ibid*., 15 November 1905.
 6 *Ibid*., 1907–8, Appendix I.
 7 Each year the college issued a prospectus, printed in the GPC Minutes, which detailed for each course the subjects of study and the hours allotted to them.
 8 GPC minutes, 1907–8. Appendix I.
 9 *Ibid*., 1913. Director's report, pp.177–80.
10 Statistics from the tables of student numbers published annually in GPC minutes.
11 GPC minutes. Meeting of the Joint Committee of the Provincial Committees, 2 November 1907.

12 *Ibid.* Letter from SED to GPC, 22 September 1911.

13 *Ibid.* Chairman's Sub-committee, 10 March 1911.

14 *Ibid.* Special meeting of GPC with architects, 10 February 1913.

15 CCES annual report 1921–22. Report by J.C. Smith, HMCI.

16 GPC minutes. January-June 1920 contain the CCES minute of 10 February 1920.

17 Of the 21 members of the CEC, 9 were clergy in 1939, 11 in 1946.

18 CCES annual report 1922–23. Report by J.C. Smith, HMCI.

19 *Glasgow Herald*, 23 June 1924.

20 CEC minutes, 10 November 1934, 5 June 1937, and 14 January 1939.

21 Rae, G. Interview with W.B. Marker, 16 June 1993.

22 CCES annual report 1919–20. Report by J.C. Smith, HMCI.

23 *Ibid.* 1928–29. Report by J.C. Smith, HMCI.

24 CEC minutes. 16th annual report, 1935–36.

25 Wilson, J.D. The junior student system in Bone, T.R. ed. *Studies in the history of Scottish education, 1872–1939.* London: ULP, 1976.

26 CCES annual report 1924–25. Report by J.C. Smith, HMCI.

27 Wood, H.P. 'It is assumed in Scotland that the ideal is that all academic or practical or aesthetic qualifications should be obtained in a university or central institution'. Notes on the training of teachers in Scotland. Unpublished mimeo in Jordanhill Archives.

28 CEC minutes 1929–31. 11th and 12th annual reports. The hostel was built in brick, rather than stone, and work slowed down, to save money.

29 In 1933–34, for instance, there were 86 honours graduates taking both Chapter III and Chapter V and only 22 taking Chapter V alone. The following year the figures were 107 for both courses and 8 for Chapter V.

30 Moffett, J. Interview with W.B. Marker, 7 July 1994.

31 Tribute by W. Kerr in the *New dominie*, March 1940. Jordanhill Archives.

32 Livingston, A.E. *A personal approach to outdoor education.* Uddingston: Paperfold, 1987, p.87.

33 MacFadyen, A. and Adams, F.H. *Dance with your soul.* Edinburgh: RSCDS, 1983.

34 GPC minutes. Finance, Property and Law Committee, 21 March 1941.

35 Wood, H.P. Interview with W.B. Marker, 8 February 1993.

36 Before coming to Jordanhill, Kerr had been a popular and inspiring English teacher at the High School of Glasgow. He was also an accomplished writer of light verse. There was a well known poem (quoted in Scotland, J. *The history of Scottish education.* London: ULP, 1969, vol.2, p.122) poking fun at the easy life of teachers, whose refrain ran: 'And aye the pay gaun on'. Kerr wrote a parody of it for *The New dominie* which began:

> Oh, wha would be a dominie,
> Could licht on decent wark?
> He's trauchelt frae the peep o' day
> Till lang 'oors after dark
> Five days in schule, and i' the Kirk

Wi' fashious loons is he
On Saturdays he weets his sark

As fitba' referee
Leezie, Leezie, maist uneasy
Is a life like yon –
He's need be twenty men at aince
To keep the pay gaun on'.

37 Although 1946 was unique, the turnover of staff between 1945 and 1959 was markedly higher than pre 1939. For instance, between 1949 and 1958, 77 new members of staff were appointed.
38 Wood, H.P. MS notes on Jordanhill. 1993.
39 Wood, H.P. Interview with W.B.Marker, 8 February 1993.
40 GPC minutes 26 November 1948 and CEC minutes 11 December 1948. The posts reserved for men were those of Director and Deputy Director of Studies and the Principal Lectureships in Methods, Education and Psychology.
41 Cruickshank, M. *History of the training of teachers in Scotland*. London: ULP, 1970, p.189.
42 See for instance CEC. 32nd report, 1951–52 for revision of the syllabuses at Moray House College.
43 CEC minutes. 31st annual report, 1950–51.
44 *Ibid*. 33rd annual report, 1952–53.
45 *Ibid*. 34th annual report, 1953–54 gives a survey of the research activities of the colleges.
46 *Ibid*. 38th annual report, 1957–58.
47 Wood, H.P. Interview with W.B. Marker, 8 February 1993.
48 Wood, H.P. Interview with W.B. Marker, 6 November 1989.
49 In 1950 there were 90,639 live births in Scotland. By 1960 there were 101,292 and the trend was still upwards.

4

The Golden Years, 1959–76

Willis Marker

The new administrative framework

The year 1959 marked a watershed in the history of the college. As part of a general trend which subsequently saw the setting up of the Scottish Certificate of Education Examination Board (SCEEB), the General Teaching Council (GTC) and the Consultative Committee on the Curriculum (CCC), new Regulations were made which altered the status of the college.[1] The old centralised system of National and Provincial Committees was swept away. The college, now renamed a college of education, was given its own governing body, which was to be a 'body corporate' and as such the employer of the staff. The college was given powers to provide preservice and inservice courses for teachers and community workers, and to award its own certificates and diplomas. As a symbol of this change of status, the college devised its own rites of passage into the teaching profession: the annual ceremonies at which the successful students, suitably gowned and hooded, were presented with their diplomas.

One reason for these changes was Brunton's wish to make the Scottish education system more of a partnership.[2] So the Board of Governors was made broadly representative of local interests: the local education authorities, the Senate of Glasgow University, the Church of Scotland and elected teachers from the south west of Scotland.[3] Internally, to involve staff more in running the college, the Regulations provided for a Board of Studies, 'to advise upon, and assist the Principal in relation to the coordination of studies, including teaching method and practice, in the various courses, the maintenance of standards ... and generally questions falling within the ambit of teaching staff.'

However, this move towards greater independence for the college was still within a framework of central coordination. In an attempt to strike a balance between the former detailed control and the widely held view that the same general regulations should apply nationally, the Regulations created a new coordinating body, the Scottish Council for the Training of Teachers (SCTT). This proved to be short-lived, disbanded in 1967 as a consequence of the setting up of the GTC. The SED then created the Joint

Committee of Colleges of Education in Scotland (JCCES) as an intermediate body but this met only once a year and was of little practical consequence. The real link beween the SED and the colleges became the Committee of Principals (CP) which, unlike the SCTT, was not a national and representative forum. So, for the first time, there was no real buffer between the college and the SED.

During its short life, the SCTT played an important part in several developments which affected the college.[4] Indirectly Jordanhill was affected by the decisions to build new colleges at Hamilton, Callendar Park and Craigie and to confine their work to the training of female primary teachers. More directly, it was affected by the long overdue reform of the 1906 Regulations. In 1965 these were replaced by the Teachers (Education, Training and Certification) (Scotland) Regulations which created the system which has lasted until the present day. The old terminology of 'Chapters' and 'Articles' was swept away and replaced by three Teachers' Certificates: for primary, secondary and further education. The primary certificate could be obtained by following either the three-year diploma course, or a four-year BEd course, or by taking a university degree followed by a one-year course at a college of education; the secondary certificate by either the BEd, or a university degree and a one-year college course, now quite separate from the primary course. These changes focused attention on the question: what was the appropriate training for the certificate in further education? Prompted by SED, the SCTT created a standing committee to examine this question, which reported in 1965 recommending that the training of FE lecturers should be centralised in one specialist unit attached to Jordanhill,[5] a recommendation which led to the creation of the School of Further Education.

The external environment
Throughout the period from 1959–76 the college, in common with teacher education institutions throughout the UK, was subject to some inescapable pressures for change. One came simply from the demographic trends. After their postwar peak, live births in Scotland declined but, from the mid 1950s, they began to rise again, topping 100,000 between 1960 and 1966. They then declined with gathering momentum, so that by 1977 they were down to a postwar low of 62,000, from which they never recovered. The big rise in pupil numbers began in the mid 1960s. In 1965–66 the number of pupils in local authority schools was about 875,000, much the same as in 1960–61. By 1975–76 the number had risen to 1,053,000, an increase of 20% in ten years. Given this pattern, the national problem for most of the period was that of teacher shortage, especially in the west of Scotland, and the pressure on the college was to expand and to provide the teachers needed by understaffed schools.

In addition to these demographic factors the college was also affected by changes in the schools. The 1960s saw widespread challenges to established tradition and a push for modernisation, which made themselves felt in efforts to reshape and renew the curriculum. In primary education, the key document was the Primary Memorandum.[6] In an attempt to loosen up the rigidities of a curriculum thirled to the 3Rs, this swung to the opposite extreme and put forward the view that the needs of children could be discovered by research and the curriculum then based on them. Even if philosophically unsound, the push towards a more 'child centred' form of education was necessary and desirable at the time. It certainly presented a challenge to the ideas and practices of many teachers and so placed the college in a difficult position (one where it has often found itself), caught between the desire to innovate and the need to train students for the schools as they were.

Reform of the secondary curriculum proceeded quite independently subject by subject, without any coordination with the primary. In the 1960s one impetus came from the SED report *From school to further education,*[7] which advocated using 'the vocational impulse as the core round which the curriculum should be organised' to meet the needs of the majority of pupils. A stronger one came from the new O grade syllabuses being developed by SCEEB, developments in which college staff played an important part as examiners and members of panels. More fundamental questions about the secondary curriculum then arose as secondary schools became comprehensive and as the school leaving age was raised to 16 in 1972: questions about the curriculum for mixed ability classes or for those pupils in S3 and S4 for whom the 0 grade syllabuses were inappropriate. In response, two weighty committees were set up, Munn on the curriculum[8] and Dunning on examinations.[9] Both reported in 1977 and excited a great deal of discussion, but their practical impact did not come until the 1980s. Meantime college staff, many of whom had taught only in senior secondary schools, had to wrestle with the problems of preparing students for the comprehensive schools.

Expansion
The immediate problem for the college in the 1960s was the rapid rise in student numbers. From 1927 in 1959–60, the number soared to 2813 in 1963–64—a 46% increase in four years. Then the opening of the new colleges at Craigie and Callendar Park in 1964 and at Hamilton in 1966 took some of the pressure off and numbers fell back slightly. In 1969–70 they stood at 2687 but the increased demand for secondary teachers created by ROSLA then led to a further upsurge which took the student population over 3500 in 1971–72 to a peak of 3713 in 1975–76.

The 1960s also saw a number of significant changes in the composition of the student body. The most contentious was the admission of men to the primary diploma course in 1967. This had long been resisted by the teachers' unions which saw it as 'dilution', a step back from their cherished goal of an all-graduate profession. This change brought into primary teaching a number of mature and motivated students who were an asset to the schools but, in the long run, men did not come into primary teaching in any numbers. For the first five years, the average intake was only about 30 and they never represented more than 9.5% of the intake. Less contentious but more important in the long run was the addition of new groups of students: speech therapists, social workers, youth and community workers. These too brought in more mature students with a wider range of backgrounds. As a result the pastoral work of the college increased, throwing into greater prominence the role of the Dean of Women, which was most capably filled by Joyce Moffett from 1959–71. These new groups made Jordanhill much less exclusively an institution for the initial training of primary and secondary teachers.

Diversification

On the teacher training side, the important developments were in further education and inservice training. Further education had always been one of Wood's particular interests and, with his support, the college made rapid progress in developing training for lecturers in further education. Added stimulus came in 1965 from the new Teaching Qualification in further education. Although this was not compulsory, it gave an incentive to further education lecturers already in post to undertake training. By 1964–65 a pattern of training had already been established which was to last for the next 20 years: eight weeks full time attendance in college, followed by a year of supervised teaching in post and then by a further eight weeks in college. The SCTT recommended that all FE training should be centralised at Jordanhill. The importance of this was recognised by the Governors, who elevated further education from a department into a School of Further Education which, like the SSPE, had its own Director and its own sub-committee of the Board of Governors.

Inservice, unlike FE, had always been an aspect of the college's work but it was given added importance in the 1960s by the increased pace of change in schools, associated with such developments as the new O grades and the Primary Memorandum. One obvious response to this was to expand the traditional provision of short courses and conferences. In 1962–63 the college ran 42 courses and 19 conferences for 3541 teachers; by 1966–67 this provision had become 107 courses and 39 conferences for 5614 teachers.[10] Another response, typical of Wood's vision, was to create a separate department of Inservice Training in 1963, which was and remained unique within the Scottish system, and to make it the responsibility of the Vice principal, John A. Smith.

Before coming to the college as Principal Lecturer in Methods, Smith had had a very varied career.[11] A native Gaelic speaker from Mull, he was devoted to the promotion of Gaelic language and culture. After teaching and war service in the Royal Navy, he served briefly on the staff of Moray House, before being successively Assistant Director of Education in Fife and the first HMI with special responsibility for the handicapped. He therefore brought a wealth of experience, and a very shrewd mind, to the development of inservice. His great contribution was to see beyond the traditional provision of courses. As he wrote in his second report to the Governors:

> It can no longer be expected that the provision of inservice training is simply a business of holding courses and conferences. There are other types of provision, working parties, discussion groups, panels and committees, staff tutor arrangements, which may be even more effective for certain purposes.[12]

To put these ideas into effect, he arranged for the appointment in 1964 of Bill Michael as a full time staff tutor in art 'to work with the local authority in the field and with the individual teacher in the classroom in dealing with particular teaching problems on the spot'.[13] This work was so successful that two more staff tutors (Fred Rendell and Steve Bell) were appointed in 1967, thus creating the nucleus of the staff tutor team which was to have such a wide and valuable influence on primary schools in the west of Scotland for the next two decades. In 1972 inservice received another boost with the publication of the James report[14] which promoted the idea throughout the UK that inservice was a necessary part of the career development of every teacher. Briefly there was much optimism about expansion and SED actively promoted the development of one-month full time courses. In anticipation of this, the college created a new post of Principal Lecturer in Inservice in 1972. This eased the burden on Smith and expansion seemed to be proceeding smoothly until he retired in December 1975, just before the situation was radically changed.

Smith also played a major part in the diversification of the college's work into fields beyond teacher training. The departments of Youth and Community and of Social Work owed a great deal in their early days to the close personal interest which he took in their development.[15] The first step was the appointment of John Round as a youth tutor in 1964 to create a two-year course for youth and community workers. The original plan was for a small intake every two years but demand increased so quickly that there was soon an intake every year. By the end of the decade, a three-year course and a one-year postgraduate course had been added, and a staff of six had been recruited to teach them. The next step came in 1967 when Smith persuaded Vera Hiddleston to bring her course for probation officers from the Scottish College of Commerce, which was in the throes of merger with Strathclyde University. Following the reorganisation of social work in Scotland in 1968, Hiddleston developed a two-year course leading to the Certificate of Qualification in Social Work.

The third strand in diversification, the coming of the School of Speech Therapy, was largely the work of McAllister and Wood. The School had been Anne McAllister's creation and had been sustained throughout its life by her drive, enthusiasm and prestige. Since 1952 the Glasgow School of Speech Therapy had been based at 25 Athole Gardens, but by the early 1960s it was becoming clear that the future of speech therapy training lay within higher education. So Wood persuaded the Governors to make the School part of the college from 1963.[16] Diversification beyond teacher training does not seem to have been part of any strategic development plan, locally or nationally. The youth and community course, it is true, was started at the request of SED as part of a national initiative but the other developments came because Wood and Smith took opportunities when they saw them and SED, well disposed to the colleges in those days, saw no reason to object. The results were certainly very beneficial to the college. The new courses brought staff and students with different backgrounds, attitudes and skills. Whether this had much influence on the work of teacher training is doubtful; but when teacher training was cut back it was certainly a source of strength that the college was not exclusively a teacher training institution.

Improved facilities

Expansion and diversification would not have been possible without a major building programme. In 1959 Brunton and Rodger had been convinced that, to relieve the pressure and to provide capacity for expansion, Jordanhill would have to have new buildings and that a new college would have to be built in the west of Scotland. SED then had to extract the necessary money from an unsympathetic Treasury.[17] This meant that the planning of new buildings did not start until 1960. In the meantime, the pressure from rising student numbers had to be met by two expedients: the erection of temporary huts for use as classrooms and the manipulation of the timetable, which forced the college to do things which were educationally undesirable. The worst was probably the division of the secondary graduates into two groups so that only half of them were in college at any one time. The unfortunate students in the first group therefore had to undertake their first spell of teaching practice after only a one-week introductory course.

From 1960 to 1975 the campus was never free of building works or of temporary huts, as the building programme always lagged behind the rising student numbers until the mid 1970s. The first phase of the building programme[18] saw improved facilities for the SSPE in the shape of a swimming pool and a games hall. Also, on the site of the old mansion house, a new tutorial block and theatre were built and named after Thomas Crawfurd, a 16th-century owner of the lands of Jordanhill. All these buildings were officially opened by HM Queen Elizabeth II in July 1963, a ceremony which symbolised the political importance then attached to teacher education.

Despite the temporary relief provided by the opening of the new colleges, facilities at Jordanhill remained overcrowded and inadequate. So a second and more ambitious phase of building was planned. By 1968, the SSPE and College PE departments were able to move into one new building and the Mathematics and Science Departments into another (the Smith Building).[19] Next in the pipeline were plans for purpose-built accommodation for Inservice and for the SFE. Unfortunately, the proposed Inservice Centre was postponed in 1969[20] and was never built. Work went ahead, however, on the new School of FE, which was opened in 1972. Meanwhile work had begun on a six-storey extension to the main building, incorporating a lecture theatre and a spacious library. Departments were able to move into this in January 1973. In March 1974 it was officially opened by Wood, in whose honour it was named the Sir Henry Wood Building. That honour could not have been better earned. On the present campus everything except the original building (now the David Stow Building) is a legacy of his time as Principal. *Si monumentum requiris, circumspice.* The net result was to provide the college with greatly extended, much more spacious and flexible accommodation for both staff and students.

Improved facilities did not come only in the form of buildings. This was the period in which the college first felt the impact of educational technology. In 1966 David Butts, who had had experience both of teaching and of working for the BBC, was recruited as 'Officer for TV'. With great skill and enterprise, he began building up what became the Audiovisual Media Department in 1969. By this time the College had its own mobile unit and its own TV studio linked to a network of points throughout the buildings, which allowed the use of closed circuit TV. The Department was therefore able to perform two roles: to produce programmes to support preservice and inservice courses and to train staff and students in the educational use of the media. The hope at that time was that independent learning would be encouraged by adding a purpose built Resource Centre as an extension to the library. Plans for this were drawn up but, like the Inservice Centre, it was never built. Whereas educational technology was beginning significantly to permeate the work of the college, if sometimes only at the humble level of using the overhead projector, the impact of computers had hardly begun. In 1971, Hawthorn was appointed as Senior (and sole) Lecturer in computer education and in 1972 the college acquired its first IBM mainframe. To most staff, this was an esoteric and inaccessible mystery. In its early days, computer education was confined to contributing to the secondary course and providing a schools computing service.

Changes in the curriculum

Improved facilities did in time facilitate changes in the curriculum and in approaches to teaching and learning but the effects of these improvements were only being felt towards the end of this period. The general picture throughout the 1960s and early 1970s is of an overcrowded college, with poor working conditions for both staff and students. These hampered curriculum innovation, as did the sheer weight of numbers, which meant that many staff were on a constant and time consuming round of visits to students in schools. Nevertheless innovations did take place, in response to changes in schools and in the education system.

The first major change was the introduction of a BEd course. In 1963, the Robbins Committee produced its wide ranging report on higher education in the UK.[21] Its key proposals for colleges of education were that colleges should develop four-year concurrent courses leading to the degree of Bachelor of Education, open to men and women, and that 'selection for it should depend on the standard achieved in the work of the first two years and ... should not be limited to those who had university entrance qualifications at the beginning of their college course'. These recommendations offered the college an opportunity which it was keen to grasp. As the degree had to be awarded by a university, this meant negotiations with Glasgow University, in which a number of issues had to be resolved, particularly:

(a) Should the degree be largely academic, modelled on the traditional Scottish Ordinary degree? Or should its main focus be on the professional training of teachers?

(b) Should the BEd students be required to have university entrance qualifications and pursue a separate course? Or should there be a common BEd/Diploma course for two years, at the end of which students would be selected for the BEd?

In Scotland (except at Dundee) the pressures were towards conservative answers to these questions, as teachers, college and university staff, themselves products of the Scottish system, saw the traditional Scottish degree pattern as the norm against which all proposals should be judged.

The first formal move in these negotiations was a special meeting of the Board of Governors in January 1964, which set up a small sub-committee to meet a committee of the University Senate. Meanwhile the Board of Studies had come out strongly in favour of a degree which would be 'very strictly a professional degree, with a course more akin to a medical course than to an arts or science course'.[22] Proposals on these lines were sent to the university in May but for nearly a year there was very little response. However, eventually the Principal wrote Wood a conciliatory letter and negotiations were resumed, but on the university's terms, which the college had to accept if it wished to have a degree. So, instead of a professional degree, what emerged was an academic one, based on the seven graduating passes of the Ordinary MA. The only concession which the university made was that students might choose in their fourth year to do a college study in physical education, youth service or the education of young children in place of one of the graduating courses. Practical and aesthetic subjects were completely squeezed out; professional studies and teaching practice were to be a college concern and were not to count towards a degree; college proposals for a first-year foundation course were replaced by a third-year course called 'Background to modern society', which the university insisted should be taught by its own staff, as it was not prepared to validate a purely external degree.

On this basis the college took in its first BEd students in 1966. Despite its limitations the BEd did have some beneficial effects. The fact that the college was now running a degree course probably raised its status a little. It certainly raised the sights, academically, of the staff involved and was therefore a vital stage in the development of degree work. It also brought the immediate benefit of the better staffing ratios which degree courses then attracted and which SED was willing to support as long as it believed that the BEd might help to alleviate the shortage of teachers. So initially it was a source of stimulus and excitement, which perhaps clouded the danger that some staff might become more interested in teaching academic subjects than in the professional training of teachers.

In the 1960s the bulk of professional training was done through the three-year diploma course. Once the college was free of the tutelage of the CEC, Wood placed reform of the diploma course on the agenda of the Board of Studies[23] but its discussions were shelved pending publication of the Robbins report. There was then further delay due to the negotiations about the BEd but a new stimulus to action came in 1965 from the Primary Memorandum.[24] So three committees were created for the revision of the diploma course. The composition of these was unusual in what had hitherto been a very hierarchical organisation and probably reflected the more radical views of James Miller (Vice principal, 1966–72). He himself chaired Committee C, but Committee A was chaired by Alasdair Nicolson (then a young and very junior head of department) and Committee B by Barry MacDonald, an unorthodox young lecturer in education, supported by other young and unpromoted staff, like Bell and Rendell.

The outcome was a new course, which started in 1969. It broke with the long tradition that students had to study every subject they might have to teach in a primary school, which meant that they were all studied superficially. The main changes were that all students in Year 1 had to take an interdisciplinary course in modern society. In Year 2, they chose one academic and one aesthetic option, which they then studied for four hours a week for the next two years. New courses were included, like language arts and environmental studies, which reflected the thinking of the Primary Memorandum. Very importantly, the students were given more study time. These changes broke new ground in a number of ways. They were a step towards more staff involvement in curriculum planning; they brought departmental schemes of work under wider scrutiny[25]; they provided an opportunity for higher standards of work within the options which, like the BEd, were important for raising the sights of both students and staff.

Before long it seemed possible that the new diploma would lead fairly quickly to a BEd designed specifically for primary teachers. When SED saw the demand for primary teachers falling and began to reduce the intake to colleges from 1972 onwards, it saw an opportunity to upgrade the diploma to a degree. What it wanted was a three-year vocational degree developed out of the diploma course and quite unlike the existing academic BEd. Faced with opposition from the universities, the GTC and (more vehemently) from the EIS, the government decided not to press for the three-year degree and the chance of an all graduate profession was postponed for another decade.

Uncertainties about its future inhibited review of the diploma course but, in view of its recent revision, this was less serious than in the case of the secondary course. Questions about it had been raised nationally, partly because of concern that it was not preparing students for the challenges of the comprehensive school. As a result, the GTC set up a working party under Brunton, which reported in 1972 in favour of a contentious and potentially costly sandwich course.[26] SED sat on the report for three years, thereby creating a period of planning blight, and then rejected it. Only then could any serious revision of the structure of the secondary course get under way, although before then many individual departments had been revising their courses to take account of mixed ability classes and of the situation created by the raising of the school leaving age in 1972.

The biggest change in the secondary courses was in the training of PE teachers. Their basic course was the three-year diploma course, which gave them a sound practical training without stretching them intellectually. A degree route had been opened up for them but, because it only consisted of Ordinary and Higher classes within the structure of the Glasgow BEd, it was far from satisfactory. As degree courses in PE were developing throughout the UK, change was necessary if the SSPE was not to be left behind. The opportunity was taken, when Hugh Brown retired as Director in 1974, to recruit Bernard Wright, who came from south of the border with knowledge of the new developments. Because Glasgow University would not contemplate a professional degree in PE, an approach was made to the CNAA and, after much hard work by the staff of the SSPE and of the departments of Education and Psychology, a new four-year BEd in Physical Education and Human Movement was validated to begin in October 1975. So started the college's involvement with the CNAA, which was to have such an important influence on its development in the future.

Staffing

The growth in student numbers, diversification, the launch of the BEd— taken together these necessitated a dramatic increase in the number of academic staff. In 1958–59 there had been 123. By 1970–71 there were 312, of whom 237 were new. The turnover was even more rapid than this suggests. Because the 1960s was a period of general expansion, some staff stayed for relatively short periods before moving on. Some went to the Inspectorate or to the advisory services which the larger authorities were beginning to develop; the greater number went to the new colleges, which recruited from Jordanhill all three Principals (Walker at Hamilton, Rennie at Craigie and Leggatt at Callendar Park) as well as many of their senior staff.

In one respect this expansion did not lead to an improvement. The proportion of women staff slipped back to pre-1914 levels. In 1970–71, for instance, there were 93 women (31%) in an academic staff of 301 and only 7 women heads of department, all (with the exception of social work and speech therapy) in areas like needlework, womens' PE or the education of young children. What it did do was to improve promotion prospects, particularly after the Houghton report of 1974 with its recommendations for relating senior lectureships to student numbers.[27] As these were at their peak in the mid 1970s, the college was able to make a large number of promotions (32 in 1976); special procedures had to be created by the Governors. A Promotions Board was set up in 1975,[28] which brought the Governors more actively into the management of staffing and prepared the way for their important role in the period of contraction.

A further effect of expansion was on the communal life of the college. Until the early 1960s Jordanhill had been a close-knit community. There had been strong continuity in staffing; everyone had worked in one building;

and Wood and his wife had successfully fostered a family atmosphere. With the influx of new staff and their dispersal to buildings around the campus, this community spirit became more difficult to sustain. However, there were compensatory benefits. Some very able staff were attracted by the new BEd course; new staff brought fresh ideas to a rather conservative institution. One feature of it had been that almost all the staff (Wood himself was a notable exception) had trained at Jordanhill, taught in the west of Scotland and then come back to Jordanhill. The influx of the 1960s broke this closed circle. The outstanding 'outsider' was Lawrence Stenhouse but other figures—Round, Butts, Mangan, Marker and Wright—came from south of the border and made a mark on the college. This was a brief and untypical interlude. When the college contracted, the circle tended to close again.

Changes in college organisation
The same factors that led to an increase in staff also affected college organisation, which became more complex. In the late 1950s two new departments had been created, Further Education and Remedial Education. This period saw another seven: the five already mentioned (Youth and Community, Social Work, Speech Therapy, Inservice, and AV Media) plus Modern Studies and a separate department for the Education of Young Children. To cope with this complexity, Wood persuaded the Governors to appoint a second Vice principal in 1966, thus allowing Smith to concentrate on the developing areas of inservice, social work and youth and community. The new Vice principal was James Miller, who brought to the post not only a very acute mind but, like Smith, very useful experience of local government and of the Inspectorate.

In 1959 the college had also become more autonomous, with its own Board of Governors and Board of Studies. Although the Governors had the right to discuss any aspect of college affairs, in practice they confined themselves, like a university court, to such issues as finance, buildings, staffing and student welfare. Issues about courses and curricula were left to the Board of Studies.[29] As there had been no formal arrangements for staff participation in policy making prior to 1959, this created a new situation to which both the Principal and the staff had to adjust. After a decade of running the college in a different way, Wood had to open up to wider and more regular consultation, while staff used to more hierarchical arrangements had to learn to take their part in this. These adjustments were not made without difficulty. In 1961 Sillito (Head of Mathematics) was moved to write a letter to Wood suggesting that more needed to be done to encourage discussion in the Board.[30]

This letter was discussed and led to an agreement that there should be fuller agendas and more work done in committees. This was just the start of the pressure towards greater staff participation. In 1967 the Regulations were altered to make the Board more democratic. The number of elected members was now to be at least one-third and only lecturers and senior lecturers were entitled to vote for them. Four elected staff members were also added to the Board of Governors. By this time too the complexity of the college's work was producing a more formal committee structure, which drew more staff into discussion. The Board of Studies minutes list 13 of them: AV Education, Programmed Learning, BEd, Library, Linguistics, Further Education, Primary, Secondary, Physical Education, Examinations, Youth Service, Social Work and Inservice.[31] Throughout these changes Wood's management style was that of benign paternalism: willing to encourage discussion and to listen, but reserving the final decision to himself. This was generally accepted because most staff saw him as a wise and enlightened leader, for whose judgement they had great respect.

By the time Wood retired the pressure for a more democratic approach was building up. The memorandum which the Board of Studies submitted to the Select Committee on Education and Science argued that 'the powers of the Board of Studies should approach more closely those of a university senate'.[32] The convener of the group which prepared that submission was Tom Bone (then Head of Education). So when he succeeded Wood as Principal in 1972, he immediately declared that his policy would be to regard the Board as the policy making body and to accept its decisions. From then on, his management style was always to seek consensus in the Board, in which he was normally successful thanks to his skill as a chairman and to the thought given to planning agendas and to the presentation of issues. On the rare occasions when the majority of the Board went against him, the view of the Board was accepted.

The issue of student participation was more difficult. Demand for this really began to build up after the great wave of student protests in 1968. At first the college responded by encouraging departments to set up a network of staff student consultative committees and by offering the students places on some committees which seemed most relevant to their concerns, like the Student Welfare Committee of the Board of Governors.[33] What the students, or at least the SRC representatives, wanted was direct representation as of right on the Board of Governors and the Board of Studies.[34] This was more difficult to concede because it involved changes in the Regulations but Bone moved quickly to bring the students in as far as possible. At the first meeting of the Board after he became Principal he presented a paper on the options for student representation.[35] By January 1973, it had been agreed that there be five student observers on the Board and that they should have observers on appropriate sub-committees.[36]

Conclusion

These were in many ways the golden years for the college. This was partly because, in the post Robbins years, higher education in general was high on the political agenda and received more generous treatment than ever before or since. Within that political agenda, the colleges were in a specially favourable position:

> 'It was a golden age for the colleges in Brunton's time. In a sense they got away with murder. There was such a desperate shortage of teachers ... that they could get almost anything they wanted ... And there was very little control'.[37]

This does not necessarily mean that they were golden years for the students, who were sharply critical of many aspects of the college in the evidence which they presented to the Select Committee on Education and Science in 1970.[38] Staff too might grumble about overcrowding and delays in providing new facilities, but they could see that improvements were on the way. With student numbers increasing, new staff coming in, major changes taking place in schools, and the start of degree work in the college, the general feeling was one of old moulds being broken, of being at the start of a march towards a better and brighter future.

If the environment in which the college worked was uniquely favourable, nevertheless morale would not have been so high without the wise and humane leadership of Wood, who guided the institution with great skill and foresight through these changes. A rather shy and retiring man, who never really sought the limelight, he became a highly respected figure in Scottish education, sitting on many important committees (eg Appleby, Wheatley, Brunton) and invited by the British Council to give advice to education systems in developing countries. Recognition came in the form of a CBE in 1960 and a knighthood in 1976. When he retired, the chairman of the GTC paid this tribute: 'He had become the Principal to whom all the others for many years looked for inspiration and advice'.[39] Such things are often said in valedictions. In this instance, they have the ring of truth.

When Wood retired, there was little sign that the golden years might come to an end. Bone succeeded him in an atmosphere of optimism, which lasted for several more years. In addition to inheriting greatly improved facilities, he was also fortunate in being able to reshape much of the senior management team. At the end of 1972 Miller left to become Registrar of the GTC. George Riddell, his successor as Vice principal, came to the college from a headship in Shetland via a Principal Lectureship in Education at Craigie. Behind a rather stiff exterior, he was a man of very sound judgement with a slightly impish sense of humour, whose deep understanding of primary education was a great asset to a management team whose background otherwise was entirely secondary. Moffett had retired at the same time as Wood, and was replaced as Dean of Women by Marion Baillie. Then, in December 1975, Smith retired and his work was divided between two Assistant Principals, Willis Marker taking charge of inservice and Alasdair Nicolson taking a general oversight of social work and youth and community. Along with Robin McArthur, the team remained unchanged for the next ten years, except for Riddell's retiral in 1983.

Though the mood of optimism continued, there were already some small signs in the mid 1970s of the difficulties ahead. As the pressure on teacher supply eased, SED began to tighten its control by instituting, in 1973, new formal procedures for the approval of courses, by which the college had to submit to the Department all proposals for new courses leading to qualifications and for inservice courses not leading to qualifications, lasting one month or more. In one sense this was only a formalisation of existing arrangements; in another it was a warning that the college was not moving, as many had hoped, towards becoming an independent degree-granting institution.

The real storm cloud, however, was the approaching end of teacher shortage. As early as 1972–73, SED imposed a limit on the primary intake to the colleges as a whole, which was gradually reduced in the following years. These reductions were very tentative. Despite the warnings from their statisticians, ministers and officials had lived so long with teacher shortage that they could hardly believe it was coming to an end, and were reluctant to face the political outcry if they cut too much or too soon. Such cuts as were made did not affect Jordanhill, cushioned by the particular difficulties of teacher supply in the west of Scotland. So intake to the primary diploma course remained at around 350 a year up to 1975–76 when, bolstered by the continuing high demand for secondary teachers, student numbers reached their peak at 3713. Because up to that point there had been almost two decades of expansion, the shock was all the greater when that trend was sharply reversed.

Notes and references
1 The Teachers (Training Authorities) (Scotland) Regulations, 1959.
2 McPherson, A. and Raab, C.D. *Governing education*. Edinburgh: EUP, 1988. Chapter 5.
3 One consequence of the new composition of the Board of Governors was to diminish the clerical influence which had been so strong on the GPC.
4 Marker, W.B. *The spider's web: policy making in teacher education in Scotland, 1959–81*. Glasgow: University of Strathclyde, Sales and publications, 1994. Chapter 2.

5 SED. *Future education and training of teachers for further education in Scotland.* Edinburgh: HMSO, 1965. (Robertson report).

6 SED. *Primary education in Scotland.* Edinburgh: HMSO, 1965. (the Primary Memorandum).

7 SED. *From school to further education.* Edinburgh: HMSO, 1963. (Brunton report).

8 SED. *The structure of the curriculum in the third and fourth years of the Scottish secondary school.* Edinburgh: HMSO, 1977. (Munn report).

9 SED. *Assessment for all.* Edinburgh: HMSO, 1977. (Dunning report).

10 JBG minutes, 28 September 1967. Appendix II. Department of Inservice Training report for 1966–67.

11 Obituary in *Jordanhill Journal,* 20, Summer 1993.

12 JBG minutes, 27 November 1964. Appendix III. Department of Inservice Training report for 1963–64.

13 *Ibid.* 26 November 1965 ... report for 1964–65.

14 DES. *Teacher education and training.* London: HMSO, 1972. (James report).

15 'It was due to Mr Smith's initiatives that social work was established at Jordanhill ... he nurtured the growing department and personally chaired panels for the selection of students on Saturday mornings for several years'. V. Hiddleston. MS letter in author's possession, 25 March 1993.

16 JBG minutes, 20 September and 22 November 1963.

17 Marker, W.B. and Raab, C.D. Advise and construct: the expansion of the Scottish colleges of education. *Scottish educational review,* v.25:1, May 1993.

18 Fairley, J.A. *Jordanhill College of Education, 1921–71.* Glasgow: Jordanhill College, 1971. Chapters 8 & 9.

19 Named, like the Crawfurd Building, after a previous owner of the Jordanhill estate.

20 JBG minutes, 27 February 1969.

21 Committee on Higher Education. *Report.* London: HMSO, 1963. Cmnd 2145. (Robbins report).

22 JBS minutes, 25 February 1964.

23 *Ibid.,* 18 May 1959.

24 *Ibid.,* 15 June 1967. Appendix 9 is a very interesting paper by Stenhouse on the issues raised by the Primary Memorandum.

25 *Ibid.,* 17 April 1970.

26 GTC / SED. *The training of graduates for secondary education.* Edinburgh: HMSO, 1972. (Brunton report).

27 Committee of Inquiry into the pay of non university teachers. *Report.* London: HMSO, 1974. Cmnd 5848. (Houghton report).

28 JBG minutes, 19 September 1975.

29 Select Committee on Education and Science. *Teacher training* vol.2. Scottish sub-committee 1970. Evidence of Wood, para.929 and Bone, para.841–2.

30 JBS minutes, 10 January 1961.

31 *Ibid.,* 2 December 1966.

32 SCES. *op.cit*. Memorandum by Jordanhill Board of Studies.
33 JBG minutes. Student Welfare Committee, 14 November 1969.
34 SCES. *op.cit*. Memorandum by Jordanhill SRC.
35 JBS minutes, 19 January 1972.
36 *Ibid*., 24 January 1973.
37 HMCI J. Sandison. Interview with W.B. Marker, 14 May 1991.
38 SCES. *op.cit*. Memorandum by Jordanhill SRC.
39 GTC minutes, 2 December 1971.

5

Contraction and Take-over, 1976–81

Willis Marker

The sudden switch from expansion to contraction and its consequences for the college can only be understood within the wider political context. In 1973, the Yom Kippur War triggered a rise in oil prices and a bout of inflation which by 1975 was running at 25%. The Labour government was forced to adopt new measures to control public spending, including a switch to a system of cash limits, a change in the direction of policy which has lasted until the present day.[1] The Labour government, moreover, was not in a strong position politically. Since 1974 its overall majority was only three, and facing it on the opposition benches were 11 Scottish Nationalist MPs. So up to 1979 the government was very vulnerable to any charge that it was not defending Scottish interests. Meanwhile, in the mid 1970s the previous network of education authorities was replaced by nine regions and three island authorities. This reorganisation was particularly drastic in the west of Scotland, where the sprawling region of Strathclyde included half the population of Scotland.

It was within this context that SED finally faced up to the problem of reducing college intakes in line with the falling demand for teachers. So early in 1976 it proposed sharp cuts in the intakes to all the colleges. These were most severe for the primary diploma course; at Jordanhill the intake was reduced from 371 (in 1975) to 220. The secondary intake was not cut so drastically, but an important change of principle was made. Instead of the open door policy in which the colleges trained all qualified graduates who presented themselves, SED established a quota system in which priority was given to shortage subjects like mathematics and physics, while the intake to subjects like history and geography was drastically reduced.

In common with the other colleges, Jordanhill tried to bring political pressure on the government to lessen the impact of these cuts in various ways: to improve staffing standards in schools; to provide extra teachers in areas of deprivation; to introduce a four-year degree for primary teachers and to use more college staff for inservice training.[2] What transformed the situation temporarily was an outburst of student unrest, sparked off by the looming prospect of unemployment. As a result of the overproduction of previous years and of a sharp drop in wastage, Strathclyde Region was estimating that it would require only about 450 primary teachers for the coming session.[3] This came as a tremendous shock to the primary students, who had entered college confident that a teaching qualification was a job ticket for life.

In all the colleges their response was to stage a series of sit-ins and demonstrations. The sit-in at Jordanhill began early in May, led by Ian Davidson, the start of a political career that was to take him to be Convener of Strathclyde Region Education Committee and MP for Govan. The students occupied the whole of the administrative area and found convenient sleeping accommodation in the old library, recently refurbished to provide a new Inservice Suite. Although teaching and examinations were allowed to continue, for several weeks the students brought the administrative work of the college to a standstill, while trying to draw attention to their cause by marches in the city centre and even by a brief occupation of the City Chambers.[4] At the same time a flurry of questions was asked in the Commons. The government, however, stood firm and the sit-in crumbled away in early June. Its main effect proved to be in discouraging student recruitment, and the college failed to reach even its reduced quotas for 1976–77. Many staff, of course, were personally sympathetic to the students[6] but there was little the college could do. Its most positive response was to take advantage of the job creation schemes being promoted by the Manpower Services Commission. As a result over 20 projects were mounted over the next three years, giving temporary employment to over 700 students.[5]

When announcing the intake figures for 1976, SED had promised that this would be followed up by a review of their implications for the future shape and size of the college system. This eventually appeared in January 1977.[6] The Department forecast that for the next few years the colleges' intake of primary students (both diploma and postgraduate) should be about 1,000 and that the demand for secondary teachers would fall steadily. At the time these forecasts were much criticised. In reality, they turned out to be too optimistic and therefore too generous to the colleges. Even so, the clear implication was that there was massive over-capacity in the system and that the only sensible course of action was to close unwanted colleges.

The SED therefore proposed to close Craigie and Callendar Park; to transfer the training of women PE teachers to Dundee, thus allowing Dunfermline to be closed; and to merge Craiglockhart with either Moray House or Dundee, with safeguards for the Roman Catholic element in training. The threatened colleges at once began to mount strong campaigns against closure, which placed the other colleges in an awkward position. The main fear at Jordanhill was that the college would suffer disproportionately in order to give Craigie a viable intake. However, at a meeting between the JCCES and the Secretary of State in March 1977, Alan Mill (Chairman of Governors) raised this point and was given assurances by Bruce Millan that any cuts would be spread across all the colleges.[7] Other than that, there was little the college could do except watch and wait while the political battle raged. In the end, the government was forced to back down and all ten colleges survived. As the cutbacks in intake continued, this meant that a dwindling number of students was spread around more thinly. By 1980–81, the intake to the primary diploma course at Jordanhill was down to 90; the total number on the course to 280; and the total student population to 2064—a 44% decline from the peak of 3713 only five years previously.

Contraction on this scale was bound to create all sorts of pressure for change but SED policies left little room for positive responses. Publicly, the SED urged the colleges to seek to diversify, but in practice blocked every attempt to move into niches already occupied either by the universities or the central institutions. Even niches they might reasonably have expected to move into were denied them in the interests of reducing government spending. For instance, faced with cuts in the quota of PE students, the SSPE proposed to develop a degree course in sports studies and recreation but that proposal was rejected. Jordanhill was relatively fortunate: it was not completely dependent on teacher training and the demand for social workers, youth and community workers and speech therapists remained steady. The best it could do in the way of further diversification was to begin to seek overseas students and to second staff for training in teaching English as a foreign language, so that it could move into that market. These were interesting developments but on a very small scale.

The development of inservice education
The one area in which SED positively encouraged development was inservice education. Up to 1975, the college's provision of inservice took five main forms: the school-based work of the staff tutors; courses leading to a special qualification (eg the ITQ or the Diploma in Special Education); short courses in college either during the day or in the evening; the summer school; and the Saturday conferences for subject teachers, which were a special feature of the work at Jordanhill. Provision was therefore extensive, but it was largely unplanned. Most initiatives came from individual departments and were simply advertised to see what the response would be. A good deal of it also took place outside normal working hours. As a result, it was paid for as overtime and could not count towards the college's staffing complement. In the mid 1970s it began to be recognised that this pattern of provision had to change and that better planned and more effective forms of inservice should be developed.

At the end of 1975, Smith retired and Marker took over the inservice part of his work. Almost immediately, several new factors began to have a powerful influence. Strathclyde Region began to build up its own inservice programme, to which it gave priority over college courses. At the same time, the cutbacks in public expenditure from 1976 onwards made it more difficult for authorities both to fund release and to pay the expenses of teachers attending courses in their own time. Any expansion of full time courses therefore became very difficult. Nevertheless, the Region did support the development of courses in those areas which it regarded as vital. So substantial day release courses were developed jointly with Strathclyde, notably those in management for senior promoted staff in secondary schools and in guidance (in which Notre Dame was the third partner).

For these courses Strathclyde's policies were very positive; for award-bearing courses they were completely negative. For instance, the college joined with Notre Dame and the Open University in a scheme (unique in the UK) to base courses for Modules 3 and 4 of the OU Diploma in Reading Development in the two colleges. A similar scheme in Dundee was enthusiastically supported by Fife Region, but Strathclyde would have nothing to do with it and so very few teachers were willing to participate.[8] Award-bearing courses therefore could only be developed on a limited scale and on a part time basis. The most imaginative development was due mainly to Butts, whose department launched a college Diploma in Educational Technology, which in 1977 became the first predominantly distance learning course to be validated by the CNAA, and went on to become one of the most highly regarded and durable of the college's inservice courses. The most popular was the part time Associateship in Upper Primary Education, first offered in 1976.

Amidst these difficulties, SED came forward with an initiative which drastically changed the nature of inservice provision. In 1977–78 it allocated to the college the full time equivalent of 27 members of staff (later increased to 48), provided that they were used for school-focused inservice (SFIS), ie either directly for working with teachers in schools or for running courses in teachers' centres. This initiative was partly an expedient to cushion the impact of the cuts in initial training, but the HMCI in charge of teacher education also undoubtedly saw it as a genuine opportunity to use spare capacity in colleges to improve inservice provision. To justify this allocation, closely monitored by SED, to whom elaborate returns had to be made detailing how staff time had been used, SFIS had to be rapidly expanded. Some part of the expansion was achieved by building on the success of the staff tutors' workshop course. Members of staff from other departments were encouraged to become involved so that more courses could be run and so that follow-up in schools could be more intensive. Another part was achieved by developing some joint projects with Strathclyde. However, most of the SFIS came from a large number of small scale departmental or individual initiatives.

This expansion of inservice represented a massive shift in the allocation of college resources. From being a peripheral activity, it quite suddenly became (in terms of its demands on staffing) more important than any single college course. For an institution dominated from its outset by courses for the initial training of primary and secondary teachers, this was bound to be an uncomfortable change, and it sparked off some intense debates about whether there should be a much extended cadre of staff devoted full time to inservice, so that the college could respond flexibly to the needs of the schools.[9] This idea was opposed by most heads of department, reluctant to lose staff when preservice was contracting, and by staff, who were wary of committing themselves to the unpredictable demands of inservice. These structural and attitudinal problems in the college were compounded by those of Strathclyde Region, which never managed to find ways of articulating its inservice needs with any precision or far enough in advance to permit the rational planning of college resources.

There was indeed a basic flaw: that Strathclyde was responsible for the staff development of its teachers, while the colleges controlled the major resource. As a result, SFIS never realised its full potential. Nevertheless, thanks to the talent and commitment of many of the staff involved, a great deal of valuable work was done in schools, which helped them and the college by stimulating staff and by offering them possibilities for growth and development in a time of contraction.

Management of resources

As the expansion of inservice could only mitigate the severity of the cuts in preservice, the college was put under pressure to take a more systematic approach to the way in which it managed its resources. When SED reprieved the colleges, it insisted that they should all carry out an accommodation review. The college benefited from this by abandoning most of the remaining prefabs and substandard buildings and by centralising nearly all departments in the college buildings proper from 1978–79.[10]

Management of staffing resources was much more controversial. During the years of expansion, the college had not felt the need for any strategic plan nor for any mechanism linked to it for the management of staffing. Nevertheless, as the balance of work shifted, some ways had to be found of matching resources to new developments. The college therefore moved cautiously in that direction. From 1978–79 onwards, all major committees of the Board of Studies were asked to submit development plans, which were discussed by the Board. But it was not until November 1980 that a

Policy and Resources Committee was set up, following criticisms made by the CNAA during its first Institutional Review visit in the January. The most difficult problem posed by contraction was that of reducing the numbers of academic, technical and administrative staff. Since 1972, the entitlement to academic staff had been calculated according to ratios agreed with the SED, which ranged from 9:1 for the BEd to 13:1 for the diploma course. As student numbers fell from 1976 onwards, the college became overstaffed in terms of these ratios and was pressed by SED to reduce staffing until it was in line with entitlement.

This gave an added prominence to the role of the Board of Governors, legally the employers, and to ALCES, the union representing staff. The Governors' policy throughout was that compulsory redundancy should be avoided, if at all possible. Within that context, they considered what procedures should be adopted where reductions in academic staff were necessary. After consultation with ALCES, an Establishment Committee was set up, chaired by the Chairman of Governors, and including governors, senior academic staff and other elected staff. This had to consider whether SED should be asked to fill any vacancies that arose; but its main task was to consider applications for voluntary redundancy. Parallel procedures were set up for the technical and administrative staff, although in their case it was less clear what the college's entitlement should be.[11]

These procedures were very time consuming. The college was therefore most fortunate that Mill and other governors were willing to give that time and that they dealt with these delicate issues with a consideration and impartiality, which gained the confidence of the staff. The magnitude of their task can be gauged from the fact that between 1976 and 1980 the number of academic staff was reduced by 67, 50 by voluntary redundancy and 17 by non replacement of staff who had retired or taken other appointments. It was, however, made easier by the very generous redundancy terms on offer through the 'Crombie' agreements, by which staff over the age of 55 could retire with two-thirds of their salary (index-linked) until the age of 67.

If the college came through this difficult period without great damage to staff morale, a price had to be paid in some of the undesirable consequences of contraction and voluntary redundancy. Recruitment of staff with recent experience of schools stopped. If heads of department left, they had to be replaced by internal promotions instead of by recruitment throughout the UK. Some of the staffing imbalances created by redundancy were offset by transferring staff between departments. For instance, people from overstaffed secondary departments were moved into departments like Primary Education and Special Educational Needs. Even with retraining, such transfers were not always satisfactory. There is little doubt that these factors weakened the college, but a more ruthless approach by the Governors would probably have weakened it more without affecting the main problem—the inability to recruit new staff.

Contraction and the students

Contraction brought more tension for the students than for the staff. Less so for the secondary students, for whom it was easier to make rapid adjustments between supply and demand through the system of subject quotas. The main effect of these was a beneficial one: that most college departments could now select students instead of having to train any graduate who chose to come. For the large numbers of primary students in the pipeline and aware that their employment prospects were poor, it was a different story. Suddenly their grades for teaching practice acquired a crucial importance and their relationships with the tutors changed accordingly. For decades the tutors had been able to assume the role of counsellor and friend; now they were thrust into the uncongenial role of judge, a throwback to the situation in the 1930s, but with the added difficulty that the students of the 1970s were more likely to challenge their tutors' judgements.

An added source of tension came from attempts to create a fair national system. To help them with the difficult task of selecting the best students, the education authorities negotiated an agreement with the CP that all students would be placed in four bands: 15% in Band I, 15% in Band II, 40% in Band III and 30% in Band IV.[12] Some scheme of this sort was essential if colleges were not to inflate their students' grades in an attempt to give them an edge in a highly competitive market; but it was unpopular with staff and students, as those with good college grades were forced by the norm-referenced national system into lower bands. There were several heated debates on the subject in the Board of Studies in which the system was attacked, particularly by those in departments with small numbers of students, who argued most strongly against its distorting effects.[13] They failed, however, to propose a better alternative. Good grades were one way of getting an edge in the market; a degree rather than a diploma was another. So another effect of contraction was to encourage more primary students to opt for the BEd degree. The BEd however had been devised mainly as a degree for secondary teachers; this shift underlined its unsuitability as a preparation for primary teaching, and attempts were then made to reform it.

One unintended effect of cuts and unemployment was to discourage men from entering primary teaching. In 1975–76 there had still been an intake of 22 men to the diploma course. By 1978–79 it was down to 5; by 1981–82 to 1. The number on the postgraduate primary course fell almost as drastically. Contraction therefore reinforced the stereotype of primary teaching as a woman's world.

Developments in difficult times

These years of contraction and uncertainty were never likely to be marked by major innovations. Even outside teacher education, where the environment was less unsettled, progress was difficult because of restraints on government spending, which blocked attempts to develop degree courses for social work and youth and community students. The only important change was in speech therapy, where a specialised degree in Speech Pathology and Therapeutics, with an honours route, was approved to start in 1978. Within teacher education, despite the difficulties, attempts were made with varying success to improve all the major courses.

The future of the BEd had been put in doubt by the SED's suggestion that the secondary BEd should be discontinued.[14] Although this suggestion was not pressed in 1977, it had the effect of discouraging applications. By the end of 1977, the Board of Studies was already noting that many of the BEd classes had very small groups and that it was overstaffed at the expense of other areas of work.[15] So it set up a working party on the future of the BEd, which suggested that its future might be secured, either by having a joint foundation year with social work and youth and community students or by making it more suitable for primary teachers.[16] Nothing came of the first alternative, but some progress was made with the second. As had been the case when the BEd was set up, developments were inhibited by the conservative attitude of Glasgow University. The university did make some concessions: two college courses instead of one could count as graduating passes and students were to be allowed to transfer to the BEd after the first year of the diploma course with credit for one graduating pass. But attempts to relate the two college courses more closely to the primary curriculum ran into difficulties. The university accepted a course in reading, but not in environmental studies.[17] This was as far as change went but at the end of 1980 a joint working party was set up with the university to discuss ways of adapting the BEd to the needs of primary teachers and the college began to develop ideas for a new structure.[18]

Attempts to reform the primary diploma course were inhibited by the expectation that it would soon be replaced by a degree. The secondary course fared better. Once the SED had rejected the Brunton report, steps were taken to tackle some of its weaknesses, notably those of college/school liaison and of the fragmentation of contributions from education, psychology and the subject departments. A move to improve college/school liaison had been taken in 1973, in response to the Brunton report, when a small number of schools agreed to designate staff as 'teacher regents'.[19] The basic idea of the scheme was simply that in each school there would be a senior member of staff (typically an AHT) with a dual role: pastorally, as the person to whom students turned for advice; professionally, as a tutor running seminars on general aspects of the working of the school. The regent scheme was an interesting and worthwhile initiative, but its effectiveness was limited by Strathclyde Region's refusal to give it any official recognition.

The problem of fragmentation was tackled by a working party chaired by Colin Holroyd. On its recommendation, all the one-year secondary courses were amalgamated from 1976–77, putting an end to the distinction (rooted in the old system of Chapters III, V and VI) between courses for honours graduates, ordinary graduates and diplomates. An attempt was made to break down the barriers between Education, Psychology and the subject departments through an interesting scheme for a 'coordinated day', ie on certain days the students in college were put into interdepartmental groups to study and discuss themes. Although this scheme had to contend with the familiar difficulties of interdepartmental cooperation, it was nevertheless an imaginative step.

Such moves towards a more systematic form of course planning would probably not have been so quick or so strong without outside influences. Indirectly there was that of the Open University, which in the 1970s was setting new and higher standards for well-planned course materials. More directly, however, there was the influence of the CNAA. Since the BEd in PE and Human Movement in 1975 several other courses had been validated by the Council: a postgraduate Diploma in Educational Technology (1977); an Inservice BEd in PE (1978) and a postgraduate Diploma in Computer Education, run jointly with Paisley College (1980). These, however, were confined to two areas, the SSPE and Inservice, which were often seen as outside the mainstream of preservice teacher education. Moreover to many staff with personal ties to Glasgow University and comfortable with its undemanding approach to validation, the CNAA seemed an unwelcome, English-dominated body.

For over 20 years, since the end of inspection, the college had really had no outside scrutiny. It was therefore not fully prepared for the sort of questions raised when the CNAA came for its first Institutional Review visit in 1980. Although the visiting party's report praised the commendably high academic standards of the college courses, it went on to make trenchant criticisms: that the college did not have an adequate forum for strategic planning, that planning was hampered because the Board of Studies played no part in resource allocation, that there was no agreed plan for staff development and that the Board of Studies did not effectively exercise its responsibility for maintaining academic standards.[21] These criticisms could not be ignored and the college's response to them led to important changes in internal organisation and course planning, whose main effects were not felt until the 1980s.

A more indirect effect of involvement with the CNAA was to encourage research, because the Council took the view that this was an essential feature of an institution of higher education. Pressure came more directly from the need to justify staffing in a time of contraction. In December 1978 the Research Committee urged that more should be done to safeguard staff time for research.[22] By 1980 the Institutional Review report was able to list 9 major funded research projects. Although its research record compared favourably with those of other Scottish colleges, research remained a marginal activity, because of the difficulties of securing funding and of allocating staff time in usable blocks. There was also the inherent difficulty that most of the staff had been recruited for their practical expertise and saw their main task lying in the improved performance of their students. They had less interest in the sort of research which led to academic publication. The college research community was therefore concentrated almost exclusively in the departments of Education and Psychology.

The need to meet CNAA criteria for the validation of courses and for the organisational structures which underpinned them was one example of the way in which, during this period, the college saw its autonomy reduced. The severer constraints, however, came from the SED. Contraction brought tighter control of staff numbers and monitoring of staff utilisation, while cuts in public spending brought reduced resources. To control developments that would require resources, the SED introduced a new two-stage procedure for the approval of courses. Bone took the lead in the CP in protesting against this, both as an increase in bureaucracy but 'mainly on the basis of the undermining of academic freedom'.[23] The CP's protests left the SED unmoved. The college might complain that SED was hampering its development, but it also used its power to insist that new courses should be externally validated, a policy in the college's long term interest.

The take-over of Hamilton College
The general election of 1979 brought to power a Conservative government, with the declared aim of reducing spending on public services. By this time, the cuts in intake had made the overcapacity of the college system even more glaring than it had been in 1977. So it was only a matter of time before the question of college closures came back on the agenda. The expected government announcement came in August 1980. In most respects, it was a repeat of the proposals made by Labour in 1977. The only differences were that Dunfermline was to be reprieved and that Hamilton was to be closed instead of Craigie. Naturally, the Hamilton staff launched a vigorous campaign, similar to that which had saved other colleges in 1977. This time the political situation was quite different. Early in 1981 it became clear that there would be no serious backbench revolt, and that the government was bound to get its way. In March, the Hamilton Governors conceded that

closure was inevitable and opened negotiations with SED for the sake of the staff and students.

Behind the scenes, informal talks were taking place between Jordanhill and Hamilton. Once the Hamilton Governors had conceded defeat, these informal talks were followed up by more formal meetings, and from that point on events moved swiftly, driven by the government's political imperative to be seen to be closing Hamilton at the end of the session. By June the negotiations had been completed. It had been agreed that the Hamilton Board of Governors would be wound up and that the college would become the responsibility of the Jordanhill Board (enlarged by four additional members from the Hamilton Board) on the following conditions:

1 that Jordanhill took over the Hamilton College buildings, but would dispose of them after the end of session 1981–82;
2 that the Hamilton academic staff were all to be transferred to Jordanhill, with their salaries conserved;
3 that the non academic staff could be transferred to Jordanhill if vacancies arose;
4 that the primary diploma students entering their final year in 1981–82 would complete it at Hamilton. Those entering their second year would continue their course at Hamilton in 1981–82 but would then transfer to Jordanhill;
5 that the BEd students in Year II at the end of 1981–82 should be allowed to transfer either to Jordanhill or Craigie;
6 that inservice provision would be maintained in the Lanark Division, using the college in 1981–82 and thereafter an outstation to be established in Lanarkshire.

The Hamilton campaign had failed to keep the college open but it had been sufficiently effective to win a number of significant concessions. What SED gained from these was that Jordanhill took over the responsibility for Hamilton, including the problems of selling the Hamilton buildings and possibly of making staff redundant.

Notes and references

1 Midwinter, A. et al. *Politics and public policy in Scotland*. London: Macmillan, 1990. p.110.
2 JBG minutes, 15 April 1976. Appendix.
3 GTC. Minutes of Supply Committee, 26 May 1976.
4 *Glasgow Herald*, 27 and 28 May 1976.
5 Jordanhill College. *Report for the Institutional Review visit of the CNAA*. 1980. p.53.
6 SED. *Teacher training from 1977 onwards*. January 1977.
7 JPC minutes, 8 March 1977.

8 Marker, W.B. The Open University and teacher education in Scotland. *Open learning*, v.6:1, 1991.
9 JBS minutes, 14 October 1976 and 22 March 1979.
10 *Ibid.*, 16 February 1978.
11 Jordanhill College. 1980. *op.cit.* pp.44–51.
12 CP minutes, 14 December 1977.
13 JBS minutes, 11 October 1979 and 23 October 1980.
14 SED. 1977. *op.cit.*
15 JBS minutes, 10 November 1977. By 1978–79, there was only one BEd class with ten students or more, five with between five and nine; and six with under five.
16 *Ibid.*, 8 December 1977.
17 *Ibid.*, 23 March 1978 and 20 March 1980.
18 *Ibid.*, 11 December 1980 and 23 January 1981.
19 Archer, E.G. and Peck, B.T. *The Jordanhill regent scheme.* Glasgow: Jordanhill College, 1982.
20 JBS minutes, 12 November 1975.
21 *Ibid.*, 23 October 1980. Appendix on CNAA Institutional Review report.
22 *Ibid.*, 7 December 1978.
23 J.P.C. minutes, 25 February 1981.

6

From Take-over to Merger: 1981–93

Willis Marker

From 1981 to 1993 Britain was ruled by Conservative governments, which tended to look at higher education with a critical eye. As a result there was pressure to cut costs and increase efficiency, driving the unit of resource gradually down. Institutions of higher education were told that their first purpose was 'to serve the economy more effectively'.[1] In order to do so, they were encouraged to make closer links with industry and to seek more of their funding from private sources. Some were indeed successful in doing so but there was little opportunity for this in teacher education. There, as elsewhere, the financial pressures meant worsening staff student ratios, less money for books and equipment, and a relative decline in the value of academic salaries. Until late in the 1980s the SED sought to implement government policies by tightening central controls. In 1983, it revived formal inspection of the colleges. The Department insisted on national guidelines for all the major courses of initial training and tried to extend them to award-bearing inservice courses. Course approval procedures therefore became more elaborate and time-consuming.

As always, the college had to look two ways, both towards other sectors of higher education and towards the schools, where the 1980s saw some very important developments in the curriculum. The new Standard Grade examinations, designed for the full range of abilities in secondary schools, began to replace O grades in 1986 and by the end of the decade the process was complete. The secondary schools were also affected by the SED Action Plan. Launched in 1983 with the FE sector mainly in view, this replaced the existing confusion of courses by a system of 40-hour modules, leading to a National Certificate. The schools soon realised the value of these for the growing number of pupils who wished to stay on into S5 but for whom Higher Grade courses were not appropriate. These changes in the secondary and FE curricula raised questions about their articulation with what went before. In response, SED set up working parties which drew up national guidelines for the age range 5–14 in five currricular areas: mathematics, language arts, environmental studies, expressive arts, and religious and moral education. Their implementation was then gradually phased in by schools.

All these changes greatly affected the work of the college. In 1981, however, its most immediate problem was that of completing successfully the take-over of Hamilton College. On the whole this took place very smoothly, helped by a great deal of goodwill on both sides and by the fact that many of the staff had worked together on committees. Some of the Hamilton promoted staff naturally felt their reduction to lecturer status but the pain of transition was eased by the avoidance of compulsory redundancies, by conserved salaries and by the opportunity, as promoted posts fell vacant, to compete for them on equal terms. The only controversial aspect of the take-over was the sale of the Hamilton site and buildings. In December 1981, against the advice of their Chief Valuer, SED agreed that the Governors should advertise the sale through the college solicitors and, in October 1982, the Governors accepted an offer of £270,000 for the college building from a private school company and of £410,000 for the residences from a property developer.[2] This provoked such an outcry that the Public Accounts Committee decided to mount an enquiry. Its report was very critical of SED for ignoring the advice of the Chief Valuer and allowing the sale to the private sector at knock-down prices of buildings which the Valuer estimated might have fetched £6 million.[3]

Numbers and types of students
After the cutbacks and closures, the college system could only have expanded again if the birthrate had risen. Instead it remained at a low and stable level throughout the 1980s. In the early years of the decade, the effects of the decline in the birth rate which had begun in the late 1960s were still working their way through the secondary schools, only partly offset by the higher staying on rates. Throughout most of the 1980s, therefore, the student numbers in the college were declining. Exact numbers are difficult to calculate because of changes made by SED in the way it arrived at the FTE for FE students. Leaving aside FE, inservice courses and overseas students, the number of students on other courses went down from 1726 (1981–82) to a low point of 1175 (1988–89) before increasing again to 2025 in 1992–93. These fluctuations were outwith the college's control, as SED continued to impose quotas (or from 1989 only slightly more flexible 'targets') and to turn the tap of teacher supply off and on in unpredictable ways, which made forward planning difficult.[4]

Within these numbers, the stable elements were the speech therapy, social work and community education students. Other groups, however, saw significant changes in their fortunes. In 1981, the primary students were outnumbered by the secondary, but their numbers thereafter steadily increased and in 1992 the 761 students on the primary BEd course were the largest group in the college. Even so, the quotas for the BEd and the primary

PGCE were quite small and the competition for places so strong that the academic standards required for entry rose considerably.[5] At the same time, in common with other institutions of higher education, the college tried to open up entry routes for mature students and / or those with non traditional qualifications. It joined a consortium, the Scottish Wider Access Programme (SWAP) offering courses whose successful completion guaranteed students a place on the BEd course. These programmes began to feed students into the BEd from 1990. None of this, however, made any difference to the gender balance on the primary courses. In 1981–82 there had been only four men on the diploma course. The change to a degree course failed to attract any more. In the 1985–86 intake, there were four men out of 145 and the proportion on the PGCE course was similar.

While the primary numbers rose, the numbers on the one-year secondary course roughly halved from about 400 in 1981–2 to around 200 in 1984–85, and they remained at that low level until the end of the decade. In addition, there were two further losses: the ending of the secondary BEd and the closure of the SSPE. The future of the secondary BEd had been in doubt since 1977 and these doubts had led an increasing proportion of the BEd students to opt for the primary route. When an SED consultative paper proposed that it should be ended, the college tried to defend it[6] but, whatever the merits of concurrency, the course was so obviously uneconomical that SED ignored the protests and announced that there would be no intake to it from 1983.

The loss of the SSPE was a much greater blow. From 1981, a cut in the intake to the BEd in PE had left the School vulnerable. Wright and his colleagues saw the obvious danger and diversified. In cooperation with the Community Education department, they started a BA in Sport in the Community in 1982 for both male and female students. Again this was farsighted, because equal opportunities legislation pointed to a future in which both the SSPE and Dunfermline were mixed. In view of these developments and of the high reputation of the SSPE, it came as a shock when the Secretary of State (Malcolm Rifkind) announced in 1986 that the training of all PE teachers was to be centralised at Dunfermline. The college protested[7] and a deputation of Governors went to meet Rifkind, who claimed that the decision was purely educational, taken on the advice of the Inspectorate in response to the falling demand for PE teachers and the requirements of equal opportunities legislation. These claims, however, rang hollow when the intake to Dunfermline was doubled in 1987, making it large enough to support courses in both the east and the west. The SSPE staff therefore felt betrayed. They did not even have the satisfaction of seeing the college fight a campaign to save them as Bone and the Governors judged, correctly, that it would have been futile.[8]

Alongside these major losses there were developments in recruiting overseas students. Efforts to do this were set back when the government decided that overseas students should pay full-cost fees. However, under Nicolson's leadership, the Committee for the Education of Overseas Students continued to develop international links. The strongest of these were in the field of environmental education in which the college built up a reputation based on Jim Dunlop's work in the Jordanhill Project in International Understanding and on the involvement of others in the CADISPA (Conservation and Development in Sparsely Populated Areas) project. Important links were also made with the World Wide Fund for Nature. These strands came together in the late 1980s, when CNAA validated a modular award-bearing course for overseas students, and when the WWF Environmental Education Resource Centre was created, officially opened by Lynda Chalker (the Minister for Overseas Development) in 1990. By 1992 a Master's programme in environmental education was under way.

The fall in student numbers and, in particular the loss of the SSPE, left the college with a surplus of accommodation. Following the Inspectorate report,[9] SED sought to solve this problem, and that of the shortage of accommodation at Queen's College, Glasgow, by persuading the Governors to lease most of the Crawfurd Building to Queen's. The Governors were reluctant to do so unless SED agreed to convert three of the now surplus gymnasia into a integrated arts area.[10] A deal was eventually agreed on these lines. Queen's moved into the Crawfurd building and part of the library; the Arts Division moved into the converted gymnasia in 1991.

Changes in courses: initial training
In 1981, the college faced the problem that two of the main routes into primary teaching needed revision: the primary diploma course because it had been devised nearly 15 years before and the BEd because it was now mainly taken by primary students. Anticipating that the diploma course would be replaced by a degree, the college decided that the best way forward was to make the BEd a more satisfactory preparation for primary teaching. This revision was underway when, in 1983, the government announced that the secondary BEd was to end and that a four-year BEd degree was to replace the primary diploma from 1984. When the national guidelines for the new BEd appeared, it became clear that the revised course did not meet them and that course planning would have to start again from the beginning. The result was that, in 1984, the college found itself committed to running the two former versions of the BEd course, the last year of the diploma course and the first year of the new degree. This difficulty resolved itself in time, and in the end the primary students gained a degree course genuinely geared to their professional needs.

SED then followed up its guidelines for the degree with another set for the postgraduate primary course. One feature of these (and of the subsequent secondary ones) was their emphasis on the practical. In accordance with UK-wide trends, the course was lengthened to 36 weeks, and 18 weeks of school experience were stipulated. Also, the role of the GTC as gate keeper to the profession was strengthened by giving it the task of accrediting courses against the criteria of the guidelines. The new BEd had been taken for validation to the Scottish Council for the Validation of Courses for Teachers (SCOVACT) as the college wished it still to be a Glasgow degree. This experience convinced many of those involved that SCOVACT lacked the expertise of CNAA in primary education.[11] So the new PGCE was taken to CNAA and validated in 1986.

Reform of the one-year secondary course presented even more difficulties than the primary courses. Because of falling student numbers, the number training in many subjects became very small. So, from 1982 onwards, the SED began to suggest that the teaching of courses with small numbers of students should be concentrated in certain colleges. Others would lose the right to teach certain subjects or only be allowed to offer them on a rota basis. The college's immediate response was to claim that it should continue to offer courses in all subjects.[12] These discussions finally came to a head in 1986 when the college lost the SSPE, and for several years, the training of secondary art teachers.

The subject departments had the threat hanging over them of losing their postgraduate students at the same time as they were losing the Ordinary and Higher classes of the BEd. Inevitably this created some defensive attitudes. It was perhaps a symptom of this that the arrangements for the coordinated day broke down in 1982.[13] In any case, because of its fragmentation among subject departments, the secondary course had always been difficult to plan as a whole, and made more difficult by the fact that students could take the Glasgow University DipEd concurrently. In these circumstances, it was positively helpful that there should be national guidelines and that the course should be taken to CNAA (in 1987) and therefore planned more coherently from the students' point of view than ever before.

Alongside this revision of the basic secondary course, there were important new developments in specialist areas. Because of the rapid advances in technology and of the introduction of the new Standard Grade examination in technological education, there was a national consensus that the training of technical teachers needed substantial revision. SED therefore encouraged colleges to seek the cooperation of local universities in mounting a new four-year degree, Bachelor of Technological Education. The college approached the Engineering departments at Glasgow University and, with their enthusiastic support, the new degree was ready for its first intake in

1987. The same year saw the beginning of another example of inter-institutional cooperation, a BEd degree (CNAA) in Music run jointly with St Andrew's College and the Royal Scottish Academy of Music and Drama. In the 1980s the School of Further Education began to find it difficult to recruit students for an initial training course which required attendance for four terms spread over two years. The response was to offer an innovative scheme, starting in 1986, in which part of the work was to be done through distance learning or through the support of a mentor in the place of work, thereby reducing the time spent in college.

Outwith the field of teacher education, changes were slower in coming. The least problematic area was that of speech therapy, where there was a well established degree. In 1982 its title was changed from BEd to BSc in line with UK-wide practice. Otherwise there was simply the normal process of course review, which led to a major revision in 1989. Progress towards upgrading qualifications in social work and community education were held back for several reasons. Some employers doubted whether they wanted an all graduate entry. Certain politicians were less than enthusiastic about social workers and community educators; while SED was concerned about the resource implication of longer courses. In the end the Department could not hold out against the general trend to make a first degree the benchmark for entry to any profession. So the college was at last allowed to offer BA degrees in Community Education (1991) and in Social Work (1992).

Tight central controls continued to give the college little leeway to diversify in response to falling numbers on initial teacher training courses. The main thrust came in physical education. Once the training of PE teachers had been transferred to Dunfermline, it became vital for those PE staff who stayed in the college to build on the success of the BA in Sport in the Community. So, as the BEd in PE ran down, they entered into cooperation with other departments to devise a new structure for BA degrees. What emerged was a core course leading into three specialist outlets in Sport in the Community, Community Arts, and Outdoor Education. Validated by CNAA in 1989 these proved very popular and by 1992–93 there were 167 students on course. Planning also began in cooperation with the Universities of Aberdeen and Strathclyde which was to lead to the Scottish Institute of Sports Medicine and Sports Science. These developments, however, only compensated for the loss of the SSPE. To compensate for other losses, the college remained heavily dependent on developments in inservice education.

Changes in courses: post-initial training
In the inservice field, this was a period of fluctuating fortunes: on the one hand, the rise and fall of school-focused, later to be called school and agency focused inservice (SAFIS); on the other, the burgeoning of award-bearing

courses. The take-over of Hamilton raised the college complement for inservice to 68 FTE. At this level, inservice represented about a quarter of the college's work and, unless it had been on this scale, contraction would have been very difficult to manage. This complement had to be earned and college staff made strenuous efforts to do so. In every session up to 1983–84 the staffing targets for inservice were achieved or exceeded. The Inservice Department also tried hard to channel those efforts into structured projects and did achieve some improvement even though too much of the matching process was outwith its control.[14]

These encouraging developments were blown off course by the protracted teachers' dispute from 1984–87 during which the unions urged their members to boycott development work and inservice. So, from 1984–86 the college could not meet its staffing targets. Meanwhile, SED was becoming dissatisfied with the deficiencies in the matching process and, following UK-wide trends, began to move away from a system in which resources were controlled by the providers (the colleges) to one controlled by the clients (the education authorities and eventually the schools).

In 1986–87, the college was asked to draw up contracts for SAFIS with the education authorities and to submit them to SED for approval. By 1988–89, all SAFIS was brought within this contractual system. The college was also asked to allocate staffing to certain national priority tasks: 'top-slicing' in the jargon. This was a source of strength to the college because staff were closely involved in major developments in Scottish education, like the development of Standard Grade, in a way which had no parallel in England.[15] Hardly was this system of control fully in place, when the government decided to replace it with the discipline of market forces. Funding was switched to the education authorities in 1991, who could then use it to purchase inservice from any provider they wished. To cushion the blow, the education authorities were obliged initially to spend most of the money on services provided by the colleges at full economic cost. By 1992–93 that safety net had been withdrawn and the volume of SAFIS declined sharply, with a serious loss of income to the college.

So ended the high hopes engendered in the late 1970s when the college received its big allocation for SFIS. To some extent it was a story of missed opportunities. It was never going to be easy for the college to devise an organisation which supported equally the provision of predictable, timetabled preservice courses and the flexible provision of inservice. None of the colleges succeeded in doing so and, through the staff tutor team and other arrangements, Jordanhill probably did it better than any other.

The development of modular award-bearing courses continued to be difficult in the 1980s. The only area where the education authorities would consider releasing teachers was that of special educational needs and it was there that the first progress was made. The Diploma in SEN (Recorded Pupils) was validated by CNAA in 1983 and that for Non Recorded Pupils in 1985, the latter run both for Strathclyde and, on an outreach basis, for Dumfries and Galloway. In other fields progress had to be through part time or open learning courses. The major difficulty here was that courses outwith the college day or year could only be staffed by volunteers paid for overtime. Fortunately, there was a strong tradition of enthusiastic volunteer staff. So, when SED decided on the change to all graduate entry to primary teaching and recognised that this must be accompanied by opportunities for diplomates to upgrade their qualifications, the college was able to start a part time Inservice BEd degree (CNAA) in 1984.

This was always intended as the first stage in a more extended modular scheme. The next stage was not long in coming—a Diploma in Professional Studies in Education with specialist components in Community Education and Education Management—a CNAA validated modular structure into which further specialisms and options could be slotted and through which people could chart a variety of pathways. The first such pathway, the Certificate in Further Studies in Education, was opened up straight away but after that progress was held up for several years, while SED refused to approve any new courses unless they met national guidelines drawn up by SCOSDE. However, as with SAFIS, it then switched from bureaucratic to financial controls and allowed colleges to offer any courses which were self-financing. Iain Smith and Bill Thomson seized this opportunity and devised a modular scheme, within the SCOTCAT framework, in which credits could be earned to build up through certificates and diplomas to a Master's degree. As by this time validating bodies were more sympathetic towards the accreditation of prior or experiential learning, the scheme was very flexible and soon proved so popular that by 1992–93 nearly 2,000 students were enrolled on it. This timely growth helped to counterbalance the decline in SAFIS.

The development of modular Master's degrees was paralleled on a smaller scale by that of research degrees. The first one or two students had registered with the college for CNAA research degrees in the mid 1980s but there was little development until Douglas Weir was appointed Director of Research in 1988. This coincided with the encouragement of research by CNAA, which pushed the idea that research degrees should be part of the activities of a mature institution. So by the early 1990s there were about 20 people registered for research degrees, either PhDs or MPhils.[16]

The influence of the CNAA
One common feature of all these new or revised courses was that they were externally validated. Until 1982, external validation, except for the Glasgow

BEd, meant validation by the CNAA. In that year, the Scottish universities came together to create SCOVACT, and this gave colleges a choice. Most other colleges chose to remain with CNAA, but in Jordanhill opinions were divided. Some staff argued for SCOVACT validation which would lead to Glasgow awards and others argued for the advantages of being part of CNAA's UK-wide network of peer review. The outcome was a mixed economy in which the primary BEd, the BTechEd, and the TQ(FE) were validated by SCOVACT but all other courses were validated by CNAA.

The process of external validation had extensive internal repercussions. Before a course could be submitted to external scrutiny, convincing documentation had to be prepared and the course team had to be ready to answer the probing questions of the visiting party. The validating bodies, particularly the CNAA, therefore had a powerful influence on course planning. Although CNAA always disclaimed any intention of imposing a particular model of course design, its visiting parties certainly came with certain expectations. They looked for a course which had been planned as a whole by the team that was to teach it. There should be a rationale for the course design and clearly-defined aims and objectives, which described what the students would learn. The various elements in the course should be inter-related: the buzz words were 'coherence' and 'progression'. Procedures should be in place for evaluation and review.

For most members of staff, accustomed to considerable freedom in deciding what they would teach and how, this was unfamiliar territory. It was, however, vital that the college should be successful in it. So, in 1982, after a staff conference devoted to validation, an Internal Validation Procedures Committee (IVPC) was created.[17] This had the delicate task of developing a culture in which colleagues accepted the need to specify in detail what they intended and then to explain and justify it. Inevitably, questioning by the IVPC created some tensions, but most colleagues saw the necessity and benefits of the new procedures. Their success can be judged by the fact that the college never failed to have a submission validated first time. Naturally there were criticisms of these procedures for the amount of time-consuming documentation which they required and for the rigidity which might come from adherence to the approved course. Initially, however, there can be no doubt that scrutiny by the CNAA and dialogue with its visiting parties greatly improved the standards of course design, to the benefit of the students, and raised the level of professional dialogue among colleagues in different departments.

Internal validation, however, was only a first step. In the 1980s, the CNAA was developing a policy of 'Partnership in Validation', in which it was looking for institutions to take more responsibility for the quality of their courses. It was shifting its focus from individual courses to the institution as a whole and asking whether it was organised in such a way as to assure the quality of its courses. As part of this, it carried out two further Institutional Reviews in 1985 and 1990. The first of these proved very important. The college came out of it well in that the visiting party concluded 'that the college had shown through its critical appraisal that it was capable of reviewing its operation and . . . ensuring that academic standards overall were being maintained'.[18] Approval of the college as appropriate for the conduct of CNAA courses was therefore unhesitatingly given.

Within this general approval, there were a number of criticisms, some of which had been anticipated in the college's own critical appraisal.[19] A crucial one concerned the setting and maintenance of academic standards. While the IVPC procedures for the scrutiny of new courses were generally satisfactory, the procedures for monitoring and review of courses were less systematic. The college responded immediately by setting up a Courses Review Committee which developed a system in which annual reports were submitted by all course committees for scrutiny and, if necessary, the course teams questioned about them. In 1989 it was amalgamated with the IVPC to become the Academic Standards Committee.

Another criticism was that the college needed to develop its 'capacity for purposeful forward planning', that it tended to be too reactive and to plan over too short a timescale. This point was contested by the Board of Studies, which felt that CNAA had taken insufficient account of the constraints imposed by SED.[20] Nevertheless, pressures for corporate planning mounted and became irresistible when, in 1989, SED began to demand the submission annually of an institutional plan. Even before that, the Academic Board had begun to draw up systematic forward plans and to hold regular discussions on the extent to which the college was achieving its declared aims.[21]

The influence of the CNAA was also felt on the internal organisation of the college. Its expectation that courses would be planned and taught by a team, fitted uneasily with the departmental structure which had been essentially unchanged since 1906. Other factors were calling that structure into question. Among the most important were 'the development of inter-disciplinary courses, the increasing proportion of inservice work which demands flexible groupings of staff, and the fall in student numbers which has led to a situation in which 14 out of the 17 secondary departments have less than 10 staff and are likely to become smaller'.[22] In 1984 therefore the Governors set up a review body, chaired by J.L. Brown (Chairman of Governors, 1983–87), which proposed a matrix structure. Along one axis were 17 divisions into which the 34 previous departments were grouped; along the other a new breed of Course Directors in order to shift the emphasis to the management of courses. Such a change raised difficult issues about status and conditions of service but, after a lengthy period of consultation, the new structure was implemented in session 1987–88.

For an institution whose prime purpose was vocational training, this structure was almost certainly a move in the right direction. However, because of resistance from defenders of the status quo, it was a compromise which left some issues unresolved. The obvious difficulties were in the potential for conflict between the Heads of Division and the Course Directors, and in the complexities of the chain of command. These difficulties were commented on by CNAA in the 1990 Institutional Review. As the college was then seeking the right to award CNAA degrees on the strength of its own quality assurance procedures, Bone suggested further reorganisation which would base the academic structure on 'a fairly small number of Schools'.[23] Although there was initial resistance to another reorganisation, a working party was set up, which reported in favour of grouping the divisions and courses into Schools, each headed by an Assistant Principal, to create a clearer line management structure. This was accepted and in 1991–92 five Schools were set up: Primary, Secondary, Further Education, Educational Studies, and Applied Human Studies. It could be argued that this was a useful and far-sighted step in preparing the college for entry into the university sector; it could also be argued that in its last years the college spent too much time and energy on internal debates about restructuring.

One piece of internal reorganisation was unavoidable. In 1987, SED issued new Regulations[24] as part of the government's policy, throughout the public sector in general, of trying to tighten management by reducing locally elected elements. These had the effect of reducing the size of the Governing Body and eliminating the elected teacher representatives. The Board was no longer to elect its own Chairman, who became instead a nominee of the Secretary of State. The Board of Studies was also reduced in size to 25 members and renamed the Academic Board. It remained an advisory body. These changes had little practical effect. The first nominee as Chairman of Governors was Professor George Gordon who, as a respected member of the previous Board, might well have been elected. In 1983, the Board of Studies had itself decided that it was too unwieldy and had delegated most of its work to an Executive Committee of 20 members. So the new Academic Board was virtually the Executive under another name.

Changes in finance and staffing
Until the mid 1980s the college was funded in a basically simple way. The number of staff was worked out by dividing the number of students by the agreed staffing ratio for each course and adding allowances for equipment, maintenance and such activities as inservice or research. SED then met the costs of the staffing complement and the college negotiated for funds to

meet its other needs. This was an incremental approach, which perpetuated historic funding patterns. It did not, in the government's view, provide an incentive to achieve economies or to improve efficiency.

The first warning shot came in 1986, when SED refused to meet the full cost of the negotiated salary award, thereby destroying the concept of a staffing complement. The college was told that it must employ only the staff it could afford and that it should be looking for ways of cutting costs and increasing income from other sources.[25] To bring home the message, SED stopped funding overtime for inservice work so that course fees had to cover their costs. The next step was to bring the Scottish centrally-funded institutions into line with those elsewhere in the UK. This meant that the college received a grant for teaching purposes calculated by multiplying the student costs for a particular category of course by the number of students. To this might be added earmarked grants for specific purposes. The SED announced the change to the new system in December 1987 and it began in the financial year, 1989–90. This marked an easing of the centralised controls which had been such a feature of the 1980s, a move to replace detailed bureaucratic controls by the discipline of the market.

The introduction of this new system combined with the switch in inservice funding to the local authorities put considerable financial pressures on the college in its last years, though no more than were felt generally throughout higher education. It tried to respond by better marketing (a Marketing Unit was set up 1989); by recruiting more overseas students; by attracting more external funding; and by increasing the income from its facilities. It had some successes in all these fields but, compared to those of the universities, they were bound to be modest. The only field in which real economies could be achieved was that of staffing.

The college began the 1980s with a generous staff student ratio of 1:8, the consequence of the fall in student numbers being dealt with by voluntary redundancy. The takeover of Hamilton brought an influx of staff, younger on average than those at Jordanhill, and so made the situation more difficult. The college therefore had to encourage staff to leave and 74 did so without replacement between 1980 and 1984. The Governors continued to manage this awkward problem with great sensitivity, while the college coped with its undesirable consequences. For instance, 'At the time of the inspection, one-third of those in the Department of Primary Education had had no experience of teaching in primary schools'.[26]

The real squeeze on staffing, however, came with the new system of grant in aid. In 1986–7 the staff student ratio was still 1:9.3; by 1990 the college was on target for a ratio of 1:11.1 and later reductions in the real value of the unit of resource were to worsen that ratio further. This intensified the pressure to persuade staff to take early retirement. The new financial regime also made it imperative to have more flexibility in staffing. So where staff were recruited they were often secondees or on short-term contracts, latterly some 10% of the staff. With so many people leaving in the 1980s, there were bound to be changes in the senior staff. Riddell retired in 1983 and McCall became Vice principal. McArthur and Marker left in 1986, Baillie in 1987, Wright in 1989 and Nicolson in 1991. The management team which took the college through its last years and into the merger with Strathclyde University therefore had a new look, consisting of Bone, McCall and the heads of the five Schools: McKay, Nimmo, Niven, Smith and Weir.

Having piloted the college successfully through the crucial phases of the merger with Strathclyde University, Bone retired in 1992. Like Wood he had been a major figure in Scottish education and beyond. To mention only his major offices he had been, at various times, Chairman of the GTC, of SCET and of the CNAA Teacher Education Committee; Vice chairman of the Dunning Committee, of SCEEB and of STEAC (Scottish Tertiary Education Advisory Council). The knowledge this gave him of the world of education and the range of his contacts were undoubtedly of great benefit to the college. He had had to lead the college in more difficult times than any of his predecessors. Up to the postwar period, they had been largely concerned with administering a stable state. Wood had had to grapple with the problems of expansion, but in a favourable climate. Bone had to manage contraction under renewed external scrutiny. To this task he brought outstanding qualities: an enormous capacity for work; a clear mind that saw quickly to the heart of issues; great skills as a communicator and as a chairman. Moreover, from the beginning, he encouraged in the Board of Studies and other committees the sort of open discussion which gave staff a sense of participation and did much to sustain staff morale. This consensual style worked well in the 1970s and early 1980s but, in the harsher climate of the later years, the Inspectorate judged it to be somewhat too laisser-faire.[27] A distinction is sometime made between two types of leadership—transactional and transforming—and it is rare to combine the two. In these terms, Bone was undoubtedly a superb transactional leader, highly skilled in analysing situations, judging what policies were feasible and guiding them to fruition.

The last years of the college, as it wrestled with the problems of contraction and of financial pressures, were difficult ones. They were also years of real achievements. The college extended and developed its influence in the wider world. Mangan went as a Visiting Professor to Berkeley (a high scholarly accolade). The staff tutor team won disciples for their topic approach as far afield as Iceland, Hong Kong and Oregon. The college as a whole became more involved in the European dimension through exchanges with Hamburg and Holland, and through the institutional networks set up by the Council of Ministers.[28]

The major achievements, however, were in course developments. Between 1981 and 1993, every course was revised, successfully taken to external validation and, in many cases, upgraded to degree level. The modular award-bearing scheme for inservice courses had been developed up to Master's degree level and the first doctorates had been awarded. To underpin all this, a systematic and robust system of quality control had been created. This progress had been achieved by staff who saw their workloads steadily increasing as the staff student ratio became less favourable but who continued to work with their traditional commitment. It is greatly to their credit that in the early 1990s the college's portfolio of courses was so much stronger than it had been ten years before. The intended beneficiaries of this were the students, but it also meant that, when questions of merger arose, the college was in a stronger negotiating position.

Merger with Strathclyde University[29]

In the 1980s there was much debate about the structure of higher education in Scotland. When STEAC reported in 1986, it took the radical view on planning and funding that all Scottish higher education should be under one Council, but on structure accepted the traditional view that it should be divided into three separate parts: the universities, the CIs and the monotechnic colleges of education. Although Bone was a member of STEAC, the college's submission questioned this separation and looked towards an 'extended university system' in which the colleges of education might seek closer relationships and/or amalgamation with appropriate universities.[30]

By the late 1980s, Bone came to judge that the binary line would be abolished and most of the CIs be given the status of a university. If this were to happen, the college could not hope to become a university in its own right; its range of courses was too narrow. He therefore analysed the options open to it as:

a) to seek the right to award its own degrees. This did not seem an attractive option, as the degrees would be regarded as inferior and the college disadvantaged in the competition for students.
b) to merge with one of the CIs (Paisley or Glasgow Polytechnic) to form a new university, again with the difficulty of establishing the status of new degrees.
c) to seek merger with an established university.

This latter seemed by far the most attractive option and, in view of the college's long association with it, Glasgow University seemed the obvious partner to approach. So, in September 1989, Bone sought and obtained the permission of the Governors to discuss with Glasgow the options for future relationships.[31] A working party was quickly set up, but progress was very slow, the university displaying the same lack of urgency as in the negotiations for the original BEd. So it was not until March 1991 that the senior management of the university decided that their preferred solution was that Jordanhill should remain a separate institution but should become an Associate College, with its degrees validated by Glasgow and linked to the university by a Joint Council. This fell far short of the college's aspiration to become a full Faculty of Education but, when the proposals were put to the Glasgow Senate in May, the view of the senior management prevailed and the idea of working towards a merger was rejected,[32] the main argument being that Jordanhill was essentially a teaching institution which would lower the university's research rating.

When Bone reported this decision to the Jordanhill Academic Board, its unanimous view was that the Glasgow offer was unacceptable and Bone then wrote to Sir William Kerr Fraser, Principal of Glasgow University, that, unless the university was willing to offer merger, Jordanhill would have to look elsewhere.[33] By this time action was becoming urgent, as the government had produced a white paper[34] in May announcing its intention to abolish the binary line, phase out the CNAA and establish a new Higher Education Funding Council for Scotland, intentions put into effect by the Further and Higher Education (Scotland) Act of 1992.

Fortunately for the college, a new opportunity immediately opened up. John Butt, then Vice principal of Strathclyde University and a former Chairman of Governors of Craigie College, took a keen interest in teacher education and was convinced that its future lay within the university sector. As soon as the negotiations with Glasgow broke down, he approached Bone informally and suggested that the college might find Strathclyde more receptive to the idea of a merger.[35] From the college's point of view, such a suggestion could hardly have been more welcome or more timely. It quickly led to a more formal exchange of letters between Bone and Sir Graham Hills (Principal of Strathclyde University) and then to a series of meetings between senior staff of the two institutions, in which John Arbuthnott, then Principal designate, was invited to join. These were so successful that, by September, Bone was able to put a merger proposal, in principle, to the Academic Board. This was discussed at a two-day residential meeting which ended with a unanimous vote in favour of exploring the possibility.[36] From that point on events moved very quickly and very smoothly. A joint working party was set up which produced a report in January 1992 in favour of the college merging with Strathclyde and becoming its Faculty of Education from April 1993. This was accepted without any opposition by all the internal bodies concerned—the Governors and Academic Board of the college and the Senate and Court of the university.

It is easy to see why, having been rebuffed by Glasgow, the college found Strathclyde's offer so attractive. The interesting question is why Strathclyde was not swayed by the same arguments that had led Glasgow to rejection. There were a number of reasons for this. Because of its origins, Strathclyde was more sympathetic towards a vocationally-orientated institution like Jordanhill. It looked more closely at the college's research record and found it to be stronger than Glasgow had realised, as the college's Grade 3 rating for educational research in the Research Assessment Exercise confirmed. It had no departments which overlapped directly with those at Jordanhill and so the two institutions were complementary. Above all, the merger was driven by academic considerations, the belief that the combined resources of the two institutions would produce better courses for the students.[37]

After internal approval, the merger successfully negotiated the external scrutiny of the Scottish Committee of UFC and of the SOED. In June 1992 the college became an Associate Institution of Strathclyde so that the university could take over the validation of its courses and, under the newly agreed procedures, McCall was elected as the first Dean of the Faculty designate. It then only remained for joint working groups to continue sorting out the details over the period until the end of March 1993. On 1 April, at a Merger Congregation in the beautiful and impressive setting of the Barony Hall, the independent existence of Jordanhill came to its close.

Notes and references

1 DES. *Higher education: meeting the challenge.* London: HMSO, 1987. Cm114.
2 JBG minutes, 29 October 1982.
3 TESS. 5 & 19 November 1982; 24 February 1984.
4 JBS minutes, 20 December 1990.
5 *Ibid.*, 26 March 1992 reported that there had been 945 applicants for 183 places on the BEd, for which 4 Bs at H grade was now the normal entry requirement.
6 JBS minutes, 25 March 1982.
7 *Ibid.*, 9 September 1986.
8 Bone, T.R. Interview with W.B. Marker, 18 January 1995.
9 SED. *Report of an inspection of Jordanhill College of Education.* 1987. p.2.
10 JBG minutes. Chairman's Committee. 8 September 1989.
11 JBS minutes. BEd Committee. 24 April 1984.
12 *Ibid.* 25 March 1982.
13 *Ibid.* 18 February 1982
14 *Ibid.* Inservice Committee reports, 1983–5.
15 Smith, I.R.M. Interview with W.B. Marker, 20 July 1995.
16 Weir, D. Interview with W.B. Marker, 3 July 1995.

17 JBS minutes, 10 June 1982.
18 CNAA. *Report of an Institutional Review of Jordanhill College of Education.*
    1985.
19 Jordanhill College. *Report for the Institutional Review Visit of the CNAA.*
    1985. pp.57–60.
20 JBS minutes, 3 October 1985.
21 *Ibid.*, 11 February 1988.
22 Jordanhill College. *op.cit.* 1985. p.62.
23 JBS minutes, 25 October 1990.
24 *The Colleges of Education (Scotland) Regulations*, 1987.
25 JBG minutes, 12 May 1986.
26 SED. *op.cit.* 1987. p.5.
27 *Ibid.*
28 I am grateful to Bryan Peck for the information on which this paragraph is
    based.
29 Arbuthnott, J. & Bone, T.R. Anatomy of a merger. *Higher education quarterly*,
    v.47:2, 1993.
30 JBS minutes, 8 November 1984.
31 JBG minutes. Chairman's Committee. 8 September 1989.
32 Glasgow University. Minutes of Senate. 16 May 1991.
33 JBS minutes, 6 June 1991.
34 DES. *Higher education: a new framework*. London: HMSO, 1991. Cm1541.
35 Butt, J. Interview with W.B. Marker, 31 August 1995.
36 JBS minutes, 17/18 September 1991.
37 Butt. *op.cit.*

7

Far from Elementary:Initial Training for the Primary Sector

Molly Cumming

At the turn of the century the teaching force in Scotland's elementary schools consisted mainly of certificated, uncertificated or pupil teachers. Graduates also held (mainly promoted) posts but since 1846 the pupil teacher system had been the major route for access to what we would today term primary education. Acknowledgement of the need for a structured training system for a new century came with the introduction of the 1906 Regulations[1] for teacher training. Pupil teachers were replaced by junior students who required the Intermediate Certificate to enter a three-year combined course of initial professional training and general education to the age of 18 years. The Student Certificate gained on successful completion of this course gave the holder senior student status and access to a recognised training centre. The pattern of training which these students then followed was to remain largely unchanged for the next 50 years. Control of courses was centralised under the National Committee for the Training of Teachers (NCTT) in 1921, and would remain in its hands until 1959. Graduate status for all entering the teaching profession was 80 years in the distance, but new courses were just over the horizon.

Courses under Chapter III Regulations

Chapter III of the 1906 Regulations was concerned with qualifications to teach in primary schools. They provided for a two-year non graduate course for applicants who held the Junior Student Certificate or the Higher Leaving Certificate. Article 73f of Chapter III allowed existing certificated teachers access to this course and, on condition of meeting the requirements of Article 71a, uncertificated teachers were able to join assistants qualified under that Article in a programme of study lasting not more than one year. (This provisional registration of uncertificated teachers expired in 1914.) A three-year concurrent course permitting attendance at university classes, or a one-year course for graduates (Article 15) were the other qualifying routes for the primary sector. The concurrent course was phased out and the

95

two-year course was extended to three years in 1931. The three courses followed mainly the same curriculum, the shadows of which are still recognisable in the courses of today.

In 1924 the Regulations were amended to restrict male entry to Chapter III courses to degree holders, effectively limiting their access to one route, namely the graduate course.[2] At the same time, the Regulations amended Article 39[3] to give Chapter III graduates the opportunity of obtaining a qualification to teach in the lower classes of secondary schools. Men qualifying under Article 39 would dominate primary headteacher posts for many years, having followed a career in junior secondary schools and often having little or no experience of primary education. This situation was strongly resented by many female colleagues, seemingly unable to break this male domination of senior posts in a sector where the majority of teaching posts were held by women. Promotion prospects for women were best among those who held the Chapter VII Infants Mistress endorsement qualification established in the 1906 Regulations. Entry required the General Certificate plus two years' service as a qualified teacher in a primary school. This would later develop as an end-on full time one-year course, following the three-year certificate (and later diploma), commonly referred to as the 'endorsement' or 'Froebel certificate' (when it became associated with that Foundation).

Those enrolled on the two-year certificate were taught a heavy 1500 hour course[4] comprising professional subjects (600 hours, including 270 hours of methods and practice of teaching), general subjects (580 hours), supplementary studies (240 hours) and 80 hours of religious instruction, a pattern still visible six decades later. Article 22 of the Regulations required all primary courses to include hygiene, psychology, logic, ethics, education and methods and practice of teaching, under the heading of professional subjects. As supplementary studies, non graduate Chapter III students were required (until 1964) to cover Part A of courses in music, junior educational handwork, physical education, art and arts and crafts. They then opted to study Part B in only one of these areas, the successful completion of which gave them recognition under Article 37(b) to teach that subject and have it included in their qualification. The curriculum for general subjects covered a wide range of topics. Although not academically demanding, it was designed to equip students for their generalist role in primary schools.

Surviving student notebooks give some notion of the content and structure of these early courses. Florence Adams[5], a non graduate student in 1919 and Margaret Dundas[6], a Chapter III graduate of 1923, (whose brother had followed the graduate course at Dundas Vale in 1912) kept meticulous notes which reflect a full lecture programme, and there appears to have been little difference in the content and structure of the two courses.

Marie McDougall[7] followed a similar course in 1945–48. Subjects included history, geography, English, mathematics, arithmetic, natural science, botany, zoology and phonetics. Science subjects required meticulous line drawings and sketches, with watercolour and crayon finishes unlikely to have been completed in the lecture room. The notebooks served as a resource which the students could use as a detailed reference later on in their teaching career.

Teaching practice notes were compiled under specified headings, in a notebook provided by the GPC, and included evaluative comments by students, tutors and class teachers. The headings used in these lesson notes, 'Lesson aim', 'Main ideas' and 'Procedure', are recognisable today; they may be paraphrased in a different way, but fulfil a similar purpose. Students taught some lessons to classes of children, in front of an audience of tutors and other students, a continuation of the public criticism lessons advocated by David Stow. The 'crit lesson' was defined as 'a joint investigation of teaching', aimed at 'correcting and explaining errors in practice and benefiting both the onlookers and the student teaching' and showing 'the application of educational theory to actual teaching'.[8] Interestingly, this 'joint investigation' seems to have required that students evaluate their tutors' performance in demonstration lessons.

There are other clues to the assessment of the Chapter III courses in those early days. Certain examination papers, eg psychology, were set centrally by the NCTT, and posed such questions as, 'Define character and give an analysis of the psychological factors which go to form it'.[9] There were also internal examinations for other subjects, and perhaps a form of continuous assessment. The students' lecture notebooks contain critical comment by tutors on quality ('VG', 'excellent', etc.) and accuracy.

The restrictive regulations and the relatively unchanging curriculum in primary schools did not encourage innovative development. A surplus of teachers, leading to teacher unemployment in the 1920s and 1930s, had its effect on student morale. One Chapter III graduate was advised in 1931 that there would be 'no jobs for two years',[10] although she did gain a teaching post in a junior secondary school, 'as I was £19 cheaper than a man'. The shadow of war intervened and it was the 1950s before the system saw any serious movement to update and improve the curriculum and methodology which had been its hallmark for over 40 years. The postwar period brought new hope, and a fast rising birthrate which affected the intake to primary schools by the early 1950s. An expanded teaching force was urgently required and a special recruitment scheme was introduced to help meet the demand.

Recruitment was encouraged from men returning from the war, married women (who had been barred from teaching since the 1920s) and people with non-standard qualifications. The course for these students was almost identical to the non graduate certificate course,[11] which by then included general, infant school and rural school methods in the first year, with observation of practice in schools. Junior methods followed in the second year, supported by an early attempt on the part of staff to provide structured resource material in the form of a seven-page booklet entitled 'Notes on beginning teaching', with the foreword, 'Remember that you cannot learn the lesson for your pupils'. The student experience was becoming more than attending classes where staff 'lectured the text'. Students were still compliant in satisfying the demands of lecture programmes and teaching practice but the early postwar period saw some experiments with tutorials and workshop approaches to student learning.

Curricular movement began with the introduction of new topics, such as child welfare and storytelling, to the Chapter VII Infant endorsement course, which by the early 1950s had a ceiling entry age of 40 years in a course for women only.[12] The first changes to Chapter III courses were more organisational than curricular. The publication of the 1950 Memorandum[13] led to minor adjustments in the course. Professional subjects, recognisable from the 1920s, still underpinned the course timetable and the non graduate course continued to consist of general subjects and the Article 37(b) requirements. The expectation remained that students would cover a wide-ranging programme with a practical rather than an academic focus. Subject areas changed, eg art and arts and crafts became art and junior educational handwork; religious education was included as an element of the general subjects programme; Part B of Article (37b) became an aesthetic option, a terminological change which was, however, underpinned by progressive ideas. An in-depth academic option was also introduced for study in the third year and at the student's own level. Hygiene became health education and now dealt with issues relevant not only to pupils in schools but to the students themselves.

There was the beginning of a workshop approach, a slight loosening of teaching and organisational approaches, yet the 1950 Memorandum did little to encourage radical changes in thinking about the primary curriculum. It reads as a pessimistic document, ideologically humanist with emphasis on the teacher and instruction, and consequently knowledge and facts, showing scant regard for the Advisory Council's innovative attempt four years previously to 'discard with little regret the narrow and obsolete view that reading, writing and arithmetic are the three fundamentals of education'.[14] It may have been an attempt to reconcile the traditional with the progressive in terms of educational philosophy, but it was too weak to have any real impact on the schools and on training centres like Jordanhill. Yet, in fairness, this document widened the door for debate about the future of the primary curriculum. For teacher training, however, the change in status of the training centres themselves would prove to be the impetus for progress.

The diploma course

As soon as Jordanhill College of Education gained self governing status in 1959, the Board of Studies began to give high priority to debate concerning the organisation and structure of initial training for the primary sector. Wood began discussion about the nature of the three-year course as far back as 1959[15] but the report of the ad hoc committee formed to undertake this task was shelved in 1963,[16] pending the publication of the Robbins report. This would prove to be the first of a long list of delays.

In 1965 the system for teacher training which we know today was set in place.[17] The 566 third year certificate students and 25 Article 39 primary graduates of 1964–65 were the last to qualify under Chapter III regulations. In future, graduates were restricted to a teaching qualification for the primary or secondary sector, as the dual qualification of Article 39 was abolished in the 1965 Regulations. The 497 first and 670 second year students began their courses under Chapter III but ultimately graduated with the diploma of a College of Education (Jordanhill). The main influence on the development of initial training at this time was the publication of another SED Memorandum on the primary curriculum.[18] It was soon required reading for all primary courses and a member of the Education department produced a summary of key points for students.[19] His comparison of the 1965 Memorandum with its 1950 predecessor emphasised the shift from a view which 'clearly owed much to the doctrine of original sin' to 'emphasis on the learner, on participation, on enquiry'. Yet it would be almost a generation before it truly impacted on the curriculum of the primary courses at Jordanhill.

In 1965 the College Committee on Primary Education was revived, just ahead of publication of the Primary Memorandum. Three sub-committees were formed to look at the existing course and its future. With vision the Board gave Barry MacDonald leadership of one of these groups, while the Primary Methods department was considered inappropriate as a source of leadership and inspiration, damned as 'a relic of the 19th-century training system' which had 'become a supervisory and demonstrating department with little opportunity to influence the approach of students to method and curricula in the primary school'.[20] After two years of discussion committees were formed to revise the diploma course[21] and 15 months later the Board received draft proposals for its reform.[22] After final revisions[23] the first cohort joined the revised diploma course in October 1969.

The curricular structure of the revised course marked a watershed in thinking, not only about the course but about the deployment of staff and other resources. Individual subjects were submerged in interdisciplinary groupings, in terminology guided by the 1965 Memorandum.[24] Environmental studies and language arts entered the timetable, while mathematics remained a discrete subject, along with those subjects which would later come under the umbrella of the expressive arts. A course on modern society was established, to provide a wider view of the world for diploma students who were, in the main, school leavers. This, along with the introduction of an academic and an aesthetic option, broke with the tradition of students following a broad course which had no pretensions towards academic study in depth. It was a radically new opportunity, permitting study at an academic level and it represented a step on the way towards an all graduate course.

Staff delivering the revised diploma course could 'no longer labour under the fiction that one department may convey information to the student while another restricts itself to methods of passing it on'.[25] Jordanhill had entered the age of interdepartmental and interdisciplinary teams for planning and delivery of its primary courses. New staff were recruited from schools directly involved in the developments which emerged from the 1965 Memorandum. By the mid 1970s these included staff who had previously held promoted posts in open plan schools, which had been experimenting with the then 'state of the art' innovations in curriculum and organisation.[26]

The Board kept an keen eye on the progress of the course.[27] When Stitt retired Richardson took his place as Head of Primary Education, bringing new ideas for organisation and planning, which would prove to be the main thrust behind many of the innovations which we take for granted today. The Centre for the Teaching of Reading was developed in the former Methods department staffroom. Behind its success was a team which had developed the language arts course for the revised diploma. Centres for Environmental Studies, Mathematics and Early Education followed. These innovations led directly to the establishment of the Primary Curriculum Centre which exists today.[28] Richardson encouraged these developments, which gradually led to the predominance of primary education staff in the teaching of primary courses at Jordanhill. There was some resistance to generalist primary-trained staff teaching on the mainstream programmes of the primary courses, just as there was to the idea that secondary-trained subject staff were equipped to prepare and assess primary course students in school experience. The focus of courses was now more professional and Richardson, although not always a popular leader, was a major inspiration and facilitator of change.

A further review in 1977 would once again focus on the diploma course, in the light of a national campaign for the introduction of a four-year primary degree. A series of delays impeded progress, and the Board took the decision to suspend the review pending the government's announcement on an all graduate profession.[29] In the meantime, the planning teams continued the task of improving and developing course content and resources. Course materials began to take on a new look.[30] Booklets and other resources were compiled to support course delivery, which was increasingly dominated by seminars and workshops. Participation and interaction among staff and students was encouraged, at a level which 20 years previously would have been inconceivable. Assessment of student experience in schools now had a more open agenda. Preparation was supported by informative booklets which guided students in requirements for each year, and which were the basis for the checklists used today. Jordanhill staff were now relatively well equipped to respond to the requirements of an all graduate profession.

All graduate primary training
The 1965 Regulations had added a new, third, route to the Teachers' Certificate (Primary), via a four-year BEd degree, essentially a secondary course which accommodated an option to train for the primary sector. This Glasgow University validated BEd was essentially an academic course based on the traditional Scottish ordinary degree. It was not an ideal preparation for primary teaching and it attracted only a few to the primary route, in comparison with the high numbers who enrolled for the diploma course. The course did offer an option to study education of young children in the fourth year, the first time such a specialism had been included as part of an initial training course. A department of the same name emerged within the Primary Education department to teach this part of the BEd, drawing on the expertise mainly of those who had previously worked with Chapter VII (Infant endorsement) students. Diploma students had the option to take a further year end-on to their three-year course, giving them access to similar, specialist training. Whatever it promised, this BEd was not destined to be the degree so many had hoped would replace the three-year diploma. It was not designed as a professional degree for those entering the teaching profession, nor was it oriented to the needs of those entering the primary sector.

After many years' campaigning by the teaching profession, the government at last announced the phasing out of the diploma course and introduction of a four-year degree for primary teaching. By 1982 the college had argued its case for a revised BEd, to be offered from October 1983,[31] in a form better suited to the needs of primary students and taught entirely by Jordanhill staff. The dilemma now was whether to proceed with a restructured BEd or wait for the guidelines to be issued for the new four-year degree. The Board opted for the former,[32] and began preparation of a short-lived interim BEd, an ill-judged decision in retrospect. The guidelines,[33] when they were published, left planning teams with no option but to prepare a new course from its foundations, as the interim BEd was out of step. The course was subject to external validation (a new experience for most involved in its preparation) and approval by the GTC before it could be implemented. The degree was validated by SCOVACT as the BEd in Primary Education (Ordinary) and enrolled its first students in October 1984. Session 1984–85 saw staff teaching students finishing the interim BEd, those in the final year of the diploma and those enrolled on the first year of the new degree together with their commitments to the one-year graduate course and the last presentation of the end-on endorsement course.

Experiments in course design and development, together with the SED guidelines, had resulted in a course structure radically different from that previously experienced by staff at Jordanhill. The revised diploma course had introduced departmental cooperation in course planning and delivery. The BEd degree shifted the philosophy from 'utility' to 'relevance'.[34] The new course was a vocational degree, specifically designed to prepare students for teaching in the primary school. Education, psychology and preparation for teaching were now integrated as a professional studies course of 21 components over four years. For the first time, staff in primary education worked hand in hand with colleagues from education and psychology.

The experience gained by staff in adapting the original BEd curriculum to become more professionally relevant proved a worthwhile rehearsal for this new course. Music and drama were introduced, as was the scientific and technological environment. The emerging four-year course would include:

Induction and professional studies	21 units
School experience	121 days
Curricular studies*	30 units
Elective studies	17 units

*Language and communication, mathematics for the primary school, the environment (social and scientific), expressive arts and health education.

The second year of the course developed the idea which had begun in the diploma course, whereby students followed an academic option. Scottish and Celtic studies, along with children's literature, proved to be particularly popular. The 'list C' and 'list D' options of the final year of the new course presented opportunities for staff and students to explore and promote current issues, including:

List C	List D
Computer education/educational technology	Multicultural education
	European perspectives
Chemical world	
Making sense of our environment	Working with people

Guidelines[35] also appeared for the reform of the graduate course as a Postgraduate Certificate in Education (Primary) (PGCE) of 36 weeks' duration. The experience of the SCOVACT validation of the BEd[36] convinced the PGCE planning team that this course should be taken to the CNAA, which was considered to have a superior record in the validation of primary courses. There was a major shift in philosophy and structure, reorganising the PGCE (primary) as a course of three elements, viz. school experience (86 days), professional studies (100 hours) and curricular studies (280 hours), as an interrelated programme, taught by an interdisciplinary team.

Student progress on both courses was measured by continuous assessment, set by staff, a situation very different from that of their counterparts of even two decades before. School experience in both courses incorporated training for the nursery sector, for the first time as part of an initial training course. Both the BEd and the PGCE henceforth prepared students to teach three to twelve year olds. The end-on infant endorsement year was phased out, leaving the part time inservice courses in infant and nursery education for those who sought specialist qualifications after entry to the profession.

External validation brought with it another phenomenon new to staff, the regular course review. For both courses this was more than a simple exercise in fine tuning. The BEd underwent its first review in 1987, the major change being the increase of school experience for students from 121 to 142 days. The review suggested that health education would be more appropriately incorporated as an element of the environment course and that computer education should be allocated more time in the induction course. Both courses now benefited from formally-appointed Course Directors as part of the matrix structure introduced by the college in the late 1980s. They also drew on college-wide expertise and experience. Reviews became a positive contribution to course development and the advice of colleagues at such events was considered constructive, if sometimes critical.

By the end of the 1980s initial training for the primary sector was no longer an elementary preparation for the exposition of facts, as had been the major focus of the early Chapter III courses and their predecessors. The two routes of entry to the primary education sector had now evolved into a rigorous professional training of which David Stow would have been proud. All graduate primary training was firmly established, yet there was one further development which would give future primary teachers an academic and professional status to which they had not previously been able to aspire.

The 1990s saw a further revision and upgrading of the BEd as a degree with Honours. The length of the course remained at four years, but the final year now required that students undertake individual research projects, assessment of which would contribute to their final award with Honours classification. The dissertation was underpinned by a study of research methods, part of the professional studies programme, and by support from a supervisor on a one to one basis. Students in the final year of this course could now assert with confidence that they were academically and professionally as well equipped as their graduate counterparts for their chosen career.

The last awards ceremony held under the name of Jordanhill College of Education fittingly included a group of students who graduated with a first class honours BEd degree in primary education. Jordanhill's reputation and status could now claim to be far from elementary.

Notes and references

1 SED. *Regulations for the preliminary education, training and certification of teachers for various grades of schools.* 1906.
2 CCES annual report, 1924–25. Report by HMCI J.C. Smith.
3 *Ibid.*
4 GPC minutes included each year the prospectus detailing courses and subjects taught, with allocated hours.
5 Adams, F.H. 1919–21. Methods notebook. Jordanhill Archives.
6 Ken Dundas, senior lecturer, department of Primary Education, loaned surviving materials from his father's and aunt's student days as a contribution to this research. This material will be donated to Jordanhill Archives.
7 McDougall, M.M. 1945–48. Lecture notebooks. Jordanhill Archives.
8 Adams, F.H. *op.cit.*
9 Crawford, E. 1928–29. Notebooks and examination papers. Jordanhill Archives.
10 Brown, J.F. 1930–31. Letter 1 March 1985. Jordanhill Archives.
11 Taylor, A. 1946–48. Lecture notebooks. Jordanhill Archives.
12 Glasgow Training Centre. *Prospectus.* 1949–50.
13 SED. *The primary school in Scotland.* Edinburgh: HMSO, 1950.
14 Advisory Council on Education in Scotland. *Primary education.* Edinburgh: HMSO, 1946.
15 JBS minutes, 18 June and 10 November 1959.
16 *Ibid.*, 10 October 1963.
17 SED. *Teachers (Education, Training and Certification) (Scotland) Regulations.* Edinburgh: HMSO, 1965.
18 SED. *Primary education in Scotland.* Edinburgh: HMSO, 1965.
19 MacDonald, B. *Primary education in Scotland.* Student handout issued by the Education department in 1966. (From personal material which will be donated to Jordanhill Archives).
20 JBS minutes, 12 January 1965.
21 *Ibid.*, 8 November 1967.
22 *Ibid.*, 12 February 1969.

23 *Ibid.*, 12 March 1969.
24 The 1965 Memorandum had introduced the terms 'environmental studies' and 'language arts' for the first time and primary schools had already responded by dropping the traditional, compartmentalised subject areas of, eg history and geography.
25 Nisbet, J. and Kirk, G. (eds.) Teacher training in *Scottish education looks ahead*. Edinburgh: Chambers, 1969.
26 Graham White came from an open plan school in Aberdeen. Glenda White and Molly Cumming had been in Mark I and Mark II open plan schools in Glasgow, respectively. All joined the staff at Jordanhill from promoted posts which had kept them at the 'leading edge' of developments at that time.
27 JBS minutes, 17 April and 21 October 1970.
28 Ken Dundas was instrumental in the design of the current Centre, which required the demolition of two main lecture rooms and two tutorial rooms and their reconstruction in the current open plan form.
29 JBS minutes, 16 September 1980.
30 From personal resources gathered at the time. These will be donated to Jordanhill Archives.
31 JBS minutes, 21 January 1982.
32 *Ibid.*, 17 February 1983.
33 SED. *Guidelines for the primary BEd degree 1982–83*.
34 Nisbet, J. and Kirk, G. (eds.). *op.cit.*
35 SED. *Guidelines for the Postgraduate Certificate in Education (Primary). 1984*.
36 JBS minutes. BEd Committee, 24 April 1984.

8

The Training of Secondary Teachers

Gordon Kirk

The tradition of secondary training at Jordanhill, reflecting the general pattern of teacher education in Scotland, was strongly influenced by two crucial developments in the first decade of this century: the transfer in 1905 of responsibility for training to four 'Provincial Committees' and the introduction of new Regulations in 1906. While, ostensibly, these changes sought to maintain the involvement of universities in teacher training, there is evidence[1] that both Craik and his successor as Secretary of the Department, John Struthers, believed that, if what was needed was a broader conception of education for teachers, 'the university is the last agency in the world through which we are likely to obtain it'. The Departmental strategy, therefore, was to restrict teacher education to specialist training institutions independent of the universities. Inevitably, secondary training for the most part had to be 'consecutive', undertaken after the degree or other qualification had been acquired.

The pattern of secondary training that emerged from these formative years was differentiated to reflect the prevailing ideology which required separate courses for different categories of pupil.[2] Accordingly, three categories of teaching qualification for secondary school work were established. The qualification for teachers of 'higher subjects' (Chapter V of the Regulations), was intended for honours graduates in one or two subjects, those who were destined to provide secondary education with what the Advisory Council's report of 1947 referred to as its 'incorrigibly academic' bias. The General Certificate (Chapter III), when supplemented by additional work as prescribed in Article 39, entitled a person to teach in the lower years of the secondary school. Finally, Chapter VI, which dealt with teachers of 'special subjects', entitled diplomates of central institutions to teach such lower status subjects as art, technical subjects, agriculture and 'domestic economy'.

What form did that training take? Article 22 of the Regulations specified that the curriculum of professional training should include 'instruction in the elements of school and personal hygiene, psychology, ethics and logic, and also in the principles of education and in the history of educational systems and theories'. Teaching practice 'under proper supervision' was also required. The Glasgow Provincial Committee prospectus for 1907–08[3] includes the following curriculum for graduates:

WINTER SESSION:	Hours per week	SUMMER SESSION:	Hours per week
1. Logic and Psychology or Ethics	5	1. Psychology (experimental)	3
2. Education	5	2. Education—present-day problems	2
3. Methods and Practice	4	3. Methods and Practice	12.5
4. Hygiene	2.5	4. Hygiene	2.5
	Total: 16.5		Total: 20

The same curriculum was prescribed for those qualifying as teachers of higher subjects and those qualifying as teachers of special subjects.

The curriculum for session 1925–26[4] for Chapter V students was as follows:

	Average hours weekly
1. Logic and psychology (unless taken already)	3 (or 4)
2. Ethics (unless taken already)	1
3. Psychology (experimental)	2/3rds
4. Education (unless taken already)	3 (or 4)
5. Methods and practice in teaching	12
6. Secondary school organisation and management	1/3rd
7. Hygiene	1
8. Physical training	2
9. Phonetics and voice training	1
10. Religious instruction	1

There was little change over the years. In 1935–36 provision was made for nature study, laboratory arts for science students, and music ('unless exempted')[5] and in 1945–46 'educational psychology' was substituted for 'logic and psychology' and 'ethics'.[6] The entry for 1952–53, in language that clearly echoed the 1906 regulations, confirmed the curriculum as 'instruction in health and physical education, in the principles of teaching, in school management, in methods of teaching, in the history of educational systems and theories, and in phonetics and voice training', as well as 'teaching practice under supervision'.[7]

While the pattern of training in the first half of the century was therefore relatively static, certainly when judged by the standards of today, some reminiscences of life at Jordanhill in these years provide a more encouraging picture. For example, Russell, looking back 30 years to his time at Jordanhill in session 1924–25, described it as 'a year of real vintage class'.[8] He enthused over the distinction of his classmates, one of whom was Dr Inglis, who was later to be Principal at Moray House, and refers admiringly to such lecturers as Pender Crichton, Dr Patton, Dr Carstairs Douglas, and Todd Ritchie. Similarly, in his history of the first 50 years of the college at Jordanhill, Fairley identified a number of respected members of staff, such as Rusk, Dawson and Pritchard.[9] These and other personalities were vividly recalled by Moffett[10] and by Miller.[11] However, these reminiscences perhaps demonstrate not a vibrant institution but rather one in which traditional ways were occasionally enlivened by charismatic teachers and colourful personalities.

The student experience in those years was, by all accounts, a somewhat unhappy one. Referring to her training in 1931–32, Moffett reported, 'We were lectured to as the sole method of instruction. And we were not lectured to as adults. We were lectured to as if we were really ignorant.' Miller, evoking his training in the 1940s, recorded the same reaction. Others objected to the college's 'clanging hour bells for class changes and its rigid timetables and regulations' compared to the environment of the university. Apart from the alienating ethos, students experienced the understandable anxieties about performing well enough to be sure of obtaining the high grades that would facilitate a speedy appointment to a post. All in all, according to Moffett, 'College, to the incoming honours student or graduate student, was regarded as a necessary penance'.[12] Indeed, that perception of Jordanhill formed part of the undergraduate folklore at Glasgow University for decades and was at least part of the explanation for the popularity of the DipEd course at the university which, when taken concurrently with the training year, exempted a student from major parts of the Jordanhill course. What is more, the experience of the college year clearly affected attitudes to the institution subsequently and surely influenced the staff room advice which the experienced teacher offered the new entrant to the profession: 'Forget the high-faluting methods they tell you about in college. They don't work here.'[13] Comments of that kind, whether or not they were justified, discouraged many teachers and damaged Jordanhill's reputation. They elicited Wood's despairing observation: 'Teachers give us an incredible amount of help with students but, in their public utterances and conversations with students, they do anything but create a decent public image of the work of the colleges.'[14]

At the same time, the anecdotal evidence is supported by wider surveys of opinion. Elliot[15] and Ashley[16] both found that for a substantial proportion of graduate entrants teaching was a 'second-best': they merely drifted into teaching without any strong commitment to it. Moreover, the report of the Advisory Council of 1946 criticised educational theory and history for its preoccupation with details of the life and work of the great educators, and castigated the psychology course as one in which the student 'makes careful scientific studies of sensation and perception, learns about psychologists' quarrels as to the nature of instinct, about conditioned reflexes in dogs, and so on'.[17] The evidence before the Robbins Committee, 1961–63, pointed even more forcibly to difficulties and inadequacies in secondary training.[18]

It is reasonable to conclude, therefore, that secondary training of teachers in Scotland was not in good health. A combination of factors appear to have created a degree of institutional stagnation: the central control of the Scottish Education Department; the equally pervasive dominance of the Central Executive Committee; the academic isolation induced by low staff turnover and local recruitment; an over-regimented ethos; the denigration heaped on it by its own graduates; and a body of recruits to teaching who were relatively uncommitted to the profession. To that catalogue may be added the relative stagnation of the education service itself, which provided no spur to change and innovation. In consequence, Jordanhill in these years, like its sister institutions, could be described as a conservative and compliant institution, whose initiative was curbed by excessive central control.

The BEd and the concurrent principle
Appearing as it did so soon after the revised Regulations of 1959 gave colleges their own Boards of Governors and Boards of Studies, the Robbins report stimulated discussion about how teacher education might develop. One of its key recommendations was that a BEd degree should be introduced for students in colleges of education, a concurrent programme combining academic and professional studies with experience of teaching throughout, rather than postponed till an academic qualification had been obtained. That was not a new principle. For example, it had been advocated by the 1946 Advisory Committee, which had been strongly critical of 'the crowded postgraduate course', and maintained that the integration of academic and professional knowledge was 'best secured if the students' course is planned as a whole and not as two separate parts'.

What was new was the Robbins idea of a concurrent **degree**. In formulating that recommendation the committee was influenced by two sets of considerations. Firstly, there was a need, in line with its egalitarian philosophy, to create opportunities for students in non university institutions to work for a degree, especially when more than 40% of those taking the primary diploma met the standard university entrance qualifications. Secondly, it was necessary to find a way of minimising the impact of the much criticised postgraduate year, particularly for teachers 'whose work in the schools will not necessarily be highly academic in character'.[19] The Robbins report therefore recommended a course 'of a balanced, concurrent nature, liberal in content and approach, although directed towards the professional work that lies ahead'.[20]

The Jordanhill Board of Studies had its first discussion of the Robbins report at its meeting in December 1963 and minuted the view that the new degree 'should be thought of as a professional degree rather than an alternative to the ordinary arts or science degree'.[21] The college found it difficult to persuade the university to accept a distinctively professional degree. In its memorandum to the Board of Governors in September 1965, the Board of Studies suggested, perhaps rather timidly, that the Governors 'should remind the university that, since graduates will not merely be dealing with the academically able, the university might give sympathetic consideration to the idea that some subjects not hitherto regarded as degree-worthy might find a place in the BEd course'.[22] The Board's pleas were obviously unsuccessful, for the scheme ultimately agreed by the Senate was directly in line with the traditional university undergraduate programme, with seven graduating courses, one or two of them taken to Higher level. Teaching and related studies were marginalised and would not count towards the degree. The only concession made by the university was that a college study in the fourth year—physical education, or the education of young children, or the youth service—could replace one of the graduating subjects. The university insisted that one of the compulsory graduating courses should be Background to modern society, to be taught entirely by the university.[23] The new course took its first students in October 1966, in line with Moray House and Dundee, but a year behind Aberdeen College.

The enquiry into teacher training by the House of Commons Select Committee on Education and Science in 1970[24] provided the opportunity for a national review of the BEd. The submission from the Jordanhill Board of Studies, while affirming a commitment to the concurrent degree, identified several shortcomings: low numbers threatened the course's viability; there was insufficient time for teaching practice and related work; 'the restrictions imposed by working with an ancient university' made it impossible to develop BEd programmes in other areas such as PE or technical subjects; students were denied the opportunity to transfer to an honours programme; and it was impossible for students who were performing well on the primary diploma course to transfer with credit to the BEd. It was disclosed that these difficulties had led to some 'disenchantment'. In his evidence to the committee, Wood made it clear that he regarded the structure of the BEd adopted as far from ideal. And there is a poignancy in his analysis of the college's failure to create a fully professional degree, implying that that failure was at least partly attributable to the fact that 'the staff are teachers, whose own profession will not support them', a reference to the opposition of the teachers' professional associations to degrees other than those of the traditional university type.[25]

A subsequent study of the BEd was undertaken by the Visitation Committee of the GTC in 1975[26] which reported very favourably on the reaction of students and staff to the course. Yet within four years of that report, the SED proposed[27] that there should be no further intake to the secondary BEd after session 1982–83. The case for phasing out the degree was a strong one: there was a need to continue reducing intakes; the BEd output had reduced in 1981 to only 5.4% of the total of those obtaining a secondary qualification; and since the available students were distributed across six colleges, invariably they were taught in small uneconomic groups of fewer than ten. The usual robust submission to the SED was sent from the Board of Studies and the Board of Governors.[28] The case was based on the desirability, on educational and economic grounds, of keeping the BEd (Primary) and BEd (Secondary) as a single group, and on the need to retain choice of method of entry to secondary teaching. However, the Secretary of State was not to be deflected from his purpose.

Views differ on the impact of the BEd on the work of Jordanhill. Miller and Marker both agree[29] that the introduction of the BEd perhaps sharpened the dichotomy between teaching practice and academic work since it led the college to recruit a number of academically able members of staff with very little experience of the schools. More seriously, on completion of the programme, students received two awards, the degree from the university and the teacher's certificate from the college, symbolising in that arrangement that performance as a teacher was an appendage to the degree programme. On the other hand, it was popular with many staff, who welcomed the opportunity to demonstrate the capacity to teach to university degree level and many benefited from the frequent interactions with university staff on the Joint Board, and in other contexts.

The one-year secondary course
Whichever view is taken of the impact of the BEd on Jordanhill, as in other colleges, it always constituted a small minority of those graduating with the secondary teaching qualification. The overwhelming preponderance of those taking that qualification took the one-year postgraduate/post-diploma course. In the early 1970s, the number of such students was just under 1500 and, while that progressively reduced to 188 in session 1988–89, it has, since then, increased to just over 500 students. Throughout its history Jordanhill has been the largest single provider of this course in Scotland. Inevitably, therefore, particularly in view of the criticism the course has attracted over the years in all Scottish institutions, the one-year secondary

course has been a major focus of development work since the 1960s. In all, there have been five major reviews.

The first of these took place in session 1965–66 and was the first serious opportunity the Board of Studies had to exercise its responsibility with regard to secondary training. The remit of the working party, chaired by John A. Smith, was to consider the implications for teacher training of the Brunton report of 1963[30] with its innovative proposals for the education of pupils ill-suited to the traditional secondary curriculum. However, the working party judged it necessary to consider the changes to be introduced by the new Regulations of 1965 which established a single qualification to teach in the secondary school, the Teacher's Certificate (Secondary Education).

The working party's report, which was surprisingly conservative,[31] proposed a programme that differed in no significant respects from that which it was supposed to supersede. By contrast, the review conducted in session 1975–76 represented perhaps the most profound transformation of the course in its history. The college had before it the evidence of the Brunton report 1972[32] and of the Select Committee[33] that the one-year secondary course had many shortcomings and was subject to widespread criticism. Despite the change in the Regulations of the mid 1960s, ten years later the departments of Education and Psychology were still differentiating between honours graduates, ordinary graduates and the various specialist teachers that were formerly categorised as Chapter VI. There was no coordination between the programmes offered by the departments of Education and Psychology. Worse still, there was a clear tension between the subject departments and the professional subjects departments. Finally, the college still operated the familiar 'box and cox' arrangement whereby at any one time half of the cohort were in college and the other half were in schools, an arrangement forced upon the institution by overcrowding: it was a clear example of the way in which curriculum design was determined by the physical accommodation. All of these factors, then, created powerful pressures for change.

Consequently, when in 1975 the Secretary of State decided not to proceed with the implementation of the Brunton proposals, there was much relief in the Board of Studies that at last the uncertainty was ended and it would be possible to review the course.[34] The Secondary Sub-Committee agreed to undertake 'a complete reappraisal of the course' and made that recommendation to the Board of Studies.[35] In due course, the Review Group, chaired by Holroyd, embarked on its task and was able to report to the Board of Studies a matter of months later. In introducing the topic, Bone stated that it was 'one of the most important items to have appeared on the Board's agenda for many years', and even in advance of the discussion suggested that the working party had carried out its review 'with imagination as well as thoroughness, radically overhauling the course'.[36]

While the report provided a persuasive rationale for secondary training in the light of the new demands placed on the schools, it did not offer a blueprint for a new course. Rather, it offered a framework within which a new course could be developed. Designed for an intake of 1,000 students, the course included five components: teaching practice, specialist subject studies, elective studies, professional studies and the 'coordinated day', which was intended, in response to criticisms made by the GTC, to relate the work in professional studies with that in the specialist subject areas. The Board of Studies agreed to the overall framework for session 1976–77 and to the establishment of five interdepartmental working groups to undertake the detailed planning for each of the major components of the programme to be introduced as and when these became available and had the confidence of staff and cooperating teachers.

The 1982–83 review, which sought to address some of the unresolved difficulties of the previous review, particularly with regard to the coordinated day, is perhaps best regarded as a fine tuning exercise. By contrast, the reviews of 1986–87 and 1992–93 were radical and were the direct result of the Secretary of State's increased involvement in teacher education. The closure of colleges in 1980–81 had demonstrated to SED that there were widespread variations in teacher education programmes between colleges. The Department's response was to generate national 'mandatory' guidelines for courses, seeing these as an important way of ensuring that programmes of teacher education were broadly comparable across the country.

Several external pressures have influenced the various reviews of the one-year postgraduate course at Jordanhill. The first of these was the changing pattern of secondary education itself. If the first half of the century was a period in which secondary education developed only slowly, the second half has been marked by a series of major and profoundly dislocating changes. Over these years, there has been the development of comprehensive schooling, the common course, the introduction of O Grade, the raising of the school leaving age, the abandonment of corporal punishment, the major transformation of curriculum and assessment through the Munn and Dunning Committees that resulted in Standard Grade, and the equally wide ranging national initiative of the 5–14 development programme. In addition, there have been important developments in connection with pupils with learning difficulties, information technology, equal opportunities, social education and a wide range of other issues. Obviously, a college of education charged with the responsibility of preparing teachers had to ensure that the training took account of these changes.

The partnership principle

The second pressure for change derived from the acknowledgment that teachers cannot be trained within the walls of a college of education alone: they require sustained periods of supervised practice in schools. Accordingly, it has been essential to develop ways in which the college and its cooperating schools can work together in partnership to ensure that the training provided by each partner contributes to a coherent educational experience for the student. The General Teaching Council has been particularly insistent on the partnership principle and, indeed, has interpreted many of the criticisms that are levelled against the colleges as evidence of their failure to develop appropriate collaborative arrangements with schools.

The Council's first formal statement of the partnership principle was in the Brunton report of 1972,[37] which made radical proposals for change covering three phases:

phase 1: two terms in college
phase 2: three school terms
phase 3: one term in college.

By that arrangement, students would be given a basic introduction to teaching during phase 1 and then, working as fully paid teachers, would develop the experience that would make the further theoretical analysis of the third phase more appropriate and acceptable. The stronger involvement of the schools implied by these proposals would be established through a formal system of cooperation involving 'regents', who would carry responsibility for coordinating the work of students throughout the whole training process, and be the focal point for collaboration with the college.

While waiting for the Secretary of State's response to these proposals, Jordanhill established an ad hoc committee to explore with education authorities ways in which the Brunton idea of a regent could be taken forward. As a result, in November 1973,[38] the Board set up an experiment in sessions 1973–74 and 1974–75 in which nine schools participated. Archer and Peck's detailed and comprehensive study of the development of the regent scheme[39] indicates that agreement was reached between the college and the authorities that the regent would have three responsibilities: 'pastoral tasks', taking a general interest in the student's wellbeing; 'professional tasks', ensuring that the student's programme in school was properly coordinated and devoting time to the study of whole school as opposed to subject teaching issues; and 'linking tasks', acting as the principal link between the school and the college and helping to ensure that the professional studies courses in the college could be illuminated by appropriate learning experiences in the school.

Following a review in 1976, a progressive extension of the scheme was agreed, with the aim of adding another 15 schools to the scheme each year.[40] By 1980–81, 41 schools were involved. Annual meetings of the regents were held in the college, to discuss the scheme. In addition, members of staff in education and psychology each had a number of schools with whom they were expected to maintain a closer relationship. However, some heads of subject departments objected to the involvement of professional studies staff in schools, on the grounds that already the pressures on students' main teaching areas were substantial.[41]

While the Secretary of State was unable to agree to the implementation of the Brunton report, he nevertheless accepted one of its central thrusts, that there was a need for a closer involvement of experienced teachers in the training of student teachers. Accordingly, in January 1976, a joint SED/GTC working party was set up under Sneddon[42] to consider, 'the need for the introduction of a more structured relationship between schools and colleges and a clearer definition of their individual and joint responsibilities'. Its report concluded that despite substantial improvements 'an important residuum of justifiable criticism remains'.

Between 1979–81 the GTC undertook a follow up study, 'to ascertain the extent to which the arrangements in the different colleges embodied the recommendations made in the Sneddon report'.[43] When the GTC panel visited Jordanhill, the Principal listed the most important developments in recent years: the ending of the 'box and cox' pattern of teaching practice; the introduction of a common programme for all secondary students; the increased contact between Education and Psychology departments through the 'coordinated day' and the development of the regent scheme. Nevertheless, the committee found that at Jordanhill 'there is a long way to go', and one Principal of another college on the panel felt that during his visit he had met 'able people all going their own way, sometimes at variance with each other'.[44]

National guidelines and external validation
Without doubt, the most formative influence on the secondary course at Jordanhill, as elsewhere, were the national guidelines. In 1982, the government embarked on a strategy for enhancing the quality of teacher education and saw it as a necessary part of that strategy that national guidelines should be established and that the Department should only approve courses which were compatible with the guidelines. In June 1984, the Secretary of State announced the setting up of a representative working party to review the one-year postgraduate training course. The main features of the guidelines, which were published in 1985[45], were as follows:

1. the specialist nature of the training was confirmed;

2. the length of the programme was extended from 32 to 36 weeks, and not less than 50% of the programme had to be devoted to school experience;
3. the partnership principle was affirmed by stipulating that school experience should be jointly planned by college, school and education authority;
4. the professional studies element of the course was required to form 'a coherent programme of study explicitly concerned with the classroom and the professional needs of the teacher ... and related to the other components of the course and, in particular, to school experience';
5. the course should be validated by an external body;
6. the course should be acceptable to the General Teaching Council.

These guidelines called for a major change in the course. They represented the Department's considered response to the Sneddon report, acknowledging the crucial importance of school experience, and affirming that teachers should play a fuller part in the training programme. That principle was even more strongly emphasised in the revision of the guidelines which took place in December 1993.[46]

The requirement in the 1985 guidelines that the course should be submitted for external validation exerted a further powerful impetus for change. That requirement meant that all programmes would be subjected to three levels of independent evaluation before a student could be enrolled: they would require to be approved by the SED to ensure that they were compatible with national guidelines; they would require to be accredited by the General Teaching Council as courses which met professional expectations and were appropriate for the changing circumstances of the schools; and, thirdly, it would need to be judged, by an appropriate validating body, that their academic standards were high.

The decision to have the one-year postgraduate programme validated by CNAA was significant in two ways. Firstly, the college had to subscribe to the nomenclature used by the CNAA for such programmes and, for that reason, the course had to be designated the Postgraduate Certificate in Education (PGCE) (Secondary), following practice south of the border. Secondly, the CNAA had developed a distinctive philosophy about one-year courses which, with its emphasis on integration of studies and partnership with schools, had the effect of reinforcing the mandatory guidelines stipulated by the Secretary of State. Documentation submitted to CNAA in January 1987[47] was approved subject to the condition that a full evaluation of the programme should be developed for submission to CNAA by December 1989.[48] The institution's response to that condition is a powerful vindication of the CNAA approach[49] portraying, as it does, that

Portrait of David Stow by John Graham Gilbert.

The first Normal School at Dundas Vale.

Interior of the new College building, 1921.

PROGRAMME

Organ Recital - - from 7 to 7.30

Mr. ROBT. McCOLL, M.A., L.R.A.M.,
Principal Lecturer in Music, Glasgow Training Centre

Sir HENRY S. KEITH, LL.D - - will preside
Chairman of the National Committee for the Training of Teachers

Addresses will be given by

Sir GEORGE MACDONALD, K.C.B., F.B.A.
Secretary of the Scottish Education Department

Dr. CYRIL NORWOOD
Headmaster of Harrow School, President of the Educational Section of the British Association

Mr. PETER COMRIE, M.A., B.SC., F.R.S.E., F.E.I.S.
President of the Educational Institute of Scotland

Dr. R. R. RUSK
Principal Lecturer in Education at Glasgow Training Centre

Dr. ALEX. MORGAN
Emeritus Principal and Director of Studies, Moray House Edinburgh

Rev. ALEX. ANDREW
Chairman of Glasgow Provincial Committee, Convener of Education Committee of Church of Scotland

Dr. DUNCAN MACGILLIVRAY
Late Headmaster, Hillhead High School, Glasgow, and Member of Glasgow Provincial Committee

Mr. GEORGE A. BURNETT
Director of Studies, Glasgow Training Centre

National Anthem

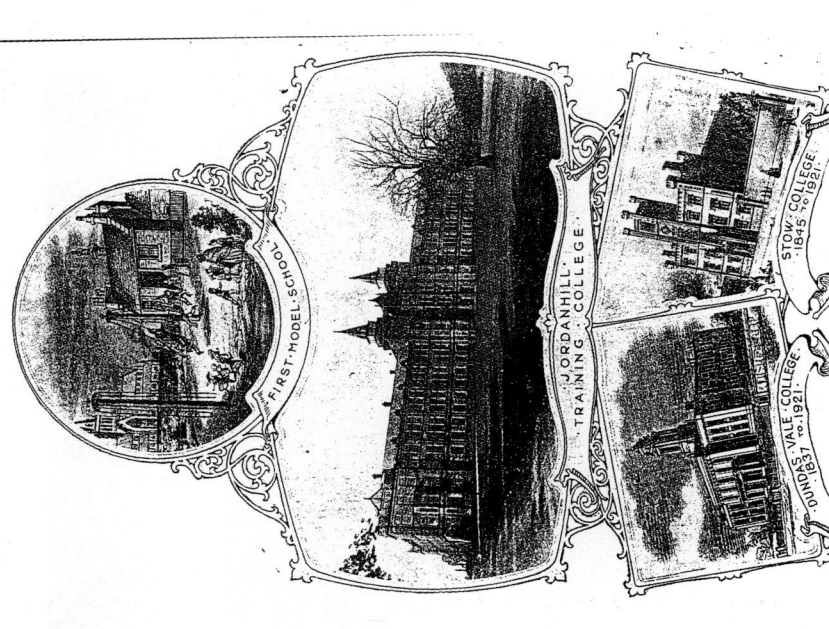

Centenary celebrations, 1928.

Students in the 1920s with Anne McAllister, Jean Milligan and K.G. Smith
(*Reproduced by courtesy of Miss Eliza M. Crawford*).

William Kerr, Director of Studies 1940–49.

A biology field trip in the 1930s with Dr D. Patton (in background).

Henry P. Wood, Principal 1949–71.

Dr Anne McAllister, founder of the School of Speech Therapy.

Miss Jean Milligan honoured by Aberdeen University.

Formal opening of the Crawfurd Building by HM the Queen, 1963.

Principal Tom Bone conferring awards at a college diploma day.

Formal opening of the Wood Building in the new Library, 1974.

Joe Casciani (left) and Iain Anderson in a College production of *Othello*.

Student in a primary classroom.

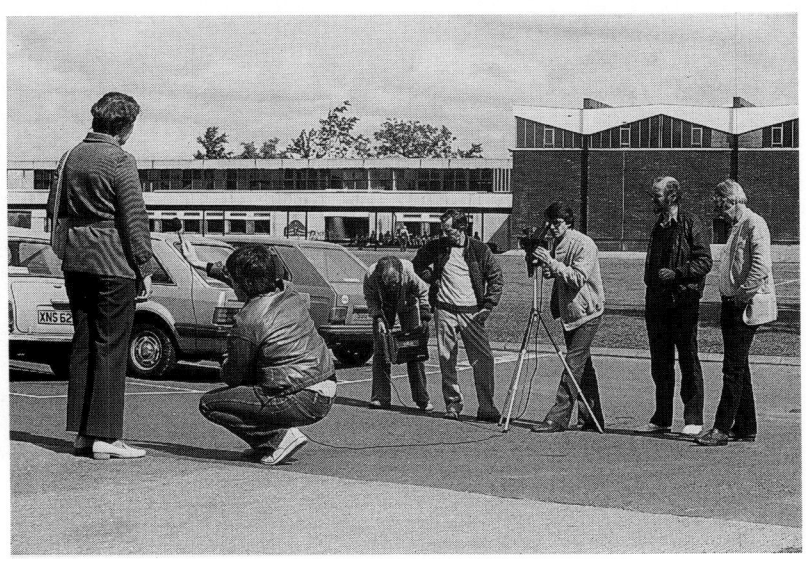

Dip Ed Tech students making a videotape.

Music tuition with Tommy Smith.

Students on rock climbing course.

HRH the Princess Anne and G. Bernard Wright at the
Commonwealth Games conference, 1986.

Tom Bone, Principal 1972–92.

Graduation is a family occasion.

Merger with the University of Strathclyde. Congregation in the Barony Hall
(*Photograph by Neil Maclennan*).

culture of critical discussion which is essential to the development of strong courses.

Two persistent themes

Throughout the successive reviews of the one-year secondary course at Jordanhill over the past 30 years, and in similar reviews elsewhere, there have been two predominant and pervasive themes: the relationship between college based studies and school experience, and the relationship between the various strands of college based studies. Arguably, the college has been successful in fusing college studies and placement studies into a single curriculum. It has achieved that through the widespread adoption of its regent scheme, through the intelligent design of placement itself, through the adoption of appropriate administrative arrangements intended to ease communication, and, most of all, through the kind of collaboration between college and school staffs which allow shared understandings to develop and roles and responsibilities to be agreed. Moreover, the shift from 'teaching practice' to 'school experience' acknowledges the wider range of objectives of the one-year secondary programme, as well as the need for students in training to acquire a critical understanding of how the school operates as an environment for learning. Cameron-Jones[50] has characterised the most appropriate relationship between an institution of higher education and schools as one of 'complementarity', which recognises the distinctive contributions made to training by school on the one hand and higher education institution on the other. There is evidence of that approach in the 1993 definitive document of the Jordanhill PGCE course.

If the college has made significant advances in implementing the partnership principle it has perhaps achieved only qualified success with regard to the integration of studies. The 1945 report of the Advisory Council, in what is still an impressive analysis of teacher education and its institutional context, was concerned to find ways in which the main components of 'education', 'psychology', 'methods' and 'practice' could be integrated. Its suggestion was that all four might be placed in the hands of a single lecturer and, failing that, responsibility might be shared between staff involved in professional studies and those involved in the practice of teaching. That dichotomisation, which was well established in the 1940s, has bedevilled secondary training in the Scottish teacher education colleges. In 1967, Nisbet wrote: 'What would first strike the visiting educationists from England is the widespread assumption that 'education', 'psychology' and 'methods' are three very different things'.[51] As a result, lecturers in education rarely see their students in schools and deal with issues that have very little impact on the students' practice.

Jordanhill's first attempt to overcome the institutionalised separation of theory and practice was in the 1975–76 review. It was recognised that 'there is need for an identifiable area of the course where the work of the professional subjects and of the teaching subjects develops in a structured relationship'. The coordinated day was intended to achieve that integration of the studies. The programme for session 1977–78 identified three areas for coordinated treatment. These were: discipline and class control; aims and objectives and their assessment; and social education. The evaluation[52] showed that the reaction of students was not very positive. Besides, the response of the staff in the departments of Education and Psychology showed that they were not altogether happy with the contents of the programme, and some staff felt 'that the coordinated day was imposed on them from above and that they had little possibility of influencing either organisation or content'. Notwithstanding that uneven evaluation, it was agreed to run the coordinated day for a second time in the course of session 1978–79 and to introduce a much more comprehensively radical approach in 1980–81.[53]

The hopes expressed in 1980–81 were not fulfilled, but there was still a commitment to integrate the work of professional studies and subject departments, and in the 1983 review the coordinated day gave way to what was called 'synchronisation'. This involved the joint exploration of the themes of language and learning, mixed ability teaching, primary/secondary liaison and learning difficulties. In due course synchronisation gave way at the time of the 1987 review to professional issues and teaching strategies (PITS). In response to student feedback about overlap PITS gave way in the 1992–93 review to generic issues and strategies for teaching (GIST). While GIST may be said to represent a significant step forward, in the sense that it entails collaboration between staff in the now unified department of Education and Psychology and staff in methods, both in college and on placement, arguably it is open to the same criticisms as were levelled at the very first coordinated day. At the time of the GTC visit in 1978 one member of the visiting panel asked informally if the existence of the coordinated day was intended to signal that the remaining days were uncoordinated. If the college is able to devise close professional and effective collaboration for the GIST component, why cannot that be extended to the whole of the programme?

The university connection

As has been noted, in the course of the last century and at the beginning of the present one, universities had a strong involvement in secondary training. That continued throughout the present century, principally through the Diploma in Education, which was intended to give those teachers in training who wished it an opportunity for a more academic study of education.

When moves were made to ensure that the professional studies programme was more closely coordinated with subject studies, the pressure arose to make the DipEd separate from postgraduate training and, when SED financial support was withdrawn, that change eclipsed the universities from any involvement in teacher training. However, with the merger of Jordanhill College as the Faculty of Education of Strathclyde University, the wheel has come full circle: secondary training now falls within a university context, and leads to a university qualification. It will be important, as the pressures mount to give schools a stronger role in the training process, for the university to ensure that the involvement of the teaching professional in training is protected while, at the same time, ensuring that an award made in its name devotes appropriate attention to the theoretical underpinnings of teaching.

Acknowledgment
I am grateful to Mrs Margaret Harrison, Librarian, and Professor James McCall, Dean, for facilitating my access to archive material.

Notes and references
 1 Stocks, J. Broken links in Scottish teacher training. *Scottish educational review*, v.18:2, November 1986, pp.110–120 and Cruickshank, M. History of the training of teachers in Scotland. London: ULP, 1970, p.145.
 2 Paterson, H.M. Incubus and ideology: the development of secondary schooling in Scotland 1900–1939 in Humes, W.M. and Paterson, H.M. (eds.) *Scottish culture and Scottish education 1800–1980*. Edinburgh: John Donald, 1983.
 3 GPC minutes, 1907–08.
 4 *Ibid.*, 1925–26.
 5 *Ibid.*, 1935–36.
 6 *Ibid.*, 1945–46.
 7 *Ibid.*, 1952–53.
 8 Russell, J.A. Jordanhill: thirty years back. *The new dominie*, March 1957, pp.14–15.
 9 Fairley, J.A. *A history of Jordanhill College 1921–1971*. Glasgow: Jordanhill College of Education, 1971.
10 Moffett, J. Interview with W.B. Marker, 7 July 1994.
11 Miller, J. Interview with W.B. Marker, 2 November 1994.
12 Moffett, J. *op.cit.*
13 *Ibid.*
14 Quoted in Scotland, J. *History of Scottish education*, vol.2. London: ULP, 1969.
15 Elliot, J. Drifters will make up the bulk of future graduate teachers. *Times educational supplement Scotland*, 3 May 1968.
16 Ashley, B., Cohen, H. and Slater, R. Why we are teachers. *Times educational supplement Scotland*, 12 May 1967.

17 SED. *Training of teachers: a report of the Advisory Council on Education in Scotland*. Edinburgh: HMSO, 1946. Cmd 6723.

18 Committee on Higher Education. *Higher education*. London: HMSO, 1963. Cmnd 2154. (Robbins report).

19 *Ibid.*, p.362.

20 *Ibid.*, p.363.

21 JBS minutes, 9 December 1963.

22 *Ibid.*, 22 September 1965.

23 Resolution of the University Court, 13 July 1966.

24 Select Committee on Education and Science (Scottish Committee), Session 1969–70. *Teacher training: minutes of evidence*. London: HMSO, 16 March 1970.

25 *Ibid.*

26 GTC. *Report by the Visitation Committee on the BEd courses in the Scottish Colleges of Education*, 8 September 1978.

27 SED. *Rationalisation of secondary teacher training in Colleges of Education in Scotland*, March 1982.

28 Letter from Dr Bone to Mr Orde, SED, 29 March 1982.

29 Miller, J. *op.cit.*

30 SED. *From school to further education*. Edinburgh: HMSO, 1963. (Brunton report).

31 JBS minutes, 15 March 1965.

32 GTC. *The training of graduates for secondary education*. Edinburgh: HMSO, 1972. (Brunton report).

33 Select Committee on Education and Science (Scottish Committee). *op.cit.*

34 JBS minutes, 15 October 1975.

35 *Ibid.* Secondary Sub-Committee, 5 November 1975.

36 JBS minutes, 24 March 1976.

37 GTC. *The training of graduates*. 1972.

38 JBS minutes, 7 November 1973.

39 Archer, E.G. and Peck, B.T. *The Jordanhill regent scheme*. Glasgow: Jordanhill College, February 1982.

40 JBS minutes, 29 June 1976.

41 *Ibid.*, 29 June 1976.

42 SED/GTC. *Learning to teach*. Edinburgh: HMSO, 1978.

43 GTC. *Investigation of teaching practice arrangements in the one-year postgraduate secondary course at the Scottish Colleges of Education*. May 1982.

44 GTC. *Report of Visitation Committee: visit to Jordanhill College of Education on 13 February 1980 and 13 March 1980*. 6 May 1980.

45 SED. *Report of the working party on secondary postgraduate preservice training*. June 1985.

46 SOED. *Guidelines for teacher training courses*. January 1993.

47 Jordanhill College. *Postgraduate Certificate in Education (Secondary): submission to the CNAA and the GTC*. January 1987.

48 CNAA. Report of validation of Jordanhill College's PGCE (Secondary), 20

February 1987. Letter 22 June 1987 from Mr L. Wharfe, Registrar for Education, to the Principal.

49 Letter from J.D. Kilgariff, Registrar, to Mr L. Wharfe, CNAA, 15 December 1989.

50 Cameron-Jones, M. *The Scottish pilot PGCE (Secondary) course, 1992–93.* Edinburgh: Moray House Institute, 1993.

51 Nisbet, S. The study of education in Scotland. *Scottish educational studies*, v.1:1, June 1967, pp.8–18.

52 Megarry, J. and Hewitt, C. *Coordinated day evaluators' report.* Glasgow: Jordanhill College, 1978.

53 JBS minutes, 1 November 1979.

9

Inservice and Special Needs

Gerald Mortimer

Articles and endorsements

Jordanhill became involved in the inservice training of teachers as soon as it came under the direction of the Glasgow Provincial Committee (GPC) in 1905. Prior to 1905 the responsibility for the 'further instruction of teachers in actual service' had lain with the County Councils but under Article 55 of the 1906 Regulations this responsibility passed to the Provincial Committees and the training colleges established under them. Thus these regulations signalled the beginning of the college's involvement with inservice work which was to continue up to the end of its independent existence.

Article 55 stated that the initiative and expense of running inservice lay with the Provincial Committee, but in practice the Committee reacted to requests from School Boards or County Councils. The process was formal and bureaucratic, with a sub-committee vetting the requests and setting fees and minimum enrolment numbers, before submitting the amended proposals to the SED on a specific form known as Form 6T. The Department in its turn reserved the rights of 'approval, inspection and certification'.[1] As with other aspects of college provision at this time, inservice training was kept under close central control. In its turn the GPC jealously guarded its own newly acquired rights. Thus when in 1906 Kirkcudbrightshire County Council requested that classes in cookery should be run in Kirkcudbright and Dalbeattie and offered to manage them, the Director of Studies was instructed to point out that 'only the managers of the institution in which the classes were being held could act as agents of the Committee'.[2]

This incident serves to illustrate other features of the early provision. Firstly, although the bulk of requests for inservice came from Glasgow and Lanarkshire, others came from farther afield. Requests in 1906–07 included submissions from Dumfriesshire, Inverness-shire, Ross and Cromarty and Stornoway School Board. Secondly, requests were for classes held locally, either in the evening or during the school holidays. Classes held in local centres were often conducted by local staff. Even within Glasgow the college had little option but to farm out such work. Thus in 1907 science inservice was offered at Anderson's College, while a class in physical training was approved for Maryhill Public School.

In 1920 the training colleges came under the control of the National Committee for the Training of Teachers (NCTT). This body's rules for the conduct of Article 55 classes clarifies the pattern which had emerged over the previous 14 years and demonstrates the format that was to last for the next 40. Classes for the further instruction of teachers were established in two main categories, those held during the school and college session and those held during the vacation. The initiative for sessional classes lay with the education authorities, who applied for courses to the Provincial Committees and their Training Centres, and who were responsible for paying the costs. The arrangements for sessional courses were subject to the approval of the NCTT and of the SED. The Provincial Committees did, however, have sole responsibility for the appointment of those who were to teach the courses. The Provincial Committees had more control over vacational classes in that they could propose the subject and location as well as determining the costs. Proposals for courses and their staffing had still to be submitted for approval to the NCTT, who would not normally sanction courses unless the fee income balanced the costs.

The sessional classes, which were held in the evenings or on Saturdays, were solely concerned with the enhancement of teachers' qualifications under either Article 37(b) for primary teachers or Article 39 for secondary, with the majority of the classes aimed at the former. This explains the annual diet of needlework, woodwork, drawing and domestic science which ran for over 50 years. The vacational classes which were held over several weeks of the summer holidays had the same emphasis but also included topical interests which did not count towards an award, for instance courses on the teaching of reading offered in 1910 and on sociology in 1921. This division between award-bearing and non award-bearing provision was to remain for as long as the college existed.

Within this framework the provision of inservice remained in a predictable routine from its inception to the 1950s, with several generations of teachers undertaking classes in needlework, drawing and domestic science to gain endorsements under Article 37(b). Nevertheless there were significant developments in this period, especially in the 1920s. In 1921 the NCTT decided that an Infant Mistress endorsement should be made available under Article 51 to certificated women teachers who completed a vacation course on infant teaching methods. The first such class at Jordanhill was held in summer 1924. 91 undertook the course and 86 passed, including three teachers from the Gold Coast. This marked the start of an enduring feature of inservice provision at Jordanhill. The Infant Methods course, with some change of title and content, was the longest running inservice course offered by the college, continuing beyond the merger of 1993.

The second development was the decision of the GPC in 1924 to recognise Article 55 classes in the methods of teaching mainline subjects in the Advanced divisions (ie secondary) as qualifying for endorsement under Article 39. Sessional classes started in the methods of teaching English, history, geography, modern languages, mathematics and science in 1924–25 and by 1926 vacation classes were offered in English, history, geography and mathematics. This marked the start of what became known as the Additional Teaching Qualification classes, another element of inservice provision which was to continue, although in a changed format, up to the merger with Strathclyde University.

The third major innovation arose from a conference held by the Central Executive Committee (CEC) and Glasgow Education Authority in November 1921. At this meeting it was agreed that specific training should be given to teachers of mentally defective children and that the course should be taught by a specially-appointed lecturer who would teach the required didactic element at Jordanhill, while at the same time acting as adviser to Glasgow Education Authority on arrangements in its special schools. By March 1922 it had been decided that there should be a one-year full time course for teachers throughout Scotland under the GPC, containing not less than three months' continuous teaching practice and leading to endorsement under Article 51. It was to be open to certificated teachers who had completed their probation and had been nominated by their authority.

After an unsuccessful attempt to interest some eminent London psychologists in the position, the CEC decided to offer it to David Kennedy Fraser, a qualified psychologist, who had been Principal Lecturer in Education at the Edinburgh Training Centre since 1920. He accepted and was appointed from January 1923. Because the MD course was full time, the student numbers were to be tightly limited throughout its history. In 1925 this was confirmed by a decision of the GPC that the recommended number in the class should be 16 and the absolute maximum 20. At the same time, however, the Committee did agree that an Article 55 course should be run as a refresher for teachers already working with mentally defective children. In this way started the long association of the college with the training of teachers of children with special needs, a field in which Jordanhill was eventually to exercise considerable initiative and influence.

Change and developments in educational thinking during this period were signalled through the interest or 'other' courses. For example, one in experimental science started in 1921 was still among the vacation classes of 1936 along with one on physical training and games (men), a reminder that the Scottish School of Physical Education was located at Jordanhill from 1931. In 1936–37, courses were offered on Dalcroze eurhythmics and on child guidance. In the 1944 vacation, the list of other courses included: modern methods in the primary school, speech training for primary schools, problems and possibilities of the junior secondary school and play centres and recreational activities for children, while vacation 1945 featured visual methods in modern education and vocational guidance.

Expansion and development

Although developments in inservice were to be a major feature of the energy released after Jordanhill became a self-governing college of education in 1959, some significant changes had begun in the mid 1950s. Up to this point enrolments in the interest courses had remained low in comparison to those for the endorsement classes. Suddenly this was reversed as new courses aimed at secondary teachers commanded a great deal of interest.[3] In 1955 a course on recent developments in physics was attended by 239 teachers while one on modern developments in chemistry held in 1956 attracted 290. During 1959–60 there were 49 such courses offered and a total of 3841 teachers attended. It is significant that half of that number were recruited for ten one-day conferences on aspects of the new O Grade Certificate. The new wave, however, included courses on other developments as well. In the late 1950s and the early 1960s the Mathematics Department ran a very successful series of courses on the Cuisenaire method of teaching arithmetic.

It is worth noting that the staff concerned were qualified to offer this help because they were involved in these new developments at national level. This participation was a new feature, but one which remained for the rest of the college's existence. Whether as panel members of the newly formed Scottish Examination Board or of national working parties and task groups or later as national development officers, many of Jordanhill's staff were to make significant contribution to the implementation of central policy and in some instances to its formulation. By 1965 a report on the inservice work of the college could refer to 'the large mass of activity ... which flourishes everywhere, under the names of panels, working parties, discussion groups, committees and with which the college has become more and more closely associated at national, regional and local level'.[4]

Another aspect of inservice, which was to become a major characteristic of Jordanhill for two decades, was the series of annual subject conferences, such as the annual conference of history teachers, held for the first time in 1956. Practising teachers learned about the latest developments in their field and from the start the conferences proved very popular. By the early 1970s some 15 or more conferences were being held on Saturdays throughout each year. Jordanhill was the only college which organised such gatherings and they were one of the college's unique contributions to inservice. This programme eventually fell victim to the discontent and industrial action of teachers in the mid 1980s but a few conferences survived.

A third and perhaps the most significant change of this period came in the field of special education. In February 1951 the CEC agreed that a new course be instituted under the revised training regulations of 1949 leading to an Article 51 endorsement in the teaching of physically handicapped children. The course was to be four months in length, the first part dealing with aspects of teaching both physically and mentally handicapped and the second part specialising in the teaching of the former. The course was to be centralised at Jordanhill and the existing MD course changed so that it also had an initial part dealing with teaching physically and mentally handicapped and a second part concentrating on the mentally handicapped. Its duration was also to be shortened to four months. As a result what were essentially two new courses began in October 1951, with 13 teachers enrolling for the physically handicapped course and 11 for the mentally handicapped version.

The next move in this field came as a result of an approach from the Director of Education for Glasgow in 1957, which Wood referred to the CEC. That body agreed that the PH and MH courses should be merged into a single course leading to a qualification to teach handicapped children, including those termed maladjusted. The new course was to be in two parts, the first consisting of four months at Jordanhill, the second of six months teaching under supervision. The SED gave approval in March 1958 so that the new unified course came into operation in the autumn of that year with 30 students. The college had already made its own internal arrangements in readiness for this. A new Department of Remedial Education was created, led by John A. Smith, who before his appointment to the college had been the first HMI appointed with special responsibility for the handicapped.

Smith was also prominently involved in inservice provision after 1959. The demand for inservice had continued to increase and education authorities were taking steps to provide their own inservice training. Although the college had endeavoured to meet some of the demand for courses outwith college by mounting residential courses in Argyll, Ayrshire and Dumfriesshire, Wood and Smith had already considered a more radical approach. This was to follow the example of Durham University's Institute of Education in appointing staff tutors dedicated to inservice provision. The Jordanhill tutors would be deployed partly in conducting inservice courses in the college and partly in organising and conducting courses for teachers across south west Scotland. These tutors were to form the core of a new Department of Inservice Training, through which all Article 55 provision would be coordinated. In 1964 Bill Michael was appointed as the first staff tutor in the new department, under Smith. By 1967 the work done by

Michael had proved sufficiently convincing for two further staff tutors to be appointed, Fred Rendell and Steve Bell. Although Michael was soon to depart for the recently-opened college of education at Hamilton, Rendell and Bell, along with Sallie Moodie, were to form the basis of a team which was ultimately to expand to five full time members.

The inservice staff tutor team was unique to Jordanhill. For some 20 years this team was to be at the forefront of developments in primary education in the west of Scotland and its influence extended to Europe and North America. The intention from the start was that the tutors would work with teachers and pupils in their own schools around issues arising from the Primary Memorandum, functioning as on-the-job consultants, and much of their work was left to their own initiative.[5] The main focus of their work centred on devising a holistic approach to topic work in the primary school. This enabled children to build their own conceptual model of situations using their own experience and problem-solving abilities. From the mid 1970s to the mid 1980s this unique methodology was incorporated into a very effective workshop course, arising from a collaborative experiment with Renfrew primary schools which had started in 1973. The headteachers of selected schools were introduced to the methodology. Thereafter teachers from the upper stages of the same schools were released in turn to take similar courses. The great merit was that a team was built up with a unified approach to topic work. As a result the workshops were soon being offered throughout Strathclyde Region and proved extremely popular. By the early 1980s the staff tutors were being invited to run workshops abroad on the 'Glasgow method', which built up a considerable following in Denmark, Germany, Iceland and the USA. Rendell then worked with Tricia Watterson in producing computer-assisted topic packages which were still proving popular at the time of merger. There is no doubt that some of the most enduring and widespread effects arising from Jordanhill inservice came from the work of the staff tutors.

This work sat alongside the provision of an increasing number of weekend conferences and a growing range of short courses offered as evening classes and as part of a summer school. Not all of this programme was focused on professional development, however. From 1960 there was a distinct rise in the number of courses in outdoor activities offered by the staff of the SSPE. Although some of these enabled teachers to obtain or improve qualifications in that field, most of them provided opportunities to engage in new recreational pursuits such as canoeing and rockclimbing.

By this time the Inservice Department was also organising Jordanhill's share of a programme of national courses promoted by a National Committee for the Inservice Training of Teachers (NCITT) formed in 1967. This Committee identified national priorities, arranged an annual programme of courses to meet these and requested the colleges of education to run them. In 1987 NCITT was replaced by the short-lived Scottish Committee for Staff Development in Education (SCOSDE) and under the title of SCOSDE seminars the national course programme continued until 1991. Whatever the nomenclature it seemed to the staff involved that Jordanhill always had more than its fair share of these courses.

By the early 1970s, therefore, the inservice scene was a busy one and the emphasis given to continuing professional development in the James Report indicated that it was likely to become busier still. Although the department had acquired an office and, from 1967, the support of an administrative assistant, Ian Caldwell, the growth in the quantity and diversity of the work made it clear that more support was required at a senior academic level. To provide this, Willis Marker was appointed to the department as Principal Lecturer in 1972. When Smith retired in 1975 Marker was appointed as Assistant Principal with specific responsibility for inservice training, separating this clearly from the many other remits which Smith had accumulated. The level of the new appointment was an indication of the importance of inservice in the work of the college, much of which was owed directly to the foresight, initiative and industry of Smith. Another indication was the decision that the old library in the David Stow building could be refurbished as an Inservice Suite. When completed in 1976 it contained a conference area, a workshop room, a store / office for the staff tutors and a coffee bar. It gave the college a flexible area outwith timetable constraints.

Changing goalposts and the enterprise culture
The session of 1975–76 was significant because of external factors also. The reorganisation of local government meant that most of the traditional province of the college was now composed of the monolith of Strathclyde Region. The new region held a virtual monopoly over release of teachers for inservice and saw more of its emerging priorities being met by its own developing advisory service. At the same time the shortage of teachers in the west of Scotland suddenly came to an end and the pressure on the college to concentrate its efforts on initial training eased. In these circumstances, Marker advocated that the college should create a range of award-bearing courses to be validated by the CNAA and should develop school-focused inservice training of the kind already undertaken by the staff tutors. The former aim was to be delayed by the policies of the SED and Strathclyde Region; the latter became an urgent priority far sooner than was anticipated, when the SED reduced the intake to the preservice courses and reallocated staff funding to school-focused inservice work (SFIS). By 1978 Marker was reporting that the 1977–78 session had

undoubtedly been a watershed in the development of the inservice work of the college. Previously it had seemed of minor importance compared to the preservice training of primary or secondary teachers, but this situation has been transformed by further cuts in preservice projects and by the allocation of 27 staff for school focused inservice. As a result, inservice had now become probably the largest single element in the work of the college'.[6]

For many staff this meant that they had quickly to redirect their attention from training as many qualified teachers as possible to working with serving teachers in a great variety of schools across the Strathclyde landscape. In the primary area there is no doubt that the process was greatly eased by the good relationships which had been established with education authority advisers by the staff tutor team. In the secondary sector the difficulties were greater.

In 1981 the situation changed again when Hamilton College of Education was closed and Jordanhill became responsible for fulfilling a government guarantee that the inservice provision made by Hamilton to Lanark Division would be maintained via a centre established for that purpose. Fortunately most of Hamilton's inservice had been linked to a Lanark development plan for primary school curriculum work and this was initially sustained by former Hamilton staff who had transferred to Jordanhill. The establishment of the centre took a good deal longer to achieve but after some time in temporary accommodation it was eventually located adjacent to St Mary's Primary School in Hamilton and courses were delivered there until the merger.

Much of the early SFIS work did not have the planned continuity of the Lanark programme and it became one of the major aims of successive development plans for the Inservice department in the late 1970s and throughout the 1980s to make SFIS work relevant, effective and embodied into structured and sustained programmes agreed with education authority staff. Despite the assiduous 'milk round' tour of the Strathclyde divisions by Marker and others each year this was never successfully achieved. Because the Region did not specify inservice needs sufficiently clearly or in sufficient time, it was difficult for the college to allocate staff. Attempts to make the college more proactive, especially in cross-curricular aspects of inservice, did not have much success either because for many college staff inservice work remained a much lower priority than departmental commitments to preservice training.

The SED was also concerned that inservice work be geared to appropriate national priorities and that ad hoc approaches to SFIS be eliminated. Accordingly in 1984 the Department made available to regional authorities specific grants whereby 75% of expenditure on inservice work identified as meeting defined national priorities could be reclaimed and in 1986 a procedure was introduced whereby, to obtain funding, SAFIS work, as it came to be known, had to be arranged through contracts between college and authority staff. Although both developments certainly encouraged concentration on national and regional priorities they also marked the reassertion of central government control over inservice work.

The changing emphasis in the inservice work of the college was reflected in the changes made in its organisation and management. In 1981 the position of Principal Lecturer was restored, to assist with the coordination of the SFIS programme and especially with the additional work in Lanark Division. Shortly before, a lecturer had been appointed to organise the national course programme and the short courses and conferences. In 1986 Gordon Wilson, who had been Principal Lecturer since 1982, took over as Assistant Principal (Inservice) on Marker's retiral. In the following year he reorganised the management structure of what was now the Division of Inservice Education. Three coordinators were appointed, one for primary inservice contracts, another for secondary SAFIS work and the third to maintain the national and short course programme as well as assisting with the administration of the award-bearing courses.

From the inception of SFIS the college had been funded directly for this work, an annual budget being allocated against a staffing target set by SED. In 1991 this policy was altered and the money was given directly to the education authorities, to use for the purchase of services from colleges. To allow the colleges to adjust to the new situation the change was to be phased in over three years. Although this did give some protection it meant that Strathclyde and Dumfries and Galloway Regions, which had made up the specific province of Jordanhill since 1905, could contract inservice work from the other colleges of education. The corollary was that Jordanhill in its turn was able to market SAFIS and other inservice contracts across all the regions of Scotland.

The short course programme had entered the cash nexus several years earlier. In 1986 funding for the payment of overtime to college staff teaching outwith normal college hours was withdrawn, and the effect on the programme of evening and weekend courses was considerable. From 1959 the college had used this funding to offer courses free of charge to the teachers attending, but from session 1986–87 the programme had to be self-funding. This financial constraint did not, as many anticipated, kill off the programme, which had been such a prominent feature of inservice work for the previous three decades, but it did reduce it to very modest levels. By 1990 the summer school was restricted to the vacation elements of award-bearing courses, and in 1991–92 the sessional short course programme consisted of only 21 courses attended by a total of just over 1000 teachers.

Modules and credits

Although through the work of the staff tutors, and through the range of short courses and conferences and SAFIS, a vast amount of valuable inservice training had been provided, all of these developments were eventually destroyed or diminished by external changes. Some compensation, however, was provided by the development of award-bearing inservice. In 1965 the changes in the training regulations had swept away many of the endorsement courses, leaving the college with the special qualification courses in infant methods, nursery education and special and remedial education. The initial priorities of the Inservice department had been the establishment of the staff tutor team and the organisation of the expanding short course programme, but from the early 1970s the annual forward plan of the department consistently included proposals to develop a range of new award-bearing courses, preferably externally validated.

These proposals ran into difficulties because of the policies of the SED and of Strathclyde Region. SED was giving priority to SFIS and was unwilling to see resources allocated to long, full time courses. Strathclyde would have found difficulty in funding release even if it had not opposed 'credentialism'. So, in the mid 1970s SED rejected proposals for an Inservice BEd and for Diplomas in Management and Guidance, validated by CNAA. Only the development of part time courses was possible. The most popular was the Associateship in Upper Primary Education (AUPE), which ran from 1976–83, when it was phased out to make way for the Inservice BEd. The most innovative was the Diploma in Educational Technology, which relied heavily on distance learning materials and was the first course of that kind to be validated by CNAA.

Only in the field of special education did it prove possible to develop full time courses. After the Melville report[7] in 1973 the combined PH and MH course became a one-year full time course leading to a Diploma in Special Education and following an Inspectorate report[8] in 1978 it was decided that the Special Qualification in Remedial Education should be phased out and replaced by a Diploma in Learning Difficulties (DLD). The college was approached by Dumfries and Galloway Region to develop a DLD course there. G Howel Jones, the Head of Department, decided to take both the existing Diploma in Special Education and the new Dumfries course to the CNAA for validation. The former was validated as the Diploma in Special Educational Needs (Recorded Children) in 1983 and the latter as the Diploma in SEN (Non Recorded) in May 1985. Almost immediately Strathclyde indicated an interest in the Non Recorded Course if it could be amended to involve a different pattern of release. A new version of the course was written over a weekend, proved acceptable to both Strathclyde and the CNAA and commenced in September 1985. These courses were of major significance, as they provided the basis of the college's provision in special needs until 1992.

As work was proceeding in the area of special needs, the view of what would prove acceptable to the SED was gradually clarified by a series of reports[9] prepared by NCITT, which developed the concept of a three tier structure of award bearing courses, incorporating credit accumulation and transfer. These were accepted by the Secretary of State and opened the way to courses based on modularity and credit transfer. The college then put forward a range of modular courses in areas such as computing but the key development was of a generalist Diploma in Professional Studies in Education (DPSE) open to teachers, FE lecturers and community educators, which came on stream in October 1985. This drew on some of the strongest features of existing courses such as the Dip Ed Tech and the special needs diplomas, in that it was made up of core studies, a specialist component, optional studies and a project, but its main feature was its modular structure which was deliberately designed, 'to combine with other modular courses ... to create a structure through which people can chart a variety of pathways leading to certificates.'[10] By January 1986 the DPSE had been joined by a generalist Certificate of Further Studies in Education which could be gained by completing four modules of any existing award-bearing inservice course with CNAA validation, or by a combination of three such modules and an Independent Study Module.

Further development became possible in the late 1980s when SED changed its policies to allow colleges to run any course which was self financing. This allowed Iain Smith to develop a scheme of free-standing modules modelled on programmes in operation at English institutions such as Thames Polytechnic. To avoid any potential delays or restrictions the Inservice Awards Scheme (IAS), led by Bill Thomson, was planned as a full-cost entrepreneurial venture and, after CNAA validation in March 1991 it was widely publicised through a series of high profile launching conferences with education and social work officials from the regions. Although it built on earlier developments, the scheme contained many features which were new to Scotland. All the modules within the IAS were validated at postgraduate M level. Successful completion of any four modules gained a Postgraduate Certificate in Advanced Professional Studies; completion of an additional three gained a Postgraduate Diploma. Holders of this could proceed to take the MSc by completing a research methods module (the only obligatory module) and a research study equivalent to another four modules. The most novel aspects of the scheme were that entry with advanced standing could be obtained from the accreditation of prior experiential learning and that modules devised and taught by agents external to the college could be validated and accredited within it. The new scheme proved a great success; by the time of the merger almost 2000 students had registered on the programe.

The national contribution

Although inservice never quite achieved parity of esteem with preservice, Jordanhill made a contribution to national developments which went well beyond its programme of courses. For two decades the Saturday conferences made the college virtually a national inservice centre. John A. Smith and Willis Marker were both in their day leading figures on the national scene, while Howel Jones played a significant part in developments in special education. The staff tutor team influenced developments in primary education, not only in the west of Scotland but in parts of Europe and North America. Over the years a great many other members of staff were involved in working parties engaged in curriculum development, in the formulation of guidelines and in the construction of training packages. Whatever its failings, it is a record to be proud of.

References

1 GPC minutes, 1905–06. *Regulations for Article 55 classes.*
2 *Ibid.*, 1906–07.
3 Fairley, J.A. *Jordanhill College of Education 1921–71.* Glasgow: Jordanhill College, 1972.
4 J.B.G. minutes, November 1965.
5 Bell, S. Interview with G. Mortimer, 1995.
6 Jordanhill Inservice department report 1978.
7 SED. *The training of staff for centres for the mentally handicapped.* Edinburgh: HMSO, 1973. (Melville report).
8 SED/HMI. *Children with learning difficulties in primary and secondary schools in Scotland.* Edinburgh: HMSO, 1978.
9 NCITT. *The future of inservice training in Scotland.* HMSO, 1979. (Green report); *Development of three tier structure of award-bearing courses.* 1984; *Arrangements for the staff development of teachers.* 1984.
10 Jordanhill Inservice committee report 1985.

10

The School of Further Education

Magnus Ross

Early history of further education

It has been suggested by Ross[1] that the provision of further education in Scotland has twin roots. One was derived from the inadequacies of school education to meet the legitimate needs of employers for increasing levels of competence, particularly in technical areas. This led to the development of evening continuation classes, based in schools, from the end of the 19th century. Evening classes developed and expanded and in some instances led to the creation of specific institutions. At the same time John Anderson's bequest in 1796 and the practical application of his ideas by George Birkbeck can be seen in the origins of the Mechanics Institutes. Ross argued that further education in Scotland grew just as much from this root as it did from evening class expansion.

Much of the early provision was carried out in central institutions such as the Royal Technical College, but as local authority provision of non advanced further education developed and grew the CIs began to concentrate on higher level courses. The further education service as it exists today is very much a creation of the post World War II era. It was only in 1946 that the title 'further education' first appeared in the Scottish legislative framework.[2] However, no resources were available to develop FE provision at that time, since social welfare was seen as the main priority.

Early further education emphasised technical education, such as welding, engineering and construction, because of the heavy industrial base of the Scottish economy at that time. At the same time, evening continuation classes run by the local authorities gave people a second chance to obtain qualifications. Birkbeck had argued for broadening the personal educational horizons of working people by providing access to a wide range of courses. Although he was enthusiastic about using direct vocational relevance, the aim of a broader and more liberal curriculum was important to Birkbeck. His vision was much greater than that of simple vocational education to meet immediate industrial and economic needs.

Later on, in 1952, the Advisory Council on Education in Scotland in its report *Further education*[3] embraced a similarly broad vision. It envisaged

FE as an integral part of the whole education process and not just as a means of meeting narrowly-defined industrial training needs. The need to maintain this breadth of vision against the interpretation of vocational education in a very restricted sense has been a continuing theme in the development of the FE service as we know it today. It is an issue that still creates tensions and conflicts in the FE world. The pace of development was slow until the 1956 White Paper *Technical education*[4] provided the impetus for growth throughout the UK by committing large scale funding to FE for the first time. Expansion was necessary at that time, since the children born postwar, the 'bulge' generation, would attain the school leaving age of 15 from 1960 onwards. Courses for secretarial and business studies, nursery nurse training, and many other occupations which had traditionally been regarded as female began to appear around this time in the local authority FE service. Student numbers in these areas grew rapidly.

A teaching qualification for further education

The lack of sustained development of further education before the 1956 White Paper meant that, despite the traditional emphasis on the importance of teacher training for the primary and secondary sectors in Scotland, there had been no systematic approach to teacher training for the further education sector. Until 1949, most FE teachers were untrained, but a few had been trained for secondary education under Chapter VI, Article 47(b) of the Training Regulations for teachers holding a diploma of a central institution in subjects such as art, music, domestic science and technical subjects. The last of these predominated. The revised Regulations in 1949 introduced the possibility of training under Article 47(bb), which allowed people with an HNC, a Full Technological Certificate of CGLI, or equivalent to be certificated. The gates were opened for a wider range of people to become properly certificated teachers in further education.

The National Committee for the Training of Teachers showed little enthusiasm for the idea of a separate certificate for teachers in FE, possibly perceiving no real need, since the FE sector was very small until the 1960s. Early training designed specifically for FE began in 1946 with courses being provided on an ad hoc basis at Dundee, Jordanhill and Moray House Teacher Training Colleges. Before the 1946 Education (Scotland) Act there had been no financial provision for the training of teachers specifically for FE, since there had been no legal recognition of the term until then. Provision for FE teacher education in those early days was very much an offshoot of the courses for technical teachers for schools. The three centres organised their courses in their own different ways and at Jordanhill Saturday morning courses for FE teachers began in session 1946–47. When the Article 47(bb) training became possible it consisted of Saturday morning attendance during two successive sessions. The pattern of inservice training with blocks of attendance interspersed with supervised teaching practice was to prove an enduring one[5] and continued in various forms right up to 1994.

It has never been a condition of employment in FE that a teacher must achieve full certification although it has in practice now become a condition that they must be qualified to enter such training. Some incentive was therefore needed to encourage the uptake of training. The 1946 Act enabled separate salary scales to be introduced for teachers in FE. Glasgow Corporation became the first authority to create a new scale for FE teachers, which paid 10% on top of the secondary scale plus an addition for teacher training, which by national agreement later became a fixed sum of £50 pa.

Variations between the early training courses were considerable, as the different institutions providing them had failed to adopt common duration and attendance patterns. With rapid growth imminent after the 1956 White Paper it was time for a more systematic approach to the training of teachers for FE. In 1957 the Secretary of State for Scotland set up a Standing Committee on the Supply and Training of Teachers for Further Education, chaired by Sir David Anderson, Director of the then Royal College of Science and Technology. The Anderson Committee,[6] reporting in 1959, urged that a separate certificate should be introduced for teacher training specifically for the FE sector. A Central Register was proposed of people who were otherwise qualified for teaching posts but who lacked teacher training. They would be able to seek employment in FE and, once in post, would become eligible to attend a teacher training course. Anderson also, however, recommended that facilities for training for FE should be available in both the east and the west to 'make it easier to train part time teachers, should such a step be later decided upon'. It is interesting to note that a much later Anderson report[7] would make not dissimilar suggestions.

In Jordanhill College the decision was taken in 1957 to appoint W.M.T. Mason as Principal Lecturer in Further Education. He was to establish and develop FE training until 1970, when he retired as first Director of the School of Further Education. He was succeeded by Dr Dennis Griffiths and then in 1972 by Dr James Stark. A former HMI, Stark was widely respected in Scottish further education. His gentlemanly style and his eye for detail characterised the management of the SFE during the period of growth and consolidation up to the early 1980s. Stark retired in 1983 and was succeeded by Stuart Niven, who was to have to deal with what was in many ways a more difficult period of increasingly rapidly changing demands from the FE sector. This has been worsened by the recent threat to the long-standing position of the School as the sole provider of basic teacher education for the FE service in Scotland.

Although the 1959 Anderson report provided some encouragement to the training of teachers for FE, it was not until the 1960s that development really took off. The expansion of provision triggered by the 1956 White Paper was now well under way. New colleges were opening throughout Scotland[8] and older ones were expanding, with a consequent rapid increase in the numbers of students and teaching staff. Most of these staff were recruited from industry or commerce on the strength of their technical qualifications in their own subjects. Although many had satisfactory general educational qualifications, they did not usually have any experience or qualification in teaching. At the same time, the Robbins report[9] was to bring about a dramatic expansion of the higher education system. The movement of some institutions into the HE sector was to bring even greater pressure for expansion of FE. Behind all the expansion in post school education was the demographic change associated with the late 1940s population bulge reaching school leaving age.

New regulations introduced full certification for FE teachers in the form of the Teaching Certificate (Further Education) in 1965. A year earlier, in March 1964, the Secretary of State for Scotland, in consultation with the Scottish Council for the Training of Teachers, had reconstituted the Standing Committee on the Supply and Training of Teachers for Further Education, under the chairmanship of Robert Robertson, then Chairman of Renfrewshire Education Committee and later for many years Chairman of the FE Committee of Jordanhill Board of Governors. The Committee reported in 1965, recommending that, in view of the uncertainty concerning numbers of FE staff likely to come forward for training, and the consequent difficulty of providing training for a wide spectrum of subjects, FE training should be located in a single comprehensive unit in close association with an existing college of education.

Such a location was desirable, since the Committee concurred with Brunton's view[10] of further education as an extension of secondary. Residential facilities would be required, to allow it to cater for students from all over the country. The Committee further recommended that the unit be located at Jordanhill, on the grounds that

> (a) It is centrally placed to a very large number of further education centres ... 60% of the teachers in further education centres are employed within its 'province'; and
> (b) the staff already have had considerable experience both of the mixed course and of courses of post-initial training.[11]

A significant note of reservation,[12] disagreeing with the proposal for a single unit, was added by W.B. Inglis and D.E. Stimpson, Principals of Moray House and Dundee Colleges. Their concern was that a strong, self-contained unit within one college would not in fact interact or integrate successfully with the rest of the college as the Committee envisaged. They saw a risk that such a unit could, in attempting to assert its own identity, lose some of the essential sense of belonging within the overall framework of the college and of the system of teacher education in Scotland.

From 1965 until the opening in 1973 of a new building on the campus dedicated to FE training, the courses were provided in a range of premises of varying degrees of suitability, not always on the Jordanhill campus, and sometimes even in the centre of Glasgow. Staff and students had to travel between buildings and this did nothing to enhance the status of the FE teachers' course. When Sir Edmund Hudson opened the new purpose-built facility in September 1973 it was hailed as a great advance for the provision of teacher education for the FE sector, for the staff involved and for Jordanhill College itself. The new building certainly did enhance the self esteem of the staff, who had been working under great difficulties before that time. The building had its own library, AV support and office services. In addition it interconnected with its own new and comfortable multi-storey hostel accommodation with full independent catering facilities.

Full time and day release attendance patterns had been rejected by the Robertson Committee in favour of mixed preservice and inservice provision and this was to be made more attractive by offering the course with three different starting dates each year. A full time staff of 28 lecturers and an annual intake of around 250 students spread between the different intakes was anticipated. The largest intake in a year was expected to be no more than 100. The idea of mixed pre- and inservice provision was unworkable. There was a lack of financial support for students to take the preservice courses and no guarantee of employment at the end. In practice the provision rapidly became inservice only, a situation that continues to the present day. Students coming on the course would already be employed as teachers in FE, and their employers would meet the cost of training.

By 1973 the course provision had settled into a thick sandwich pattern of two eight week blocks of attendance and two terms of supervised teaching practice in the intervening period, with intakes to the course in January, May and September. The course covered teaching methods, educational studies and psychology and curricular studies. In the early 1970s the need was recognised to bring the course into line with practice south of the border, where recognition by the Burnham Committee required 600 class contact hours. To achieve this necessitated the expansion of the full time attendance blocks to ten weeks each. With the staffing available in the School of Further Education the tutorial visiting programme had to be drastically cut, despite the fact that students consistently reported this as being one of the most valuable aspects of the course. The different intake dates were never equally attractive to employers and in practice the intake immediately after Easter had become the main intake for the year. This made sense in FE colleges at a time when a large part of teaching commitments ended with external examinations, often run by professional bodies, traditionally taking place in the third term and often starting just after Easter. It was a time when it was much easier to release staff with little or no inconvenience or additional cost.

New modes of learning
That situation changed dramatically in the early 1980s after the introduction of the new National Certificate following the 16–18 Action Plan.[13] The traditional quiet time in FE colleges disappeared almost overnight and colleges became more reluctant to send students to the School of Further Education in the numbers that they had in the past.

Other factors had also had an effect. The salary differential between FE and schools had been eroded steadily over a longer period but, more importantly, after the Houghton report[14] in 1974 the specific additional payment for teacher training ceased. The payment of a year's increment in its place meant that at the top of the scale, salary would be the same with or without teacher training. An incentive for staff to undertake training had effectively been withdrawn. The costs involved for the FE colleges were also considerable. Not only had the course fees to be paid but travelling and subsistence expenses were substantial. The halving of the course fee in 1982–83 led to a peak in enrolments in 1983 but the figure rapidly slipped back again in the following years.

The changed needs of the FE service coincided with the requirement to secure external validation for the course, in line with government policy in teacher education generally. The result was that a completely new form of provision was validated by SCOVACT in January 1986 and subsequently accredited by the General Teaching Council. This was seen as a course which could be suitable not only for teachers in FE but also to meet growing needs within higher education, not least because many FE colleges were developing their own provision of higher level courses.

This course extended over five consecutive terms, with full time attendance at Jordanhill for four weeks in the first term, one week in the second, another four weeks in the fourth, and one week in the fifth. Two intakes each year were provided, very close together, one in late April and the other just four weeks later in May. Although the equivalent of 600 hours of class contact was maintained, there were now only 300 hours actually in the Scottish School of Further Education. 276 hours of distance teaching/ learning activities were provided and 24 hours of tutorial visits by the staff of the School made up the balance. The course was innovative in its use of senior staff in FE colleges as mentors for the trainees, in the tutorial visits to students by Jordanhill staff and in the repackaging of the course to make it suitable for a distance learning mode. The purpose was to reduce the backlog of FE teachers awaiting training by reducing the direct costs to the sponsoring colleges, and the employers liked it. This course was subsequently revised for a modular pattern of delivery and written in terms of competencies. This was a pioneering initiative which came into effect in summer 1994, offering far greater flexibility in training to FE college staff. It was now also a form of provision which was much closer to the expectations and professional practice of FE lecturers themselves.

Alongside the provision for teachers and lecturers in further and higher education there has been for many years (since the 1970s) successful provision for teachers of nursing and midwifery. The implementation of changed policies in the training of nurses, especially Project 2000, and the move to an all graduate profession has meant that nursing education is now rapidly relocating within mainstream higher education. The future of specific provision for the training of teachers in nursing and midwifery at the Scottish School of Further Education is therefore under some doubt at the time of this study. It may or may not be that the new pattern of provision to be introduced in 1994 can succeed in retaining this particular student group at the Scottish School of Further Education.

Post-initial courses, conferences and research

Recognition of the importance of these activities was made in the Robertson report.[15] To the extent that these activities took place at all they had been very much an ad hoc response to quite specific circumstances. Robertson recognised that they would be vital to meeting the rapidly changing needs of the FE service and the report argued that they could only effectively be provided in a single national centre. This was not only a major plank in the report's advocacy of a single centre, it was also a major reason behind the argument that such a centre be located within an existing college of education. This would ensure access to a broader range of facilities and resources and of course to much wider research experience.

From its earliest days the staff of the School of Further Education were involved in running short courses and conferences to meet specific needs among FE staff, despite the heavy demands of running the teaching qualification course for rapidly increasing numbers. The staff were uniquely well placed to become aware of these needs as a result of their frequent visits to colleges throughout the country. Major conferences were run on topics such as manpower planning, coping with change and the management of FE, while individual staff became involved with various curriculum development initiatives such as unified vocational preparation (UVP) in 1976. Two things in particular were lacking. There was no overall planning or structure designed to provide continuity and systematic provision at post-initial level, and there was no way of rewarding those who took part in short courses by recognising the work they had done and its contribution to their professional development. This might have been done by giving credit within a modular awards scheme, but no such schemes were sanctioned by the SED until the mid 1980s.

The impetus to address the problem came in the aftermath of the 16–18 Action Plan, when the SED set up three task groups concerned with curriculum and assessment, teacher education, and guidance and counselling. Curriculum and assessment was to become the province of the Curriculum Advice and Support Team (CAST). Guidance and counselling was to lead to major initiatives in the FE service as a whole and within the SSFE would ultimately lead to a collaborative effort with Strathclyde Region to develop a new Certificate in Adult Guidance. From the teacher education task group came recognition that not only would it be necessary to introduce changes to the initial training of FE staff, but there would be an even greater need to provide courses for staff who had been in the FE service for a long time. The need for a more systematic approach to continuing staff development in FE was by now becoming widely recognised and the SSFE proposed a flexible programme of modular courses which would earn credits which could accumulate and lead to recognised awards. This scheme was eventually approved by the SED and introduced in 1989.

30-hour modules were available in five broad areas and they could be delivered in a variety of modes, either at the SSFE or on an outreach basis in response to specific requests. Teaching was done by the staff of the SSFE but could also include input from other Jordanhill staff, staff from FE colleges themselves and outside contributors. An additional 30 hours of study was required from students for each module. An accumulation of four module credits would qualify for a certificate award, 12 would qualify for a diploma and 16 would lead to the degree of BEd, at that time from Glasgow University. All the awards were in Post School Education Studies. This scheme was designed to assist non graduates to upgrade their qualifications. Very large numbers of staff in FE have original technical qualifications which are not at degree level. There was, therefore, considerable attraction in the idea of gaining a degree award from undertaking further study which would at the same time be of direct relevance to their normal work. Enrolments on the programme rapidly increased and there were soon over 1000 teachers from FE, community education and nursing and midwifery engaged on the programme.

It was perhaps unfortunate that the programme could not have been more fully integrated with the Inservice Awards Scheme that was developing elsewhere in the college. The latter was entirely a postgraduate scheme, aimed at the 'reflective practitioner'. This was eventually dealt with by making different levels of study possible to achieve the different awards within the same modular structure. This created the possibility of further study up to Masters level, and the opportunity of higher degrees by research, some of which have been based on study within the field of further education. The emerging weakness of the post initial award-bearing courses offered by the SSFE was that of appearing to be qualification-led and depending on the personal development goals of individuals, rather than being demand-led by the FE colleges. As college managements became more careful about spending scarce resources on staff development, this made it more difficult to attract enrolments on the programme. Equally there is no guarantee that a demand-led system would be any better at meeting needs, especially longer-term development needs, both of the FE service and of the individual staff involved.

The die is CAST: an opportunity lost
In the aftermath of the 16–18 Action Plan it quickly became apparent that a major effort must be launched to meet the resulting curriculum development needs within the FE service. Initially those needs had been met by the appointment of national and territorial development officers on short-term secondment from their own colleges. By summer 1984 most of these appointments were coming to an end and there was then no national focus for the support of curriculum development in FE. On 31 March 1985 the Scottish Office announced the setting up of CAST which would be financed for a two-year period to 31 March 1987. Its remit was to be specifically Action Plan related in the first instance. HMI J. Hay was seconded to lead a unit of six development officers, and there was also an office manager. The unit was to operate from the SFE; CAST was born.

Generations of students of education had long learned from Lawrence Stenhouse that curriculum development and staff development were quite inseparable. The staff of the SFE had always been overstretched simply in maintaining the delivery of the basic TQ(FE) course to an ever-increasing number of FE lecturers. The demands of the course were heavy and a large tutorial visiting programme was carried out in the supervised teaching part of the course. In consequence it is not surprising that the SFE had not been able to meet all the curriculum development needs of the colleges and the corresponding continuing staff development needs. However the staff of the School had achieved a considerable amount in this field, and continued to do so after the establishment of CAST. External examiners frequently commented favourably on the School's curriculum development work with students, and there had been some notable successes, such as the UVP initiative. It appeared to staff in the School that successful efforts such as this were not perhaps given the recognition they deserved in the decision making that led to the creation of CAST.

CAST was a success. By August 1987 it had produced a 23 point Action Plan Staff Development resource covering all aspects of curriculum delivery. It was also embarking on the training of staff development tutors. Some of what was offered by CAST may have appeared to be very much based on ideas that the staff of the School had long promoted. They in turn may have felt disappointment at not being more directly involved. The big difference was that CAST now had the resources to do this much more thoroughly and to present it in a much more attractive and professional manner.

CAST had been located at Jordanhill in the early days, but had not been at this stage regarded as an integral part of Jordanhill, although administered by the college. When the initial period of funding expired in 1987, SED proposed that CAST be assimilated into the SFE, and from April 1987 it became the Curriculum Services Unit of the SFE, although retaining the name CAST, which had become familiar in the field. This was seen as a 'golden opportunity'[16] by the college authorities. The Director of CAST (Ian Natusch) was accountable through the Director of the SFE to the Principal of Jordanhill College. In day to day practice, however, CAST operated semi autonomously and there was comparatively little formal collaboration with the SFE, although individual staff did develop constructive informal contacts.

Once the tone had been set, for whatever reason, CAST and the SFE developed in their own ways. CAST rapidly expanded. Its remit was now much wider, being

> To promote the implementation of vocational education and training by providing an advice and support service to teachers, lecturers and others engaged in it by:
> - preparing and publishing curricular support materials
> - maintaining a national information and resource centre
> - organising and servicing working groups for specific developmental tasks
> - organising and participating in relevant staff development and inservice activities
> - maintaining close contact and collaborating with SED, LEAs, SCOTVEC, SCCC and others concerned with vocational education and training.[17]

It would not have been an enormous leap of imagination to interpret this remit as being quite complementary to the original remit of the SFE in the Robertson report. The possibility might have opened up of creating a unified organisation with access to a vast and unique pool of experience in all levels of staff development and curriculum development, to the benefit of the FE service and of Jordanhill College. The work of CAST rapidly grew and its success can be judged by the fact that within two years it was able to support almost 40% of its total budget from externally-funded projects.

Management of FE colleges was a major concern of government policy in the late 1980s, in the light of forthcoming changes in funding and the future incorporation of the colleges as independently constituted organisations. In a report[18] published in June 1989, Miller and Neil recommended that a Scottish Further Education Unit (SFEU) be set up, by analogy with the FEU in England, to support FE colleges and their then new College Council management regimes. Consultation in the field suggested that greater independence and a wider remit were necessary and the SFEU was accordingly established on 1 April 1991.

The new SFEU had its own steering group chaired by an Under Secretary in the SOED and was now free of any kind of accountability to Jordanhill College. Increased accommodation was made available in the Scottish School of Further Education building, causing more pressure on accommodation for the rest of the School. The publication of the White Paper *Access and opportunity*[19] and the subsequent Further and Higher Education (Scotland) Act, 1992, meant that there were huge opportunities, as well as challenges, to help support the FE service through the major changes in its management and organisation. SFEU soon found ample scope to expand its work again. In 1992, however, the SOED decided that SFEU should become a non departmental public body managed by a Board of Management. It continued to occupy its rented accommodation at Jordanhill but decided to investigate relocation elsewhere. (The decision was subsequently taken to move to Stirling in early 1996). To the observer it may seem that a golden opportunity to combine the strengths of the two organisations has slipped away.

Conclusion

The SSFE has grown from insignificant beginnings to a position where it was a major part of the work of Jordanhill College at the time of the merger with Strathclyde University. The contribution it has made to the FE sector as a whole has been vast. FE has always regarded itself as the Cinderella of the education service, never accorded the status of school or higher education, yet often taking the failures of the former and turning them into successes. During the past 20 years, FE has been subject to virtually constant change. In that environment, there have been constant pressures on the SSFE to adapt and develop in new ways.

To a very large extent it has succeeded in meeting those challenges. Teacher training has never been made compulsory, yet the training given by the SSFE has contributed to raising the status of FE lecturers and enabling them to converse with their counterparts in other sectors of education on more equal terms. A later Anderson report[20] would challenge the concept of a single centre for FE teacher training, but bring in its wake, for the first time, the possibility of training for part time lecturers. The SSFE has constantly adapted its provision to meet changing needs in the FE sector and it will now have to demonstrate this ability once again. All its history suggests that the staff of the SSFE will rise to the new challenges and again turn these challenges into opportunities.

Acknowledgements
Much of the information for this chapter was obtained from S.M. Niven's account, *The first twenty-five years*, SSFE, 1992. The interpretation of the information and opinions expressed are entirely the responsibility of the author.

References
1 Ross, M. *The evolution of further education in Scotland from 1956–1972*. MEd thesis, University of Glasgow, 1984.
2 Education (Scotland) Act 1946.
3 Advisory Council on Education in Scotland. *Further education*. Edinburgh: HMSO, 1952. Cmnd 8454, p.24.
4 Ministry of Education. *Technical education*. London: HMSO, 1956. Cmnd 9703.
5 Logan, J.L. *The training of teachers for further education in Scotland*. MEd thesis, University of Glasgow, 1974.
6 Advisory Council on Education in Scotland. *Teachers in Scotland: measures to improve the supply* …. Edinburgh: HMSO, 1959. Cmnd 644. (Anderson report)
7 SOED. *Initial training of further education college lecturers*. Edinburgh: SOED, 1993. (Anderson report).
8 Ross, M. *op.cit.*
9 Committee on Higher Education. *Report*. London: HMSO, 1963. Cmnd 2154. (Robbins report).
10 SED. *From school to further education*. Edinburgh: HMSO, 1963. Cmnd 2154. (Brunton report).
11 SED. *Future recruitment and training of teachers for further education in Scotland*. Edinburgh: HMSO, 1965. p.26. (Robertson report).
12 *Ibid*. p.30.
13 SED. 16–18 Action Plan. 1983.
14 Committee of inquiry into the pay of non university teachers. *Report*. London: HMSO, 1974. Cmnd 5848. (Houghton report).
15 Robertson report. op.cit. pp.21–22.
16 JBS Executive minutes, 29 January 1987.
17 JBG. SFE Committee minutes, 20 February 1987.
18 Miller, E. & Neil, J. *Management of further education in Scotland*. Edinburgh: SOED, 1989. 3v in 1.
19 Scottish Office. *Access and opportunity*. Edinburgh: HMSO, 1991. Cm 1530.
20 Anderson report 1993. *op.cit.*

11

The Scottish School of Physical Education

Roy B. Small

From 1931 until 1989 the Scottish School of Physical Education at Jordanhill College was the centre for the training of male teachers of physical education in Scotland. For almost 60 years it mirrored and responded to the demands of Scottish society. In the early years the students learned to recognise and counter the effects of poverty and deprivation; in the middle period, as society became more affluent, the curriculum was shaped and broadened to include a wide range of physical activities. In the last 15 years courses became more academically orientated to allow graduates to participate with confidence and effectiveness in the widest educational context. The School and its purposes, however, could trace its roots directly back to the first 'college' for training physical education specialists, set up in the town of Dunfermline in Fife in 1905, through the beneficence of the Scottish American philanthropist, Andrew Carnegie.

Origins of the School
At the turn of the century the investigations and subsequent reports of two medical practitioners, Hay and McKenzie, had highlighted the imperative need for a structured, rational policy which would improve the health of the populace.[1] The poor state of health of volunteers for the Boer War had given great cause for concern throughout the country, and it was argued that the notion that 'society must provide' superseded the strongly held view of the day that an individual was responsible for his or her own destiny.[2] The Royal Commission for Physical Training (Scotland) was set up in 1901. The Commissioners' report described the deplorable living conditions which existed in many towns, and was instrumental in preparing public opinion to support legislation for a school meals service and medical inspection in schools. Although the report covered a wide range of important issues, and stated that physical education should be an essential part of education, it was the recommendations relating to the inspectorate, medical inspection, teacher training and certification and the setting up of physical training institutions, which had the greatest impact on the formal training of teachers of physical education.[3]

In August 1903 Andrew Carnegie had supported the Dunfermline Trust with a gift of $2,500,000 and from this source the Trustees built the swimming baths and gymnasium, and the College of Hygiene and Physical Training opened in 1905.[4] The excellent facilities at Dunfermline, together with the ideas, energies and abilities of the leaders of the town and staff of the gymnasium, made the new institution an immediate success. The use of the word 'Hygiene' in the title (which survived in the Scottish School of Physical Education and Hygiene, Jordanhill College, until the mid 1950s) reveals the medical emphasis of physical education at that time. It also indicated a change in official thinking, from physical education as a means of discipline to physical education as a way of improving general health.

A study of the prospectus for 1905 illustrates very clearly how Dunfermline College attempted to respond to the social ills created by poverty and deprivation. The theoretical course in the new curriculum comprised anatomy, physiology and remedial gymnastics, and the practical component included Ling's gymnastics and massage.[5] The bias was heavily weighted towards the remedial aspects and scant attention was given to educational or recreational considerations; methods of teaching and participation in games, dancing and swimming occupied only half of the total practical time allocation.

Training for men at Dunfermline, which had been available from 1908, was suspended during World War I. When it resumed in 1919 pressure was brought to bear on the National Committee for the Training of Teachers to reconsider the arrangements for the training of male teachers of physical education. In 1929 the idea of a separate college for men was first mooted, and in January 1930 the Special Committee set up to consider this reported, 'that it would appear that because of limitations of training accommodation and opportunities for teaching practice there would be a need for separate colleges in the near future'. On 30 September 1930 the Central Executive Committee (CEC) agreed to transfer the men to Jordanhill Training College, Glasgow.[7] Dr Alastair MacKenzie was invited to take over as Medical Officer and Principal Lecturer in Hygiene and to transfer with him two members of staff, Frank N. Punchard as Master of Method and Oswell Rosser as Lecturer in Physical Education. A Devonian, Punchard had trained at St Luke's College, Exeter, as a general teacher. His ideas had been strongly influenced by Niels Bukh at the Folk High School, Ollerup. Very capable physically, he had a deep interest in gymnastics, swimming and wrestling, and his reputation was 'deservedly international'.[8] Rosser, a Welshman, was in many ways complementary to Punchard; his philosophical and liberal nature and his love of words acted as a counterbalance to the exact technical and precision teaching of Punchard.

The high noon of gymnastics

On 1 October 1931 the Scottish School of Physical Education and Hygiene took up residence at Jordanhill College and established a continuity which existed until 1990. The three members of staff went to very primitive conditions, having no proper dressing room and sharing the limited facilities offered by the four womens' gymnasia available in the Glasgow centre. Not until 2 May 1932 were the new gymnasia and dressing rooms completed and on 5 September 1932 the Scottish School made ready to move into the accommodation which had cost the then very considerable sum of £6,750/8/4d with adjustments being made to the playing fields on the campus at a cost of £723/16/11d.[9]

The curriculum still had a strong medical bias and instruction in anatomy, physiology and medical gymnastics was conducted externally by the Managers of Glasgow Royal Infirmary, in conjunction with their course for the Certificate of the Chartered Society of Massage and Remedial Gymnastics. The CEC decided, however, 'that the study of massage be not obligatory', a decision which placed physical education firmly within the educational camp.[10] In a letter to the President of the Scottish Association of Physical Education in 1963, Punchard, then 75 years old, commented, 'Essentially one aims at producing a teacher—the reason why I favoured the attachment to Jordanhill Training Centre'.

This early period at Jordanhill from 1932 until 1939 was described by Hugh C. Brown, a later Director of the Scottish School of Physical Education as, 'the high noon of gymnastics'.

> We were taught gymnastics with total dedication by two important Danes. They taught it efficiently but without humour, and they taught it painfully. My most pungent memory is of 45 minutes of free-standing exercises, followed by a session that invariably overran the period time, and without question the accent was overdone ... Whilst games were 'recognised', little more could be said for them. For example, playing in a competitive game where both teams operated in the same colour of jersey, making it difficult to distinguish friend from foe, indicates better than anything where the emphasis lay. Such a confusion would not have been permitted in the gymnastic situation where attention to detail was total and deviation from the accepted norm of training and performance totally prohibited.[11]

George F. Orr, on the other hand, a student in 1933–36 and a member of staff from 1946, had a totally different perspective from Brown.[12] He referred to this period as the 'superlative days'. The gymnastics referred to by Brown were Swedish in origin, and differed from the early concept of military drill. Evolved between the wars, the essential concept was one of free-flowing rhythmical movement, designed to develop joint mobility, local and general endurance linked to the development of fine skills on apparatus. Unlike the German form Swedish gymnastics stressed swift, skilful movement rather than the more static strength requirements of the Eastern European variety.

But if Brown and other Scottish students were dissatisfied, the international reputation of the School was growing rapidly; in the 1930s Egyptian, Indian and other colonial students were admitted to the Scottish School of Physical Education.[13] In 1935, the School was invited by the Ling Association to represent Great Britain at the Southern Swedish Gymnastic Festival at Revingehed,[14] but without question the climax of recognition came in the acclaim the School received at the Lingiad in Sweden in 1939. The Scottish School represented Scotland at the last Lingiad ever to be held, in 1949. Whilst Swedish gymnastics were practised in schools throughout Scotland there may well be justification for the belief that they were foreign to the Scottish culture. Educational gymnastics gradually gave way to more inventive forms of movement and with greater diversification into games and outdoor activities physical education changed dramatically.

The halcyon days of games

After World War II, Punchard and Rosser were joined on the staff by George Orr and W. Dickinson and during this period the curriculum was broadened. Games coaching became more systematic and strong links were established with the governing bodies of sport, particularly with the Scottish Football Association, the Scottish Rugby Union and the Scottish Amateur Athletic Association. In 1950 Scottish School students went for the first time to Glenmore Lodge at Aviemore for skiing instruction.

In 1953 Brown was appointed Master of Methods on Punchard's retiral. Brown was aggressively Scottish. Born in Dunlop, Ayrshire, he trained at Jordanhill from 1933–36 and spent two years as Physical Education Organiser in Lanarkshire. Brown was a dynamic, charismatic figure who was held in great respect and affection by Scottish School students. He had a strong influence on professional standards in dress, conduct and achievement and did a great deal to establish a strong, independent Scottish School ethos. One of his primary aims was to root the curriculum of the School in the culture of Scotland.

A great deal happened during Brown's administration and many of the improvements were without question due to the increasing availability of money and the support he received from the then Principal, Henry P. Wood. New buildings in the late 1960s incorporated teaching accommodation, physiology laboratories, swimming pools and games halls. Brown made games compulsory for all students who did not already have a professional games commitment. He was 'strongly of the opinion that compulsory Saturday games with teams from outside college was a necessary part of the training of physical education specialists'.[15] An analysis conducted in 1969[16] revealed that from a possible 3000 units of extra curricular participation there were an actual 2040 during that academic year. (A unit of participation was calculated as a college team taking part in a game or event in formal competition within a recognised league or association outside college.) These activities involved soccer, rugby, hockey and outdoor activities but many activities which occurred mid-week, for example basketball, volleyball, swimming and badminton, were not recorded in the survey. There is no question that this policy was effective in many ways since it brought the Scottish School into direct contact with the community at an adult level and did much to enhance the reputation of the School and break down its previous insularity.

From 1956 six soccer teams participated in the Combined Reserve League of the Scottish Football League, the Scottish Amateur League, the West of Scotland League and the Glasgow Colleges League. In seasons 1956, 1957, 1958 and 1959 the college first eleven was successively first in Fourth, Third and Second Divisions of the Scottish Amateur League and second in Division One. From 1957–58 until 1965–66 in the Scottish Amateur cup, the soccer team were finalists in 1956, semi-finalists in 1963 and 1964 and winners in 1966. Rugby was equally prominent and from 1957, when they first gained full membership of the Scottish Rugby Union, Jordanhill subsequently became one of the leading clubs in the country. In 1959–60 the team were third in the Unofficial Championship, in 1961 and 1962 they were runners-up and in 1968–69 they were Unofficial Champions. The Jordanhill College Hockey Club played two elevens. The first eleven played with distinction in the 1st Division of the West District of the Scottish Hockey Association. Outstanding players within the Club gained representative honours at District, Full International, British and Olympic level.

Swimming had always occupied a prominent place in the programme of the Scottish School. With the opening of the new pool in the mid 1960s a swimming and water polo club was formed. Between 1975 and 1985 they won the British Colleges Water Polo Championships on nine occasions and two wins were gained in the British Colleges Team Swimming Championships, making Jordanhill the leading college for swimming in the United Kingdom. College teams were also prominent in basketball, volleyball, cricket, tennis, athletics and outdoor education. Perhaps the most significant indication of the Scottish School's influence on sport in Scotland is that Jordanhill students represented Scotland at the highest level in almost every sport, and former students became national coaches to national associations for long periods.

Brown, like Punchard before him, saw his primary function as being the training of teachers, and there is no doubt that the Scottish School earned a high reputation for producing very able 'on the floor' teachers, who were warmly welcomed by headteachers throughout Scotland. But the winds of change were blowing and the sound pragmatism that had been the strength of the Scottish School began to be seen, both in Scotland and furth of Scotland, not as a strength but as a weakness. From 1966 onwards students of physical education in England were able to take a degree course, and had a broader and deeper understanding of their subject and were thus more capable of initiating change. As early as November 1961, Wood had set up a Special Committee of the Jordanhill Board of Studies to discuss the content of the physical education courses. This Committee proposed two alternatives: (a) a revised form of the three-year course, and (b) a four-year course within which it would be possible to provide a specialist qualification in physical education covering primary and secondary education, and an endorsement in one other major subject, which might be taught in the first three years of the secondary school. Detailed curricula were drawn up, but the notion of an Associateship for Colleges of Education, with which this course was to be linked, did not come to fruition and the Jordanhill course was never mounted.

In 1966, however, Jordanhill College achieved a BEd degree in conjunction with the University of Glasgow, but this only included physical education as a special college study, which did not allow it to be taken at Higher Ordinary level. Bone, who succeeded Wood as Principal, put forward proposals for modifications to the BEd degree in 1971, permitting the study of physical education at Ordinary and Higher Ordinary levels. This course ran parallel with the traditional diploma course.

Neither of these courses was totally satisfactory. Although the diploma course provided a sound practical basis for teaching physical education, it did not extend the intellectual capacity of the candidates or enable them to obtain qualifications comparable with those in other subjects. Similarly, the rigid structure imposed by the Glasgow University BEd degree made it extremely difficult to establish a balanced and meaningful relationship between practical and academic studies. The proportion of time allocated to physical education was far from adequate and it was imperative that a new structure be designed. Whilst the reputation of the Scottish School had been based on a first class specialism, it was clear that neither of the existing courses provided a training fully adequate to the demands made upon a teacher of physical education in contemporary society.

Academic rigour

In March 1974, Brown retired from the post of Director, having served for 21 years. His successor was G. Bernard Wright, a Welshman, trained initially at Caerleon and Cardiff Colleges of Education, before completing professional training at the University of Leeds. He had been Principal Lecturer in Physical Education at Borough Road College in London, where he had been responsible for designing and introducing their new Honours degree in Physical Education; his experience was to prove invaluable to the Scottish School. An initial approach was made to the CNAA, proposing a BEd degree in Physical Education and Human Movement at both unclassified and honours level. Three main areas of study were envisaged—educational studies, academic studies in physical education and human movement and practical studies in physical education. Practical studies and teaching would be a fundamental part of the course and would provide the foundation upon which academic studies would be built.[17]

Validation by CNAA, particularly at this time, was difficult to achieve. Detailed documentation for the proposed degree course, quality of staff, student recruitment and the organisation of the institution, were all subjected to intensive scrutiny. It was not unusual for institutions to be required to reconsider their proposals several times, and validation was often delayed for a considerable time. However, the Jordanhill degree was granted approval at first attempt commencing 1 October 1975, with an intake of 90 students. This was the first Jordanhill degree course submitted for external validation to the CNAA, and given that the Scottish School had no previous documentation or experience to draw upon from within the college, the achievement was considerable.

It is significant to examine the aims of this course and relate them to the ideas propounded by the early pioneers in the field. The general aim of the new degree course was to prepare students to become teachers of physical education with appropriate physical skills and knowledge. Students would follow a basic course, then choose, from a range of elective courses, those studies which would meet their personal interests and aptitudes in the field. This would enable them to extend their intellectual capacity and allow them to obtain the highest qualification of which they were capable, either at unclassified or honours level. The goals were those of continuing study of education and enhanced professional preparation with the added dimension of depth.

The new beginning was based upon a sound foundation. Whilst the Scottish School staff at that time had little experience in planning or teaching degree courses, they did have a great deal of experience in practical work in physical education and in the preparation of teachers in their subject. The School also had the benefit of the resources and support of the whole college. Roy Small was appointed Head of Academic Studies, Bob McKay, Head of Practical Studies, and seven additional lecturers were appointed, with the emphasis on academic qualifications in a wide range of disciplines. They balanced well with the existing staff and together created a team well equipped to teach the new courses. Diploma students on course at the time were consulted and their views, particularly concerning practical studies, were taken into consideration in the planning of the new courses.

All of this intensive effort produced an exciting new degree. All elements of Part I (years 1 and 2) were compulsory for all students, and were designed to provide students with a basic foundation in essential knowledge and skills. At the end of year 2 students were required to choose between an honours degree programme and an unclassified degree programme. The unclassified degree was designed to develop skills and knowledge in a broad area of study, whilst the honours programme concentrated in greater depth on a narrower field of study. In years 3 and 4 essential elements were still compulsory, but in both degrees the emphasis was on student choice. Approximately 80% of the programme was elective in nature. In academic studies in the honours degree programme, for example, there were ten courses available from which a student was required to choose three. Students were thus in a position to work in areas appropriate to their aptitudes and interests.

Wright was determined to ensure that degree study would not detract from the well established pride in quality of practical performance and teaching skill. The games involvement that had been so much a part of previous decades continued, and an International Honours Board was established, to record the name of every SSPE student who had represented his country in every recognised sporting activity. New procedures were devised to monitor and evaluate the progress of all aspects of the degree programme, and detailed student profiles were designed, to provide precise information concerning individual student progress. Given the quality of students seeking entry to the School, it was decided to proceed with degree courses only and discontinue the diploma course. From the 1975 entry, the SSPE achieved an all graduate profession for male teachers of physical education, and gradually all other PE colleges in the United Kingdom followed their lead. Research opportunities were also afforded students of the SSPE from 1978, with joint supervision by University of Strathclyde and college staff.

Immediately the preservice degree courses were validated, the Scottish School began to make provision for an inservice degree. Following prolonged discussion with education authorities concerning release of teachers for study, proposals were submitted to CNAA for a part time modular course leading in three years to a BEd honours degree in Physical Education

and Human Movement, the first such course in Scotland. The proposals
were accepted and the course validated on 23 May 1978. The course ran
successfully for a number of years and allowed serving teachers, both men
and women, to upgrade their qualifications to an honours degree. The
dedication of these students, who had to carry out their teaching duties
combined with intensive study, was one of the major factors in the success
of this venture, but it proved shortlived. Local authorities were increasingly
unwilling to release teachers to attend, even for short periods, at college.

Contraction and diversification
By the mid 1970s there began to be a steady fall in the need for teachers,
and the intake to the specialist degree courses in the SSPE gradually declined
in parallel with the national trend. Since 1975 the School had been considering the need to diversify. The Director had established a Course Development Committee to investigate the need for new courses in Scotland, courses
appropriate to the strengths of the School. The most important recommendation was a degree in sports studies, and a professional market researcher
was employed to determine the need for such a degree. The consultant's
report[18] analysed employment prospects and concluded that they would be
very good.

A proposal was submitted to the SED on 25 October 1979 for a BA
degree in Sport in the Community. Following protracted negotiations a
modified proposal was submitted in October 1982 and approval was
granted for a submission to CNAA in February 1983. The BA degree Sport
in the Community was validated by the CNAA Recreation and Sports
Studies Board in May 1983 and the first students enrolled in September
1983. The new degree involved collaboration with other college departments—Community Education, Art, Speech and Drama and College PE,
who taught important elements within the programme. The BA degree was
an immediate success and attracted very large numbers of applications for
the small number of places available. The performance of students produced
highly complimentary reports from external examiners. Graduates quickly
found posts in the field of sport and recreation and were accepted at
universities throughout the United Kingdom for higher degree study. The
course was revised in 1988 with diversified pathways into Community Arts
and Outdoor Education, and continued, highly successfully, after training
for secondary physical education ceased at Jordanhill.

Although female teachers of physical education had enrolled on the first
inservice degree course in 1978 they had attended college at weekends and
in the evenings. The BA course brought female students to the SSPE on a
full time basis for the first time in its history and it was no surprise to staff
and male students that they integrated immediately and made a major

contribution to the life of the college. Equal opportunities legislation passed in the mid 1970s rendered a review of physical education training for secondary schools inevitable. It was no longer defensible to educate men and women separately, the women at Dunfermline College of Physical Education and the men at the Scottish School. Both Jordanhill and Dunfermline were prepared to become coeducational. Mergers and closures in England followed the DES announcement of a complete rationalisation of PE training in 1983 and the threat of similar closures in Scotland naturally initiated action both by Jordanhill and Dunfermline.

There followed a period of uncertainty and protracted formal and informal negotiation, as both institutions attempted to enlist the aid of local and national politicians. There was a belief in Glasgow that Lord James Douglas Hamilton, the constituency MP for Cramond in Edinburgh, the home of 'Dunfermline' College, lobbied strongly in favour of that college. Under the pretext that there were insufficient student numbers to support two centres, and creating a monopoly in physical education training although monopolies elsewhere in public life were regarded as unacceptable, the Secretary of State on 17 July 1986 announced in Parliament[19] the closure of the SSPE. The timing of the announcement was particularly unfortunate, coming at a time when Jordanhill was host to the Commonwealth Games Conference, public recognition of the status which the SSPE enjoyed in the world of sport. Strenuous efforts were made to have the decision reversed, but to no avail, and the sense of betrayal at Jordanhill was further heightened when the student intake figures the following year were doubled, and it became obvious that two centres could have been supported. In retrospect, Jordanhill might have shown more political awareness by moderating its pursuit of sporting excellence in favour of the more fashionable 'sport for all'.

Perhaps the last word should be accorded Professor W.W. Fletcher, Convener of the SSPE Committee of the Board of Governors from 1967–83,

> Many difficult battles were fought at St Andrew's House, but the writing was on the wall; the decision had been taken even before discussions were underway. The Scottish School was unjustly sacrificed on the altar of rationalisation and it closed in June 1990 when the last cohort of students graduated. I was glad that I was not the chairman to see its demise. That outstanding School meant much to me … But the man who was really, almost mortally, wounded was its Director, Bernard Wright.[20]

It is important to acknowledge the drive, enthusiasm, insight, intensity and industry of Wright. He came to Jordanhill at a time when change was necessary and he effected it speedily and efficiently. He brought a wider experience to a School then staffed largely by its own former students, yet was able to perpetuate the close relationship the School enjoyed with its current and former students.

To understand the ethos of the Scottish School it is important to have been part of it. Since 1931 it had been an integral part of Jordanhill, yet it had always had a very strong individual identity. Part of Jordanhill—yes, but different too. Whilst students were proud to be called Jordanhill students there was never any doubt about their being different. It was not only their dress that set them apart, there was a pride in having been selected from ten times as many candidates as applied for admission, as Thomas B. Robertson (a student in 1956–59) acknowledged,

> Our leader Hugh Brown left us all in no doubt
> He expected the best, or he'd soon kick us out.
> After all there were men with five Highers or more
> Who hadn't been able to get in the door.

By studying together over a period of three or four years, through shared, intense experiences in public and competitive situations, both nationally and internationally, the corporate spirit was reinforced. During the last decade of the Scottish School's existence students and staff made a number of educational tours, throughout Scotland and England, to Denmark and Sweden, Hungary, Czechoslovakia, the Federal Republic of Germany and the then German Democratic Republic, to investigate physical education in these countries. Sporting links were established with students in the Netherlands and Germany. Few other institutions had such close staff student relations, by the very nature of their work in formal and informal situations. Students were proud of their standards and proud of their differences, robust, tough minded, opinionated, but with a strong sense of humour and fun. At reunions each year the old ethos is reinforced. There has always existed a sense of identity and exclusiveness, not because they believed themselves to be superior but because they believed themselves to be different.

References

1 Royal Commission on Physical Training (Scotland) 1902. Reported in McNair, D. *The development of physical education in Scotland before 1916.* Unpublished thesis. University of Manchester 1961.

2 *Ibid.*

3 *Ibid.*

4 MacLean, I.C. *The history of Dunfermline College of Physical Education.* Edinburgh: Blackwood, 1976.

5 *Ibid.*

6 *Ibid.*
7 CEC minutes, 30 September 1930.
8 *Sir Henry P. Wood in conversation with Marion Baillie.* Glasgow: Jordanhill College, 1990. (videocassette).
9 GPC minutes. Report of Chairman's Sub-Committee, 5 September 1932.
10 GPC minutes, 3 June 1932.
11 H.C. Brown interview by R. Small. 10 June 1975. (audiotape).
12 G.F. Orr interview by R. Small. 12 June 1976. (audiotape).
13 GPC minutes, 26 February 1937.
14 Orr interview. *op cit.*
15 JBS minutes, 15 January 1965.
16 Survey by J.F. Donnachie. Glasgow: SSPE, 1969.
17 G.B. Wright interview by R. Small. 31 October 1991. (audiotape).
18 Macfarlane. *Sport studies degree: market research report*, presented to SSPE, 30 November 1979.
19 SED. *Working party on the centralisation of the training of physical education teachers and the merger of Dunfermline College of Physical Education with Moray House College of Education: final report.* Edinburgh: SED, 1986.
20 W.W. Fletcher letter to R. Small, 4 April 1995.

12

The Glasgow School of Speech Therapy

Elspeth McCartney

The relationship with Jordanhill College

The Glasgow School of Speech Therapy began at Jordanhill sometime in the 1920s, moved out for a time, maintaining links, in the 1950s, and moved back to the campus in the 1960s. Because of this continuity the Glasgow course for the training of the profession which has become speech and language therapy (SLT)[1] is one of the oldest continuously accredited courses in Britain, and arguably in the world. The outline given in this chapter is the first approach to a history, and much further work remains to be done. Access to historical information is made easier by the fact that SLT education in Glasgow was set up, developed and run by one woman, Dr Anne McAllister. From the 1920s to the 1960s, she provided the emergent profession in Scotland with much of its early academic canon, its ethos and curriculum. Because of her prominence, it is possible to trace some of the early history of SLT education in Glasgow through printed sources relating to the development of the profession in Britain.

McAllister was appointed Lecturer in Phonetics at Jordanhill in 1919. According to Wood's obituary[2] her appointment was to Stow College, that is the Stow building of the Glasgow Provincial Training Centre. Phonetics was one of the seven education subjects taken by General Certificate student teachers under the 1906 regulations, and reflected a concern with spoken English and 'correct' standards of speech which remains a matter of educational debate to this day.[3] McAllister's post was concerned with trainee teachers; her interest in pathological speech and language difficulties developed in parallel with this main activity, and was concerned principally with the problems of school children. The training of practitioners to work in the relatively new SLT profession was carried out for a long time at Jordanhill, using Jordanhill staff, and indeed training many former Jordanhill students, but not as part of the actual college curriculum. This unofficial element in SLT training is alluded to by Wood in his comment that McAllister started the Glasgow School of Speech Therapy in 1935 and operated it 'with the connivance of successive Principals of Jordanhill'. This confirms a comment by McAllister herself that the School had its origin 'as a day school' at Jordanhill 'due to the indulgence and help of the then Director of Studies, Dr William Kerr'.[4]

Early work in speech and language pathology, 1920–35
18th and 19th century work on speech in association with handicapping conditions was carried out in Scotland, mainly involving work with deaf children and to some extent with stammering. Pioneers included the Braidwoods, and the Bell family, including Alexander Graham Bell, inventor of the telephone.[5] Early wax-cylinder voice recording was used by Dr John Macintyre, a throat surgeon at Glasgow Royal Infirmary, around the turn of the century, foreshadowing later interest in voice work.

During the 1920s, Anne McAllister gained a 1st class Honours EdB degree at Glasgow University, and worked with a psychology lecturer, Dr Henry Watt, in his laboratory on rhythms of speech. On his death she carried out a study of the speech of 21,000 Dunbartonshire school children, which became the basis for her book *Clinical studies in speech therapy*, accepted by Glasgow University in 1937 for the degree of DSc.[6] The pioneering aspect of McAllister's work was the application of phonetic knowledge to the alleviation of speech difficulties. *Clinical studies in speech therapy* also contained a section on work with 'stutterers', in which McAllister's interest in psychological and emotional aspects was prominent. Further early work was carried out in association with Dr William Boyd, Lecturer in Education at the University of Glasgow and a part time member of Jordanhill staff from 1910–23, who had an interest in 'infantile paralysis'. This work led to collaboration in a Saturday morning children's clinic modelled on that of Cyril Burt in London, which was one of the earliest child guidance clinics in Scotland. Norman Walker and William Inglis of Jordanhill were also involved, and teachers brought children with a variety of disabilities. The notion of a distinct specialism of SLT must have emerged around this time, paralleling developments in London. The role and professional specialism of self-taught SLT was sufficiently developed for McAllister later to give her own date of qualification as 1924.[7]

Medical aspects of speech difficulties also assumed early importance. Matthew White, a specialist in cleft palate surgery at the Glasgow Royal Hospital for Sick Children, persuaded McAllister to open a clinic at West Graham Street, a city-centre outpatient department of the Hospital. Run by Jordanhill staff and Glasgow teachers, the speech clinic was allowed to use the premises on Wednesday afternoons only. SLT training became centred there. The Wednesday afternoon clinic started some time in the 1920s, and ran for over 20 years.

Despite the innovatory and exploratory nature of the work, there was a demand for training early on. During the 1920s, some informal courses were set up to teach SLT techniques, and around 1929 teachers who had become involved with the West Graham Street clinic began to be trained as speech therapists by McAllister. The mix of SLT, medical, psychological and educational personnel, and the application of phonetic and educational studies, psychology, anatomy, neurology and speech pathology techniques which was in place by the early 1930s has informed SLT professional knowledge ever since. The emerging discipline of SLT had also developed its clinical basis and a client-centred approach, and those factors, discernible from the earliest days, crystallised to form the core of the SLT curriculum when training developed in earnest.

The beginning of formal training, 1935–45

By the start of the 1930s, two professional bodies concerned with SLT had been established. One was the Remedial Section of the Association of Speech and Drama, formed in 1930 and renamed the Association of Speech Therapists (AST) in 1935. The other was the British Society of Speech Therapists (BSST), formed in 1934 and considered to be the more medically oriented of the two associations.[8] From 1935 the BSST published the journal *Speech*, the first UK journal concerned exclusively with SLT issues,[9] and a useful source of information about SLT training under the auspices of the BSST. The contribution of the Glasgow School can be clearly traced. Volume 1, July 1935, listed Anne MacAllister MA (*sic*) as being on the Executive Committee, and gave her affiliation as the Royal Infirmary, Glasgow (probably in error for the Royal Hospital for Sick Children, Glasgow). In addition, five of the medical members were from Glasgow, including Matthew White. In 1937 McAllister was listed as a founder member of the BSST.

Associateship and Membership were offered to those who passed the Society's and the Association's examinations, following an approved course of training and clinical practice, but experienced people and those with hospital appointments were initially offered Associateship following personal interviews, ie without sitting a qualifying examination. One of the Society's objectives by 1937 was the preparation of a syllabus of training and examination, with the object of granting diplomas to successful candidates. Three centres had already organised training; Winifred Kingdon Ward's centre at West End Hospital for Nervous Diseases, London; Beryl Oldrey's at the Central London Throat, Nose and Ear Hospital and the National Hospital for Nervous Diseases, and Anne McAllister's Centre at Jordanhill. There was also a speech clinic at St Thomas's Hospital in the 1930s run by Elsie Fogerty.[10]

If professional accreditation is considered to be the real starting point for the GSST, 1935 appears to be a reasonably firm foundation date. This date was given by Wood, and it coincided with the BSST recognition of practitioners and the earliest formally accredited courses, including Glasgow. A syllabus had been developed and the notion of a more formal Glasgow School appears to have emerged around this time. The first listing of new Associates 'graduating' from Glasgow appeared in *Speech* in January 1938, when six people (including five men) were listed. The students would have qualified in 1937, and since a two-year training was required this corroborates the 1935 date. Although the early SLTs included a number of men, the profession quickly became almost totally female, perhaps because many of the recruits were teachers or elocutionists.

McAllister published a series of books and articles during the 1930s, including *A year's course in speech training, Steps in speech training* and in 1941 *The primary teacher's guide to speech training*. They were much appreciated by teachers and practitioners. The concern with speech training reflected her continuing work with non-pathological groups at Jordanhill. In an early use of mass media, McAllister broadcast radio courses in speech training to Scottish schools between 1935 and 1940.

The Glasgow influence on the developing SLT profession was strong in the 1930s, and had an educational flavour. The link between schools and clinical rehabilitation was developed, and the emphasis was on work with children. In January 1939 *Speech* published a Scottish edition, including contributions from Sr Marie Hilda of Notre Dame College, Glasgow, whose Child Guidance Clinic had opened in 1931. She described her team approach, which included four SLTs, working two week-day evenings with groups of children. There were few opportunities for SLT work in hospitals (even for those who wished to give voluntary service), with only the Royal Hospital, Edinburgh and the Royal Hospital for Sick Children, Glasgow employing SLTs. Education authority appointments had recently been made in Fife, Midlothian and Dunbartonshire, and Aberdeen was considering starting a speech clinic. The Scottish Branch of the BSST organised a series of lectures: Shearer on common neurosis; Vernon on the psychological functions of language; MacIntosh on cleft palate; Land on the physiology of hearing; Kennedy Fraser on psychological sequelae; McAllister on stuttering; Boyd on educational aspects of speech restoration; Inglis on clinical procedures, and many others.

The situation in Glasgow before World War II therefore was of an established and developing movement, with a professionally accredited training programme, sufficiently confident to call itself the Glasgow School of Speech Therapy. The training had been developed to meet the professional needs of individuals, mainly teachers or those with speech and drama interests, who wished to work as therapists. The emphasis was mainly on children, and was strongly educational. There was a prescribed syllabus and a practical component, and training lasted for two years. Teaching was carried out by well-qualified and experienced professionals, including McAllister, who was still Head of Speech Training at Jordanhill. There is little information on the content of this early course, but comparison may be drawn with the experience of a London student[11] in 1932. She recalled studying theory in first year, with observation of cases and practical experience in clinics. Lectures were on general psychology, phonetics, elementary anatomy, biology and neurology, with later an advanced course in neurology and psychopathology. Further growth, consolidation and development of qualifying training took place after World War II, but the issues which arose—curriculum, accreditation and validation, assessment and recording of students—built on the early foundations.

Professional accreditation and the College of Speech Therapists, 1945–55
The early war years brought little development and probably diminished professional SLT education, as war work disrupted training and practice: the wartime Vigilance Committee made certain restrictions on training. Professional developments did take place in Glasgow however, with McAllister being asked in 1941 by Dr Allardyce, Director of Education for Glasgow, to set up speech training and remedial help for children in child guidance clinics.[12] There was also the need further to expand SLT work in the field of adult acquired speech and language difficulties, owing to the number of combatants receiving war wounds and head injuries. McAllister worked at Killearn Military Hospital, Stirlingshire, with neurologist Dr John Gaylor, of Glasgow Western Infirmary, on the rehabilitation of men injured in aerial combat.

A major postwar impetus to training occurred with the amalgamation of the British Society of Speech Therapists with the Association of Speech Therapists in November 1944,[13] to form the College of Speech Therapists (CST), a UK-wide professional grouping, now entitled the Royal College of Speech and Language Therapists (RCSLT). There was considerable continuity between the old BSST and the new CST executive membership, and once again McAllister was a Founder Fellow of the new society. A main concern continued to be training new professionals, and maintaining standards of training, and a committee was set up to draw up a syllabus for a qualifying examination. It was agreed that 'as an interim measure, pending the publication of the syllabus, the college keep a list of those schools whose students are accepted for the Students' Register of the College and that these schools be asked to send a copy of their syllabus.' Glasgow was one of those schools. In a decision which sharply distinguishes the teaching and SLT professions, academic subjects were to be taught exclusively by professionals in the relevant discipline, with only speech pathology taught by SLTs.[14]

As part of CST course accreditation, all students were to sit the same examination papers, constructed by the Syllabus Committee, and courses were to be visited on a regular basis by CST representatives, a procedure which continued as quinquennial accreditation visits. There was some delay in visiting Glasgow. In November 1945 McAllister had written to the CST executive concerning progress in reorganising the Glasgow Speech Therapy Training School, and it was agreed that inspection would be delayed; it was later deferred until October 1946. In the meantime, the status of the School was maintained, and students became CST Licentiates if they passed the GSST examinations. The delay and the veiled disquiet expressed in the minutes suggest that the GSST was finding some difficulty in consolidating its training programme after the war. It is tempting to relate this to the rapid increase in numbers of student teachers at Jordanhill at this time, but other issues such as staffing and the new CST examination system might be equally relevant. The inspection carried out in 1946 was, however, favourable and the course has been continuously accredited ever since.

The CST syllabus included papers on Normal Voice and Speech, for which McAllister was a national examiner from October 1946 (examiners usually served for three years), Anatomy and Physiology, for which White and Dr George Beel examined, and Psychology, for which David Kennedy Fraser of Jordanhill was recommended by McAllister. McAllister argued that the standard for the paper on Normal Voice and Speech should be very high, as speech therapists should be prepared to take classes in normal voice and speech as part of their professional duties. This reflected her own background in speech training, but the SLT profession's concern was with pathology only. Written examinations were held simultaneously in Glasgow and London, and there was also an oral examination. There were four Glasgow candidates in 1946.

Glasgow personnel, including the original pioneers in SLT training, continued to be active in shaping the emerging profession, and in furthering its aims and expertise. The demand for SLTs was high, with the 1944 Education Act in England and Wales requiring local education authorities to provide special education for those with 'speech defects', including pupils who, on account of 'stammering, aphasia or defect of voice or articulation not due to deafness', required special education. The 1945 Education (Scotland) Act made similar requirements. Work in hospitals expanded after the National Health Service Act of 1948. However, there were still no premises for the Glasgow School. Jordanhill remained the unofficial base, but the address was given in 1944 as the Royal Hospital for Sick Children, Speech Therapy Department, and conferences were held in Glasgow restaurants. Many lectures took place in the evenings and at weekends. The setting up of a more formal educational establishment was clearly required.

Consolidation and development, 1955–65

In the postwar period, many changes occurred at Jordanhill with the appointment of a new Principal, the updating of the teacher training curriculum, an influx of new staff and a rapid rise in student numbers. In 1951 McAllister transferred from her post as Principal Lecturer in Speech Training to take charge of a new course for teachers of physically handicapped children, assuming responsibility also for the course for teachers of mentally handicapped children a few years later, when Kennedy Fraser retired. Her pioneering contribution to the development of speech therapy was recognised by the award of OBE in 1953.

A College of Speech Therapists' reinspection of the Glasgow School of Speech Therapy took place in May 1952, and the other Scottish school, by now established in Edinburgh, was also visited. The visiting panel recommended that CST should 'continue to recognise the two [Scottish] schools as effective units for the training of speech therapy students'. However, recommendations were made concerning the selection of students, medical examinations, the rearrangement of some subjects in the curriculum to prevent overcrowding and the provision of adequate premises. Pressure on space was a problem in Jordanhill at that time, and a move away from the Jordanhill campus seemed advisable. On 10 November 1952 Trustees were appointed for the constitution of the Glasgow School of Speech Therapy.

From October 1947, meetings of practising SLTs had been held from time to time at 25 Athole Gardens,[15] a large terraced house in the west end of Glasgow and the home of Mrs Murray Stewart, a teacher of speech and drama at the Glasgow Athenaeum. On 13 August 1955, the Glasgow School of Speech Therapy purchased this house from the Trustees of Colonel Ralph Robertson Stewart, the purchase price of £2,850 being raised by generous donations and a series of coffee mornings.[16] The Chair of the Board of Governors at that time was Matthew White; other members were McAllister, reflecting the professional partnership that had by then lasted for 30 years, and Gaylor. McAllister used the title Principal of the Glasgow School of Speech Therapy, but maintained her post as Principal Lecturer in charge of courses for handicapped children at Jordanhill until her retirement in 1958. She presided at the opening of the new Sub-Department of Speech at the University of Newcastle upon Tyne in 1965[17] and became the first President of the College of Speech Therapists, also in 1965.

Student training was then based in Athole Gardens. The building provided lecture rooms, offices, and common rooms. Miss Margaret Sievwright was employed to teach speech pathology, but much of the staffing was still in the early days part time and voluntary. Students were eligible for grants to attend the School, and fees were payable by local authorities. Lectures were also held outwith Athole Gardens, eg in 1956 at the Anderson School of Medicine (on brain dissection), and of course clinical placements were undertaken. Students also continued to travel to Jordanhill, for example to phonetics classes with Joyce Moffett and for anatomy and physiology with the Assistant Medical Officer, Dr Eileen Wybar. Some payment was made by the School for these services. The GSST was therefore in this period an independent establishment, at least after 1958 when McAllister retired from Jordanhill, but it still had strong links with the college.

The GSST presented students for the award of the Diploma of the College of Speech Therapists, a three-year course with examinations set by the CST. By the 1960s up to 20 students entered in each year. Curriculum and syllabus development was coordinated through the CST, and considerable expansion and revision of the course took place on a UK-wide basis.

The move to higher education, 1965–95

The GSST continued to be based in Athole Gardens until the late 1960s, but the future for speech and language therapy courses across the UK lay in higher education establishments, as part of the expansion of higher education at that time. In Glasgow, the decision was taken to integrate the School of Speech Therapy back into Jordanhill College. McAllister noted in her opening address at Newcastle in 1965, that she was 'happy and proud to have been enabled to take [the GSST] back to its first home before I finally retire'. Wood was also present on this occasion, and McAllister continued, 'I am deeply in his debt for his interest in my School, and his generosity in finding a place for it in Jordanhill'.[18]

Agreement in principle to incorporate the GSST into Jordanhill was taken in September 1963. McAllister was due to retire in 1964, but was asked to continue as Director of the School for a further year, until a worthy replacement had been found. This problem was solved with the appointment in October 1965 of Catherine McCallien. McCallien had qualified as an SLT in 1945, having, while working as a teacher, attended McAllister's evening classes in Glasgow. She had also worked in Killearn Military Hospital, and had been Lecturer in Phonetics at Jordanhill from 1946–50. At the time of her appointment as Director she was Associate Professor in the Department of Linguistics, University of Ghana. McCallien continued as Director until her retirement in 1974; she was then succeeded by Anne Wallace, who had been Assistant Director of the Edinburgh School of Speech Therapy since 1967.[19]

Despite the agreement to move to Jordanhill, there was considerable delay, and indeed rumours of negotiations with other institutions, including the newly-established University of Strathclyde. The actual move to Jordanhill campus did not take place until October 1968, when the GSST became the Department of Speech Therapy. The sale of Athole Gardens to the Scottish National Academy of Music (the Athenaeum) for the sum of £6,250 took place on 5 June 1969.[20] In 1970 an Advisory Committee was set up at Wood's suggestion, to parallel the wide professional input of the disbanded Board of Governors of the Glasgow School. Medical links were thus re-established, and also links with the University of Glasgow, where several members of the Advisory Board were based.

Throughout the 1960s, the College of Speech Therapists had been calling for an all-graduate profession. A Committee of Enquiry into Speech Therapy Services (the Quirk Committee) was set up in 1969, and its findings, published in 1972[21] recommended degree-level training for all SLTs.[22] This became government policy, and was implemented across the UK during the later 1970s and early 1980s. In Glasgow, a speech therapy degree was planned, validated by the University of Glasgow. Outline proposals for the first degree course, the BEd in Speech Pathology and Therapeutics, were placed before the BEd committee of Jordanhill College on 11 October 1971. The professional body, interested in these developments, proposed an 'inspection' visit; quinquennial accreditation visits were still CST policy, although the regularity of visits had not been maintained. The word 'inspection' had unfortunate resonances, and the Board of Studies rejected the suggestion of a visit, since at that time no other staff in the college were subject to inspection of this kind. In fact, although the course remained accredited, no visit appears to have taken place between 1952 and 1980.

The BEd degree was established in 1973, (and offered with Honours from 1979) as a four-year degree of the University of Glasgow. As with teacher education, the course had to conform to the pattern of a Glasgow University undergraduate course. Only those subjects which appeared on the Glasgow curriculum could be offered; other subjects had to be incorporated within them, or offered as 'professional studies'. The important SLT principle of having experts teach subjects was adhered to, with clinical medical courses taught by lecturers of the University of Glasgow. However, the disadvantage of this early BEd course was the excessive education content, and the balance of time in relation to such courses as phonetics. The students felt that the degree course overburdened them, and forced them to engage in studies they found to be largely irrelevant.[23] The problem was discussed at the Joint Board of Studies, and considerable changes were proposed. By 1976, the Principal of Jordanhill reported to the Board of Governors that a major revision had been approved, and the result was 'a highly specialised course in speech therapy'.[24]

The 1976 degree was adapted but not fundamentally altered for ten years. This allowed continuity, but meant that the often creative process of ongoing course review was not experienced. A one-day visit from the CST took place in 1980, and a three day visit in 1984. The designation of the degree was changed to BSc in 1982, the better to reflect the degree content, and also to conform to practice elsewhere in the UK. Students holding the BEd qualification were given the option of changing to BSc.

In 1987 Anne Wallace retired, and was replaced by Elspeth McCartney, who had been Lecturer in the Department of Audiology, Education of the Deaf and Speech Pathology at the University of Manchester. In the same year the report of the HMI inspection of Jordanhill stated that the four-year Ordinary BSc degree should be reduced to three years, the Honours route remaining at four. No educational reasons were given, but the change brought the Ordinary degree into line with similar Ordinary degrees in SLT in Scotland and England, and indeed with other Scottish Ordinary degrees. The revisions needed to achieve this change were extensive, involving a teaching year lengthened to 33 weeks, a move to blocks of clinical practice rather than weekly placements, and a considerable reduction in teaching (as opposed to student learning) hours. The new degree was validated by Glasgow University and accredited to start in 1989. Validation was transferred, following a 1994 re-accreditation, to the University of Strathclyde subsequent to the merger with Jordanhill.

Before the merger, however, the research and professional work of the GSST had been continued. As well as developing SLT education, staff increased their research and scholarship profiles, and externally-funded research contracts were won. The department supervised the first MPhil research degree at Jordanhill College, awarded by the Council for National Academic Awards in 1991, and staff were active in CSLT affairs. The notion of an academic discipline of speech and language therapy, with a sound empirical research footing and knowledge base, and with a leading role in the education and development of the profession remains, and may be amongst the happiest legacies of Jordanhill College.

Acknowledgements
The author would like to thank Roberta Lees, Irys Lindsay and Catherine Renfrew who commented on earlier versions of this paper.

Notes and references
1 The title of the profession changed from speech therapy to speech and language therapy in 1992 and the College of Speech Therapists (CST) to the College of Speech and Language Therapists (CSLT) at the same time. In May 1995 the professional body became the Royal College of Speech and Language Therapists (RCSLT). This chapter uses the historically appropriate title for the professional body, but the name speech and language therapy or therapist (SLT for brevity) unless clear anachronism would arise.

Teaching the Teachers

2 Wood, H.P. Dr Anne H. McAllister, OBE: obituary. *College of Speech Therapists bulletin*, 374, 1983, pp.2–3.

3 Ross, S., McCartney, E., Ramsay, W. & McKeating, D. Students' judgements of children based on social class-linked features of Glasgow pronunciation. *Education in the north*, new series, v.3, 1995. in press.

4 McAllister, A.H. Speech therapy comes of age: address presented at the official opening of the Sub-Department of Speech, University of Newcastle upon Tyne, October 1965. *British journal of disorders of communication*, v.1, 1966, pp.3–10.

5 McGovern, M.A. Speech and language therapy education in Edinburgh. *History of Education Society bulletin*, v.54, 1994.

6 Wood. *op.cit.*

7 CST. *Directory of members.* 1969.

8 McGovern. *op.cit.*

9 The journal *Speech* continued with this title until 1957, when it became *Speech pathology and therapy* (1958–65), then the *British journal of disorders of communication* (1966–91), later the *European journal of disorders of communication*.

10 C. Renfrew, personal communication.

11 Pick, S. Memories and impressions of a student. *Speech*, v.1:4, 1936, pp.37–39.

12 Moffett, J. Interview with W.B. Marker, 7 July 1994.

13 CST. Executive Committee minutes, November 1944—March 1946.

14 Renfrew. *op.cit.*

15 Spelled Atholl on earlier maps.

16 JBG. Finance, Property & Law Committee minutes, 23 June 1969.

17 McAllister. *op.cit.*

18 *Ibid.*

19 McGovern. *op.cit.*

20 JBG. Finance, Property and Law Committee minutes, 23 June 1969.

21 DES. *Speech therapy services.* London: HMSO, 1972. (Quirk report).

22 And also recommended that SLTs be employed in the NHS, which took place following NHS reorganisation in 1974.

23 JBS. BEd committee minutes, 11 November 1975.

24 JBG minutes: Principal's report, 1976.

13

Community Education

Terry May

The training of students in youth and community service, subsequently community education, began in the college in October 1964, when 24 students undertook the first of their two years of training under the direction of John Round, sole tutor, then head of the Youth and Community department 1968–80. The course came into existence as a consequence of pressure applied to the SED by church leaders, education officials, senior officers of voluntary youth organisations and other concerned citizens in the west of Scotland. The pressure was occasioned by the total lack of training facilities locally for full time youth and community workers, in contrast to the east of Scotland, where such training was being provided by Moray House College. Agreement was reached to begin the new course following a meeting in Stirling between H Wood, SED officials and representatives of the pressure group.

Youth leadership

In effect, the provision at both colleges was a response to the stimulation for such courses contained in the Albemarle report[1] which was, strictly, a report for England and Wales only, but whose recommendations were fully endorsed in a brief follow-up Scottish report. Albemarle was the most important report in the development of the youth service throughout Britain; it led to significant changes in the status, provision and financing of services to young people. Prior to its publication most youth work was left to the voluntary organisations: the uniformed organisations, eg Scouts, Guides, Boys' Brigade, and the non uniformed, eg Scottish Association of Boys Clubs and its sister organisation, church youth fellowships, YM/YWCA. Legal responsibility contained within various education acts was confined to ensuring that 'suitable provision' for young people was made by local authorities. Little financial help was provided, or intervention made, either by central government or local authority. The Committee appointed by the Minister of Education in November 1958 was charged with reviewing, 'the contribution which the Youth Service in England and Wales can make in assisting young people to play their part in the life of the community, in the light of changing social and industrial conditions...' Among these changing conditions, the report identified the bulge in the adolescent population, the ending of national service, the changing pattern of women's lives, a new climate of crime and delinquency and much greater spending power of young people. In summary, the image presented was of an antisocial, delinquent youth culture alienated from the rest of society, the 'teddy boy culture'.

Round was appointed to Jordanhill in April 1964 and was required, by September, to devise a suitable course, recruit students and persuade appropriate departments to service the diploma course. Prominent among the departments to respond positively to such persuasion were Modern Studies, Business Studies, Religious Education, Psychology, Art, Music, Drama, English and the College Physical Education department. The involvement of the latter as opposed to the SSPE seems somewhat surprising, as the age range catered for by SSPE was clearly more in tune with youth work. Contributions from those support departments, together with the principles and practice of youth work, constituted the academic course work and this was supplemented by a requirement for all students to work two evenings per week in a youth context. All students were required to spend a full term in each year in a youth placement and, following the recommendations for the organisation of such courses, two one-week residential experiences were included. Initially, these took place at the Inverclyde National Recreation Centre in September and at Glenmore Lodge in March, underlining the leisure activity content of the training.

Demand was such that an intake to the diploma course was recruited each year from 1964 and a postgraduate course of two terms' duration, subsequently one year, commenced in 1967. Two additional staff were recruited, first Peter Williamson and then Terry May. The qualification awarded was a Diploma (Certificate for the postgraduates) in Youth and Community Service, although as shown above the content was virtually exclusively youth leadership orientated, in line with the recommendations under which the courses were constituted.

It is an undoubted fact that the students in the new diploma course were a surprise, indeed a shock, to the college. They were, to say the least, different. Many of them had few, if any, of the educational qualifications normally deemed necessary for entry to an institution of higher education. They did have other qualifications: many had work experience, gained in shipyards, commerce, transport and a wide variety of other occupations. All had experience of the work for which they were to be trained: each one could show evidence of a number of years' working as part time paid or unpaid youth leaders in a wide variety of settings. In this way, they were unique as a group. Some student groups, eg in technical education and further education, had similar backgrounds but even in the latter, where more similarities were apparent, the students, when in college, seldom came into contact with other departments.

The first cohort of students in 1964 numbered 24, 5 females and 19 males. The imbalance is accounted for by factors operating at that time. Membership of mixed youth clubs was heavily male dominated and those clubs were the biggest employers of part time youth leaders. The staffing reflected the membership and the view that males were needed to cope with often difficult male adolescents. The change from youth to youth and community work and ultimately adult education interested more women, who saw the opportunity of managing a full time day job and coping with the demands of family life. At no time was there a policy on the balance of male/female recruitment. Over a number of years more females than males were recruited, particularly for the postgraduate course, but no positive discrimination operated. Initially entrants to the course ranged in age from 21 to the late 40s. The upper age limit was determined by the number of years any particular applicant might be expected to work after qualifying, and on the ability to satisfy employers' superannuation schemes. In a few cases, applicants aged 50+ were accepted. The average age of students in the early years of the course tended towards the upper 30s but subsequently dropped to the low 30s. The department had only one recruitment policy, which was to recruit the very best applicants available.

Community and adult involvement
In 1961, in pursuance of the policies recommended for the improvement of the youth service, the SED introduced a temporary scheme to make capital grants available to voluntary youth organisations for the purpose of acquiring or improving premises. By 1968 some 276 projects benefited from this scheme. In addition, cities and counties with large populations, such as Dunbarton, Fife and West Lothian, built new youth and community centres with funds provided by their education departments. It was for the management of such centres that the first students were trained, and in which many of them found employment, and it was as a consequence of these appointments that the first major change in the course took place. Not surprisingly, local councillors, and many members of the public, were not prepared to see new, splendidly-equipped, purpose-built buildings operating only in the evenings and at weekends. Before long, playgroups, lunch clubs and pensioner groups gained admittance. It was an initial, albeit tentative, step towards activating the 'community' in the qualification.

The content of the courses changed rapidly to accommodate this development, initially perhaps to the displeasure of some students whose previous interests and experience had been wholly concerned with youth work. Consequently in many cases the provision of accommodation to community groups became the form of community service practised. It was, however, the recognisable beginning of what was to become the second strand in the course, community work. Despite the reservations noted above, many of the graduates of the course were finding posts elsewhere. An SED report[2] published in 1970 noted that 'the employment of some of these additional members of staff was necessitated by the opening of large new centres which required full time management; but the majority of the new posts have been for organisers, assistant organisers and area organisers.' The rather different skills required for this kind of work, together with the recommendation contained in the *Community of interests* report[3] that 'all who own or control premises or open spaces which could be used for social and recreation purposes should see it as part of their trust to ensure the fullest possible use of them' ensured that community work was firmly on the agenda. This notion of community provision was examined and found helpful but wanting, in a Youth Service Development Council report[4], which advanced the notion of the 'active society' brought about by the process of community development. This form of community work became the preferred option within the course content.

The third area of work to become a major aspect of the course content was adult education. The Alexander report[5] noted among the 'determinants of change',

> the erosion of the assumption that education is a once for all experience which happens to people for a prescribed period of time during their childhood and adolescence, and that this is sufficient to equip them with the knowledge, techniques and skills needed for a good life ...

It recommended that adult education should be regarded as an aspect of community education and, together with the youth and community service, should be incorporated into a community education service. This accorded well with the decision to make the youth and community service responsible for organising the adult literacy scheme and becoming involved with essential aspects of community development work. It also strengthened the case of those departmental staff who had long stressed the educational nature of youth work, with recreational activity as the means to that end.

Course development
Although by this stage the three strands of community education were firmly in place in the course and the qualification changed to that of Diploma/ Certificate in Community Education (Youth and Community Service), the department did not change its title until 1987 and then only by administrative reorganisation, when it became the Division of Community Education.

The reluctance to change was largely due to the problem of definition, and to a lesser extent, marketing. 'Youth and community service' did convey a clear understanding of the nature of the work, whilst many staff felt that there were difficulties with 'community education'.

The addition of adult education as one of the three main components of the course led to a move away from the generic training which had been followed previously to a limited form of specialist training. Students undertook a basic course in all three of the strands of community education, but opted later to specialise in one of them, a move welcomed by employers after some initial opposition. The resurgence of interest in youth work, after its relative eclipse by community work, together with a need for workers with youth work skills in depth, made the product rare and welcome.

The way for this reorganisation had been made easier by the decision to extend the diploma course to three years from 1970. The minimum entry age of 21 to the diploma course had been determined on the basis of the perceived need for a certain level of maturity and life experience, to work successfully with adolescents in unstructured situations. In practice, the average age of entrants tended to be well in excess of the minimum requirement. However, this policy was changed in 1970 when, in response to an initiative from SED, it was decided to admit students aged 18 and over. The mature entry age was then raised to 23, and those under 23 were required to hold the same entry qualifications as students for teacher training. This innovation was greeted with mixed feelings by many, including employers, who questioned the ability of 21 year olds to cope successfully with teenagers, many of whom could be difficult. The reasons for the change of policy were twofold. On the one hand it was claimed that the service was losing well qualified entrants to the profession, as school leavers of 18 were not prepared to wait five years before embarking on training for their chosen career. It was further argued that the profession needed a coterie of entrants with greater intellectual potential (as measured by SCE Highers) than was currently being recruited. In effect, little difference was evident between the two groups in academic achievement, and once again it was shown that the birth certificate is not necessarily the best guide to the level of maturity. The fears of employers were not realised; the younger diplomates found posts and performed well.

The change did, however, pose problems in relation to the organisation of the course. The question was whether to integrate the two groups and if so, at what stage. Undoubtedly the easier organisational option was to keep them separate but this was felt to be potentially detrimental to the longer term cohesion of the service. It was argued that as the students would be working together at a later stage it would be better for them to study together. It was further argued that total separation was likely to exacerbate the polarisation of education v experience. The decision to keep the three-year students separate for the first year was taken on the grounds that what they lacked in relation to the other students was experience and maturity. Furthermore, there developed what appeared to be a pre-professional year, followed by a two-year professional course. The appointment of May to succeed Round on his retirement in 1980 coincided with a thorough review of the course. This led to the introduction of a single three-year course, from which mature entrants were granted a remission of one year, being deemed to have covered some aspects of the course by part time training and practical experience.

The degree course

The first attempt to institute such a course was made in 1968, followed by further attempts at regular intervals. That so many of these attempts failed can be traced to a number of factors: difficulties in obtaining the interest of a suitable university partner, lack of support from the SED owing to the undesirability of increased training costs, employers' concerns that graduates would be likely to seek higher salaries and a belief that the work undertaken by community education workers did not require graduate training. The first approach for a graduate course under the auspices of Glasgow University was followed by a proposal for a combined community education and social work degree, based on a common foundation course followed by specialisms. A presentation by the two heads of department to the Council for National Academic Awards was received with interest, but progress failed to materialise. A further, more radical approach, which took the form of a combined teacher/community education/social work degree, again based on a common foundation course followed by specialisms, was also submitted. This proposal did attract support from SED, but it foundered on the lack of support from teacher education departments in the college.

Support for raising the course to degree level was eventually contained in a major report on training for community education published in 1984.[6] This report recommended a core and options pattern, already practised in the diploma course, and modular provision of community education training. Yet another approach was made to the SED in March 1984, prior to publication of the report, and agreement for the development of a suitable degree course was quickly reached with SED officials, subject to acceptance of the report by the Secretary of State. Jordanhill Community Education Division, by then headed by Ted Milburn, approached SED once again, successfully arguing that,

> the effective direction of community education within the education service often lies in the hands of other professionals at directorate level, few of whom

have training in, or field work experience of, community education. It is imperative for the development of community education and for the career advancement of practitioners that those professionally trained and experienced in that field have the opportunity to compete for senior management posts on an equal basis.[7]

So the long-awaited degree course was finally introduced in 1992.

Contribution to the profession

Inservice training was, in the first instance, conducted under the aegis of John A. Smith. It took the form of contributions to the training of part time youth leaders attending 'common element' courses. Common element courses were recommended in a report[8] on training, published in response to an initiative by the Standing Consultative Council on Youth Work in 1966. It was estimated at that time that some 45,000 part time leaders were involved in youth work, the great majority of them unpaid. Many of them received training through their own organisations and some, though far fewer, through education authorities. Common element courses were so named because they were jointly planned, 'to deal with the knowledge, understanding and skill likely to be required by leaders, irrespective of the type of group with which they worked'.

The demand for part time leaders increased with the opening of new buildings and clubs, and with it the requests to the college for advice. As these courses took place in the evenings and at weekends, life for the staff was particularly hectic, and only moderated when education authorities began to appoint their own training officers. They in turn required help in training their own tutors, but at least that was manageable during the normal college day. The lessening of demand for part time leader training enabled the development of courses to meet the demand for inservice training of the growing number of full time workers. Initially many courses aimed to meet the needs of early-trained workers who lacked the skills in community work and community education. Other courses were mounted in relation to new trends and specialisms, prominent among which were management and counselling. Many such courses took place in summer schools during the vacation. Counselling was particularly popular, and considerable concern was expressed by disappointed youth workers one year, when many of them failed to secure places. It coincided with the publication of *Guidance in Scottish secondary schools*[9] and a great many teachers attended the course!

The content, provision and style of inservice work changed considerably over the years, and ultimately included long-term consultancies to authorities and groups, often with considerable success. Nonetheless, its failure to lead to a nationally-recognised qualification was a source of frustration to both students and staff. This situation was most happily resolved by the introduction in 1993 of the inservice MSc in Community Education as part of the college's postgraduate awards programme. This modular-based programme enabled students to follow a personally relevant programme of training, including a compulsory element of personal research. Research has been badly neglected in relation to community education, and its inclusion in the programme may redress the situation.

From its inception, the department pursued a policy of cooperation with other departments, initially as a recipient of services but increasingly as a provider. In addition to familiarisation talks to a number of courses, more substantial contributions were made in guidance and counselling and, particularly, to the BEd degree in Primary Education by way of an elective in community education. The most important element of this policy was undoubtedly the institution of the BA degree in Sport in the Community, which was jointly developed with the SSPE and a number of other departments. The main initiative and contribution to the course was from the SSPE, whilst the Community Education department played the major supporting role, providing courses in working with young people and adults.

Although established to meet the training needs of the west of Scotland, the department always saw its role in a much wider context. The student intake was drawn from all over Scotland and beyond, and subsequent appointments showed a similar geographical distribution. It was understandable, therefore, that student placements followed the same pattern, and it proved extremely valuable for the development of the service. Staff visits to students provided the framework for a pattern of in-situ training, together with support for the local supervisors and their colleagues. Contacts made by staff as a consequence of their own further development and training led to extensions in this policy. Placements were developed in Eire and in Germany. In the latter case two students who had taken the German language option offered by the Modern Languages Department, were able to undertake their placement in Hamburg. The department was well placed, therefore, to take advantage of the Erasmus scheme and develop links, initially with Hamburg, Cork, Oslo and Belfast, and subsequently with Leeuwarden (Netherlands) and Bielefeld (Germany). These links enabled the exchange of students and staff with institutions in those cities.

Conclusion

Brought into being in the golden years of the college, the department was extremely busy. With money available for the development of purpose-designed buildings, youth wings attached to schools and the resurrection of a moribund youth service, it could not be otherwise. Over long periods of time, the supply of trained staff lagged behind the demand, and the evolution of the youth service into a community education service, with its attendant requirement for new knowledge, skills and experience, necessitated that staff retrain themselves. As *Training for change*[10] notes with delightful understatement,

> The incorporation (ie into a community education service) which took place was not of altogether comparable interests. Youth work, adult education and community work formed three strands, each possessing its separate history and professional concern, and each differing in important characteristics.

Pressure was intense, as in other parts of the college, but if it was demanding, it was at the same time exciting and invigorating. Staff were conscious that they were helping to build a new service, a service which despite, or because of, its unusual staffing, was making a significant contribution to the quality of life for many people, some of whom were among the more vulnerable and disadvantaged in our society. It was, as one staff member constantly remarked, a seemingly ongoing, never-ending seminar. It was not confined to the staff; the students were equally excited and involved in what was happening around them. For many of them, Jordanhill College was a second educational chance, and they seized it with gratitude and enthusiasm. They have gone on successfully to an extremely wide variety of posts, many of them at a very senior level. They are an embodiment of community education.

With the differing and disparate strands of community education, it would have been possible for the department to fragment into its specialisms. That it never did so is directly attributable to the skill and wisdom of Round, who laid such a solid foundation for the department. For its first 16 years he developed the policies, found the resources and most important of all, successfully integrated the department with the rest of the college. Those who came after owe him a considerable debt.

References
1 Ministry of Education. *The youth service in England and Wales*. London: HMSO, 1960. Cmnd 929. (Albemarle report).
2 SED. *Youth and community service*. Edinburgh: HMSO, 1970.
3 Standing Consultative Council on Youth and Community Service. *Community of interests*. Edinburgh: HMSO, 1968. (Reith report).
4 Youth Service Development Council. *Youth and community work in the 70s: proposals*. London: HMSO, 1969.
5 SED. *Adult education: the challenge of change*. Edinburgh: HMSO, 1975. (Alexander report).

6 Scottish Community Education Council. *Training for change*. Edinburgh: SCEC, 1984.
7 Jordanhill Community Education Division. Submission to Scottish Education Department. 1984.
8 Standing Consultative Council on Youth and Community Service. *Progressive joint training of part time youth leaders*. Edinburgh: SED, 1966.
9 SED. *Guidance in Scottish secondary schools*. Edinburgh: HMSO, 1968.
10 Scottish Community Education Council. *op.cit.*

14

Social Work at Jordanhill

Janice Thomson

Since its arrival at Jordanhill in 1967 social work education has been engaged in a continuous process of change and development. The influences for change have come from many sources: from politics and government, from increased knowledge gained by research in related fields, and from the growth and development of the social work profession itself. Looking back, however, it still appears that the most fundamental changes were experienced by the pioneering social work educators who created the first generic social work training course in the late 1960s. The failure of the government of the day adequately to resource the major training implications of reorganisation of the personal social services created an immense challenge for educators, social work agencies and students alike. To understand the dimension of the changes and to appreciate the achievements of those who guided the early development of social work education it is important to trace the origins of the profession.

Early social work services and training

Throughout the 1940s and 1950s social work services developed in a piecemeal fashion along with the welfare state. Individual services were fragmented and delivered by social workers employed in a range of statutory and voluntary bodies, eg psychiatric social workers, almoners, welfare officers, mental health officers and probation officers. There was no overall coordination of services and consequently gaps in provision resulted in some individuals or families in need falling through the net, while others received a service from several agencies.[1]

Social workers were acutely aware of these shortcomings, and during the 1950s and 1960s the movement towards a unified system of personal social services gathered momentum. The Labour Party was returned to power in 1964 and the political climate was set for change. The Kilbrandon report,[2] in looking at services for children coming before the courts in Scotland, proposed to link child care with the probation service through the creation of a Social Education Department. Social workers in the field, whilst welcoming these proposals, felt that they had not gone far enough. In

179

response to Kilbrandon the Association of Child Care Officers recommended that all the social services should be concentrated in one department.[3]

In 1966 the Scottish white paper *Social work and the community*[4] proposed that, 'the local authority should in future have power to provide all citizens of whatever age and circumstances, with advice and guidance in the solution of personal and social difficulties'. The resultant legislation, the Social Work (Scotland) Act 1968, created within each local authority a Department of Social Work which would ultimately take over all social work functions in statutory services and be given the general duty to promote social welfare.

Early training of social workers was very uneven. Psychiatric and medical social work had the longest history of professional training, which was normally university based and lasted at least three years. However the 1960s saw a significant increase in the size and number of training courses to meet the demands of the services which had grown in response to the welfare reforms of the previous two decades. In Glasgow in 1960 the Scottish Home and Health Department set up a one-year course for the training of probation officers. This was directed from 1962 by Vera Hiddleston, an Edinburgh graduate with several years' experience as a child care officer. Her direction of this course has been described as, 'the largest single contribution to social work education in the 1960s in Scotland'.[5]

The Younghusband report[6] of 1959 proposed a new general training in social work of two years' full time study for workers in local authority health and welfare services. In Scotland one such Younghusband course was set up in 1960 at the Scottish College of Commerce. When in 1964 this college became part of the University of Strathclyde an attempt was made to redesign the training by creating a four-year degree course leading to a professional qualification in social work. The degree proposal however was not accepted by the accrediting body, the Council for Training in Social Work. It is clear from letters and minutes of the Scottish Advisory Committee of the Council that the university did not wish to continue the Younghusband course as it stood, although two cohorts did qualify with a professional certificate from Strathclyde University.

Beginning at Jordanhill
Under the Health Visiting and Social Work (Training) Act 1962 the Council for Training in Social Work, advised by its Scottish Advisory Committee, had the responsibility of securing suitable facilities for training social workers. The Scottish Advisory Committee in May 1965, discussing alternatives to the training at Strathclyde University, considered that Jordanhill College offered the best prospect for future development.[7] The reasons are

not fully stated in the minutes, however it is perhaps relevant that John A. Smith was a respected member of this committee. The minute outlines the clear intent within Jordanhill College of Education to become involved in a range of social work training: a one-year course for experienced but unqualified child care officers, a two-year Younghusband course for the Certificate in Social Work, and a one-year refresher course for approved school staff.

This was a period of diversification for the colleges of education and social work was an expanding field. Donald MacCuaig, a former psychiatric social worker, was appointed to lead the child care course in 1966 and in 1967 Hiddleston agreed to head the social work course, bringing with her the Scottish probation and after care course of which she had been director since 1962. MacCuaig sadly died after less than two years in post and thereafter the child care course also came under the direction of Hiddleston. Both the Younghusband and the child care course enrolled approximately 12 students per year. The probation course had two intakes each year, the number varying according to the needs of the service. All courses started before the college academic year and indeed the one-year courses lasted a full 12 months.

The Social Work department was initially administratively linked with the Youth and Community department under the leadership of John Round. In practice the departments ran independently with Smith retaining the overall management role, a role in which he is remembered for his 'support, encouragement and wise counsel'.[8] When Smith retired, the management role was taken on by the Head of Department. Money was allocated by the Social Work Services Group to erect a building at 119 Southbrae Drive to house the new Jordanhill Social Work department. The main college buildings were fully occupied by the expanding teacher training programmes of the time and so the department remained in this purpose-built accommodation until 1978.

Development of the social work course
Initially Hiddleston's main concern was to administer the three very different courses and to address the curricular issues raised by the impending Social Work (Scotland) Act. The range of responsibilities for the new generic or general purpose social worker was vastly increased and it might have been logical to expect a consequent increase in the length of training at least to equal that of the former psychiatric social workers. Largely for economic reasons, however, the basic training time was held to two years' full time study for the Certificate in Social Work.

The notion of genericism in courses was not entirely new. The London School of Economics had since the early 1950s run generic training, in which 'all students had to learn about a number of specialisms, at least one in some detail, in addition to their own chosen and qualifying, field of work'.[9] Many of the other training courses contained a basic generic core, largely of social science teaching, after which specialisation took place. For the first time, however, the new courses were to equip students for generic practice in the unified social work departments, which had as yet had no time to experience genericism in practice, to identify the needs of workers or to establish standards of practice. From the outset these initial training courses were meant to form part of a continuum of training, with the expectation that workers would return to supplement their study through a range of post qualifying courses. For various reasons, such as the economic recession, the priorities of local authority departments and stretched resources in higher education, these courses did not develop as rapidly as had been anticipated.

There was little guidance available to staff in constructing a suitable course of professional training. Scotland had led the way in social services reform. In England the Local Authority Social Services Act was not passed until 1970 and the setting up of the new courses validating body, the Central Council for Education and Training in Social Work (CCETSW), was delayed until October 1971. Meanwhile the local authorities in Scotland required trained generic workers. Staff met to devise the new curriculum, decide what were the essential components of generic social work practice and find a balance between breadth in the areas of practice to be covered and the depth of study required in each to produce an informed, imaginative and competent practitioner.

Jordanhill was initially fortunate in having within the staff team representatives from four of the former specialisms, child care, probation and medical and psychiatric social work. In March 1971 Hiddleston described the attempts to plan and integrate material from a wide range of specialist disciplines. Areas such as psychiatry, human growth and behaviour, sociology, law and social administration were part of the core curriculum. Although in some of these areas, especially law, the field had widened considerably with the new responsibilities for generic workers, it was in the area of social work practice teaching that most difficulty occurred. A design of teaching in bridging concepts emerged as offering the best possibility for linking material from different areas of work. Hiddleston wrote, 'It became evident on the first run that the balance between breadth and depth required further adjustment and further cuts in specialist teaching would be required in order to allow more time for the basic principles of practice to be dealt with'.[10] The process for staff was a painful one, requiring them to give up much of the teaching they had come to value from the specialist courses.

The importance of taking on the community dimension of promoting social welfare enshrined in the Social Work (Scotland) Act is clearly acknowledged in her paper although at that time, due to lack of resources, it was not possible to give students enough familiarity with this area of work. Her conclusion was that, 'Social work education seems to me to be broadening and deepening but typically we are trying to fit it into the same span of time. Ultimately we shall have to lower standards of competence, resist pressure to widen further or lengthen training.' Her views were shared by educators and educational theorists elsewhere in the UK.

Clare Winnicott argued for 'a more deliberate effort to train students to practise a skill rather than simply to perform a function on behalf of an agency'.[11] The ability to transfer skills from one setting to another, however, requires a level of conceptual ability beyond that required in a more functionally orientated apprenticeship mode of training. It demands more of students and of teachers in developing frameworks to facilitate and support this learning. Achieving a balance between educational and training approaches when dealing with a range of students of mixed academic ability was therefore an important issue facing staff in the construction of the curriculum and in devising teaching strategies to meet the needs of all students.

The social work course originally attracted applicants from a wide variety of academic backgrounds. Although the minimum qualification for entry was only five O grades, there were many postgraduate students in the early cohorts until changes in the grants regulations in the 1980s discouraged their recruitment. Selection was not based on academic achievement alone but on personality factors such as sensitivity and flexibility which, along with a basic intellectual or conceptual ability, were thought essential qualities for someone intending to train in social work.

Very early in the life of the course the Social Work Services Group approached the college to provide an additional course for mature entrants of 30 years and over, in an attempt to attract into social work individuals whose life experience might be constructively used in working with people. With this group formal academic qualifications could be more relaxed. This course, sometimes known as the career change course, attracted former nurses, sheetmetal workers and deep sea divers to mention just a few. Initially the two courses ran separately but were later merged for sound educational as well as pragmatic reasons. The mature students course continued for a time to be advertised separately as a marketing strategy. Jordanhill maintained a commitment to mature entrants in the belief that the educational system still disadvantages those in the lower socio-economic groups. Mature students have certainly proved their worth in terms of motivation and commitment to learning and often display an academic ability at least equal to that of their graduate colleagues.

Throughout the 1970s staff concentrated on developing a workable and balanced curriculum. At that time much of the literature in generic social work emanated from the USA, where it had a longer history. Many leading American social work academics visited the UK and Jordanhill staff participated in workshops led by the systems theorists.[12] The application of systems theory to social work practice was attractive to many of the staff. It had a more sociological perspective on human problems than the psychoanalytic theories which had been the traditional basis of social work training. Systems theory offered the possibility of a unified approach to work with individuals, groups and communities and the potential to enhance student skills in promoting social welfare. Thus began the long association between Jordanhill College Social Work department and the writings of Alan Pincus and Anne Minahan,[13] perhaps the single text most remembered by any ex-student of the social work course.

The work of Ivey & Authier[14] in developing micro skills teaching also had an important impact on the curriculum. Social work practice teaching in the first year of the course was redesigned using their methods. In general staff sought to present students with a range of theoretical perspectives and methods, psychodynamic theories, problem-solving methods and task-centred practice, in the belief that the student would be most effective when adopting a style of work that fitted his or her particular beliefs and aptitudes. Teaching in specialist areas was explored in the second year of the course through electives linked to the final practice placement, eg child care and work with offenders. In 1973 CCETSW introduced guidelines for the professional award of CQSW—Certificate of Qualification in Social Work. The Jordanhill CSW substantially fulfilled the requirements, although regular reviews by CCETSW were required of all courses.

Some anxieties did emerge amongst social work managers over the competency of the new generic social workers: they were not expert in everything. The move away from teaching in the more detailed and procedural aspects of the job was bound to have 'repercussions on social work agencies because students need to learn their various functions in relation to clients within the agencies themselves'.[15] This basic shift was not universally welcomed by the hard-pressed local authority departments. At that time there were two main strands to the employers' involvement with training, firstly through the provision of practice placements and secondly through inservice training.

Training the trainers
Practice teachers, the agency-based supervisors, had always been important in social work training and, following the 1973 CCETSW guidelines, approximately one-half of the students' time was required to be spent on placement in a social work agency. In addition, the balance of responsibility

for helping students link theory and practice was tipping more heavily in their direction. The practice teacher was therefore a vital figure in the students' learning. The importance of good quality practice teaching was widely recognised and Jordanhill became involved in early initiatives in training. In 1975 Jordanhill, along with Glasgow University, provided a short course for intending practice teachers, looking at issues such as the relationship of theory to practice, styles of supervision and assessment of students. Later, social work agencies introduced their own practice teacher training in conjunction with colleges. Jordanhill staff have taken an active part in the development and implementation of these courses, which have grown from a few voluntary sessions to an extended period of assessed study and supervised practice leading to a post-qualifying award.

Practice teachers were responsible for the grading of their students' work on placement. In order to ensure appropriate and equitable standards of assessment, Jordanhill initiated a system of quality control through the creation of the 'Practice Panel'. This innovative scheme, widely replicated in other institutions, drew on the skills of experienced practice teachers from a range of social work settings. The Panel of 6–8 members scrutinised all final assessment reports completed by practice teachers and students. Where they felt that there was a significant discrepancy between the evidence presented and the student's grading, members might interview those concerned or ask for additional written material in support of the grading. The Practice Panel's final decision was then recommended to the Board of Examiners.

As the immediate crisis of local government reorganisation receded, the need for social work departments to support new staff through workload supervision, inservice courses and secondment to further training began to be given greater priority. Training departments within agencies were encouraged to develop induction training and to monitor and support the professional development of newly-qualified workers. Perhaps the most significant and innovative contribution to the education of social work trainers was the introduction at Jordanhill in 1980 of the Post Qualifying Course in Social Work Education. Drawing on the expertise of education and psychology staff in the college as well as social workers, Hiddleston constructed the course which became the first CCETSW accredited post qualifying social work course in Scotland. It was designed to enhance the teaching ability of agency-based social work educators by providing for the systematic development of relevant skills. The course was directed at practice teachers, training officers or CSS study supervisors.[16] Local authorities and voluntary agencies soon subscribed, sending a constant stream of trainers from a variety of backgrounds. The course was eventually staffed entirely from within the Social Work department, but it remains an important model of interdepartmental cooperation and achievement.

In 1974 CCETSW recognised the CQSW as an appropriate qualification for residential social work and so Jordanhill began to provide college-based teaching and placement experience in the residential sector. Practice teachers were thin on the ground in residential care, where the vast majority of staff were untrained, and this limited the numbers able to take up this option. Staff were also involved extensively in inservice initiatives within the residential sector, notably the course for heads and deputes developed in response to the *Home or away* report.[17]

Jordanhill contributed to national policy making throughout this time. Acknowledgement of the wisdom and experience of Hiddleston led to her membership of CCETSW's Scottish Advisory Committee, in which capacity in 1979 she chaired the Working Group on Practice Teaching in Scotland. In 1976, in recognition of her immeasurable contribution to the field of social work education, she was awarded the OBE. Hiddleston retired as Head of Department in 1987 and Mono Chakrabarti, lecturer in social work and social policy at Glasgow University, was appointed to the post. As his first priority he sought to become more involved nationally, believing that the department had an important role to play in influencing the direction of future policy. He was appointed to a number of CCETSW committees, one of which, the Black Perspectives Committee, was influential in ensuring the inclusion of anti-discriminatory values in the Diploma in Social Work. He also forged links with social work agencies nationally and through his connection with the Association of Directors of Social Work became a member of the Training Committee of COSLA.

The Diploma in Social Work

Chakrabarti's arrival preceded the next major directional change in social work education. The roots of this change can be traced back to developments in 1975 when CCETSW introduced a second-tier qualification, the Certificate in Social Service or CSS. This was intended to offer social work assistants, residential social workers and home help organisers a form of training which was less academic and more practical than the CQSW. With the existence of this new reference group the reservations expressed by employers over the competence of newly qualified CQSW students re-emerged. Some managers doubted the value of the more academic educative approach of CQSW courses, feeling that 'the education they receive makes them difficult employees, more concerned to change the system than get on with the job'.[18]

The variety of influences which led CCETSW to move from its commitment to CQSW to a reappraisal of social work training and hence to the competency-based DipSW are too extensive to be mentioned here. Suffice to say that in the 1980s CCETSW, spurred by the criticisms in the Barclay report,[19] undertook a review of qualifying training and produced a series of consultative papers inviting comment on their intent to introduce a new unified national qualification in social work in which minimum standards of competence would be assured. The final outcome was Paper 30[20] which contained a statement of the knowledge, values and skills required by a qualifying social worker, expressed as a set of minimum competencies. It was intended to lengthen the period of training in order to ensure the achievement of minimum standards. The proposals for a three-year Quali-fying Diploma in Social Work were rejected by the government on economic grounds. However the competencies remained relatively unchanged, to be achieved in two years rather than three.

Central to the new DipSW was the notion that the responsibility for training should reside within a partnership between academic institutions and social work agencies. These bodies were required to work together in consortia to construct and implement courses which would enable students to demonstrate the competencies outlined in Paper 30. Thus the entire training process was to be seen as a shared commitment. In the west of Scotland the sheer size of Strathclyde Region and its influence as the major placement agency enabled it to determine the organisation of partnerships. Uniquely in the UK, Strathclyde Region joined with Dumfries and Galloway Region and the West of Scotland Voluntary Agencies Forum in partnership or consortium with all of the participating institutions[21] within its bound-aries.

The West of Scotland Consortium proposal was accepted by CCETSW in 1991 just in time for the first intake of students. The first year of the course was of a general nature, while in the second year students were to complete a specialised module in one of five areas of particular practice, with each college taking responsibility for running one or more of these modules. Jordanhill ran two specialist modules, one on working with children and families and the other on the criminal justice system. Implementing the programme at Jordanhill involved considerable changes in the organisation of teaching material. The old subject areas such as psychology, sociology and social policy were swept away, appearing in the new course as aspects of the modular themes of, eg, poverty and discrimination, human behaviour, family and life cycle. Valuable inputs from other departments within the college were lost when they did not fit within the boundaries of the new curriculum. Despite the many organisational complexities, however, the new diploma became gradually more embedded in the life of the department as staff became familiar with the new structures, built up the programme in their own style, explored the boundaries for change and innovation and found them more flexible than had at first been feared.

One of the positive aspects of Paper 30 was that it brought to the fore the consideration of values in social work practice. There was increasing awareness in social work literature in the 1980s of the oppressive role of racism, sexism and other forms of discrimination in the structure of society and within social work institutions and practices. The anti-discriminatory principles of social work were clearly stated in Paper 30 and the identification and challenge of all forms of discrimination set as a competency for a qualifying social worker. This was a bold step, which has had considerable effect in raising awareness of these issues within agencies. Unfortunately it has sometimes had a negative effect in driving aberrant attitudes underground. The pursuit of political correctness in some quarters has led to an atmosphere in which students may be afraid to express their true feelings on certain issues lest they be perceived by staff or colleagues as discriminatory. They are thus denied the opportunity to examine important areas of their personal and professional development.

Degree level and postgraduate studies
The department had been pursuing a policy of diversification since the early 1980s, so that the pre-qualifying courses had become a smaller part of the total workload. This diversification accelerated in the 1980s and 1990s with the development of post qualifying training courses, employment-based learning programmes and research initiatives. In line with national trends towards improving educational standards in the workforce CCETSW in 1990 encouraged developments in post qualifying training by introducing in Paper 31[22], *A framework for continuing professional development*, a new system for evaluating practice-based learning for social care and social work staff, leading to awards at post qualifying and advanced levels.

The development at Jordanhill of the Post Qualifying Awards Scheme provided a useful mechanism for linking training initiatives in social work to a system of advanced academic awards at certificate, diploma and Masters degree level. The Postgraduate Certificate in Social Work Management, initially funded by the Social Work Services Inspectorate (formerly Social Work Services Group), was developed jointly with social work agencies in the field. While requiring participants to expand their knowledge of management principles in a general sense, it aimed to ensure that course work was relevant to their workplace experience and tackled the issues facing them in their daily work. Some of these issues concerned fairly traditional areas for management courses, eg team work, but the expansion of the role of social work agencies following the Community Care legislation[23] of 1990 brought a challenging new dimension to other modules. This four-module course set within the PQMSc programme at Jordanhill proved highly successful, with over 400 students enrolled in the first two years of the courses. Research funding steadily increased as the department gained recognition in this field. One of its major successes was the Centre for Residential Child Care, for which much of the planning was done in the years leading up to the merger with the University of Strathclyde.

Two attempts had been made to introduce a four-year degree course in the 1980s. Both proposals included a joint first year with Youth and Community students, followed by two years spent in establishing basic social work skills, and thereafter a final year of specialisation in a chosen area of work. The second proposal coincided with the development of the BEd and went further in its interdisciplinary aims by including joint classes with primary teaching students in year one. Both proposals were unsuccessful. However the commitment to establishing degree-level training remained strong in the department, and when the political climate seemed more favourable new plans were drawn up. It was decided to approach Strathclyde University for validation as the proposed merger of the two institutions was imminent. The BA in social work was validated in 1991 and the first cohort enrolled in September 1992.

The approach to curriculum design this time was significantly different. The two years of higher education required to gain the Diploma in Social Work were taken as the foundation of the new degree. Using the CNAA framework for awards in higher education one further year of advanced study was then required to achieve degree standard. Given the continuing commitment to the diploma programme this model was attractive. It was economic in use of staff resources as all students could be taught together for the first two years and from the student's point of view it cut the training time required to gain a degree to three years. Although removed from direct practice experience in year 3, students are able to develop expertise in research methods and extend their understanding in earlier fields of study to enable them to meet the ever-changing challenges of social work.

Conclusion

The department established many productive and often creative partnerships both within the college and with agency training departments, field workers, residential staff and managers. It was able to provide a widely-respected initial education in social work, high quality post qualifying training and a growing body of research material. Most importantly perhaps the department provided a continuous stream of professional social workers who in their turn made a real difference to the lives of the communities they served. John Haines in 1967 wrote of social work education: 'It is important that in teaching a subject matter that is concerned with change and itself liable to change that educators should retain a flexible and dynamic approach and a readiness to make use of new evidence as it becomes available'.[24] Although the past 30 years have seen many challenges for educators and practitioners, Jordanhill can be confident that its record of development has been in accord with Haines's principles.

Notes and references

1 Donnison, D.V. *The neglected child and the social services*. Manchester University Press, 1954.

2 Scottish Home and Health Department. *Children and young persons, Scotland*. Edinburgh: HMSO, 1964. Cmnd 2306. (Kilbrandon report).

3 Quoted by V. Hiddleston in a paper to the BASW conference 1988. *Rostrum*, 16, 1969

4 Scottish Home and Health Department. *Social work and the community*. Edinburgh: HMSO, 1966. Cmnd 3065.

5 Murphy, J. *British social services: the Scottish dimension*. Edinburgh: Scottish Academic Press, 1992.

6 Ministry of Health/Department of Health for Scotland. *Social workers in the local authority health and welfare services*. London: HMSO, 1959. (Younghusband report).

7 Scottish Advisory Committee to the National Council for Training and Education in Social Work. *SACSW*, 66:3, 1965.

8 Hiddleston, V. MS notes on the early development of the Social Work Department at Jordanhill.

9 Ford, J. Social welfare provision in the United Kingdom in Ford and Chakrabarti, M. *Welfare abroad*. Edinburgh: Scottish Academic Press, 1987.

10 Hiddleston, V. *The broadening scope of social work education*. 1971. Unpublished paper.

11 Winnicott, C. Conference paper in Central Training Council in Child Care. Joint conference of tutors: conference papers. 1970.

12 Parsons, T. *The structure of social action*. New York: McGraw Hill, 1968.

13 Pincus, A. and Minahan, A. *Social work practice: model and method*. Itasca: Peacock, 1973.

14 Ivey, A.E. and Authier, J. *Microcounseling*. Springfield: Charles Thomas, 1971.

15 Winnicott, C. *op.cit.*

16 The role of workplace supervisors for CSS was outlined in CCETSW paper 9.1, *The Certificate in Social Service: a new form of training*.

17 Edwards, F.E. *Home or away: residential child care strategy for the eighties*. Glasgow: Strathclyde Regional Council. Social Work Department, 1984.

18 CCETSW second annual report, 1975.

19 National Institute of Social Work Training. *Social workers: their role and tasks*. London: Bedford Square Press, 1982. (Barclay report).

20 CCETSW. Paper 30. *Requirements and regulations for the Diploma in Social Work*. London: CCETSW, 1989.

21 Teaching institutions in the consortium were: Jordanhill College, the Open University, Glasgow University, Paisley College, Queen's College Glasgow, Clydebank and Langside Colleges of Further Education.

22 CCETSW. Paper 31. *The requirements for post qualifying education and*

training in the personal social services: a framework for continuing professional development. London: CCETSW, 1991.

23 The National Health Service and Community Care Act 1990.

24 Boss, P. and Haines, J. *Administrative studies for social workers: a report on the teaching of organisation theory and administrative processes to social work students.* 1967.

15

The Academic Services

Margaret Harrison

The academic services may be taken to comprise the college library, AV Services and Computer Education department, all of which, by the time of the merger with the University of Strathclyde, were substantial services, each with a reputation which extended beyond the bounds of Jordanhill. The three services were of varying antiquity, having developed as the college curriculum evolved. The library dated back to the 19th century, and audiovisual resources, while present in the early days, became significant only in the mid 20th century. Computing was the youngest of the services, but quickly established an important role in support of teaching and administration.

Small, but well chosen
From its earliest days, the Normal School building included a room containing a few bookcases, described as a library, but mainly used for instructional purposes. The training course was of such short duration, and the days so fully timetabled, that little opportunity was afforded the students to read independently. The college library in the 19th century contained only a few hundred books, invariably described by HMIs in their reports as, 'Small but well chosen', but in fact containing often a random collection of varying suitability. An appeal for books for the library at Moray House gives an indication of the subject matter: history, civil and ecclesiastical; natural history and science; books illustrative of the natural history of the Bible; practical theology, and above all, books on the different systems of education, and its theory and practice.[1]

A similar appeal was made for the Glasgow Free Church College, where the sum of £40 was spent to establish the library.[2] By 1861 it contained 1200 volumes on history, geography, science and general literature.[3] The Church of Scotland College at Dundas Vale appeared not to value its library quite so highly, although it contained 1300 books.[4] Private study time was described by the college managers as being whatever time the students chose to allow before arriving at the Seminary at 8am and after leaving it at 9pm.[5] HMI John Gordon, in several of his reports, expressed concern about this situation, and in 1865 the Rector responded by assembling the students to hear public readings of improving works. The books read were Abercrombie's *Culture and discipline of the mind*, Carne's *Account of missionaries*, Barrow's *Discourses on diligence in our calling as students* and 'the most suitable of the *Exhortations* of Leighton'. The Rector reported that the readings 'were received with reverence'.[6]

The merger of the two Church Training Colleges, and relocation in the new building at Jordanhill, presented an opportunity to plan a new library. An early photograph shows a long, airy, room with dark tables, bentwood chairs and a cheery open fire.[7] The first professional librarian was appointed at Jordanhill in 1925: Miss Williamina Rait MA, of Glasgow Public Libraries, and daughter of Principal Rait of Glasgow University. She recorded her dissatisfaction with the ill-matched assortment of bookcases of differing sizes, removed from the former colleges of Dundas Vale and Stow, and the collection of books, many of which were obsolete or duplicates.[8]

The NCTT recognised that library facilities must be improved in all the training colleges. Those students attending concurrent classes at university required better study facilities and a wider range of books than had been provided hitherto, and planning was in progress to extend the two-year non graduate training course to three years from 1931. Library grants had been made on an ad hoc basis, and some colleges asked for very little. As an initial step towards a more systematic library policy, the NCTT ordered a survey of library provision in 1925.[9] This found that library accommodation in Glasgow, Edinburgh, Aberdeen and Dundee was suitable and adequate, their bookstock numbering 5567, 6000, 3281 and 1909 volumes respectively. Provision in the smaller colleges was less generous. Dewey Decimal Classification was brought in at Glasgow and Edinburgh, the libraries were converted to the open access system and the benefits of the card catalogue introduced. Miss Rait was succeeded after a short time by Miss Ellen Wright, who remained in post until 1964.

A Special Committee as to Libraries was formed, to consider what action should follow the report. Library grants were to be awarded on a regular basis, the amount to be determined by the size of the college and the current state of its library. However, these good intentions were thwarted by the economic difficulties of the 1920s and 1930s, and later by the austerity of the wartime years, and the college libraries appeared able to provide only essential books for their students. Alternative means were explored of supplying books for wider reading, including a subscription to the London Library, in order that Directors of Studies might borrow books on behalf of their students,[10] an appeal to the Carnegie Trust[11] and a central education library, to be shared by all the colleges.[12] None of these ideas was ever adopted. The library was moved to the college Board Room in 1935, to make way for teaching accommodation, and the cramped accommodation and inadequate staffing prevented large scale development of the collection and inhibited use of the library for research type investigations by students, until the spacious new library in the Sir Henry Wood Building was occupied in 1973.

Planning for the enhanced library began in 1964, on the appointment of a new Librarian, Peter B. Clarke. Library accommodation at Jordanhill was clearly inadequate, in the light of the published recommended standards for college libraries,[13] and compared with provision made in the new college at Hamilton, which Wood, as a member of the Special Building Committee, had helped to plan. The new library comprised a ground floor and an upper floor in the form of a gallery, to maximise floor area and to provide space for future expansion, utilised in 1981 to incorporate an AV Library. The outcome was a spacious and impressive building five times the size of the old library,[14] which at last gave students and staff of Jordanhill a fitting study environment. Peter Clarke retired as Librarian in 1983 and was succeeded by Margaret Harrison, formerly Librarian of Hamilton College.

The new media and methods

Visual aids had been employed in the training system from the earliest times. Stow's philosophy of education included the technique of 'picturing out', meaning the description of an object or concept in order to convey its meaning, and also literally showing the children pictures of objects, to stimulate their interest in the lesson. Charming illustrations were used to great effect in the *Glasgow Infant School magazine*[15] which published sample lessons, poetry and prose which the classroom teacher could use to enliven his or her teaching. Stow advocated for the same reason the collection of objects of natural history, reflecting the general Victorian interest in museums of all kinds. For the next 100 years there was little fundamental change, but by the 1950s gramophone records, 16mm filmstrips and slides were in use by lecturers and students. Larger scale development of learning resources at Jordanhill had to await the period of expansion of the 1960s and 1970s, when national standards and strategies were published for libraries, educational technology and computing, and revision of the curriculum incorporated an important role for those services.

A staff conference at Jordanhill in 1963 discussed new developments in teaching, such as 'modern mathematics', audiovisual methods in modern languages and teaching machines. The Research Committee subsequently approved the purchase of a teaching machine by the Psychology department[16] and John A. Smith encouraged the establishment of a Programmed Learning Research Unit headed by Peter Hodge, with the remit to train students and teachers in the preparation and use of programmed materials in schools. The Unit was equipped with Grundymaster linear and other teaching machines. By 1967 a graduate optional course in programmed learning, inservice courses and research projects were under way, and programmes such as *The rise of heavy industry on Clydeside* were being produced, for testing in schools.[17] The programmes organised subject material into a series of units or steps, with provision for student responses, which could reinforce the learning or correct errors. Interest generally in this form of self instruction, with its 'wind-on' technology, waned after a few years, although the college retained a keen interest in student-centred learning, and the concept re-emerged later as computer-assisted learning.

Audiovisual methods proved to have a more lasting impact. There had been early experiments in the use of video at Dundee College in 1962 for pupil observation, and at Notre Dame College in 1963 for scientific demonstrations, but in 1964–65 the SED decided to fund relatively sophisticated services at two colleges, Jordanhill and Dundee. David Butts, an experienced producer from the BBC, was appointed to lead the new Television department, and production began in April 1966. Butts was an able and inspired Director, who strove to define a strategic plan for AV work, rather than simply permit ad hoc developments, and strongly emphasised the need for research into the effectiveness of TV as a method of teaching. A prestigious conference on educational technology as a broad discipline, aimed at senior management in local authorities, was organised at the Thomson Foundation College in the 1960s and this conference established Jordanhill's reputation as a leader in the field.

The Audiovisual Committee of the Board of Studies set out a development plan for experiment with television.[18] Observation of classroom situations, although not particularly exciting, was a basic need, facilitated by the new mobile television unit which enabled recordings to be made in schools. Recording of student performance in teaching situations, or 'microteaching', was a stimulating update of the public criticism lessons of olden times, but required sensitive handling. The History department conducted a research study into the effectiveness of microteaching in graduate training[19] at this time, but in general research never received the emphasis that Butts would have wished.[20] Direct teaching programmes were made, notably by the History department, using the medium of television to present material in a new and imaginative way, and incorporating filming on location. 16mm and super 8mm was also promoted, but these media proved less popular with lecturers than television. Synchronised tape/slide sequences in their turn enjoyed a vogue. Video was first used in the inservice training of teachers in 1967, when a series of programmes was broadcast on the Glasgow ETV network. Equipment in the early days was all monochrome, and without editing facilities every programme had to be made in one go.[21] A four channel cable system transmitted programmes, which had to be watched in their entirety, before portable VCRs were available.

The department was renamed Audiovisual Education in 1969, with the expanded remit of running courses in audiovisual work, providing a central servicing unit for equipment, organising a film and photography service and building up an audiovisual library. This combination of teaching and service function remained a particular strength of the department for many years. Courses for college staff and students were offered, firstly on television, radio and film as media of communication, and, more practically, on the handling of audiovisual material and its applications in the classroom. Out of this grew a Diploma in Audiovisual Communication (later Diploma in Educational Technology) which was validated by CNAA on a distance learning basis, and ran successfully for many years.

A television studio, film editing and graphics facilities had been acquired, and accommodation for the department in its expanded role was proving problematic. In 1971 Butts commenced planning for a new Audiovisual Centre adjacent to the Wood building. This would have contained teaching and production facilities, reprographics and an audiovisual library. However the project was cancelled at an advanced stage, in the renewed austerity of the mid 1970s. Attempts were made on a national and regional basis to share expertise and equipment. The report[22] of the National Inter College Committee on Educational Technology (NICCET) in 1972 set out to consider the impact of educational technology on teacher training in the ensuing decade. It recommended that all colleges be equipped and staffed to a basic level, more expensive facilities being shared on a regional basis. The west of Scotland group contained Jordanhill, Notre Dame, Hamilton and Craigie Colleges. Limited sharing of college-produced resources took place, facilitated by a union catalogue, but the proposals to close and merge some colleges in the late 1970s militated against effective cooperation. A later NICCET report[23] in 1980 took a more realistic view of educational technology provision.

It is difficult to recreate the excitement experienced by those involved in the new media in the early years. Butts described the qualities required as, 'a massive attention to detail [combined] with an unflagging creativity'.[24] The initiative in many of the developments at Jordanhill came from Butts, and he saw a national and regional role for the college in sophisticated film and television production. In his time, and under his successor, George Kirkland, the department had a number of successes in this field.

Computing

Computer education at Jordanhill began shortly after publication of the interim report[25] of the Bellis Committee. The Committee, set up in 1967 to consider the implications of computers for the schools, recommended that an introductory course in computer studies be provided for the majority of pupils, that teachers of other subjects, not just mathematics, should teach these courses and that three educational computer centres be established. It was clear that the college must provide computer courses for students and for teachers in service, and a Senior Lecturer, John Hawthorn, was appointed in 1971 to establish the new subject. Additional staff were recruited as the need arose. The new venture took some time to become established. It was five years before the subject attained the status of a department in its own right and therefore representation on the Board of Studies. The first computer, an IBM 1130, was hired rather than purchased. 'If there was a real need then the college would later buy a suitable computer'.[26] In retrospect, this cautious approach seems strange, but the unwillingness to invest in expensive technology is perhaps understandable in the light of the shortlived experiment in programmed learning.

Jordanhill (along with Moray House, Aberdeen and Dundee Colleges of Education) was designated as one of the four educational computer centres, and local authorities in the west of Scotland (except Glasgow, which had established its own centre) were persuaded to support the Schools Computing Service. The local authorities paid a proportion of staff costs, and also part of the cost of the computer, and in return received curricular support from the college. Their interests lay in repetitive drill and practice work (eg in arithmetic) and in programming, mainly Fortran and Algol. Programs written by pupils were processed at Jordanhill.[27] The Schools Computing Service continued into the 1980s, in the form of design and writing of subject based packages for the schools, finally ending when the long-running salary dispute placed an embargo on development work by teachers.

The new department of Computer Education was situated initially in Robertson House, a handsome Edwardian villa on Southbrae Drive, and moved into the Stow Building in the late 1970s when space became available. The first computer was replaced in 1976 with an Interdata machine with a few local terminals attached. The Interdata was used for teaching purposes and for administrative tasks—invoicing, financial statements, and student records, mainly timetabling and processing of examination results.[28] An IBM 4331 replaced the Interdata in 1981, the new computer being formally inaugurated by the Rt Hon Roy Jenkins, then MP for Hillhead. This machine was used for programming, statistical packages and other software, as well as administrative tasks. External terminals were installed for the first time, in a star network, in other buildings on the campus. The replacement IBM

9730 installed in 1988 was used extensively for management information systems and supported a larger number of terminals, eventually linked on a fibre optic network.

The main work of the department lay in providing courses on educational computing, concentrating in the first instance on the secondary sector. An optional course at Ordinary level was included in the secondary BEd degree in the 1970s, in order that science and mathematics graduates especially would have a knowledge of computers. It stopped short, however, of the Higher pass which would have entitled holders to teach computing as a main subject. There was a need for this since the introduction of O grade computing studies, but the SED initially resisted pressure to approve an additional TQ subject, harking back to the recommendation of the Bellis report that all teachers, not just specialists, should teach computing. The case was eventually won and a TQ in computing was offered from 1982, with entry by one graduating pass in computing, plus another cognate subject. The way then opened for Additional TQ courses, for teachers who wished to add the teaching of computing to their existing subjects, and a great many qualified by this route over the years. Those without an academic qualification in computing had first to pass the Postgraduate Diploma in Computer Education, offered initially as a joint course by Paisley College and Jordanhill, and latterly by Jordanhill alone.

Support for primary schools began more gradually, since developments in the west of Scotland, Jordanhill's main market at that time, were several years behind those in other areas. Glasgow Corporation Education Authority had rented a large-scale Univac computer, which it was proposed to link to terminals in primary schools via ducting underneath the old tram lines.[29] There was, however, a desire to standardise provision throughout Strathclyde Region, and the Glasgow system proved too expensive to extend. The trend towards microcomputers had begun, and the sheer cost of supplying computers to all the primary schools in the Region, together with the shortage of teachers with computing skills, delayed developments for a few years. Following the appointment of an additional lecturer, Anne Ramsay, in 1984, Jordanhill embarked on a considerable inservice programme for primary teachers.

Meanwhile, microcomputers, often gifted by parents, were beginning to appear in schools. Cromemcos, a few RZ380s, PETs (which had inconvenient, tiny keyboards and required tape cassettes) and Apple IIs were in use, although some schools possessed only one computer. The first large scale provision came with government promotion of the BBC micro, which for a time became the standard, followed at a later stage by Archimedes and Macintosh. Elementary programming in BASIC (which came free with the BBCs) and simple word processing packages and other educational software were used. The early technology was expensive and, although SED provided earmarked funding for a time for information technology, as it did for educational technology, it was impossible to keep pace with the fast-changing technology and the proliferation of systems used in Scottish schools. The need to train students to use all the systems they might encounter in schools made the college perforce more reactive than it would have wished to be. Equipment purchasing had to have regard to the purchases made by local authorities, and forward planning was very difficult.

A strategy for learning resources

By the late 1970s the college possessed a considerable amount of equipment in the library, AV Media, Computer Education and other academic departments, together with extensive reprographic facilities. CNAA had pointed to the need for a more systematic policy for resources and for more effective forward planning. Further pressure came from the 1980 NICCET report,[30] which advocated rationalising educational technology provision on a regional basis, in view of the cost of equipping all colleges with the latest machines. Butts[31] raised the question of links between the learning resources departments in 1980 and shortly afterwards the Library and AV Committees were joined by the Computer Committee, to form a new Learning Resources Sub-Committee of the Board of Studies. The remit of the new Committee was to establish a coordinated learning resources policy for the college, promote the use of such resources in support of teaching and learning, and advise the Board of Studies on priorities in learning resources.[32]

This committee discussed topics such as resource-based learning, open learning, the microcomputer revolution, desk top publishing, media studies and library automation, and heard regular reports from the service departments. Mostly, the meetings were an exchange of information and views, but the Committee had little power actually to achieve developments, since funding decisions were made partly by SED (in respect of earmarked funding for educational technology and computing) and internally by the college Resource Allocation Committee. This situation changed in 1988, when convenership of the Learning Resources Committee passed from Alasdair Nicolson to Stuart Niven, Director of the SSFE. Niven argued successfully that the Committee must have powers to determine priorities and award funding, and that a proportion of capital funds each year must be allocated to educational developments. A number of successes followed on from this decision. An online integrated library automation system was installed in 1989, the first in a college of education in Scotland. Wider access to computers was provided for staff and students, in departments and in open access laboratories. Enhanced facilities in design and production enabled

AV Services to continue to produce high-quality programmes and to support media education in the college.

The Learning Resources Committee also took an interest in the Sales and Publications Unit, which was initially attached to the AV Media department and latterly a self-funded unit. From its origins in Hamilton College, the Sales and Publications Unit was soon generating an income of £1¼m a year.[33] It did this by selling 'the very best of educational materials' through an elegant catalogue. Tapping the remarkable skills of college staff and others, the unit produced classroom materials, reports and teachers' books. The renowned staff tutor topics, the beautifully produced computer-assisted topics such as *Desperate journey* and the ground-breaking *Foundations of writing* found their way into many Scottish primary schools, and to schools and colleges around the world.

Conclusion
An audit of the strengths of the learning resources departments in the 1990s would have found an up to date library of 180,000 books and an extensive collection of AV materials in all formats, acknowledged as a centre of excellence in the field of education. The AV service, reorganised in latter years purely as a service department, produced high-quality television programmes for college departments and for external clients and offered workshop facilities, loans of equipment and a sophisticated graphic design service for staff and students in support of learning and teaching. Computers were in use in all departments and courses, and the still unified Computer Education department was in great demand for advice from those keen to step onto the information superhighway. Jordanhill College had valued its learning resources departments very highly, and looked forward to raising them 'higher still' in the merger with the University of Strathclyde.

References
1 Free Church of Scotland. Proceedings of the General Assembly of the Free Church of Scotland. Glasgow: Collins, 1843, pp.79–80.
2 Glasgow Free Church Training College minutes, 7 December 1846. Jordanhill Archives.
3 CCE annual report, 1866–67, p.540.
4 Glasgow Church of Scotland Training College. Library catalogue c1880. Jordanhill Archives.
5 CCE annual report, 1856–57, p.819.
6 *Ibid.*, 1865–66, p.470.
7 Jordanhill Training College. Students' handbook, 1931–32, facing p.19.
8 CEC minutes, 1924–25, p.274.
9 *Ibid.*, 1924–25, pp.271–283.
10 *Ibid.*, 1925–26, p.89.

11 *Ibid.*, p.167.

12 *Ibid.*, 1925–26, p.314.

13 LA/ATCDE. *College libraries: recommended standards...*. London: LA, 1967.

14 Clarke, P.B. *Report on the new library by the college Librarian.* January 1974.

15 *Glasgow Infant School magazine* 1832–69.

16 JBS minutes, 18 November 1963.

17 *Ibid.*, 12 December 1967, Appendix 1.

18 JBS minutes, 15 June 1967, Appendix 4.

19 Fairley, J.A. The applicability of microteaching to the training of history graduates. *Teaching history,* v.3:4, 1975.

20 JBS minutes, 21 October 1970. AV Department report 1969–70.

21 Letter from D. Butts to G. Kirkland, 20 December 1982.

22 NICCET. *Educational technology in the Scottish colleges of education.* Edinburgh: JCCES, 1972.

23 NICCET. *Resource provision in Scottish colleges of education.* Edinburgh: JCCES, 1980.

24 Jordanhill AV Media Department. Notes on future policy: address to staff meeting, 18 November 1971 by D. Butts.

25 CCC. *Computers and the schools: an interim report.* Edinburgh: HMSO, 1969. (Curriculum paper 6). (Bellis report).

26 JPC minutes, 1 February 1972.

27 Hawthorn, J. Interview with M. Harrison, 3 May 1995.

28 Discussion paper on college computing resources, March 1980.

29 Hawthorn. *op.cit.*

30 NICCET. 1980. *op.cit.*

31 Butts, D. *A policy for AV services: paper to Library, AV and Printing Resources Subcommittee.* 15 January 1979.

32 JBS Learning Resources Sub-committee, 12 November 1980.

33 Information contributed by R. Frame, Publications Officer, 1995.

16

The Student Experience

Catherine Adams

How can one chapter encapsulate the differing experiences of students on different courses over a period of 90 years? Systematic research into the views of students past and present would have been beyond the scope of one researcher. Instead, various forms of evidence have been tapped: the Hostels Association records; the archive collection of student magazines; students who contacted the Alumni Relations Office with a view to class reunion events; interviews, sometimes unplanned, with colleagues or with busy staff in schools. As a result, what follows is inevitably impressionistic and is concerned largely with student teachers rather than with the other groups of college students.

Much of the data consists of people's recollections, often of distant times. Two factors influence their reliability. One is sheer forgetfulness; the other is that people select those memories which are important for their self image.[1] Another difficulty in writing about student experiences is that these change over time, so that one is unsure how representative any sample is. There is also the influence of 'student sub-cultures through which they interpret their experience, generate responses, and in general achieve support systems for handling the situations they confront'.[2] These subcultures emerged from the structural arrangements for dividing students into manageable groups for teaching.

Group dynamics specific to different courses, each of which reinforces a sense of professional identity as a primary teacher, FE teacher, community educator, speech therapist or PE teacher, have been accentuated in Jordanhill by the lack of shared classes, which meant that there was very little opportunity to meet students on different courses. 'I knew nothing of the primary course. The only different students I met were those graduates doing the DipEd at university because they shared some of my classes'. (1975 Sec grad) These divisions within the college have meant that recollections of student experience are fairly course-specific. What then were the experiences of different courses? Which elements were different and which were held in common? How far and in what ways did these change over time?

Primary certificate and diploma courses

The organisational structure of primary certificate and diploma courses, which kept students together within one section throughout, was of great significance. Apart from hostel life, no other planned opportunity for meeting people, for example societies, clubs or college social life, was so successful in building friendships and a support network which has seen many former students through varied teaching careers and personal ups and downs. Three other factors helped to shape the experience of students on the non graduate primary course. The simplest was that the college was largely non residential and this made the development of corporate life difficult. As William Kerr lamented:

> When I watch the outpourings at 3.45 I have wondered if, after all, the committee were right who gave us our trees and green grass, instead of planting us somewhere in the dirt of the city. We could run so many unofficial meetings in the time it takes us to reach the Central Station or St Enoch's.[3]

More fundamental were two assumptions which, although weakening latterly, have never entirely disappeared. The first was that primary teaching should be essentially 'feminised, maternal, but male regulated'.[4] Respectability, conformity, vocation were key notions of teacher training which, in the 1920s, was still strongly influenced by the former church colleges. The convent-like atmosphere of the new Jordanhill building was recalled:

> We had to wear ward shoes in the new building. On teaching practice we had to wear a simple skirt and blouse, a bit like a uniform, very plain. Discipline was very strong in college, much stricter than senior years at school. We had to speak in whispers in the corridor and there had to be silence when passing the Dean of Women's room. (1926 non grad)

Suggestions about appropriate dress for student teachers can be related to contemporary views of the status and role of the teacher. A student in 1931 recalls one lecturer's serious concern that students wear clothes long enough to maintain modesty when reaching up to write on the board. In the late 1960s, when the importance of stimulating and motivating children was to the fore, students were encouraged to wear brighter colours, a different blouse or jersey each day, and always an eye-catching piece of jewellery. Infant teachers were also encouraged to wear interesting shoes since the practice of gathering children round the teacher on the floor for a story was back in fashion.

For many years the curriculum and demeanour expected of Jordanhill students, combined with the students' own backgrounds and aspirations, accentuated rather than crossed the class divide between teacher and taught.[5] Modern equal opportunities analysis of this type of situation can be harshly critical but well-educated young women in the 1920s could not easily question their role as sustainers of the status quo without seriously damaging their careers. An oversupply of teachers meant that, 'respectable, conforming' single women were more likely to be employable and, following the death of brothers and prospective husbands in the war, they needed that employment to support parents and siblings. Many women teachers became the breadwinners for their families, on a lower salary than men, and most knew that that was going to be the case even while they were in training.[6]

The second assumption was that primary teaching was for the less intellectual and only needed a two-year (later three-year) certificate or diploma course. This was part of the rationalisation of the need for women teachers in a society which firmly believed that women should be in the home. Male access to primary teaching was restricted in the Regulations of 1924 to degree holders, thus underlining the assumption that men had 'superior' minds and creating the long-lasting rationale for male domination of promoted posts in primary schools.

Until the 1960s the curriculum for the certificate course consisted of 12 different subjects, reflecting the view that student teachers must study all the subjects they might be required to teach in primary schools. Many students had little interest in some subjects and even less use for the model of teaching by which they were conveyed. Geography came in for particularly consistent criticism over the years, even when it became subsumed under the title of environmental studies. Students from as recently as 1986 have repeated the complaint of predecessors, that they were expected to behave as Primary 7 pupils going through the information gathering for a project, rather than being taught how to teach it by analysing and evaluating the process. The danger of this approach is that it:

> discouraged opportunities for such cross-curricular issues as race and gender to emerge, which meant that not only were students not being introduced to discriminatory practices which take place in the primary school, but were also not provided with a platform upon which they could examine their own habitual assumptions regarding both race and gender.[7]

A culture of reproducing the status quo found this methodology very effective but while many students were happy to accept the content they objected to the style of delivery. 'The aim appeared to be to squash any initiative. Daughters of this generation have said the same 20 or 30 years later'. (1924 non grad) Indeed some people were making the same sort of criticism 60 years later. 'Being at college just felt like extended school, with more homework and tutors who shouted and **never** remembered your name'. (1982 non-grad) That they were not treated as adults has been perhaps the most persistent criticism made by students, across courses and over time.

Between the wars the organisation of courses, structure of employment, and the operational organisation of the college reflected society's assumptions about women's inferior role in 'feminised' primary teaching. Women students had to enter by the back door of the building for many years, classes were on a single sex basis, and even when the Students' Union was launched in February 1923 it was in the Men's Common Room, which was naturally off limits to women.

For 30 years women teachers had been expected to give up their jobs on marriage, creating a belief among some college lecturers that engaged or married students should not be admitted. This view might have been understandable during the marriage bar, but it was scarcely appropriate during a time of severe teacher shortage. 'A female tutor in a graduate history lecture told us that all females who were engaged or married were wasting a training place'. (1971 grad) Resistance to the social change of respectable married women working outside the home was perhaps even stronger than resistance to curricular change. The contradictory messages given to student teachers before the 1975 Sex Discrimination Act is best encapsulated by a description of a lecture for Douglas House residents in March 1943 by Miss Macintosh of the Methods department. Her title was 'Post war reconstruction'

> The subject matter was entirely different from what we had expected, as it dealt with future husbands, families and domestic problems. We were interested to learn that a teacher and lawyer are the ideal combination for matrimony but regret that lawyers are few and far between.[8]

Hostel life

The key difference in primary teaching students' experience of life at Jordanhill was undoubtedly whether they were hostel residents or not. Hostel life was predominantly a non graduate experience. 'Graduates, male or female, almost didn't exist as far as we were concerned. They were very different. Only one or two lived in hostel.' (1949 non grad) The comparative isolation of the site from the temptations of the city was very much in its favour as a safe, protected environment for young women, particularly those who were entering a career which insisted on celibacy until 1945. The family atmosphere created by providing new students with a 'big sister' from third year, the regular special teas with the Principal and his wife attending, the Hostel Hops, the ongoing relationship with former hostel residents, all helped to make hostel girls feel special. 'As far as staff were concerned hostel students were the chosen few. Each hall gave a Lecturers' party each year and it was a hoot. We put on entertainment and parodied the lecturers'. (1967 non grad)

The lecturers' parties originated in 1937 in a series of sketches performed by members of the Dramatic Club, supplemented with songs, and the evening finished off with country dancing. They grew into a tradition which extended to Hamilton College residences when many Jordanhill staff transferred to Hamilton. Other traditions were a House photograph, Hallowe'en parties with 'champit tatties' containing lucky charms, a meal out in a restaurant with the warden for leaving students, a gift 'to the House' from leaving students and a final year 'Midnight feast'. These traditions continued until the 1960s when, with increasing emphasis on individual freedom, the view gained ground that the strict regulation of daily life with regard to conduct, dress and the use of personal time, 'must be detrimental to personal growth and professionalism, which places emphasis on autonomy, self-regulation and the exercise of informed judgement and choice'[9]

Graduates

There is a history of tension between graduates and the college which has two main causes. One was the perception of going back to school. Responding to bells for changing classes or taking subjects such as elocution were resented by students fresh from academic studies. The other factor which devalued Jordanhill was ease of entry. Until the early 1980s, the shortage of teachers was such that graduates simply had to present themselves at the beginning of term to be granted a place. The tendency of graduates to look down on non graduates was reinforced by the college organisational policy, which kept courses completely separate. A 1924 student describes student attitudes, 'Graduates were considered to be in need of treatment for their blown up heads.' There is also a hint of resentment in the staff introduction to 1928 honours students:

> As Honours grads we were not welcome in Jordanhill. It was as though we were too conceited. Our introductory talk included the statement 'Honours students need not think they are any better than anybody else when filling in these enrolment forms because they make more mistakes. (1929 grad)

The 1946 magazine contains the following defintion of GRAD.:

> Generic term applied to students who are admitted to a limited range of lectures and not allowed to remain more than 3 terms in college. They are

often seen in the common room and are prodigious lookers at the title page of books. It is significant that grad sections are denoted by Greek letters.[10]

One of the main difficulties in establishing Jordanhill as a focus for student life was the existence of the split-site courses, DipEd and EdB. Connections with university clubs, societies and union were maintained and students worked hard at reducing their time on Jordanhill campus to a minimum. One later member of Jordanhill staff managed to reduce it to two hours per week! The excuse was well recognised :

'Attending eddbee lectures' is a phrase used by some students, especially grads, to explain absence from college lectures, unwillingness to contribute to the magazine, etc. It appears that the term was originally applied to the taking of certain advanced courses in education.[11]

However there were some graduates who enjoyed the experience. Graduates in 1926 wrote in the magazine that they had been misled by previous students that Jordanhill was a place of weeping, wailing and gnashing of teeth and that it had no social life. They found this untrue although they did get lost in the corridors as predicted![12] One postwar graduate commented:

Students who had never thought what they were going to do with their degree and simply drifted into teaching ... just did a minimum and these were the ones who generally grunted and groaned. If you put your back into it ... it was a really enjoyable course. (1949 grad)

Another was even warmer in his praise :

I had a science degree from Glasgow University and ... any education I had acquired had been in vacations. I didn't really expect to be educated in an institution and [staff such as] Ian Morris and Jimmy Scotland were eye-openers to me. (1959 grad)

One subject which evoked considerable comment in the magazine from graduate students, yet is scarcely mentioned in recollections is speech training and phonetics. The first mention is in 1927, when the subject is subtitled 'the extraction of the glottal stop'. One student's description of teaching, as taught at Jordanhill, was 'phonetics, physical education and feeding'.

Thoughts from a grad.—On entering college we enter our second childhood—even taught how to speak again, how to say Big hard words. Our only complaint about the college system is we are not taught by the methods **we** are asked to use when teaching.[13]

This complaint was echoed by graduates right through until the mid 1970s and was often accompanied by the view that the worst perpetrators were 'failed university lecturers who had no school experience either'. (1972 grad) However the mix of lectures, tutorials and tutor consultation was appreciated by some students as a more adult way to be taught than the university method. Perhaps this reflected the student experience of the group for whom the system appeared to have been designed for at least 50 years, graduate males. The bulk of female graduate students were part of the 'Senga syndrome', described as

typical Glasgow working class girl from a state school, who goes to Glasgow University, does an Ordinary degree, goes to Jordanhill College and returns, if she has ever left, to live near and teach in her old school or very close to it.[14]

That they were classed by males along with the diplomates as having inferior status is evident from the complaints made when men were admitted to the diploma course. Magazine articles of the time strongly reflect the view that gender was more important as a criterion for promotion than graduate status or teaching ability.

SSPE students
One group which had an influence out of proportion to its numbers was the SSPE students. A select band of the fittest, most athletic young men in the country, their arrival in 1931 on a predominantly female campus was bound to create a stir. Unlike the graduates this was a group of men who had undergone a varied and difficult selection process to gain entry and had every reason to be proud, considering themselves as part of an elite within Scotland. Naturally their attitudes to Jordanhill and their course were mainly positive. Like the Primary course at the time the Physical Education diploma course was intellectually limited, which was an invitation to anonymous graduates in the magazine to stereotype all PEs in a demeaning way :

PEEHEE—Tribe of wild men inhabiting the upper slopes of Jordanhill. May be distinguished by their aptitude for yelling and running along corridors as well as by their peculiar native dress, called 'traxoots'. Despite their inherent allergicity to Western civilisation many Peehees are gradually adapting themselves to 20th century conditions.[15]

Good natured rivalry between two very different groups of students was to be expected but many PE students objected to the assumption of some staff that a healthy body meant a lack of brain :

> Education and Psychology treated us like village idiots and tried to make everything virtually monosyllabic. It was really degrading and I resented it. I remember being given the exam questions on the board two days before the exam—the implication being that we couldn't pass it any other way. (1972 SSPE)

The small year group (40-60) during the years of huge numbers of Primary and Secondary students made relationships particularly close knit and most PE cohorts have had regular reunions, and old film of the preparation and performance of the PE display traditionally given on the college lawns on the summer Gala Day was transferred recently to video so that everyone could have a reminder of their youthful prowess. The presence of the SSPE students made a difference to social life on campus but was resented by some male graduates, who felt that they now had less chance to win the attention of female students. The gender divide within courses was still rigidly maintained, although eventually male PE students were allowed to teach non graduates Scottish country dancing under the watchful eye of Miss Milligan, and some of Miss Milligan's men went on to television fame in *The White Heather Club*.

Although college social life—dances, clubs etc.—is rarely identified as significant in students' lives, lunchtime and break was enough time for many relationships to develop, and each year produced its eventual crop of PE/primary teacher marriages: 'Three of our section married PE students'. (1954 non grad) Hostel dances became much more interesting when the PE men arrived but their presence was not always desired for romantic reasons:

> Suppertime at a hostel dance. After a mad scramble I find myself seated beside either a man or a PE. There are points in favour of both. A man is—well, a man ; but a PE eats more, thereby allowing time to fill my yawning cavity and lay in supplies for hours of starvation.[16]

Primary certificate or diploma students vied with one another for the attention of the PE men, and inevitably disappointment led to name-calling. 'We said they went around with their IQs on their backs'. (Each PE student had a number on his kit, generally less than 100). (1966 non grads)

Significant people

'The student population comes to constitute part of the attributes of a school and part of the culture making process, accentuating characters and reputations, modes of operating and styles.'[17] It is important therefore to highlight student comments on members of staff who made a particular impact on them. These were not always names which came to the forefront through promotion or national recognition. The memories of Miss Jean Milligan are, without exception, warm and admiring. She had an exceptional influence over a long period of time.[18] Dr Robert Rusk is a well-remembered and notable figure but many students felt that he personified the elitism of the theory/practice divide:

> He was a bit naughty in that he often mocked very amusingly some of the techniques which the Methods staff very earnestly recommended to us. We were entertained, but I remember feeling guilty about laughing about things which I knew were very helpful in their way on the practical side.' (1932 grad)

One of the main reasons speech training was feared was the formidable Dr Anne McAllister. 'She reduced strong men to states of extreme diffidence'. (1932 grad) Miss Moffett on the other hand is recalled as 'A lovely person who did not embarrass those whose diction left a great deal to be desired.' (1954 non-grad) Miss Sievwright is remembered for her ability to imitate every known speech defect.

Teddy Brown, Master of Methods, was disliked for causing potential difficulties on a crit. 'His style was to banter and joke and get the children high and then hand over to the student'. (1930 grad) Despite the power of Methods tutors over the final teaching grade (or perhaps because of it) the only other Methods tutors who are recalled are Miss Macintosh, 'a holy terror, but good for us. A tiny suggestion of a compliment put us on cloud nine' (1954 non grad); Miss Florence Adams, 'She gathered us in like a real mother hen' (1965 non-grad); Miss Cockburn, 'I had to keep the children waiting until she was settled at the rear of the class, then she tapped the desk and said 'Begin''. (1976 grad) Hugh 'the Bomber' Brown of SSPE is vividly remembered by most of his former students. He consistently reinforced the team spirit of physical education students through a highly critical but unswerving loyalty to those he regarded as 'One of our best men'. Others, principally those outside SSPE, were referred to variously as 'scrimshankers, loaby-dossers, lookers under beds, long-range melodeon players' and many other colourful names.

Naturally many former students of Jordanhill have become significant within the world of education and sport but others have made a name in other fields. Although the college magazine is scarcely remembered by most students it contains early work by Hugh McDiarmid, (*The hanging judge* appeared in the June 1926 magazine, prior to the autumn publication of *A drunk man looks at the thistle*), Gerard Slevin, actor and writer (1958), Eric Lindsay, novelist and scriptwriter (1961) and Liz Lochhead who was congratulated on winning the BBC Student poetry competition in 1971.[19] Former SSPE student Callum Macdonald is a leading member of the rock band, Runrig.

All change!

Pre- and postwar are the normal periods chosen to describe changes within society and institutions in the 20th century but the 1960s mark a greater watershed in the student experience in Jordanhill, as they did in wider social changes. Not only was this a period of rapid expansion, but the composition of the student body changed radically. Men were admitted to the primary diploma course and the huge numbers of teaching students were swelled by newer and growing groups of further education, youth and community, social work and speech therapy students, all struggling to cope in hard-pressed accommodation. A larger proportion of students in all courses were mature and had wider experience of life and other occupations before entering college. As a result the student body became more critical and 'were not willing just to accept what the lecturers said'. (1971 FE student) For instance, the youth and community students on course 20 (1970) complained in the college newspaper: 'Rather than being trained as a social rescue and reconstruction team, we are mildly taught how to run ping-pong tournaments and teach darts. Course 20 is entirely unrelated and unrealistic'.[20]

Changes in fashion also made an impact. The short skirts and heavily made-up styles of the 1960s, flaunted in trendy photographs in the college magazine of February 1967, and the mild beginnings of a 'Women's Lib' consciousness apparent in the college newspaper from 1968 onwards, were apparently threatening to some of the predominantly male staff. 'The lecturer was obviously uncomfortable around young women and always had beads of sweat on his upper lip'. (1971 non grad) Dress regulations became difficult to sustain. In February 1968 the *Daily Express* ran the story of a female student who had been reprimanded for wearing trousers. The college's policy, publicly restated, that this was not allowed was unfavourably compared to that of other colleges. This pressure no doubt led to November's statement from the Dean of Women:

> In view of the sudden onset of cold weather and representations made by women students regarding trouser suits, it is agreed that the wearing of these to lectures be accepted.[21]

As the social composition of the student body changed 'from the days when it comprised girls straight out of school and a handful of graduates returning to their own Union for social life', the demand mounted for licensed premises on the campus. In 1970 a Beer Bar was offered with a lot of restrictions and the students rejected it. It finally opened in 1971 without the controversial restrictions.

For some years, in the aftermath of the events of 1968, the Students' Representative Council became more politicised. One clear indication of this was that the student magazine changed from a once-a-term publication, full of jokes, poetry and anonymous articles, to a monthly radical newspaper, *Spectrum.* The new tone was set by its first editor : 'Comrades ... we must actively set our minds to the task of raising the level of political consciousness at the college and throughout the country.'[22] The students pressed for, and were granted, places on the Board of Studies and Board of Governors, albeit only with observer status. This political activity was male-dominated. There had been an intermittent but generally small female involvement with college magazines from the earliest days but when the paper was at its most political in 1975 the editorial team was all male, as were all the candidates for student governor. The high point of this political activity was the student sit-in of 1976, sparked off by a sudden dearth of jobs for students who had always assumed that they would be employed immediately after qualifying. The sit-in was controlled from the Tea Bar and college staff were locked out of parts of the campus. After a fortnight pickets disappeared suddenly. This was because students had been holding back the mail and consequently the bill for beer had not been paid and new supplies were needed!

La même chose?

The sit-in itself was soon forgotten, but the changes which had caused it had repercussions which lasted for the rest of the college's independent life. The ending of teacher shortage meant reduced quotas for entry to college, hence fierce competition, producing a more dedicated student body. It also meant keener competition among the students on course as they prepared for an uncertain job market. Some perennial problems remained. The social life on campus became even more difficult to sustain. The Hostels Association ceased to exist because the hostel experience was radically different due, among other things, to a change to mixed halls of residence. SSPE closed in 1990 and the men were no longer to be seen wandering around in their tracksuits. The annual Shakespeare performance ceased and other clubs and societies suffered poor attendance because of the wide catchment area of students and also because of pressures of study.

Primary courses still had to struggle against the prejudices that they were only for women and for the less able intellectually. Despite the change to an all graduate profession, the number of men entering primary teaching remained very low. The myth persisted that 'colleges are peopled with students who did not have enough Highers to gain entrance to university'.[23] This myth had caused unhappiness to a number of students in the 1970s who were guided into the BEd, with its academic structure of Ordinary and Higher Ordinary classes, because they had 'good' Highers and were advised to go for a degree.

> I hated it. I wanted to teach and the courses I had to study had nothing to do with the primary school. I failed my exams but passed my teaching. I went back to do the diploma which was what I'd wanted to do in the first place. (1972 non grad)

Even today there are still students applying for teaching who have completed an unhappy year on other degree courses where they were directed because 'My guidance teacher said my qualifications were too good for primary teaching'. (1995 applicant for teaching)

However some changes have been positive. The changing concept of 'being a teacher' produced challenging new courses in the 1980s which reflected a redefinition of professional knowledge based on research into how children learn, the importance of the social context in which children live and learn and, perhaps most importantly, the view that knowledge is socially constructed instead of 'given'. Regular review and validation has kept pace with government guidelines, eg Standard Grade and 5–14, and a growing emphasis on analysis and reflection of the teacher's role in a changing professional context has improved the student experience by encouraging students to realise their own responsibility for learning. Students who have chosen teaching despite adverse job prospects have shown the motivation to benefit from these changes.

One student who entered college just before the merger with the University of Strathclyde had left the diploma course 14 years previously due to illness. Initially the most obvious difference was the practice of calling lecturers by first names instead of Mr or Miss, but a more significant difference was that the objectives of the course and its assessment procedures were made clear and public. 'It's good to know what you are meant to be learning and how you are being judged. I know the criteria now. I used not to know what tutors wanted'. (1992 BEd entrant) Students' right of access to anything that is written about them contrasts sharply with the situation in 1928, when one of the motions at an inter college conference was: 'That students in a two years course should have some idea of their teaching mark at the end of first year'[24] or at a similar conference in 1939: 'In view of the importance attached to a teacher's training record throughout his (*sic*) professional career, a detailed written criticism and an actual mark should be given after each criticism lesson'.[25] One hopes that the student experience will not be 'All work and no play' but at least in some very important ways it seems to have changed for the better.

References
1 Stacey, J. *Women's representation of themselves through the film stars of the 40s and 50s*. Gillian Skirrow Memorial Lecture, University of Strathclyde, 1994.
2 Hunt, F.J. *The social dynamics of schooling*. Brighton: Falmer, 1990.
3 *New dominie*. Foreword, 1949.
4 Davies, L. Equal rights in teacher education. *Educational review*, v.46:2, 1994.
5 Popkewitz, T. *Critical studies in teacher education*. Brighton: Falmer, 1987.
6 Adams, C. Divide and rule: the marriage ban 1918–1945 in Fewell, J. and Paterson, F. eds. *Girls in their prime*. Edinburgh: Scottish Academic Press, 1990.
7 Skelton, C. *Whatever happens to little women*. Open U P, 1989.
8 Douglas House log book, 1943.
9 Dove, L.A. *Teachers and teacher education in developing countries*. New York: Croom Helm, 1986.
10 *New dominie*, 1946.
11 *Ibid.*
12 *Ibid.*, 1926.
13 *Ibid.*, March 1953.
14 Hills, L. The Senga syndrome in Fewell and Paterson. *op.cit.*
15 *New dominie*, 1946.
16 *Ibid.*, 1947.
17 Hunt. *op.cit.*
18 MacFadyen, A. and Adams, F.H. *Dance with your soul*. Edinburgh: RSCDS, 1983.
19 *Spectrum*, May 1971.
20 *Ibid.*, 1970.
21 *Ibid.*, November 1968.
22 *Ibid.*, September/October 1968.
23 *Ibid.*, February 1968
24 *New dominie*, 1928.
25 *Ibid.*, 1939.

Appendix 1: NOTES ON CONTRIBUTORS

Catherine Adams was a nursery school head teacher before joining the Primary Education department at Jordanhill in 1990.

Molly Cumming joined the Primary Education department in 1975. Since 1987 she has been Course Director for the BEd (Inservice) and acted as Education Management Coordinator in the Inservice Division.

Margaret Harrison was appointed Principal Librarian in 1983, having previously been Librarian of Hamilton College of Education. She is currently Librarian of the Jordanhill Campus.

Peter Hillis was Assistant Head Teacher at Gleniffer High School until 1991, when he was appointed Head of the Social Studies Division and Head of History at Jordanhill.

Gordon Kirk was Principal Lecturer in Education at Jordanhill from 1974–81. Since then he has been Principal of Moray House Institute of Education.

Elspeth McCartney was appointed Director of the School of Speech Therapy in 1987. She had previously been Lecturer in the Department of Audiology, Education of the Deaf and Speech Pathology at the University of Manchester.

Willis Marker joined the staff of Jordanhill in 1967 and was Assistant Principal (Inservice) from 1976–86.

Terry May joined the department of Youth and Community in 1967 and served as Principal Lecturer from 1980–87.

Gerald Mortimer joined the College Inservice department from Hamilton College in 1982, and since 1987 has been Coordinator of SAFIS programme, short courses and conferences.

Magnus Ross worked for ten years in the FE sector before joining the School of Further Education in 1981. He is currently Lecturer in Education Studies.

Roy B. Small became a Lecturer in the SSPE in 1956 and was Head of Academic Studies from 1976–89. Roy is also well known as a football coach and broadcaster.

Janice Thomson was appointed in 1984 to a job share post in the Social Work department, where she has a special interest in social work practice with children and families. Her previous post was in the Department of Child and Family Psychiatry at Yorkhill Hospital.

Glenda White was a member of the Primary Education staff from 1975–85. Since then she has served as an HMI and as Chief Inspector (Primary) for Strathclyde Region. She is currently Senior Depute Director of Education for South Lanarkshire.

Appendix 2: BIOGRAPHICAL INDEX OF COLLEGE STAFF AS MENTIONED IN THE TEXT

Adams, Florence H.	1956–61, 1962–63	Lecturer in methods
Baillie, Marion	1963–65, 1972–87	Dean of Women, 1972–87
Bell, H. Steve	1964–	Staff tutor, 1967–
Bone, Dr Thomas R. CBE	1962–63, 1967–92	Principal, 1972–92 (Deputy Principal, Strathclyde University, 1992–)
Boyd, Dr William	1910–23	Lecturer in education
Brown, Edward J.V.	1905–32	Principal lecturer in methods, 1920–32
Brown, Hugh C.	1953–74	Director, SSPE
Burnett, George A.	1924–40	Director of Studies
Butts, David C.	1966–80	Principal lecturer, AV media
Caldwell, Ian D.	1967–90	Administrative officer (inservice)
Chakrabarti, Mono	1987–	Head of Social Work Division, 1987–93
Clarke, Peter B.	1964–83	Principal Librarian
Cockburn, Margaret	1966–85	Lecturer in primary education
Crichton, Rev. A. Pender	1925–43	Director of religious instruction
Dawson, Dr Shepherd	1907–35	Principal lecturer in psychology, 1931–35
Dickinson, William	1952–82	Senior lecturer, SSPE
Douglas, Dr Carstairs C.	1907–31	Principal lecturer in hygiene
Dunlop, Jim	1970–	Head of International Unit
Gallie, Janet	1916–48	Lecturer in methods
Griffiths, Dr Dennis	1970–72	Director, SFE
Harrison, Margaret	1983–	Principal Librarian
Hawthorn, John	1971–	Principal lecturer in computer education, 1976–95
Hiddleston, Vera OBE	1967–87	Principal lecturer in social work, 1974–87

Hodge, Peter R.	1966–74	Lecturer in programmed learning
Holroyd, Colin	1965–68, 1971–88	Principal lecturer in chemistry, 1974–88
Insh, Dr George Pratt	1923–48	Principal lecturer in history
Jones, G. Howel	1970–92	Principal lecturer in special educational needs, 1979–92
Kennedy Fraser, Dr D.	1923–51	Principal lecturer, courses for teachers of handicapped
Kerr, William	1934–49	Director of Studies, 1940–49
Kirk, Gordon	1974–81	Principal lecturer in education (Principal, Moray House, 1981–)
Kirkland, George	1972–89	Principal lecturer in AV Media, 1980–89 (Director of AV Services, Glasgow University, 1989–)
Leggatt, Elizabeth F.C.	1955–63	Lecturer in mathematics (Principal, Callendar Park, 1963–69)
McAllister, Dr Anne OBE	1919–58, 1963–65	Principal lecturer in speech training, 1919–51; Director, School of Speech Therapy, 1963–65
McArthur, Robin	1956–86	Assistant principal, 1969–86
McCall, Dr James	1974–	Vice principal, 1983–92; Acting principal, 1992–93, Professor and Dean of Faculty, 1993–
McCallien, Catherine	1946–50, 1965–74	Director, School of Speech Therapy, 1965–74
McCallum, Hugh	1905–24	Director of Studies, 1919–24
McCartney, Elspeth	1987–	Director, School of Speech Therapy
MacCuaig, Donald	1966–67	Lecturer in child care
MacDonald, Barry	1965–68	Lecturer in education
Macintosh, Williamina T.	1936–56	Lecturer in methods
McKay, Robert	1959–85	Head of practical studies, SSPE, 1976–85
McKay, Ronald	1966–	Assistant principal, 1988–93, Head of primary education
Mackenzie, Dr Alastair	1931–48	Principal lecturer in hygiene
Macleod, Donald	1905–18	Director of Studies

Mangan, Dr James A.	1972–	Principal lecturer in education, 1981–87, Professor 1993–
Marker, Willis B.	1967–86	Assistant principal (inservice), 1976–86
Mason, William T.	1957–70	Director, SFE, 1967–70
May, Terry	1967–87	Principal lecturer, youth and community, 1980–87
Michael, Bill	1958–70, 1981–	Principal lecturer in art, 1982–93
Milburn, Robert E.	1975–83, 1987–	Head of community education, 1987–93
Miller, James	1966–72	Vice principal (Registrar, GTC, 1972–85)
Milligan, Jean	1909–48	Principal lecturer in PE (women)
Moffett, Joyce G. OBE	1941–71	Dean of Women, 1958–71
Moodie, Sallie	1963–93	Staff tutor, 1970–87
Morris, Ian G.	1952–61	Lecturer in psychology (later HMCI)
Morrison, T.M.	1905–8	Joint Rector
Natusch, Ian	1985–91	Director of CAST (later of SFEU)
Nicolson, Alasdair G.	1961–91	Assistant principal, 1976–91
Nimmo, Dr Myra	1991–	Assistant principal, 1991–93, Professor 1993–
Niven, Stuart M.	1967–	Director, SFE, 1983–
Orr, George F.	1946–76	Principal lecturer, SSPE
Paxton, Dr Donald	1923–49	Lecturer in biology
Punchard, Frank N.	1931–53	Principal lecturer, SSPE
Rae, Gordon	1947–76	Principal lecturer in geography
Rait, Williamina	1925–26	Librarian
Ramsay, Anne	1984–	Lecturer in computer education
Rendell, Fred	1962–87	Staff tutor, 1967–87
Rennie, Ethel M. CBE	1955–63	Lecturer in speech training (Principal of Craigie College, 1963–75)
Richardson, Ronald H.	1974–79	Assistant principal, primary education
Riddell, George W. OBE	1972–83	Vice principal
Rosser, Oswell	1931–59	Senior lecturer, SSPE
Round, John P.	1964–80	Principal lecturer, youth & community, 1968–80
Rusk, Dr Robert R.	1923–46	Principal lecturer in education

Scotland, James CBE	1950–61	Principal lecturer in education (Principal, Aberdeen College, 1961–83)
Sievwright, Margaret F.	1951–73	Lecturer in speech & drama
Sillito, A.G.	1953–66	Principal lecturer in mathematics
Small, Roy B.	1958–89	Head of academic studies, SSPE, 1976–89
Smith, Iain R.M.	1988–	Assistant principal, 1988–93, Vice Dean 1993–
Smith, John A.	1955–75	Vice principal, 1956–75
Stark, Dr James	1972–83	Director, SFE
Stenhouse, Lawrence	1961–67	Principal lecturer in education
Stitt, Robert G.	1949–74	Principal lecturer in primary education, 1964–74
Thomson, William P.	1967–	Director, Postgraduate awards scheme, 1990–95
Walker, William S.	1949–65	Vice principal, 1964–65 (Principal of Hamilton College, 1965–69)
Wallace, Anne	1974–87	Director, School of Speech Therapy
Watterson, Patricia	1970–	Senior lecturer (inservice)
Weir, A. Douglas	1979–85, 1988–	Assistant principal, 1991–93, Professor and Vice Dean 1993–
Williams, A.M.	1905–21	Joint Rector
Williamson, Peter	1965–73	Lecturer, youth & community
Wilson, Dr Gordon M.	1981–87	Assistant principal (inservice), 1986–87 (Principal of Craigie College, 1988–93)
Wood, Sir Henry P. CBE	1944–71	Principal, 1949–71
Wright, Ellen	1926–64	Librarian
Wright, G. Bernard	1974–89	Director, SSPE
Wybar, Dr Eileen	1949–66	Assistant medical officer 1952–66 (later Medical officer, Hamilton College)

Appendix 3: SELECT BIBLIOGRAPHY

1. *Primary Sources*
Glasgow Provincial Committee minutes, 1905–59.
Central Executive Committee of the National Committee for the Training of Teachers minutes, 1920–59. Edinburgh: Darien Press.
Committee of Council on Education in Scotland reports, 1920–. London: HMSO.
General Teaching Council minutes, 1967–.
Jordanhill college records:
  Board of Governors (JBG) minutes, 1959–93.
  Board of Studies (JBS) minutes, 1959–93.
  Principal's Committee (JPC) minutes, 1972–93.
Wood, H.P. *Notes on the training of teachers in Scotland.* Unpublished mimeo in the Jordanhill Archives. (undated).
Wood, H.P. *MS notes on Jordanhill.* 1993.

2. *Secondary Sources*
Arbuthnott, J. and Bone, T.R. Anatomy of a merger. *Higher education quarterly,* v.47:2, 1993.
Archer, E.G. and Peck, B.T. *The Jordanhill regent scheme.* Jordanhill College, 1982.
Cruickshank, M. *History of the training of teachers in Scotland.* London : ULP, 1970.
Fairley, J.A. *A history of Jordanhill College of Education, 1921–71.* Jordanhill College, 1971.
Fraser, W. *Memoir of the life of David Stow.* London : Nisbet, 1868.
Jordanhill College of Education. *Report for the Institutional Review visit of the CNAA.* Jordanhill College, 1980.
Jordanhill College of Education. *Report for the Institutional Review visit of the CNAA.* Jordanhill College, 1985.
Jordanhill College of Education. *70 years of excellence in education: Jordanhill College 1921–91.* Jordanhill College, 1991.
Jordanhill journal. Jordanhill College, 1988–93.

MacFadyen, A. and Adams, F.H. *Dance with your soul.* Edinburgh: Royal Scottish Country Dance Society, 1983.

Marker, W.B. *The spider's web? policy making in teacher education in Scotland, 1959–81.* Jordanhill Sales and Publications, 1994.

Marker, W.B. The Robbins report and teacher education in Scotland. *Scottish educational review,* v.26:1, 1994.

Marker, W.B. and Raab, C. Advise and construct: the expansion of the Scottish colleges of education in the 1960s. *Scottish educational review,* v.25:1, 1993.

Niven, S.M. *The first twenty five years.* SFE, 1992.

Rusk, R.R. *The training of teachers in Scotland.* Edinburgh: EIS, 1928.

Scottish Education Department. *Report on an inspection of Jordanhill College of Education.* 1987.

Select Committee on Education and Science (SCES). Scottish Sub-Committee. *Teacher training,* v.2. London: HMSO, 1970.

Stow, D. *The training system.* 10th ed. London: Longman, 1854.

White, G.A. *Silk and saints: David Stow and infant education, 1816–36.* MEd thesis. Glasgow University, 1983.

Wood, H.P. *David Stow and the Glasgow Normal Seminary.* Jordanhill College, 1987.

3. Transcripts of Interviews by W.B. Marker in the Jordanhill Archives
Professor T.R. Bone, Mrs M.M. Cumming, Mr C. Holroyd, Mr R.W. McArthur, Professor J. McCall, Dr J. Miller, Miss J.G. Moffett, Mr A.G. Nicolson, Mr G. Rae, Mr I.R.M. Smith, Professor A.D. Weir, Sir Henry P. Wood

Index